AMERICAN SHIPS *of the* COLONIAL
and REVOLUTIONARY PERIODS

By the Author

THE ARCHITECTS OF THE AMERICAN COLONIES

RHODE ISLAND: FORGOTTEN LEADER OF THE REVOLUTIONARY ERA

COLONIAL & REVOLUTIONARY WAR SEA SONGS & CHANTEYS

SHIPS OF THE AMERICAN REVOLUTION TO COLOR

AMERICAN SHIPS *of the* COLONIAL *and* REVOLUTIONARY PERIODS

John F. Millar

W. W. NORTON & COMPANY, INC.

New York

Copyright © 1978 by W. W. Norton & Company, Inc.
Published simultaneously in Canada by George J. McLeod
Limited, Toronto. Printed in the United States of America.

All Rights Reserved

FIRST EDITION

DESIGNED BY DENNIS J. GRASTORF
TYPE FACE IS BASKERVILLE
PRINTED BY HADDON CRAFTSMEN

Library of Congress Cataloging in Publication Data

Millar, John Fitzhugh.
    American ships of the Colonial and Revolutionary
periods.

    Bibliography: p.
    Includes index.
    1. Ships—History—17th century. 2. Ships—History—
18th century. 3. North America—History—Colonial period,
ca. 1600–1775. 4. United States—History—Revolution—
1775–1783. I. Title.
VM22.M54   623.82′2′0973   78–18742
ISBN 0-393-03222-1

1 2 3 4 5 6 7 8 9 0

FOREWORD

In 1968 I sensed, perhaps before most people, the approach of the Bicentennial of American Independence, and realized what an exciting experience the occasion could be for Americans and others. For the most part the promises for that experience have fallen through, but in 1968 there was no indication that this would be so.

For Americans who wished to explore the tangible relics of their history during the Bicentennial period, at least one important side of that history was scarcely represented: the maritime side. Apart from the display at the Smithsonian Institution in Washington, D.C., of the relatively small gondola Philadelphia, *there were no ships from the Revolutionary period for people to see, and seeing such ships could fill a real gap in the experience of their history for curious Americans. The problem was all the more serious because most Americans automatically assumed that the two frigates* Constitution *and* Constellation, *on display in Boston and Baltimore respectively, were ships from the Revolution (they were not built until 1795–97); even worse, these two ships do not represent the configurations they had at their launching, nor even the configurations they had in their finest hours (the period before 1815), but they are instead a hodgepodge of periods with a heavy accent on the mid-Victorian era. Ships of the Revolution and the Colonial period bore no more resemblance to*

Constitution *and* Constellation *(as they appear today) than a World War I destroyer bore to a modern guided-missile frigate.*

I decided to try to correct that imbalance by building full-sized reconstructions of Revolutionary period warships. The ships might possibly visit other ports, but they would be based in Newport, Rhode Island; Newport was my home, and that was reason enough, but Newport also had more pre-Revolutionary buildings still standing than any other community in the country. Further, it was because of Newport's economic ruin by a British blockade that the Rhode Island General Assembly initiated the bill in the Continental Congress that created the Continental Navy on 13 October 1775, and the first vessel authorized for that navy was "a swift sailing vessel, to carry ten carriage guns, and a proportionate number of swivels, with eighty men," which Silas Deane tells us was the Rhode Island sloop Katy, *later known as* Providence. *And it was in Newport on 9 July 1764 that the heavy guns of Fort George were fired on the British Customs schooner* St. John *by order of the governor and the General Assembly, an event that those who know about it call the "first shots of the American Revolution," twelve years before independence.*

At least one of the ships that I would build should be a ship whose plans survive, that would be big enough to persuade the curious to get out of their car to look at it,

[v]

that would be small enough that I could borrow that much money to build it, and that had been in Newport at some point during the Revolution. Of all the ships that had been in Newport in the Revolution, there were no American ships whose plans were then known to have survived. Of the French ships, a few plans survived, but the ships were all bigger than my borrowing power could afford to build. Of the many British ships whose plans survived at the National Maritime Museum at Greenwich, just outside London, I chose one called the Rose, *mainly because her name appeared on almost every page of the collections of documents about the beginning of the Revolution. I knew very little about her history and significance at the time that I chose her, so my choice later proved to be a gratifying stroke of luck, for I found out that the* Rose *was the ship whose blockade of Newport caused the General Assembly to instruct its delegates in Congress to introduce the bill that created the Continental Navy. It could therefore be said that* Rose *was the direct cause of the founding of the American navy. I could not believe my good fortune.*

Rose was variously described as a 20-gun or 24-gun frigate. She was built in 1756 in Yorkshire, and she was a little smaller than the Continental frigates Boston, Montgomery, *and* Delaware, *and a bit larger than the corvettes* General Gates, General Washington, Ranger, *and* Saratoga. *She was scuttled by her own captain in 1779 to prevent the French fleet from entering the harbor of Savannah, Georgia, and assisting an American army in besieging the British garrison at Savannah, but over the years various pieces of her have been salvaged. I was able to obtain some of these pieces, and they were incorporated into the construction of the new ship at Lunenburg, Nova Scotia. The yard of Smith & Rhuland at Lunenburg had been chosen primarily because it was*

the only one of the several yards in the United States, Canada, Britain, and the Far East, asked to bid on the construction job whose price I could afford to pay.

Rose was launched in March 1970 and sailed to Boston, and then to Newport in late May and early June of that year. With modern synthetic sails (and no engine) she sailed far better than anyone expected, a fact that has made many people wish that U.S. Coast Guard regulations and various insurance requirements were more relaxed so that the ship could sail more often than she now does. She has been on permanent display on Newport's historic waterfront, and goes out sailing on average about once a year, usually for the purpose of making a film. At this time, however, her owners have decided to sell her, so her future is in doubt.

The other ship that I had planned to have built, the sloop Providence, *had to wait a few years until money could be found to pay for her. This was accomplished by the founding of a nonprofit corporation called Seaport '76, and the sloop was launched in the autumn of 1976. Unfortunately, the* Rose *and the* Providence, *which together have such a great story to tell, will apparently never be exhibited together, at least not in Newport, owing to circumstances beyond my control, but at least they both exist and they can both sail.*

Because the Rose *was for many years the only visible part of my plan, I was heavily criticized for not reconstructing an American ship instead of an "enemy" ship. It did little good explaining that an American ship, the sloop* Providence, *was to be built as soon as money could be found for her. Nor did it make any difference when I protested that no plans existed for American ships of the* Rose's *size. A few of the critics announced that nothing short of changing the* Rose's *name would satisfy them. I can see now that it was really none of their business, but it set me to wondering whether I* could have come up with plans for an American ship of the Rose's size and period if I had spent more time on research beforehand. Naturally, the point was entirely academic for the Rose was already built, and if I had waited even one more year before proceeding with the construction of such a ship, a year's inflation would have put the cost well out of reach of my meager borrowing power, even supposing that the few skilled but aged craftsmen would still have been available.

I therefore began a period of several years' research into the appearances of American ships (American-built, -designed, or -owned) in the Colonial and Revolutionary periods, and when I found much that had never been published and that was not available to the casual researcher, I decided that my findings should be made into a book.

My decision to write such a book was reinforced by one of my findings, which began to grow into an obsession. I found that there were many representations, including pictures, plans, and models, of American ships that were obviously giving an inaccurate portrayal of these vessels' true appearance. These ranged in date from about 1800, when the pictures in the Bailey collection at the Mariners Museum at Newport News, Virginia, were painted, to the present day, when Nowland Van Powell's numerous and interesting pictures were painted. These portraits generally contained serious errors in such details as rigs, flags, color schemes, and stern windows, to mention but a few, and, since most model builders and other artists generally had neither the time nor the resources to go beyond the information provided by such popular and widespread representations as the Bailey and Van Powell pictures, other pictures and models of Revolutionary period ships were bound to be produced having Victorian sterns, dolphin strikers, spanker booms on the wrong ships, ensigns at

the gaffs, split gunport lids, and black-and-white color schemes, among other popular anachronisms. This book is an attempt to assist model builders and painters to go beyond those easy anachronisms, and may in the long run result in the public's being better informed about the ships that played such an important part in their past—a part that has been unfairly overshadowed in recent years by clipper ships, whaling ships, and other nineteenth-century craft, and of course by all the models and paintings of the nineteenth-century configuration of the frigate Constitution, as well as the ship herself.

My years of research have turned up actual lines plans of American ships of the period 1607 to 1789 that have never been published before, as well as period pictures and models. I have drawn or redrawn these plans at a scale of 1:48 (one inch equals four feet), which was the standard scale used by British shipwrights in that period, although they are much reduced to fit in the book. In some cases I have admittedly had to invent what a few of these ships looked like, based on slim evidence, such as recorded dimensions or a crude scratching on a powderhorn, and these inventions are clearly marked as such in the accompanying text; usually, but not always, these reconstructions are limited to profiles of the hull above the waterline. These reconstructions, I feel, are useful to the reader to the extent that they are my opinion (based on research and sober reflection) of the appearances of some of the more important ships of our history, some of the ships that model builders and painters would normally be more tempted to represent in spite of a lack of evidence about them.

For the sake of clarity in the drawings, and because such information was generally not available about most of the ships, I have totally omitted any information about deck plans; no doubt many model builders will resent this, but they can easily recreate deck plans by referring to some of the great standard works on ships of the period, such as the books by the late Howard Chapelle.

To my great surprise, I find that many model builders are either unaware of how to scale up drawings to the size they want to use or are unwilling to put in the effort to do so. I personally have used proportional dividers, a very useful if slightly expensive tool, which I heartily recommend to those who are willing to put the effort into it. For others, I have a suggestion: they may take the drawing in question to one of those poster houses and ask to have it photographed and blown up on a poster, although I do not know if that process can be controlled closely enough so as to meet a required scale exactly. I should mention that whichever procedure is followed, care must be taken not to infringe on the publisher's copyright; this means in particular that you may not reproduce these drawings for sale.

If I had known in 1968 what I now know about American ships, would I have found an American ship to build instead of the Rose? If I could have permitted myself the latitude of building a ship whose plans do not survive, but for which two rather vague portraits exist, I think I would have built the corvette General Washington. She was a bit smaller than Rose, but she was about the only Rhode Island ship of that period approaching Rose's size. Moreover, her history was as exciting and as long as that of any American ship in the Revolution, and she deserves to have a whole book written about her.

Very little is known about most of the ships in this book. A few previously unpublished facts—and a number of conclusions—are published herein, but nearly every one of these ships needs far more research than I have the capability or time to devote, and I fervently hope that many of these ships will eventually be the subjects of scholarly monographs by experts. Such monographs would add a great deal to what I have been able to offer in this book, and I expect that they would even refute a few of the imperfect pieces of information I have been able to present. Perhaps corrections and amendments can be made to some future edition of this book, based on research during the intervening years.

I apologize for not being a draftsman; I am self-taught, and the drawings show it, but I believe that my shortcomings in that field will not seriously hinder the reader from studying the designs.

Finally, I would like to thank my wife, Cathy, for being so patient with this lengthy project and for working as a nurse to support me financially. I also thank Barclay H. Warburton III, the loudest of the Rose's critics, for goading me into the research on American ship designs. I am most grateful to Mr. Merritt A. Edson, Jr., who read the manuscript and made some valuable suggestions.

J.F.M.

Part I
INTRODUCTION *and* BACKGROUND

THIS BOOK is about American ships of the Colonial and Revolutionary periods, 1607 to 1789, from the arrival of the first settlers at Jamestown, Virginia, and Sagadahoc, Maine, to the ratification of the constitution of a new nation. We have taken "American" to mean any ship designed, built, or owned by a resident or government of North America.

In most cases, this limitation will be seen to be more than a mere chauvinistic distinction. Most American ships were as different from European ships as the ships of the individual European countries were from each other. Putting aside the political, social, and military implications of being an American in the eighteenth century, one can easily discern a refining process at work in the American spirit that reveals itself in nearly everything the American produced. For example, American architecture of the period would generally not be mistaken for European architecture, although the parentage would be obvious; not only that, but it is usually possible to pinpoint within a few miles where a particular style of American architecture was developed. The steep, hipped roofs of Quebec, the shady galéries of Louisiana, and the heavy plantation houses of Martinique are all obviously of French parentage, but all obviously different from French designs in France and from each other, adapted to the environment and needs of their respective localities. Similarly, the step-gabled town houses and wide-gambrelled country houses of New York, the pastel, curvilinear gables of Curaçao and the elegant houses of Paramaribo are all clearly Dutch, and yet different. The neat Colonial houses of New England are as different from each other as they are from houses in England, and there are some experts who can even tell a Rhode Island house from a Massachusetts or Connecticut house.

American furniture, too, can easily be distinguished from its European equivalents, and collectors can usually tell at a glance whether a fine piece was made in Boston, Newport, New York, or Philadelphia, and whether a country piece came from Pennsylvania or Connecticut.

The reasons for the American refinement of European styles are not hard to find. By the middle of the eighteenth century the European societies had reached a plateau which could be called the highest achievement of individual man, before the advent of mass man; being so highly civilized was somewhat a bore to the European upper classes, and they sought relief from boredom by ostentatious competition with each other. With plenty of money and other resources at hand, the man who wanted a more impressive house built a larger and more massive house, and the man who wanted more impressive furniture made it more massive and ordered that it be dripping with carvings and gilded decoration. There was little refinement of design.

Such competition was not confined to Europe by any means, but it took a different form in the New World. Instead of building a more massive house, the American made his house more impressive by hiring an architect to make it look more perfect in proportion and detail. Similarly, American furniture, with its delicate but robust grace, is generally more perfectly proportioned than its European counterparts. The Townsends, Goddards, Saverys, and others were not only the best cabinetmakers in America, they were probably the best in the world.

This refinement of design in American furniture and architecture was partly the result of the lack of resources available in the New World to build something bigger at that early date, but it was also a result of the American spirit, a spirit that was shaped by the first hundred years of European life in North America, where one had to make do with what one could get, and where one seldom had more than one needed.

In the seventeenth and eighteenth centuries Americans were forced into an overwhelming dependence on the sea. It was by sea that they had arrived from Europe

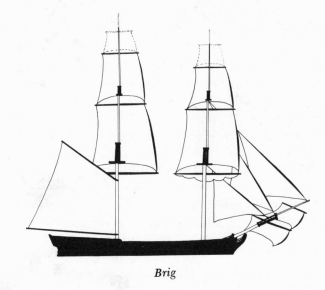

Brig

and by sea that they would have to leave if they found life too rough for them. Many of the necessities of life—and nearly all the luxuries—had to be imported by sea from Europe, just as southerners had to ship tobacco and other crops to Europe to pay for their imports, and northerners had to earn credits in Europe by fishing on the Grand Banks and by carrying anyone's cargo anywhere in the world. If an enemy were to attack, he probably would come by water (either across the ocean or a lake), and the Royal Navy was regarded as the only sure defense against an enemy attack. In addition, roads were so bad that the only sensible communications between the various American Colonies were by sea.

With the Americans depending to such an extent on the sea, we might expect to find that there emerged various recognizable features in American vessels, in the same way that we saw them in American architecture and furniture, and we would be right, at least in part.

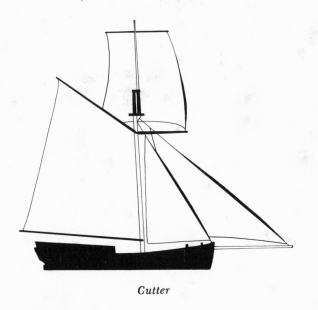

Cutter

[4]

Americans did not actually invent the schooner rig; the rig is believed to have originated in Holland. However, Americans developed the rig to a high degree of perfection and used it widely while it was virtually unknown in Europe. The schooner rig was ideal for handling coastal traders of under 130 tons with three or four men; its simplicity made it almost essential for coasters and fishermen who would be out in all kinds of weather, while its weatherliness made it helpful in furthering one of America's leading industries—smuggling.

Another rig that prospered in America more than in Europe is that of the sloop. The sloop, however, could carry a great deal more sail than a cutter, and so could be built with fuller lines for longer voyages, or with fine lines for smuggling. American sloops frequently ventured into the Indian Ocean and the Pacific, even though they were usually no longer than 60 feet on the

Row Galley

deck. Rhode Island and West Indian shipowners are known to have relied heavily on sloops, and Rhode Islanders and West Indians were more heavily engaged in smuggling than other Americans.

Americans did not limit their development to rigs, but experimented with hull shapes as well. The fishing pink was well suited to riding the sea on the choppy waters around the Grand Banks, while the sharp Marblehead "heeltapper" sped the catch back to New England ports before the fish could spoil. Further south, a sloop, and sometimes a schooner, with a high cabin in the stern came initially from Jamaica and then spread to Bermuda and the Chesapeake, and was recognized the world over as a Bermuda sloop. In Virginia, a pilot boat was developed with very fine lines, and was used for smuggling and escaping from British patrols during the Revolutionary War. Because of their fine lines and light construction these vessels could not profitably carry much cargo, but armed with a few light cannon they made ideal privateers, for they had the speed to escape from pursuers and catch up with potential victims, while with even only a few guns they were usually more heavily armed than most merchant vessels; in addition, they were nimble enough to place themselves in advantageous positions so as to rake their opponent but prevent him from returning fire.

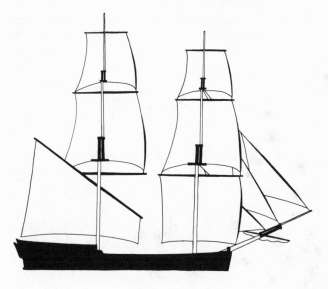

Bilander

[5]

Sloops, schooners, fishing boats, and pilot boats are all relatively small, and it was in such small craft that the majority of American commerce was carried. However, larger vessels were built in America, and after a while they developed their own special characteristics, too. The first large vessel known to have been built in North America was the 44-gun *Falkland,* built for the Royal Navy under contract in Portsmouth, New Hampshire, in 1690. She was followed seven years later by the 34-gun *Bedford Galley,* and there were others.

The navies of all the European powers were proud to the point of chauvinism of their native oak as a shipbuilding wood, but were quite worried about the growing scarcity of the wood; it took several acres of 200-year-old forest to build the hull of the largest battleships of the day (100 guns and over), and so the chauvinism was tempered with a desire to find a substitute for home-grown wood. At first it was thought that New England oak was the answer to Britain's need,

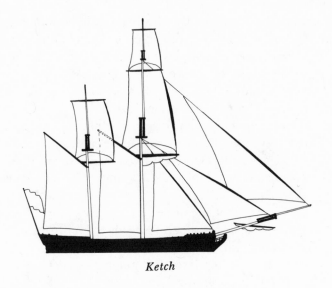

Ketch

but when the first ships built in New Hampshire for the Royal Navy showed a high rate of deterioration it was thought that American wood was inferior, and so very little attention was given to building more vessels of any size in America.

It seems likely that the problems encountered with American oak by the Royal Navy were chiefly a result of poor preparation and seasoning of the wood, as many American-built ships of later years lasted as long as their British counterparts. The British, however, had lost interest in American hardwoods, but increased instead a trade in American softwoods for spar timber. The standard British mast timber used to come from Scandinavia, where pitch pine was abundant. However, the firs and spruces of New England were a cheap and satisfactory substitute, and many pines of New Hampshire and Maine were marked with the king's "Broad Arrow," which meant that no one but the king's men was allowed to chop down the tree in question. The Ameri-

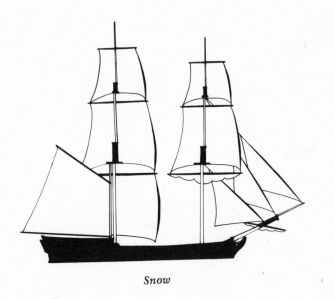

Snow

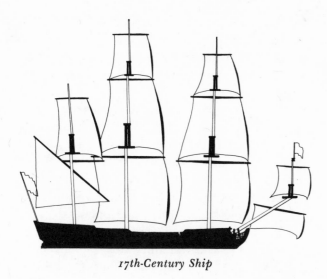

17th-Century Ship

cans themselves also used softwoods in construction of hulls. Southern builders in particular found that long-leaf yellow pine was an excellent and long-lasting wood, but it had its drawbacks in battle; yellow pine was found to splinter badly when hit by a cannonball, and more Americans were killed and injured by pine splinters than by cannonballs in the celebrated battle between the *Chesapeake* and *Shannon* during the War of 1812.

The Spanish had the exact opposite luck of the British in finding shipbuilding wood in their American colonies. A massive and dense species of mahogany grew in Cuba and Santo Domingo which they used so extensively for shipbuilding and other purposes that the wood is to all intents and purposes extinct today, although a few isolated trees may still be found in Haiti. This heavy mahogany is perhaps the most beautiful furniture wood ever found, and its shipbuilding properties were equally impressive. It seemed to be vastly superior to native Spanish oak in strength, longevity, and

ability to resist dry rot and teredo worms, and some vessels built in Havana lasted over a hundred years without major rebuilding. The West Indies, however, contained no wood suitable for use as spars, and so all mast timber had to be imported from Spain or smuggled in from New England.

Strangely enough, there are no records to indicate that the French ever made use of that same mahogany that grew in their share of Santo Domingo (Haiti), nor that the British built anything other than small sloops out of that same mahogany that they found growing in Jamaica. For that matter, it also seems that the British and Dutch settlers in the Demerara area (now Guyana and Surinam) made no shipbuilding use at all of the abundant stocks of greenheart that still grow there. Greenheart, which is virtually impervious to rot and shipworm, is said to be over twice as strong as oak, and it is one of the heaviest woods grown anywhere; it has the disadvantage, however, that it can not easily be bent, and it tends to split under certain conditions.

Gondola (or Gundalow)

[7]

Before the American Revolution, larger merchant ships could usually be divided into two categories, both ship-rigged. The East Indiaman, with its two-decked stern, generally measured between 600 and 1,000 tons, and carried enough guns to be roughly equivalent to a frigate; there were almost none of these built in America before the end of the Revolution, probably because their size and shape were better suited to the longer voyages of the Pacific Ocean and Indian Ocean than the shorter ones of the Atlantic, and trading in the Pacific area was limited to certain large monopolies which had their own shipbuilding facilities in Europe.

The smaller West Indiaman, however, was in common use in the transatlantic trade, and measured from 200 to 600 tons. These ships, of which a good number were built in America, carried as many as 20 guns, although some carried no guns at all. For the most part these ships were simple workhorses, with little elaboration. Some, resembling North Sea colliers like Cook's *Endeavour,* were extremely blunt at each end, and had neither head nor quarter gallery. Although there was little to distinguish them from their European equivalents, by the time of the American Revolution certain regional characteristics had emerged, such as the disposition of the decks of a Philadelphia merchant ship.

At the outbreak of the American Revolution, it is estimated that between a quarter and a third of all vessels under British registry were American built; this includes both those ships owned and operated by Americans, and those sold to British owners as American exports. These American-built ships ranged typically from 60-foot sloops and schooners through 80-foot brigs to 100-foot ships.

During the two wars against the French and Spanish (the War of Austrian Succession or War of Jenkins' Ear, 1739–48, and the Seven Years' War, 1756–63), Americans were quick to outfit privateers [1] and took a heavy toll of enemy merchant shipping. It is perhaps surprising to note that, with few exceptions, these privateers were tiny sloops and schooners armed with perhaps six small guns. Some of these same privateers, especially those from Rhode Island, were rightly accused by the British of trading with the enemy French West Indies (during the Seven Years' War) at the same time as they were attacking French shipping, and the truth of this accusation was one of the main reasons that the British

British Gunboat

[1] Privateers were privately owned armed vessels, licensed by their government to attack enemy ships in time of war. Captains and crews without such a license or commission were liable to be hanged as pirates if caught by the enemy. In order to get the commission, the would-be privateer owner was required to post a heavy bond in case a mistake was made and a friendly vessel was damaged. Privateering has been outlawed in modern warfare.

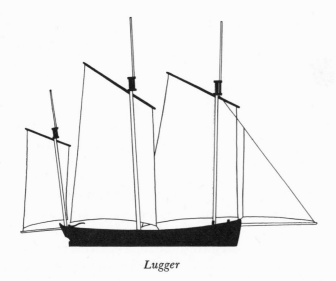

Lugger

placed severe restrictions on American trade and smuggling immediately after the Seven Years' War.

Although the Continental Navy unfortunately amounted to very little during the Revolution when stacked up against the might of the Royal Navy, yet as a shipbuilding feat it was nothing short of spectacular. With only a handful of exceptions, no vessels of any size had hitherto been constructed in the Thirteen Colonies. In the space of a few years, during which they were dragged down by the considerations of waging an exhausting war, the colonists were able to produce one 74-gun battleship (with the frames cut for several more 74s), more than twenty frigates of 24 to 36 guns, and hundreds of lesser ships and privateers.

Some of the smaller vessels revealed innovation in design, while others were merely continuations of what had been produced earlier. But it was in the frigates and 74s that American initiative is most impressive. For the most part, these vessels were marginally larger than European ships of the same rate, which showed an understanding of the long-term evolution of warship design. As for their shapes, the American ships were related more to British precedent than to the ships of any other nation, but they were by no means copies of anything in the Royal Navy. Some of the American builders had doubtless served apprenticeships in British shipyards, and were thus attracted to the British concept of the shape of the midsection, the stem, and the rudder post. Pictures of 32-gun frigates from the 1760s and 1770s from Britain, France, Holland, Spain, Sweden, and Russia have been included in this book for the sake of comparison, and it will be seen that the American designs are more closely related to the British designs than to any others, in the same way as American domestic architecture was related to British domestic architecture during this period, but it is also obviously different from the British precedent.

While the British scorned the Yankee officers and men, they sometimes praised the products of Yankee shipyards when they were able to capture them, and many were taken into the Royal Navy after their capture and their lines taken off in British dockyards so that experts could attempt to analyze why they were so fast and so stable. The British described one captured American frigate as "the most beautiful and fastest frigate that ever swam."

Since American ship designs owed a good deal to their British parentage, a quick look at British ship design would be helpful in understanding the progression of designs through the years. While the British claim that their interest in sea power goes back to King Alfred in the ninth century, they did not make much of an impression on their neighbors until the sixteenth century, when Henry VIII traveled to France on a huge ship named after him. Under his daughter Elizabeth,

British warships became smaller, faster, and more seaworthy. The exploits of the Elizabethan "seadogs" in defeating the superior forces of the Spanish Armada and in voyaging to the far corners of the globe are legendary, and the success of these intrepid mariners was partly due to the shape and size of their ships. While they had high, narrow sterns (supposedly so that they would lie head-to-wind in fierce gales), they were not top-heavy like the Spanish ships that were in effect floating castles. Serious thought had gone into their underwater lines, the theory being that they should bear some resemblance to the shape of a fish; the maximum breadth was well forward of amidships, a shape sometimes described as "cod's head and mackerel tail." They usually had three masts, of which the fore and main were square-rigged, and the mizzen had only a lateen sail on it. Merchant ships of the period looked much like the warships, and examples can be seen in the

18th-Century Ship

replicas of *Susan Constant* at Jamestown, Virginia, and *Mayflower* at Plymouth, Massachusetts. There is also a replica of Drake's *Golden Hinde* at San Francisco, but she is not quite so representative, since the designer appears inadvertently to have given her a beam about four feet too small.

Ship design continued in this fashion for about a century, with the most powerful classes of warship becoming progressively larger, but otherwise with no new ideas. Charles I took an interest in his navy, but neither seems to have benefited from that interest. His son, Charles II, on the other hand, spent a great deal of time in his dockyards, and his reign happens to coincide with both improvements in design and construction and the amending of Charles I's classification systems. At the same time, a number of wars against the Dutch and French contributed to the evolution of fleet tactics, which in turn began to influence design and classification.

As E. H. H. Archibald so well explained in his book *The Wooden Fighting Ship in the Royal Navy,* the Admiralty classified its warships in six rates. A First Rate, the largest size, carried 100 or more guns; a Second Rate mounted 90 or more, and the other rates spread downward in unequal amounts until the Sixth Rate, which carried 20 or more guns. Below Sixth Rate were any number of dispatch vessels. The battle tactics of the day called for opposing fleets to form columns, known as the "Line of Battle," and blast away at each other until one side had inflicted enough damage on the other to force it to withdraw from the conflict. Naturally, only the larger rates would be of any use in the direct line of battle.

The Admiralty would periodically issue "Establishments" for each rate. In other words, the Admiralty would decide what the minimum dimensions for each

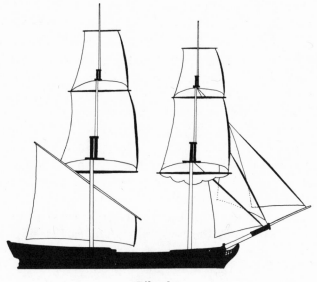

Bilander

rate would be, and how large each rate's guns would be. Almost invariably, each Establishment was for a longer and wider ship for a given rate than the previous Establishment, until by the time of the American Revolution the tonnage of a given rate had more or less doubled in ·roughly a century of development.

The Admiralty owned its own dockyards, including those at Portsmouth, Plymouth, Chatham, Deptford, and Woolwich, but it frequently purchased ships from private shipyards. These private contractors knew the latest Establishment, and were permitted to draw their own designs around the Establishments, often drawing them a few feet larger than the Establishment for good measure. In order to be awarded the contract to build the ship, the builder frequently had a model built of the hull, leaving off most of the deck planking and all the planking below the wale, thus exposing the deck beams and ribs. The Admiralty could inspect the model far more thoroughly than they could inspect a set of drawings, and then either approve the design, correct it, or disapprove it. This type of model is therefore known as an Admiralty model, Admiralty board model, or Admiralty dockyard model. Strictly speaking, Admiralty models were not rigged, because the rigging would get in the way of a close inspection, because the rig would make the model even more expensive, and because it would take up far too much room to transport or store. The rigs of the ships varied little, and in any case were usually the prerogative of the ship's first captain. Nevertheless, one finds a large proportion of beautifully rigged Admiralty models on display today, but it must be remembered that the rig was usually not part of the model's original purpose.

Admiralty models from the seventeenth and eighteenth centuries are among the finest examples of the woodcarver's art, and if they are available at all these days they sell for $50,000 apiece and more. Fine collections of them can be seen at the National Maritime Museum at Greenwich, just outside London; the Science Museum, Kensington, London; the Nederlands Scheepvart Museum in Amsterdam; the Musée de la Marine at the Trocadéro in Paris; the Museo Naval in Madrid; and the United States Naval Academy Museum at Annapolis, Maryland. There is also a splendid collection of recently built Admiralty-type models, every bit as well made as the real ones, at the Smithsonian Institution in Washington, D.C. Admiralty models were generally, although not always, built to a scale of one inch equals four feet ($1:48$), the same scale as the plans were drawn.

The arrangement inside these ships followed a definite and repeated scheme. In the bottom, near the keel, was an area running the length of the ship known as the hold. In this large space was stored all the food, drink, ammunition, and spare parts of ship and rigging that was likely to be needed on a voyage of several months' duration. Above that, on larger ships, was the orlop deck, where the boatswain and carpenter had their stores, where some cables and gunpowder were stored, and where some of the crew slung their hammocks. The headroom on the orlop, as also on all the other decks, was sometimes less than five feet, reflecting a desire on the part of the Admiralty to keep the ship's center of gravity low, the fact that the average height of a seaman was over a foot less than the average height today, and the fact that seamen were regarded as being among the lowest forms of human life in those days, so no one much cared about their headroom.

Above the orlop, and on smaller rates above the hold, was the gun deck, sometimes called the lower gun deck. This carried the heaviest battery of guns, again to keep the center of gravity low, and was so close to the waterline that its guns often could not be used in rough

Sloop

weather, thus effectively reducing the ship's fighting strength by almost one-half. More than a few fine ships have sunk because they left their lower gun deck ports open too long, allowing the sea to rush in over the sills. When the ship was not cleared for action, the gun deck would have hammocks for about half the crew slung over the cannons. At the forward end were the hawse holes, through which led the anchor cables, and a clear space was left aft of the riding bitts all the way to the capstan (a large hand-powered winch, usually located on more than one deck between the main mast and the mizzen mast). In the stern were two or four gunports facing aft, known as stern-chasers, in between which ran the huge tiller. On earlier ships the tiller was connected to a vertical staff on a pivot, known as a whipstaff, and thus the ship could be steered by men standing one or two decks above the tiller, but by the end of the seventeenth century the tiller was connected by means of ropes to a wheel on the upper gun deck or even higher.

The upper gun deck was covered only at the forward end and aft of the mainmast. The open section forward of the mainmast was called the waist, and was usually crowded in with the ship's boats and spare spars. The section of deck over the forward end was called the forecastle or fo'c'sle, while the section over the after end was the quarterdeck, so called because it originally stretched only a quarter of the length of the ship. On the larger rates, the quarterdeck was covered at its after end by another deck, known as the poop (please, not poop deck), and there were even a few First Rates that had a tiny deck above the poop, known as the poop royal.

Under the quarterdeck was the captain's sleeping cabin and great cabin (office and dining room), although on the largest rates the great cabin would be on

Schooner

the middle gun deck (in any case, this is where the modern word "quarters" comes from, describing a place to live). All these large cabins in the stern were well lit with banks of windows, which made them attractive places to live but which also made them extremely vulnerable to damage from enemy shot. These cabins were well suited for carrying admirals, their aides, distinguished passengers, and others, in addition to the captain.

In sharp contrast to the spartan living accommodations for the crew, the great cabins in the stern were frequently decorated in lavish style. For example, John Drew, a prominent house carpenter and joiner who was responsible for the excellent woodwork in many of Portsmouth, New Hampshire's finest homes, was requested by a certain Captain Warren in 1722 to do work on the great cabin of his newest ship, including "Sashes and Lockers," "a hansom beaufait" (obviously

a buffet or sideboard), "& raised Arched pannels" similar to those he had recently installed in the east parlor of the MacPhaedris House. The cabin was also to have "Mouldings" and "Collums" (probably pilasters rather than columns), a canopied bed, a table, and a chest. Captain Warren's cabin was painted in contrasting colors: "the Mouldings done with vermillion the sides or mergents with green & the Collums with blew."

First and Second Rates had three complete gun decks and an armed quarterdeck, but the difference between them was more in the weight than the number of the guns. The First Rate's lower gun deck carried 42-pounder cannon compared to the Second Rate's 32-pounders, and the First Rate's middle gun deck carried 24-pounders compared to the Second Rate's 18-pounders. Both carried 12-pounders on the upper gun deck and 9-pounders on the quarterdeck. Some French and Spanish ships even had light guns on the poop and on the gangways that led from the forecastle to the quarterdeck.

Among Third Rates were six distinct classes of ships. The three-decker, 80-gun ships were top-heavy and clumsy, and could not open their lower deck ports in any kind of wind. The two-decker, 80-gun ships, on the other hand, were too long for their height, which meant that they strained and hogged until stronger construction techniques were devised after the American Revolution. The two-decker, 70-gun ships were considered a little smaller than they needed to be, but the 74-gun ships proved to be such a happy medium that they became the workhorses of the battle fleet. The 60-gun ships, also Third Rates, were designed for the line of battle, but seem to have been better employed as independent cruisers. They were in any case largely replaced at the time of the American Revolution by the stronger and larger 64s, which, however, were still relatively much smaller and weaker than the 74s.

In practice, the First Rates usually stayed in home waters for coastal defense, while the Second Rates were the flagships of cruising fleets. Every fleet had a large number of 74s and a sprinkling of 64s, although these were phased out by the end of the eighteenth century because they were too small to stand the kind of punishment that could be dealt out by the larger ships. One practical reason for leaving the First Rates in home waters and sending the Second Rates to sea was the number of seamen required to man them. The First Rates needed over 850 men, while the Second Rates needed only 750; but since sometimes even that was regarded as extravagant, many admirals were sent off to sea with only a 74 for a flagship.

The Fourth Rates were all of 50 guns. They were originally designed for the line of battle, but as the eighteenth century progressed they were obviously too small for the task. They were, however, very useful as independent cruisers, and as flagships in peacetime on foreign stations where they were not likely to run up against any superior enemy. They carried only eighteen-pounders on their lower deck, nine-pounders on the upper deck, and six-pounders on the quarterdeck. With their smaller size, requiring only about 350 men in peacetime, they were reasonably inexpensive to maintain.

Only a little smaller was the Fifth Rate, theoretically the smallest size of two-deckers. Just as the smallest three-deckers were considered failures (80 guns), so were the smallest two-deckers, although they were still useful as independent cruisers, a number of them having been thus employed in North American waters during the Revolution. These carried 40 or 44 guns. Their death knell was sounded by the invention of the large frigate (about which more later). The Fifth Rates could not sail as well as the frigates, and in rough weather they could not even fire as many guns as the frigates. In the late seventeenth century, there were also some smaller Fifth Rates that mounted about 30 guns, but these were phased out early in the eighteenth century. When the British began to build frigates in the second half of the eighteenth century, the larger ones were called Fifth Rates out of a stubborn sense of tradition, but they bore no resemblance at all to genuine Fifth Rates.

Sixth Rates generally used their lower gun decks for oars, which helped them get in and out of harbors. They always had one loading port on each side of the lower gun deck, and sometimes had as many as four guns to a side. The main battery, however, consisted of six-pounders or nine-pounders on the upper gun deck, with occasionally a few extra guns on the quarterdeck. The stern generally had only one level of windows across it. This type of vessel was unsatisfactory in a number of ways. It was slightly top-heavy because of the height it required to keep the lower deck ports well clear of the water, and in practice its lower deck gunports and oarports leaked considerably. The concept of a Sixth Rate, with its 20 to 30 guns, was rescued by the French, with their invention of the frigate.

The word frigate, from the French *frégate,* had been around for years. Its actual meaning in earlier years was simply a small armed ship that had relatively great speed and that could be used to carry messages for the admirals. Many writers give early dates for the first frigate, but they are mistaken since the French invented the frigate (as we know it) in the 1740s. It is not entirely clear how the French arrived at their breakthrough, for while the British interpreted the new concept as being related to their Sixth Rates the French saw it as being related to the East Indiaman, a large class of armed merchant ship.

For the British, to make a frigate meant to take a Sixth Rate design and alter it. They lowered the lower gun deck until the deck itself was almost as low as the waterline. They removed all guns from that deck, except the stern-chasers, and removed all gunports, loading ports, and oarports, although they left the hawse holes, riding bitts, capstan, and tiller. The main battery was then exclusively on the upper gun deck. This caused a paradox in nomenclature, for the tradition-bound British called the lower deck the gun deck, while it had in fact no guns on it at all (other than temporary stern-chasers). Modern writers have tended to ignore this and call it a berth deck, which is what in fact it was. Oars, if retained at all, were usually placed between the gunports on the upper deck.

As a class the frigate cut across the boundaries of the rates, for frigates could have anywhere from 20 to 50 guns merely by making them longer, but still with the same deck arrangements. The smaller frigates were usually armed with nine-pounders, although a few appeared with only six-pounders, and the French preferred eight-pounders. Those of 28 to 40 guns usually carried 12-pounders for their main armament, although two American frigates built in Rhode Island in 1776 caused a stir by mounting 18-pounders, and the French-designed, Dutch-built, 40-gun frigate *South Carolina,* built in 1777, carried 36-pounders; in this, she was a forerunner of the large American frigates of the War of 1812, for they were the first to mount guns as large as 24-pounders on a regular basis, but *South Carolina* was also identical to East Indiamen being built in France at that time, so here the distinction between frigate and East Indiaman was blurred.

Frigates were fast, maneuverable, and good fighters in bad weather. Moreover, they were economical on crews. A 20-gun frigate could be manned with 70 men in peacetime, and could carry as many as 200 in wartime. The extra men were useful in manning any prizes they might capture. While frigates were extremely useful to the battle fleets for running up and down with messages in a battle or for scouting ahead for the enemy, they were also at their best as independent cruisers and as convoy guards. The British built frigates in classes of 20, 24, 28, 32, 36, and 38 guns. The French built them in classes of 26, 32, 36, 38, 40, and over.

Smaller than the smallest frigates were a variety of craft. The largest of these were known as sloops-of-war, a term that had nothing at all to do with the sloop rig. For that reason, to avoid confusion we will refer to them by their French name in this book, *corvette.* The ship-rigged corvette was not especially common in the British navy, but a number appeared in the Continental Navy, where they generally gave a good accounting of themselves. Their speed and their shallow draft enabled them to escape from larger ships, except in rough weather, when they could not carry enough sail to escape from, say, a 74. The larger sort of American privateer was usually this type of vessel, mounting anywhere from 14 to 20 six-pounders. Their deck arrangement was generally the same as a frigate's, although with even less headroom, but some dispensed with the raised quarterdeck and forecastle, preferring instead to cover the whole gun deck with a flush spar deck from stem to stern. This was an innovation that was echoed a few years later in the designs of some of the large American frigates that fought in the War of 1812.

Smaller corvettes were rigged as brigs, both in Britain and America. While a few followed the deck pattern of a frigate, the majority had only a raised quarterdeck and no forecastle. These vessels generally mounted anywhere from 10 to 18 guns, mostly six-pounders or smaller. They were particularly useful as commerce raiders. The Americans used them as privateers, and the British used them to catch American privateers, as well as for more mundane duties.

Smaller still were the various schooners, sloops, cutters, and luggers, mounting anywhere from 6 to 14 guns, mostly six-pounders or smaller. These, however, were not called corvettes or sloops-of-war. The sloops and schooners usually had either a raised quarterdeck or at least a small "cuddy" or roofed cabin in the stern, while the cutters and luggers had completely open gun decks, with cramped and ill-ventilated quarters in the hold along with the supplies. Schooners and sloops were far more common in America than luggers and cutters, which, however, were more common in European navies.

In the middle of the American Revolution, a new type of gun was invented by the Carron Foundry in Scotland, and it was therefore called a carronade. This was a short-barreled gun that could only be used at close range, but for a given size of ball the weight of a carronade was only a tiny fraction of the weight of a regular cannon. This meant that a tiny sloop or schooner could carry large-bore guns, but the practical implications were not realized until the French revolutionary wars later in the century. Only a few carronades were actually used in the American Revolution.

In the period under discussion in this book, the principal motive power of larger vessels was provided by square sails. Each of these sails was rigged in essentially the same way, so that even if a ship had a great many of these sails anyone who knew how to handle one square sail could theoretically handle all of them. For this reason, it was a relatively simple matter to train the "green" crews that usually were found for naval vessels in time of war.

Sails were set on masts above the ship. The largest ships had three masts, and rarely a fourth, as well as the bowsprit that was present on nearly every sailing vessel, large or small. The three-masted vessel was described as ship-rigged, and her masts were the fore, the main, the mizzen. Two-masted vessels could have a variety of rigs. The ketch had a main and a mizzen, but the others —brig, snow, bilander, and schooner—had a fore and a main, while the lugger was the equivalent of a three-masted schooner. Single-masted vessels were almost invariably sloops or cutters.

Since trees did not grow tall or strong enough for the required sail area to be set from one piece of wood, the mast was usually made from more than one tree, portions overlapping each other for a few feet. At the doublings or joints between the masts were a pair of trestletrees on which the second mast could stand, with a band around both masts a few feet higher up. This system enabled the crew to remove the upper masts without difficulty in case of storm or to make repairs.

As a rule, each mast had one square sail that could be set from it, although for the highest section this rule was not always observed in light weather. The lowest sail, set on the lower mast, was called the course, and this corresponded to the mainsail of medieval and earlier ships. The sail above that in late medieval times was thought to be as high as it was possible to rig a sail, so that was known as the topsail, set on the topmast. When someone eventually rigged a mast and sail still higher, it was thought that only the most gallant (meaning brave) seamen would go up that high, so it was called the topgallant sail or t'gans'l, set on the topgallant mast. Above that was flown the royal standard of the king when he was present, so when someone dared to set a sail in fair weather on the flag staff, that was called the royal (not the royal sail).

Even the bowsprit was often in more than one piece, known as the bowsprit and the jibboom, and each of them could have a square sail set under it, known as a spritsail. In the seventeenth and early eighteenth centuries, the bowsprit had a small mast stepped vertically on the end in place of the jibboom, known as the spritsail topmast, upon which was set the spritsail topsail, but this was often more trouble than it was worth.

Each square sail was suspended from a horizontal wooden spar known as a yard. All the yards were hoisted up when the sail was set by means of a rope attached to its center, known appropriately enough as a halyard. When the sails were not set, but furled on their yards, the yards were lowered to the level of the top of the mast below them, although the course yards remained where they were. One yard, however, the mizzen course yard, also known as the crossjack or cro'j'k, did not have any sail set below it; it was used simply to spread the bottom of the mizzen topsail.

In light weather, additional square sails could be set by means of extensions lashed onto the ends of the regular yards. The sails set on these extensions were called studding sails or stu'ns'ls. During the Revolution and the years immediately before it, American vessels had to be fast to escape from British patrols, and so Americans made full of their light-weather sails, such as studding sails and royals. Sometimes they held onto these sails in fresher winds with disastrous consequences; either the masts would break or the ship would literally sail herself right under—and this happened more than once. American masts were generally taller and their sails larger than those of their European counterparts; British captains complained that American ships they had captured were "overhatted." American masts were also frequently more raked than European masts, the foremast being vertical or raked slightly aft, the mainmast being raked farther aft, and the mizzen being raked even farther aft.

On all three-masted ships, the space between the foremast and the mainmast was always much greater than the space between the mainmast and the mizzen. As the eighteenth century wore on, however, the foremast was placed farther and farther aft, the Americans being leaders in this trend. Another trend was in the steeve or slope of the bowsprit; except in cutters and luggers, whose bowsprits were horizontal or even sloping downward, bowsprits sloped upward at quite a steep angle, but as the American Revolution began bowsprits started to slope a little less.

Masts were held upright by guy ropes, called stays, from all sides. The side stays, known as shrouds, were the most numerous; there were sometimes more than a dozen on each side of a main lower mast. These shrouds were kept taut by means of a tackle running between two special blocks known as deadeyes. The lower deadeyes were pushed outward from the side of the ship by a chainwale (pronounced "channel," and sometimes spelled that way too); the deadeyes were connected to the ship by means of the chains or chainplates below the chainwales.[2]

The topmasts and topgallant masts were also supported by shrouds in a similar manner. The topmast shrouds were held out by the platform known as the fighting top, and the topgallant shrouds were held out by the crosstrees. Instead of chainplates they were secured to a point on the mast below by cables known as futtock shrouds.

The backstays from every level of mast went all the way down to the chainwales on the side of the hull; to all appearances, they were merely extra shrouds placed immediately aft of the regular shrouds. So that the sea-

---

[2] Once while talking with some salty Nova Scotia riggers, I decided to play a joke on them by letting it be known that just as "chainwale" is pronounced "channel," so "chainplate" was actually pronounced "chimplet" (which it is not). A year or so later, I heard some other Nova Scotians from another part of the province talking knowledgeably about "chimplets."

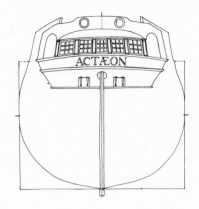

A Draft of His Majesty's 32-Gun Frigate *Actaeon,* built at Woolwich in 1775

Length on the Lower Deck	120′ 6″
Length of Keel for Tonnage	99′ 6″
Breadth	33′ 6″
Depth in Hold	11′ 0″
Tonnage	594

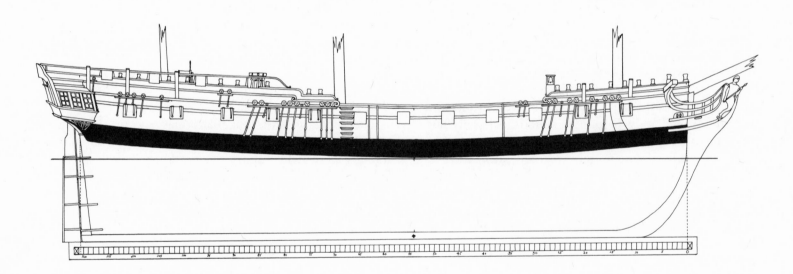

men could climb into the rigging, light lines were lashed and tied horizontally across the shrouds on each side of the ship at intervals of about one foot all the way up. These were called ratlines, and where the shrouds grew too close together to insert one's foot between them the ratlines were extended onto one or more backstays.

The forestays ran quite differently from the backstays. For the lower masts, the forestays ran over the center line of the ship until they reached a point where the next mast entered the deck, or, in the case of the foremast, where they reached the end of the bowsprit. Lower forestays were frequently doubled for extra strength. The forestays for the upper masts led to the top of the next level of the mast next forward of them, except on the foremast whose forestays went to various positions on the bowsprit and jibboom. As for the bowsprit and jibboom, they had stays as well. A heavy stay led from the stem of the ship just above the waterline to a point near the end of the bowsprit; this was called the bobstay, and there were sometimes more than one of them. Sometime in the 1790s (outside the scope of this book) a strut pointing downward from the end of the bowsprit served as a spreader to give a more direct pull to the martingale stay that held down the end of the jibboom. This is generally known as a dolphin striker for obvious reasons, and it appears in many modern models and paintings of ships from the Colonial and Revolutionary periods, which is totally incorrect. Putting a dolphin striker on models or pictures of pre-1790 ships is one of the most common mistakes found on such models, and there should be no excuse for it.

Although it took many years before the advantage of setting sails on the forestays was recognized, forestaysails, loosely known as jibs, began to appear on the various stays between the foremast and bowsprit/jibboom. These were small triangular sails that were at their most useful when the wind was coming from the side or slightly ahead of abeam. As the eighteenth century progressed, bold captains began to experiment with setting staysails between the other masts as well. The experiments were pronounced to be a success, and the staysails grew bigger and more numerous, many of them being quadrilateral. While the staysails did not have quite the driving power of the square sails, and while they were of practically no value at all when the wind was aft, there are cases on record (and I have pictures to prove it) of large square-riggers sailing to windward using nothing but staysails. It looked mighty peculiar, but on rare occasions when a ship had to claw off from a lee shore or beat into a crowded anchorage such a sail arrangement provided the right combination of speed and control to accomplish the task.

Finally, there was one more fore-and-aft sail on a ship. This was set on the lower mizzen mast. In the seventeenth and early eighteenth centuries, this was a lateen [3] or triangular sail set on a yard hung on the side of the mizzenmast, sloping in such a way as to be parallel to the mizzen forestay; about as much of the yard projected forward of the mast as aft of it, and it was thought to be a great nuisance. Its only real function was in balancing the ship to make her steer more easily. As the eighteenth century progressed, the forward end of the yard lost its part of the sail, so that a quadrilateral sail was set on the after end only. By the time of the Revolution, most, but not all, ships had replaced the lateen yard with a simple gaff, which was all the quadrilateral sail needed. The sail was known as a mizzen (loose-footed) or driver (extended by a boom);

---

[3] The word *lateen* has nothing to do with Latin, but is a corruption of *la trina,* which means "three-pointed."

we usually call both kinds by the nineteenth-century name of spanker. In light weather, a form of studding sail known as a ringtail could be added to the spanker. This was not actually an extension of the sail, but a narrow square sail that was only used for sailing downwind. In the 1790s, this sail was modified to be an actual extension of the spanker, and it could then be used for sailing to windward in light weather.

Before 1790 the spanker was quite a small sail, and almost invariably did not have a boom on ship-rigged vessels until after that date. As soon as it was married with a boom, its foot increased greatly in length until the sail projected considerably beyond the stern of the ship. Essentially the same sail had been set for years on the mainmast of brigs, snows, and schooners, and here it almost invariably had a boom, although the sail was attached to the boom only at the tack and the clew.

On a few American frigates in the Revolution, a few extra square feet of sail area was gained by the use of a fourth mast, aft of the mizzen. This was actually the staff for the ensign on which a lateen sail was set from a yard, and an extension was provided on top from which the ensign flew. The purpose of this little sail was probably to aid the helmsman in balancing the ship while she was sailing to windward. Incidentally, in this period the ensign was always set on a staff mounted on the stern just forward of the tafferel, and it was never flown from the gaff of the spanker; this is another all-too-common mistake among modern painters and model builders when they are dealing with ships of this period. This custom of flying the ensign from a staff began to be abandoned in the 1790s when the length of the spanker booms made it impractical to change tacks while the ensign staff was in position.

Brigs, snows, and bilanders were the two-masted rigs closest in configuration to the ship rig. Each was a ship rig missing its mizzen mast, and there are accounts of vessels that spent parts of their lives rigged both ways. On the brig, the spanker was borrowed from the missing mizzen and placed on the main, and therefore the main course yard became the crossjack with no sail set on it. The snow was identical to the brig except in that one place; the snow set its spanker on a vertical spar mounted only about one foot aft of the mainmast, thus allowing its gaff jaws to travel up and down without interfering with the set of the main course. The bilander, a rare rig, had no main course, but it set a huge lateen or quadrilateral sail on a lateen yard in place of the spanker.

While the previous three rigs were like a ship rig minus its mizzen, the ketch was similar to the ship rig but minus its foremast. The mainmast was stepped in or close to its usual place, thus leaving an enormous gap between it and the bowsprit. The gap was often profitably used to house one or more giant mortars for lobbing explosive shells on enemy positions; with virtually no rigging in the way, the mortar shells could be fired with relative safety.

The schooner had two masts, although in the nineteenth century there were some schooners that had three or more masts. The essence of the schooner rig was its fore-and-aft sails. The mainsail, which resembled the spanker on a ship, was slightly bigger than the foresail, but otherwise the two sails were nearly identical. There were from one to three fore-staysails or jibs. For sailing downwind, many schooners could carry a square topsail on the foremast, and some even had one on the mainmast as well. There are occasional pictures of schooners setting in a fore course as well in fine weather, but this was the exception. The schooner rig never went higher than the topmasts, and sometimes not higher than the lower masts.

The schooner is thought to have originated in Holland. A similar rig, which must have been developed over many centuries in the Mediterranean, is the lugger. This rig was used extensively by the French, both in the Mediterranean and in northern waters, but it was seldom seen on American vessels. The lugger had two masts positioned roughly as they would be on a schooner, and a third mast tacked on almost as an afterthought, just aft of the rudder post. Each of these masts carried a lugsail, which is a quadrilateral sail suspended from a tilted yard that ran fore and aft. The mainsail was slightly larger than the foresail, and the mizzen was much smaller. One jib was usually carried on the horizontal bowsprit, which carried no jibboom. In light weather, lug-topsails were set on spindly topmasts above the lugsails. Luggers were fast and light, and therefore made good smugglers and commerce raiders.

To catch the luggers, the British used the cutter. The cutter generally had an identical hull shape to the lugger, but had only one mast. On this was set a regular gaff-mainsail, similar to the spanker on a ship, but with a long boom. One or more jibs were set on the horizontal bowsprit, which, like the lugger's bowsprit, never carried a jibboom. Many cutters could set a square topsail and even a course in fine weather, and a few even had a square topgallant set above the topsail on the same mast pole. Cutters could carry tremendous sail area for their size, and they were very fast in the right conditions.

The cutter rig is thought to have been a variation on the Dutch sloop rig. Like the cutter, the sloop had only one mast, and could set essentially the same sails as the cutter. The only major difference in the rig was the bowsprit; in the sloop, the bowsprit was steeved up at an angle, and could carry a jibboom, thus allowing more jibs to be set. One might well wonder why enterprising mariners did not employ the sloop rig on a cutter hull, and vice versa, but there is no record of its ever having

been done, and the two classes of vessels developed independently; Americans preferred the sloop and the British preferred the cutter, although, of course, the British built a number of sloops and the Americans built a few cutters.

Rigs were not the only distinguishing features between ships of different nationalities. In many cases, the hull shapes were very characteristic of their countries of origin. Most of these characteristics were based on the common practice in either Britain or France, and it was not uncommon to find, say, a Spanish ship that combined obvious French features with obvious British features. This is largely because the other countries tended to hire French and British shipwrights to rebuild their navies between wars.

With warships, one of the most obvious differences between the French and British practices was that the French ships were generally much larger than the British ships of the same number of guns. Theoretically, this made the French ships faster and more weatherly than the British, but the French frequently threw away their advantage through poor seamanship and lack of experience. Nevertheless, the British kept enlarging their ships throughout the eighteenth century in an effort to keep up with the French.

The midship section of French ships was frequently different from that of British ships. The French section had a nearly flat floor, followed by a pronounced knuckle, followed by a fairly flat slope up to the waterline to another knuckle. The supposed advantage of this shape is that the ballast could be kept lower, contributing to stability, but the more simply rounded British bottoms apparently did not suffer greatly from lack of stability.

Other national characteristics will appear from time to time in the commentary on individual ships later in the book. Among those to look for and compare are the

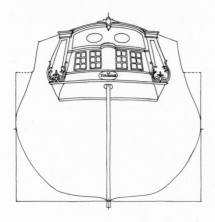

A Draft of the 32-Gun French Frigate *La Sirenne,* built in France
before 1768˙

Length on the Lower Deck	130'
Length of Keel for Tonnage	115'
Breadth	35' 2"

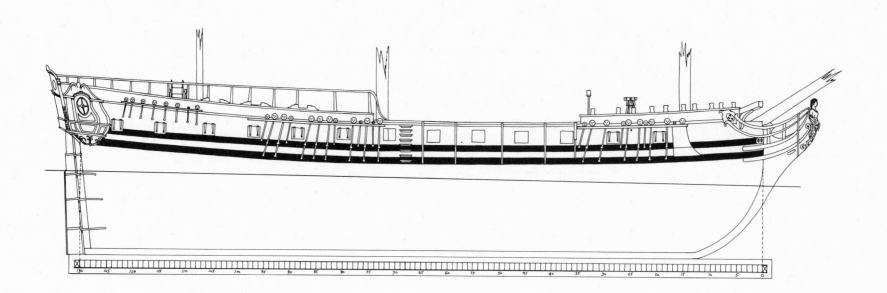

shape of the tafferels, the head rails, the quarter galleries, the rake of the stem and sternposts, the degree of sheer, the fineness of the entry, and the number and placement of fenders and wales along the topsides. While the French seem to have been largely the innovators—and indeed they explored the science of ship design and construction far more thoroughly than did the British—the British did invent one important advance in design which nearly everyone copied. This was the round tuck stern. Previous to the middle of the seventeenth century all ships had square sterns, which caused a great deal of drag in the water. The British invented a means of fairing the underwater part of the stern upward to a horizontal transom beam, which made for rounded underwater lines in the stern, hence the name "round tuck stern." By the early nineteenth century, nearly every major ship built anywhere in Europe or America had the round tuck stern.

Other national characteristics had to do with the proportions of the length and breadth of the vessel to each other. The Dutch, because of their shallow, muddy coastline, came up with a midsection that was shallower than others, and therefore wider in order to support the same cargo and the same rig; Dutch vessels also had much flatter bottoms than others in case they should have to sit on the mud to await the next high tide. Many smaller American craft also had great beam, particularly at the time of the Revolution, but in this case the goal was speed coupled with stability. Many late eighteenth-century American bottoms, therefore, were far from flat, but had great deadrise, almost like a *V*, and also had sharp entries to match. The American design might have caught on faster in Europe if it had not usually been accompanied by extremely light construction scantlings in an effort to obtain still more speed. Light construction did not stand up well in the foul weather frequently found in European waters. Euro-

peans were also impatient with the fact that American vessels were only fast when not overloaded, which, with their sharp deadrise, it was far too easy to do.

While the shape and appearance of ships varied somewhat from country to country, the actual construction varied little. The keel, a massive timber or timbers of oak or elm, was laid with the stern toward the water (although the Dutch launched their ships bow first). On it were mounted the stem and the sternpost. Frames were added in a sequence, usually starting from the stern.

Frames were of oak, and were sawn to the desired shape. The natural shapes and crooks of trees were a help, but only to a certain extent. Frames had to be built up out of a series of short, curved pieces, and they were usually but not always built in pairs, so that the butts or joints in one frame were overlapped by the wood of the other. Each of these short lengths of curved wood was called a futtock. The two frames were held together sometimes by iron bolts, sometimes by iron spikes, and sometimes by wooden tree nails (pronounced "trunnels"), usually of locust wood. The port pair of frames was joined to the starboard pair by a floor timber at the bottom, and by a number of temporary braces nearer the top.

When all the frames had been erected on top of the keel, another heavy longitudinal member, known as the keelson, was fastened on top of the floors. At this stage, it would be seen that there were large gaps between the forward frames and the stem, and the after frames and the sternpost. Into these gaps, where the planks would have very pronounced curves, were placed special frames and parts of frames, set at right angles to the curve of the planks. These were called cant frames, and they were usually more solidly spaced than the regular frames.

As soon as all the frames were set up, they were

joined longitudinally by temporary braces or ribbands. The first planks to be fastened to the ship were usually those of the main wale, which we have drawn as a thick dark line curving along the topsides in all our drawings. The wale planks were at least an inch thicker than the regular planks, both to provide extra longitudinal strength and also to serve as rubbing strakes when the ship was bumping against another ship or against a dock. The wale was usually situated at the widest point of the ship.

Above the wale the frames sloped inward, so that the ship was quite a bit narrower at the top than at the waterline. This is called tumblehome, and its purpose has been explained in a variety of different ways. Some say that it was to make it more difficult for an enemy to capture the ship by boarding, while others claim that it came from a misunderstanding of the principles of the center of gravity. Regardless of its origin, it was a typical feature of nearly all ships in the period under discussion in this book, and tumblehome only began to disappear in the nineteenth century. Tumblehome contributed to the rigidity of the hull, but it was also the place where rainwater could most easily get behind the planks to cause rot.

The planks above the main wale were interspersed occasionally with more wales, usually only one plank wide, and usually molded into an interesting decorative shape. These naturally provided additional strength and longitudinal rigidity to the ship, but it is hard to imagine that some of them were more than decorative, for they were often intersected every so many feet by a gunport.

In the nineteenth and twentieth centuries, when a plank had to be bent around a tightly curved part of a ship it was placed in a steam box and impregnated with steam. When it came out of the steam box it could be bent to the desired shape, and it would hold that shape after it had dried. Earlier shipwrights had a more difficult time. Sometimes they would cut the planks from a naturally curved tree, and sometimes they tried charring the plank on one side. Some used green lumber, which is more likely to bend than seasoned wood, but which is almost certain to rot in a very short time. Others soaked the wood for months in brine. Some form of steam preparation may have been available by the time of the Revolution, especially since one American frigate is said to have been launched only sixty days after her keel was laid, and yet she had not rotted appreciably by the end of the war; the shipwrights would not have had time to search for naturally crooked trees for the planking in her bow and stern and then allow it to season, so they must have used whatever wood they had on hand.

When the outside planking was complete, a similar amount of work remained to be done on the inside of the ship. Along the underside of where the deck beams would go a timber was placed along the back of the frames. This was called the clamp or shelf, and part of its duty was to provide still more longitudinal bracing. Decks were nearly flat from end to end of the ship, and did not follow the sheer line. Deck beams were frequently not long enough to stretch all the way across the ship, so they were pieced together. They were supported near the middle of the ship by two carlines, which were timbers running the length of the ship; the carlines themselves were supported at intervals by vertical posts, some of which ran down as far as the floor timbers and up as high as the upper decks, where they could be used as bitts or supports for bitts.

After the decks had been planked, the inside surface of the frames was covered over by planking as thick as the outside planking, although often of an inferior wood. These inner planks were known as the ceiling (what we normally think of as the ceiling in a house was called the deckhead or the overhead), and they served as further longitudinal stiffening. In some ships there were gaps in the ceiling to allow air to circulate between the frames, but others were completely sealed up and some were even caulked for extra rigidity. In these latter cases, salt was sometimes placed in large quantities between the inner and outer planking; this pickling was intended to preserve the wood from the rot that usually attacked it when it was denied full circulation of air.

For some ships no further construction was done, but for others knees had to be fitted. These were right-angled trusses cut from a natural crook in a tree or, more frequently, from tree roots. In America the hackmatack tree was traditionally used for this purpose. Some knees were placed under the deck beams so as to bind them to the sides of the ship; these were called hanging knees. Other knees, placed horizontally between the deck beams themselves to keep them straight, were called lodging knees.

For many of those ships that had a head, planking in the bows did not bend around to the stem for about the upper six feet of the topsides, but stopped instead at a bulkhead that was set a few feet aft of the stem. This was called the beakhead bulkhead, and it provided a small platform from which it was easier both to reach the head itself and to manage sails on the bowsprit. However, the beakhead bulkhead was a particularly weak point on ships that had it, for it was prone to leak in bad weather and it was very vulnerable to being pierced by shot from an enemy ship in a maneuver known as raking. The beakhead bulkhead began to disappear for this reason soon after 1750, and by the time of the Revolution the majority of warships smaller than the First and Second Rates were built with round bows.

The sterns, too, with their flimsy construction and wide expanse of window area, were vulnerable to raking fire from enemy ships, but the traditional sterns did not give way to solid round construction until about the 1820s.

Among the most common misconceptions about ships of the period of this book are the notions about their color schemes. Many people think that because the 44-gun frigate *Constitution,* now on display in Boston, is painted black with white trim all ships of the period were so painted. This is doubly misleading. To begin with, the *Constitution* was not painted this way until about 1830, so in terms of color (as well as countless other details, both major and minor) she is not in the slightest representative of ships of her true period (1795–1815) any more than she looks at all the way she did in that period. When she was first built, she was painted ochre with a black wale strake; the two uppermost panels of planks on the topsides were vibrant colors, probably blue and red; much of her head and tafferel were gilded, while her rails were black and her deck furniture was largely red. There are at least two period paintings showing her this way, and they merely confirm that she was painted more or less the same as other ships of her day. With an expenditure of over $4 million spent on the *Constitution* to put her in good condition for the Bicentennial it is greatly to be deplored that she has not been restored to either the shape or the colors of her original appearance, or at least of the way she looked in the War of 1812, her finest years.

How did these colors become so standardized, and where did they come from? In the seventeenth century the topsides of ships were usually oiled with linseed oil, which was available in large quantities because of the demand for linen. It was noticed, however, that the older a ship grew and the more it had to be oiled for

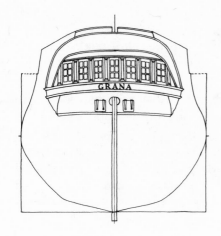

A Draft of the 32-Gun Spanish Frigate *Grana*, built in Spain about 1777

Length on the Lower Deck	118' 2"
Length of Keel for Tonnage	97'
Breadth	32'
Depth in Hold	9' 4"
Tonnage	528

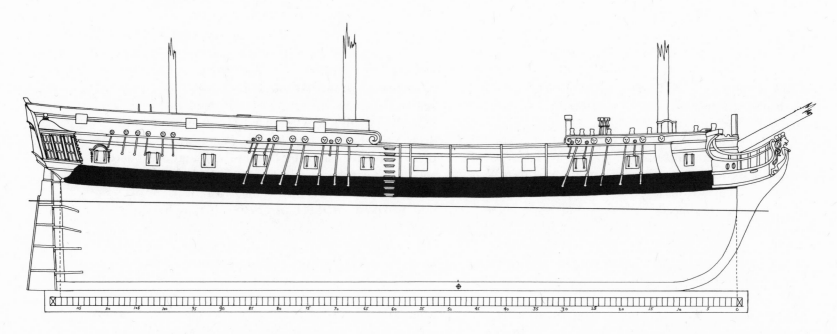

protection, the darker it became. Thus, it would be easy for a potential enemy to tell roughly how old a ship was by its color, and hence the enemy would be able to include that fact in its decision as to whether or not the ship could easily be captured. Therefore, it became the custom that ships were no longer oiled but painted to resemble the color of new oiled oak. Therefore, nearly all ships in the period covered by this book were ochre in color, varying somewhat from almost yellow to light brown, some being almost orange. There were occasional exceptions, of course; some Spanish ships are said to have been painted in red stripes, and there were a few that were all black (but the MGM copy of the merchant ship *Bounty* for the film *Mutiny on the Bounty* is ludicrously inaccurate in blue).

After the ochre, the next most obvious element of color on the topsides was the main wale. The main wale was a band of planks (thicker than the rest) that followed the sheer of the hull. The wale essentially provided longitudinal rigidity for the hull, but it also served a useful function as a rubbing strake; since it was located at the widest part of each section of the ship, it was the piece that would grind against a dock or against another ship when the ship lay alongside. Consequently, since before Elizabethan times the wale had been coated with pitch or pine tar to give it maximum wearing durability. Thus, the wale was almost always black.

The bottoms of ships were given the benefit of much experience and research, for without a healthy bottom the ship would surely sink. The greatest enemy of the ship's bottom was the teredo worm, a borer worm (related to the clam) that lives in salt water from the arctic to the equator. It does not actually eat wood, but riddles all kinds of wood with tunnels that are invisible from the outside, and feeds on microscopic organisms that float past the hull. Without protection a wooden hull would be useless in only a few years.

Since worms would not cross the layer of tar between two planks, one solution frequently used called for the bottom to be sheathed in an additional layer of planks that could be replaced every few years when the worms had destroyed enough of it. Another solution called for the coating of the bottom with an evil-smelling and poisonous substance that would discourage worms from making the ship their home. This substance was usually included in tallow, so the ships' bottoms were usually a dirty-white or off-white color. For longer bottom life, the tallow compound could be applied on top of wooden sheathing, the whole operation being done with the ship still in the water, by "careening" or pulling the ship over onto her side and doing one side of the bottom at a time. The tallow compound was also reasonably effective in discouraging the growth of seaweed, barnacles, mussels, and other marine life on the bottom that can reduce the ship's speed by as much as one-half, but the tallow compound had to be applied at least once a year.

The tallow compound was obviously far from perfect, so frequent attempts were made to find substitutes. Lead sheathing was tried, but it was both expensive and heavy, and besides it seemed ineffective against marine growth. In the 1760s, experiments were made with copper sheathing, which would quickly turn a light green in color. The copper plates were effective against borers and marine growth, but they caused all iron parts of the ship under water, such as plank fastenings and rudder hinges, to disintegrate under electrolytic or galvanic action. A few years later, all iron fastenings below the water were replaced by bronze or copper fastenings if copper plates were to be fitted. The Royal Navy made immediate and extensive use of the discovery, but few American or French ships had copper sheathing before 1790. One of history's little ironies is that during the wars of the French Revolution and

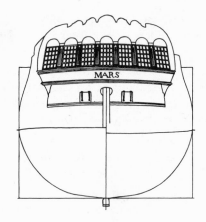

A Draft of the 32-Gun Dutch Frigate *Mars,* captured in 1780

Length on the Lower Deck	130′ 9″
Length of Keel for Tonnage	108′ 10″
Breadth	34′ 10″
Depth in Hold	11′ 10″
Tonnage	703

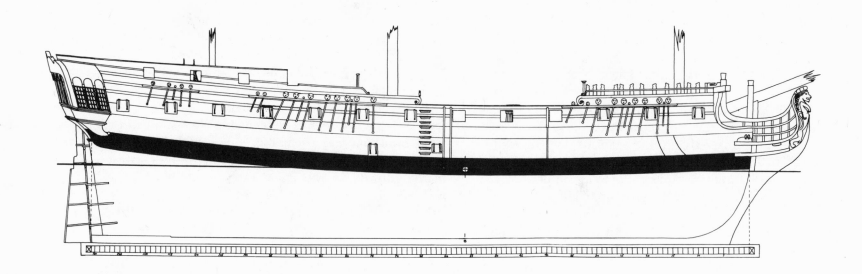

Napoleonic expansion the French continued to sell the British tons of copper (and brandy) which the British were quite openly using to make their ships go faster and last longer, which inevitably resulted in defeat for the French.

One area of the ship's hull that varied in color was the area between the main wale and the waterline in the bow and the stern. Most ships continued the ochre color down into these areas, but some continued the tallow up to the wale all the way around, thus making the areas off-white, and others continued the black of the wale down to the waterline.

Most ships were arranged in such a way as to have a panel running along the topsides immediately below the gunwale. This was often painted a bold color, such as blue or green, although sometimes it was left ochre, and sometimes it was even black, especially in later ships. Another similar panel immediately above this one in the way of the quarterdeck and forecastle was often painted a contrasting bold color, such as red, although these were also occasionally black in later ships. These bold panels were frequently decorated with leafy scrolls or classical frieze-type designs picked out in gold leaf or even carved in light relief.

Ships in the late seventeenth century were dripping with carving, but the amount of carving was cut back sharply in the eighteenth century as a cost-cutting measure. Particularly notable among the carvings on the earlier ships were the circular wreaths that surrounded the gunports on the upper decks, and the statues that filled every conceivable niche on the stern. Most of the carved parts, at least of the earlier ships, were covered in gold leaf. Later ships restricted the carving generally to the figurehead and possibly a little on the stern and quarter galleries.

Figureheads varied from ship to ship and country to country. The most common design by far was that of a crowned lion. The lion was stylized rather than sculpted from life, and resembled a heraldic lion, although at various times when national taste turned to things Oriental the lions acquired a distinctly Chinese flavor. Lookouts on a British ship could usually tell from the shape of the lion's crown if another ship were British or from a continental nation.

Lions began to give way to other designs by the middle of the eighteenth century. Gods and goddesses or other figures from classical mythology were the most popular, although an individual ship could have a figurehead that reflected her name: the frigate *Unicorn*, for example, would have a unicorn, while a ship named after a general would most likely have a statue of that general. Captain Cook's *Resolution* had a horse, as did a number of other ships. First Rates and Second Rates rarely had lions at any period; instead, they often had a collection of allegorical or mythological figures, or a member of the royal family seated on a horse.

In our practical age, we might well wonder what was the point of wasting time and money to stick a long cut-water and figurehead onto the bow of a ship some 200 years ago. While the carving itself was decorative and had no functional purpose other than as a morale builder, the space between the figurehead and the bow was extremely practical. This was called the head, and it was the lavatory facility for all the enlisted men on the ship (officers had pots in their cabins), which one might imagine could be quite uncomfortable in a cold winter storm. It was thought that having these facilities in the bow would ensure that they were kept clean by frequent large waves and hence there would be less risk of disease, but cleaning the head was a daily chore that was usually not helped much by waves. American ships, incidentally, are said to have been infamous the world over for their poorly kept heads.

On larger ships, the head was equipped with two en-

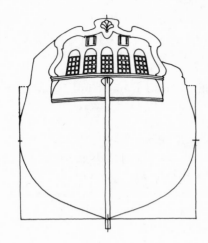

A Draft of the 32-Gun Swedish Frigate *Jaramas,* built at Stockholm before 1768

      Length Between Perpendiculars   121' 4"

      Breadth   32'

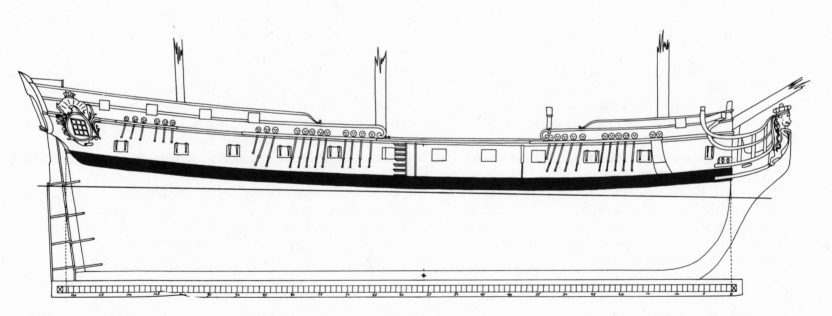

closed privies for use in bad weather, but on smaller ships everything was out in the weather. The most obvious features of the head that could be seen from afar were three curved (and sometimes carved) rails leading from the bow out to the figurehead. The lowest rail was well placed for the seaman's feet, while the middle one was for sitting and the upper served as a backrest. Head rails were gilded on some ships, and painted black or yellow, or both, on others. This whole triangular contraption was temporarily covered by a grating where men could stand to assist in weighing anchor. The grating and the headrails were supported by ribs as if the structure were to be planked (which it actually was in the Victorian era). When the ships were in port, they often disguised their heads with brightly painted canvases.

Deck furniture and the inside of bulwarks on warships were almost invariably red. Red was also used on bulwarks below decks, and on the deck itself for the deck below the lowest gun deck. It is said that the reason for this was that it was believed that seamen who were used to the color red all about them would be less likely to panic in the crucial moments of battle when they might find blood around them. As a practical matter, however, historians believe that the abundance of red paint did little that had not already been done by discipline and training. On merchant ships, the insides were usually painted a light color so that the crew could see what they were doing.

The spars, too, were painted according to an almost invariable rule. All the yards and gaffs and booms were black, probably from being coated with pitch. All the doublings, crosstrees, and fighting tops were also black. All other spars were either oiled or painted ochre; none was ever painted white until well into the nineteenth century.

This book includes drawings of about 150 ships that were designed, built, or owned by Americans in the period 1607–1789. These drawings can be broken down into two basic categories, the complete drawings and the waterline drawings. In most cases, but not all, the complete drawings reflect the fact that the original plans or a model of the ship still exist, while the waterline drawings are more conjectural, based on paintings, written descriptions, or other rather scanty data.

In a few cases, complete drawings have been included of ships for which only enough evidence exists to warrant a waterline drawing, but these are mostly ships of greater interest to model builders and artists, and the fact that the plans are conjectural is clearly stated.

The complete plans consist of three parts: the outboard profile, the plan, and the sections. The outboard profile (or "sheer" or side elevation) is simply a view of the side of the ship from stem to stern and from keel to rail cap. Many draftsmen like to include a few interior details on their outboard profiles, such as the deck levels, but it was thought that such details would needlessly complicate our drawings. For the same reason, much carving has been omitted, although figureheads have nearly always been included, contrary to the practice of the period. To emphasize the prominence of the main wale, this has been shaded dark, the way it would look on the real ship, although as a rule this was not usually done by eighteenth-century draftsmen.

Quarterdeck rails in this period were nearly always open, and have been drawn that way in spite of the fact that some surviving plans and paintings show that the rails on some ships had been lightly planked so as to form a bulwark; usually such planking was done sometime after the ship was built. On the other hand, many paintings and plans of the period omit certain details on the topsides, such as the boarding stairs, the barrel fend-

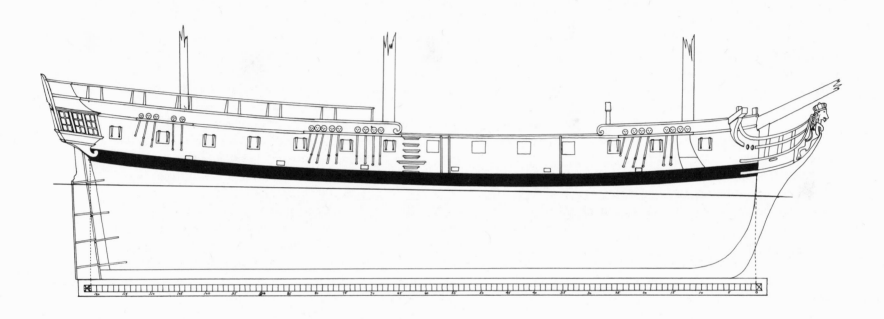

ers, the ches-trees, and the anchor fender, and such details have usually been included in this book.

The plan drawings, otherwise known as the half-
breadth, show a view of one side of the bottom of the
ship, and are located immediately underneath the outboard profile. Many draftsmen like to include details
of the deck plan superimposed on this, but we have not
done so for two reasons: (1) it would clutter up the
drawings more, and (2) there is precious little information about the deck plans of most individual ships,
although they generally did not vary much from one
ship to another within a type and period.

The section or body plan shows the shape of the ship
looking from the bow and the stern, so that the shapes
of certain selected frames (and, by extension, all the
frames) can be shown. The left half shows all the stations from the stern to the point of maximum breadth
(usually more than half the distance to the bow), while

[32]

the right half shows the stations between the point of maximum breadth and the bow. These stations are sometimes brought up to the top of the quarterdeck rail, but sometimes only to the top of the sheer.

Many modern draftsmen include diagonal lines on their drawings, used for making sure the planking would be "fair" and have no bumps or indentations in it. We have not included such diagonals so as not to clutter up the drawings.

The general practice was to draw these lines to the inside of the planking, but we have not been consistent with this practice in every case. The difference between lines drawn to the inside and those drawn to the outside of the planking would be negligible at the scale these plans are reproduced in this book.

The originals for these plans were drawn, following British and American practice, to a scale of 1 : 48, or one inch equals four feet, but they have been printed much smaller than that in this book. Because of the great difference in size between, say, a battleship and a small schooner, the plans have been reproduced at varying scales in such a way as would best allow them to fit on their particular page. However, the scale is drawn on every plan.

We have noted a number of different dimensions of these ships, which should aid in comparison. Length overall is a measurement not generally used 200 years ago, but we find it useful. It extends from the nose of the figurehead to the after part of the quarterdeck rail, and does not include any spars.

Length between perpendiculars, or length on the deck, is a measurement that varied somewhat with the whim of the measurer, and we have not been consistent. Within a few inches, it was the length of the ship from where the planking underneath the wale met the stem to a similar point on the sternpost, in which case it was

called the "length between perpendiculars." In most cases, a deck would be laid inside, corresponding roughly with the level of the ends of the lower part of the wale, and the measurement was then known as "length on the lower deck," or "length on the range of the deck." The deck, of course, was far more nearly level than the wale, which curved in imitation of the sheer.

Length of keel for tonnage was a measurement made for tax purposes, and should be of little or no interest to most readers.

Breadth was the width of the ship at her widest point, usually a point just above the waterline a short distance forward of the midpoint of her length. This measurement varied somewhat depending on whether it was made to the inside or outside of the planking. On a small boat this could mean only about three inches, but on a battleship this variation could be over a foot.

Depth in hold is another measurement that should hold little interest for most readers, since it was used primarily to calculate taxes. It varied somewhat from measurer to measurer and could be the distance from the keelson to the underside of the berth deck or even to the gun deck.

Draft, on the other hand, might be of more use to the reader, but it varied considerably, depending on how heavily laden the vessel was. We have taken the draft as the measurement from the bottom of the keel at the sternpost to the waterline, and we have drawn the waterline so as to be consistent with good trim and sailing practice; the waterline we show is not always the same as that shown on original plans of the ships, since these only reflect the trim as it was on the day the plans were made. In most cases the keel had a slight drag, which means that the draft was greater at the sternpost than further forward.

Tonnage is another figure intended for tax purposes. This was a measurement, not a weight, and it was obtained by putting the length of the keel, the breadth, and the depth in hold into a formula. This showed theoretically how many "tuns" or large casks of wine could be stowed in the available space on the ship. The actual displacement tonnage was usually a much larger figure, say, thirty or forty percent greater.

Sources for the drawings in this book are almost as varied as they are numerous. However, the majority of drawings that were done from existing plans came from the National Maritime Museum in Greenwich, just outside London. Historical researchers know that the Latin countries have kept the most thorough records of their colonial activities; such absurd figures—such as the number of nails required to build a privy for an obscure fur trader in Quebec—are carefully preserved in vast archives. However, when it comes to ship design we find that Great Britain has more plans and models than all the rest of the world put together. This is partly because most of the French and Dutch drawings were destroyed in the fighting of two world wars, and partly because the British were so keenly interested in ship design that they kept most of their own plans, and even made plans of many of the ships they captured from the French, the Dutch, the Spanish, and the Americans. The majority of these plans repose at Greenwich, and nearly all of them are available for reproduction.

A few plans were included in books over the years that do not appear in the archives at Greenwich. Most notable among them are the Swedish shipwright Fredrik Henrik af Chapman's *Architectura Navalis Mercatoria,* and *Souvenirs de la Marine* by the nineteenth-century French admiral Paris. The collection of plans in this book would probably not have been possible without the pioneering research work conducted over nearly a whole lifetime by Howard I. Chapelle, and reflected in many of his books (see our Bibliography) as well as in the superb exhibits of ship models at the Smithsonian Institution, where he was a curator.

We have tried to indicate the sources for our plans in the text that accompanies each drawing. Some of these sources are admittedly quite tenuous, for which we make no excuse, but, in explanation, shedding even this bit of light is one of the primary purposes of the book. Over the years, beginning at least as early as the first two decades of the nineteenth century when a collection of watercolor paintings of Revolutionary War ships was produced (now at the Mariners Museum, Newport News, Virginia), artists and model builders have attempted to show their contemporaries and future generations what they thought Colonial and Revolutionary period ships looked like. Unfortunately, in most cases they have been highly inaccurate and misleading. Sometimes this was only the addition of a dolphin striker or spanker boom where none existed, flying the ensign in the wrong place, flying the wrong ensign, or use of the wrong color scheme, but frequently it was more than that.

The Bicentennial of American Independence has produced a new spate of models and paintings of ships of the Colonial and Revolutionary periods. While this book is admittedly far from perfect, there should be no excuse for any model builder or artist who has access to this book to make such egregious mistakes as most (but not all, I am happy to say) have made in the past. Let us indeed joyfully celebrate the glorious—and not so glorious—deeds of men like Silas Talbot, John Rathbun, John Barry, Abraham Whipple, and John Paul Jones, but let us at least represent their ships as accurately as possible.

Part II
The SHIPS

L'ABENAKISE

THE 38-gun ship *L'Abenakise* (sometimes spelled *Bon Acquis* and even *A Bien Acquis* in the British records) was apparently built along the St. Lawrence River in Quebec Province about 1756. She was designed as a frigate for the French navy. She had the classic shape of an East Indiaman of the period, and was quite similar in size and shape to the French East Indiaman *Le Duc de Duras* which later became the more famous *Bonhomme Richard*. We suspect that her name was intended to have been *L'Abenakise* (which is French for "girl of the Abenaki tribe"; the Abenakis were one of the tribes of the Algonquin group), and that illiterate crewmembers called her *A Bien Acquis* (which is French for "cheap") in much the same way as British sailors on the ship *Bellerophon* sometimes called their ship *Billy Ruffian*. Hopefully, calling the ship by a name that means "cheap" was not a reflection on the quality of her construction.

She is reported to have been captured on 23 January 1757 at the beginning of the Seven Years' War by the much smaller British frigate *Unicorn* (although one source says she was actually captured on 24 November 1757 by the 74-gun British battleship *Chichester*). Being a powerful vessel herself, she was renamed *Aurora* and taken into the Royal Navy as a Fifth Rate of 36 guns. Her career was short-lived, however, for she was broken up at the end of the war in April 1763. The records do not state how well Quebec oak lasted, and whether she was broken up because of extensive rot; presumably she would have been sold to private owners and used as an East Indiaman after the war if she had still been sound. The Admiralty records do say that she was a fast sailer and unusually well armed.

Her plans were drawn in abbreviated form and still exist in the British Admiralty records. All that was drawn was the profile of the bow, the profile of the stern, and the body plan, all rendered on graph paper. The midship section shows the characteristic French form with the pronounced double knuckle.

Quite a number of ships were built in Quebec for the French, but no plans have been found for any others yet; they included the 500-ton corvette *Le Canada* in 1742; the 700-ton, 22-gun ship *Le Caribou* in 1744; the 22-gun ship *Le Castor* in 1745; the *Le Martre* in 1747; the 60-gun ship *Le Saint-Laurent* in 1748; the 70-gun ship *L'Original* in 1750; the corvette *L'Algonquin* in 1753; and the frigate *Le Québec* in 1757.

L'Abenakise by herself is not believed to have had any influence on the future of ship design, but the basic form of the East Indiaman did look forward to the Revolution and Napoleonic Wars when frigates assumed more of the shape and size of East Indiamen, under French leadership.

Dimensions: length overall, 168'; length on gun deck, 146'; length on keel, 134'3"; beam, 37'; depth, 15'; draft, 17'6"; tonnage, 946.

Although we have shown a standard French crowned lion for a figurehead, she may well have had an Indian maiden instead.

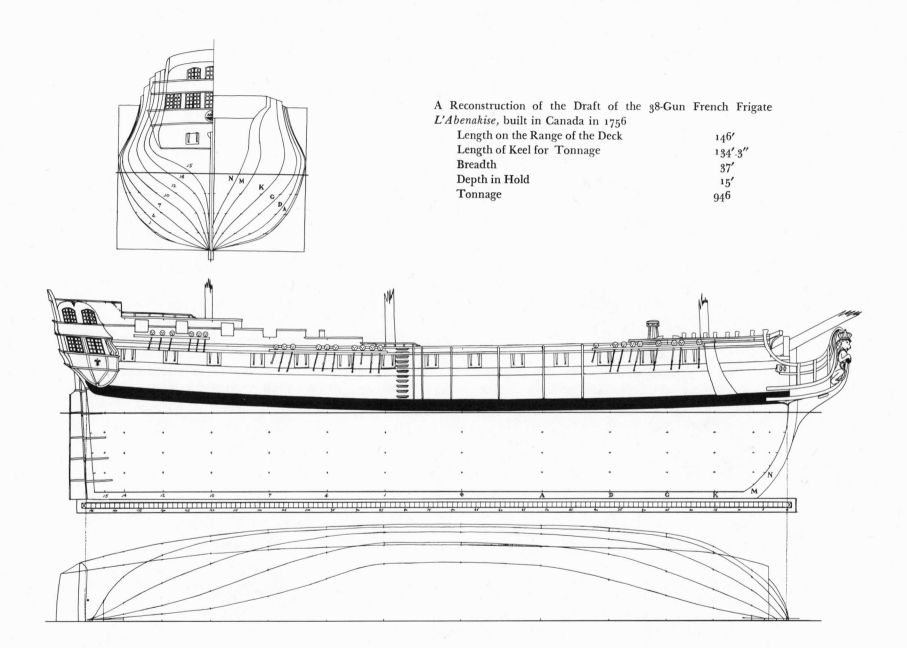

A Reconstruction of the Draft of the 38-Gun French Frigate
L'Abenakise, built in Canada in 1756

Length on the Range of the Deck	146'
Length of Keel for Tonnage	134'.3"
Breadth	37'
Depth in Hold	15'
Tonnage	946

ALEXANDER

IN 1780, the merchants of Portsmouth, New Hampshire, were sorry to learn that the British had captured the 18-gun Continental Navy corvette *Ranger* at Charleston, South Carolina. The *Ranger* had been built at Portsmouth three years earlier, and many of her crew came from the Portsmouth area. In a fit of patriotism, they commissioned a larger ship to be built at Portsmouth and presented to the Continental Navy. She was to mount 28 guns, and was to be named *Alexander,* presumably after the Macedonian conqueror. Unfortunately, when she was finished they changed their minds and decided to outfit her as a privateer, to be owned by the merchants who had put up the money. Under the circumstances, they cannot be blamed for their change of heart, since the Continental Navy was in such terrible shape as to inspire practically no confidence in the future of such a fine ship if she were to be donated to the navy. As a privateer, she would have had little trouble recruiting a sufficient crew, in contrast to ships in the navy; in fact, virtually the whole crew of the *Ranger* signed on aboard *Alexander* once they were released from British custody. Her captain was Thomas Simpson of Portsmouth, and she was bonded on 5 January 1781.

The privateer *Alexander* had few initial successes, and she was captured by the 44-gun British ship *Mediator;* in fact, *Mediator* captured *Alexander,* the privateer brig *Amiable,* the French ship *La Ménagère,* and two others—all in the same action on 12 December 1782.

It is at least conceivable that if the Allied ships had stayed together instead of allowing *Mediator* to pick them off one by one they might have beaten off their assailant, if not even captured her, but the naval history of the Revolution affords few examples of close cooperation between American ships under adversity. The battle was painted by both Robert Dodd and Dominic Serres, and prints made from the paintings are at the New York Historical Society. Since it was already 1783 by the time the captured *Alexander* reached Britain, and the peace treaty was all but signed, the Royal Navy had no use for this fine frigate so she was sold to private owners, who no doubt used her as a merchant ship in either the East Indies or West Indies trade.

Frigate *Alexander*
From an engraving after Dominic Serres, 1782
New York Historical Society

A Reconstruction of the Draft of the 28-Gun American Privateer
Ship *Alexander,* built at Portsmouth, New Hampshire, in 1780
Length between Perpendiculars   118'
Tonnage   550

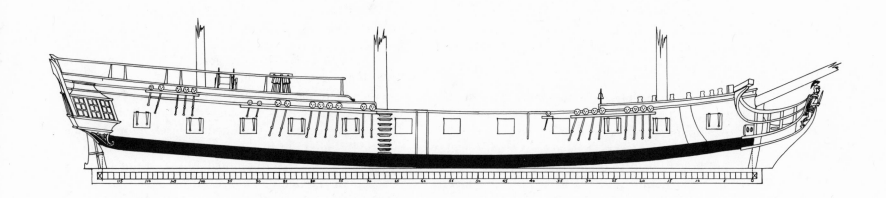

Our source for this drawing of *Alexander* is a mixture of looking at the above-mentioned paintings (the artists had without doubt seen *Alexander* when she arrived in England), the lines of the frigate *Raleigh,* which had been launched from the same yard, and a print of the bow of *Alliance* (also built by the same builder), which, being rather finer and more extended than *Raleigh*'s, shows some development from the original model over the years. Our assumption here is that *Alexander*'s design was related to *Raleigh*'s in the same way that *Virginia*'s was related to *Randolph*'s, or any 28-gun frigate to any 32-gun frigate by the same designer.

Although we could find no official dimensions for *Alexander,* we believe that these would not be far off: length overall, 140'; length on the gun deck, 118'; beam, 32'; and tonnage, 550.

[39]

ALFRED *and* DRAKE

ONE of the most easily recognizable shapes among American ships of the Colonial period is that of the Philadelphia merchant ship. Such ships were generally about 90 feet long on the deck, had blunt bows (with or without a head), usually had no quarter galleries, and were completely decked over, the quarterdeck being raised about two feet above the deck over the waist.

When the Continental Navy was established in the fall of 1775, it had ready access to smaller craft such as sloops, schooners, and brigs, all of which were suitable for certain kinds of work. The navy eventually had a number of larger warships built to its specifications, but for the first few months it had to make do with converting some Philadelphia merchant ships by adding gunports and generally strengthening their hulls. Such a ship was *Black Prince* (named after the dashing son of King Edward III), built about 1774 for a syndicate headed by Robert Morris and John Nixon, and commanded by the famous John Barry. She had a figurehead of the Black Prince in full armor.

Purchase of *Black Prince* for the navy was authorized by Congress on 30 October 1775, and fitting out began a few days later under command of Dudley Saltonstall. Commodore Hopkins came aboard early in December, and she left Philadelphia on 4 January 1776 as flagship of the first American fleet. Her name had been changed to *Alfred,* in honor of the ninth-century British king who is said to have founded the Royal Navy.

Her first navy assignment was to carry home powder and cannons acquired in a raid on Nassau, which had been captured in March 1776. While thus heavily laden

the fleet encountered the 24-gun British frigate *Glasgow* off Newport, Rhode Island, in the middle of the night. *Alfred* herself had about 24 guns (some accounts say 20, others 24, and still others 28), so she should have been able to inflict punishment on the frigate, and with the rest of the fleet in the action there should have been no chance of escape for *Glasgow*. As it happened, the fleet bungled the job; they allowed *Glasgow* to damage them considerably, and then, being slow because of their heavy cargos, they watched helplessly as she escaped into Newport. Commodore Esek Hopkins was eventually eased out of his job because of this incident.

Although Congress appointed Elisha Hinman as her new captain in October, word did not reach New England in time and *Alfred* set sail under command of John Paul Jones in company with the sloop *Providence*. She had a successful cruise of about five weeks, in which she captured a number of enemy ships, burned part of the town of Canso, Nova Scotia, and escaped from the frigate *Milford*. After her return, she lay more or less idle for the next nine months, needing repairs and being short of crew.

In mid-August 1777 she departed for France under Hinman in company with the frigate *Raleigh*. Being a slow sailer she was unable to keep up with *Raleigh,* and although they took a few small prizes early in the voyage *Alfred*'s slow speed proved a handicap when they attacked a lightly guarded convoy and were beaten off. They arrived at Lorient on 7 October and departed for home once more late in December, choosing a route that took them close to Africa.

East of the Windward Islands they encountered two

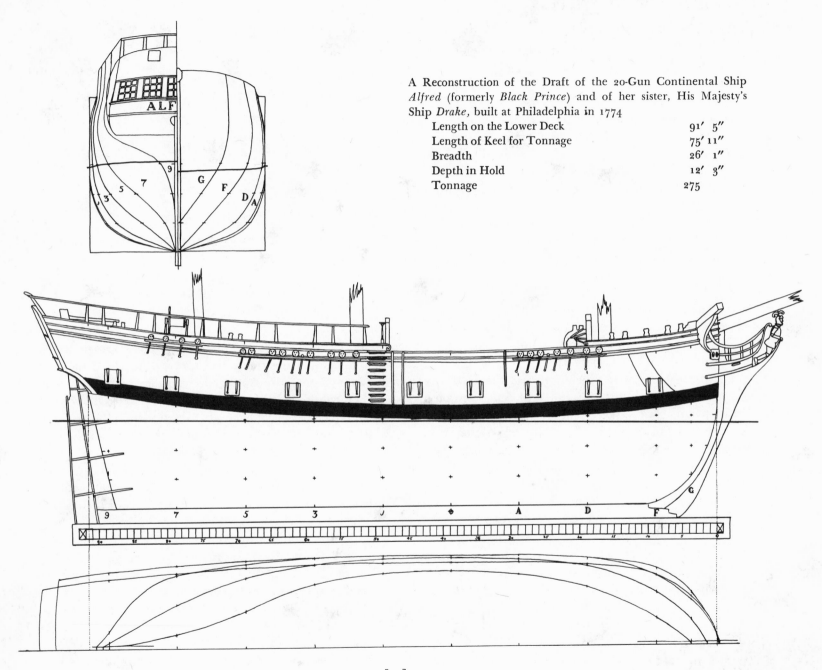

A Reconstruction of the Draft of the 20-Gun Continental Ship *Alfred* (formerly *Black Prince*) and of her sister, His Majesty's Ship *Drake,* built at Philadelphia in 1774

Length on the Lower Deck	91′ 5″
Length of Keel for Tonnage	75′ 11″
Breadth	26′ 1″
Depth in Hold	12′ 3″
Tonnage	275

lightly armed British ships, *Ariadne,* 20 guns, and *Canso,* 16 guns. *Raleigh* clapped on all sail and ran while *Alfred* surrendered without much of a fight. For this disgraceful conduct Captain Thompson of *Raleigh* was dismissed, and Hinman was absolved of all blame, so that he could turn up as an ineffectual captain of the frigate *Trumbull* later on. *Alfred* was used as an armed transport by the Royal Navy until 1782 when she was sold.

The Continental Navy was not the only navy to use Philadelphia merchant ships as warships. The Royal Navy did, too. One of these was an exact sistership of *Alfred,* so we are told, and it is possible, though not certain, that her original name was *Resolution.* She too had a figurehead of the Black Prince. When she was purchased by the Royal Navy in 1777 she was given the name of *Drake* (after the famous Elizabethan admiral) and fitted out with anywhere from 14 to 20 guns (the accounts differ). She was captured by John Paul Jones on the 18-gun corvette *Ranger* off Belfast, Northern Ireland, on 24 April 1778. He sent her to France with a prize crew under the insubordinate Lieutenant Simpson, but partway there Jones replaced Simpson with Lieutenant Hall. *Drake* was then sold.

One of the chief disadvantages of placing a heavy armament on a Philadelphia merchant ship was that the guns had to be below the main deck, both for the sake of the stability of the ship and to protect the gunners. This meant that the gunports were perilously close to the waterline, thus making it difficult for the ship to fight in heavy weather. One can well imagine that *Alfred's* men were reluctant to engage the *Glasgow* with her gunports even closer to the waterline than usual because of the great weight of captured cannons in the hold.

The plans we show here are derived from the Admiralty plans of another Philadelphia merchant ship, *Lord Camden,* whose dimensions were very close to those of the *Drake* and the *Alfred.* A confusion exists as to the dimensions of the *Alfred;* the British records

Ship *Alfred*
From a powderhorn engraving by H. Mack, 1776
U.S. Marine Corps Museum, Quantico, Virginia

say she was 440 tons, but this is a measurement to the underside of her main deck. If they had used the more common measurement to the bottom of her gun deck they would have come up with 275 tons. The length overall would have been about 110'; length on the deck, 91'5"; length on the keel, about 76'; beam, 26'; depth in hold, 12'3"; and draft about 14'6".

There are three contemporary pictures that purport to be of the *Alfred.* One, a seaman's sketch in ink and watercolors, is obviously inaccurate since it shows quarter galleries and an odd deck layout; another, a pen-and-ink sketch in the Roosevelt collection that is supposed to show *Alfred* capturing the supply ship *Mellish,* is not *Alfred* at all, but another ship. The third is a crude engraving on a powderhorn in the U.S. Marine Corps Museum. There are no known contemporary pictures of *Drake.*

I am indebted to Mr. John J. McCusker, Jr., for his careful research into the facts and myths about *Alfred's* appearance.

ALLIANCE

AFTER the initial thirteen frigates were constructed for the Continental Navy, Congress ordered several more in 18-gun and 36-gun sizes. Of the latter, only three were actually built, one of them being *Alliance*.

Alliance was built in 1777 on the Merrimack River at Salisbury, Massachusetts, by the Hackett family of builders, who came down from nearby Portsmouth, New Hampshire, to do the job. She was somewhat smaller than the other two ships of this class, but she was apparently well built, a fast sailer, and a popular ship. She was named after the Franco-American alliance that had just been concluded.

No plans of her have survived, but there are more contemporary and near-contemporary portraits of her than of any other American ship of the period. Of these portraits, some are valuable to the historian and others are useless or even misleading. The best is a view from ahead from an engraving of the battle between *Bonhomme Richard* and *Serapis* that apparently survives only at the Musée de la Marine in Paris. Another engraving and an oil painting of the same subject are not as good. Also useful are a pair of paintings dated 1789 showing the ship from astern as she approached Boston Light in 1781; one is by Captain Matthew Parke, who had been a marine in her crew, and the other, an overmantel from Waltham, Massachusetts, is by Jonathan Edes, and both are quite primitive. A watercolor at the U.S. Naval Academy Museum, showing her with all sails set, including royals and studding sails, seems to date from the 1790s and is reasonably accurate, but a "copy" of that same painting in oils at the Peabody Museum, Salem, Massachusetts, shows essentially a nineteenth-century ship. A Dutch oil painting in a private collection in Massachusetts shows a broadside view, but includes a dolphin striker, which had not yet been invented. One other contemporary picture is a small sketch of her in battle off Cuba in early 1783, but it has little detail. Our plan is based on the two most accurate pictures, plus a record of her principal dimensions, and the existing plan of the frigate *Raleigh*, which had been designed and built the previous year by the Hackett family.

Her first captain, the mad Frenchman Pierre Landais, who had been made an honorary citizen of Massachu-

Frigate *Alliance*
From an anonymous engraving, ca. 1779
Le Musée de la Marine, Paris

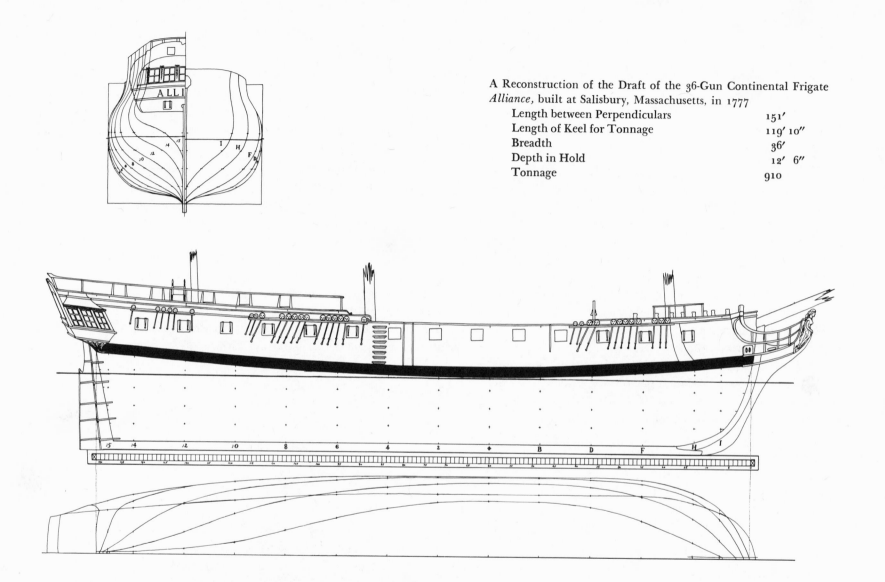

A Reconstruction of the Draft of the 36-Gun Continental Frigate *Alliance*, built at Salisbury, Massachusetts, in 1777

Length between Perpendiculars	151′
Length of Keel for Tonnage	119′ 10″
Breadth	36′
Depth in Hold	12′ 6″
Tonnage	910

setts, took her to France with Lafayette as a passenger. In August 1779, *Alliance* put to sea as part of John Paul Jones's squadron, but Landais refused to obey Jones's signals. During the battle off Flamborough Head, Yorkshire, on 23 September, Landais deliberately fired into *Bonhomme Richard* so as to sink her and then presumably gain the glory of having defeated *Serapis*. The plan did not work and Jones had Landais removed from command when they arrived at Texel, Holland. Jones himself took command of *Alliance* and on 27 December very boldly sailed right through a powerful British squadron that was waiting to catch him.

While Jones dallied with a mistress on shore, Landais seized back control of the ship, and, after being briefly detained by an irate Jones and the French authorities, set sail for Philadelphia with Arthur Lee as a passenger on 8 July 1780. On the voyage, Landais had to be replaced by Lieutenant James Degge, who brought her into Boston. At Boston, Landais was dismissed from the service for his conduct, and Degge was also dismissed because Landais had accused him of mutiny.

John Barry was made *Alliance*'s new captain, but he had difficulty finding enough crew to man her. On 11 February 1781 Barry was forced to take her to sea, grossly undermanned, to bring Thomas Paine and Colonel John Laurens to France. Many of the crew were former British prisoners and they plotted mutiny, but the ship reached France before they could do much. After they had left Lorient at the end of March, Barry found out about the mutiny and had all the plotters whipped. During the rest of the long voyage back to Boston, *Alliance* captured two brigs and the two corvettes *Atalanta* and *Trepassey*. She was then forced to remain idle in Boston for lack of crew.

March 1783 found her in Havana, Cuba, with a load of 100,000 Spanish dollars to take back to the Continental Congress. She left Cuba in company with the smaller ship *Le Duc de Lauzun* and was immediately chased by three British frigates. The appearance of a large French ship on the horizon caused the British to give up the chase, whereupon Barry turned on one of them, the 28-gun *Sybil*, and completely disabled her. This was the last sea battle of the Revolution, for when *Alliance* arrived at Newport, Rhode Island, on 20 March Barry learned that the war had ended.

The new nation felt no need to maintain a navy during peacetime, so the few remaining ships were sold, *Alliance* being the last. She was auctioned off for $26,000 at the Merchants' Coffee House in Philadelphia on 1 August 1785, even though some members of Congress had wished to maintain just one ship "for the honor of the flag" and for protection against pirates. She was bought by Robert Morris, who found her well suited to be an East Indiaman. Her first voyage to Canton, under the command of Thomas Read, was in 1787. She was eventually wrecked at the mouth of the Delaware River in 1800, probably the last warship from the Continental Navy still afloat.

According to our drawing, her dimensions were as follows: length overall, 178′; length on the deck, 151′; length of keel, about 120′; beam, 36′; depth in hold, 12′ 6″; draft, 16′ 6″; tonnage, 910. These dimensions are close to those of a typical East Indiaman.

Frigate *Alliance*
From a primitive oil painting
by Captain Matthew Parke, U.S.M.C., 1781
National Historical Foundation, Washington, D.C.

AMERICA

ONE of the few ships built for the Royal Navy in what is now the United States was the 44-gun ship *America*. She was built at Portsmouth, New Hampshire, by Nathaniel Meserve in 1748–49. A 24-gun ship, *Boston*, was built in Boston at the same time, and when the latter proved unseaworthy because of extensive rot in 1756, *America* was renamed *Boston*. She herself, however, was also rotten, and she was sold out of the navy in September 1757; she must have been in terrible shape, for the navy practically never sold anything that could float while a war was in progress.

In appearance she was fairly typical of British warships of her class, except that she was several feet longer than the Establishment then in force for 44-gun ships; this seems to be an American trait—designing ships of a certain rate to be larger than others of that rate. Her appearance is known to us through the preservation of a beautifully built model, now kept at the Athenaeum at Portsmouth, New Hampshire. The model had been allowed to deteriorate over the years, but it was carefully restored by James A. Knowles. One record states that the model was lodged at the library at Harvard College in the 1750s (along with skeletons of various animals), and that it was at that time fully rigged. The model is not now rigged.

America's first captain, Henry Barnsby, sailed her to Spithead and then to Chatham. He reported that she sailed very well, being a sharp ship with a round buttock, and that she would need very few changes. Her guns were probably eighteen-pounders on the lower deck, nine-pounders on the upper deck, and six-pounders on the quarterdeck.

Her dimensions appear to be as follows: length overall, 158′ 8″; length on the deck, 139′ 1″; length of keel, 118′; breadth, 37′ 9″; depth in hold, 16′; draft, 16′ 9″; tonnage, 863.

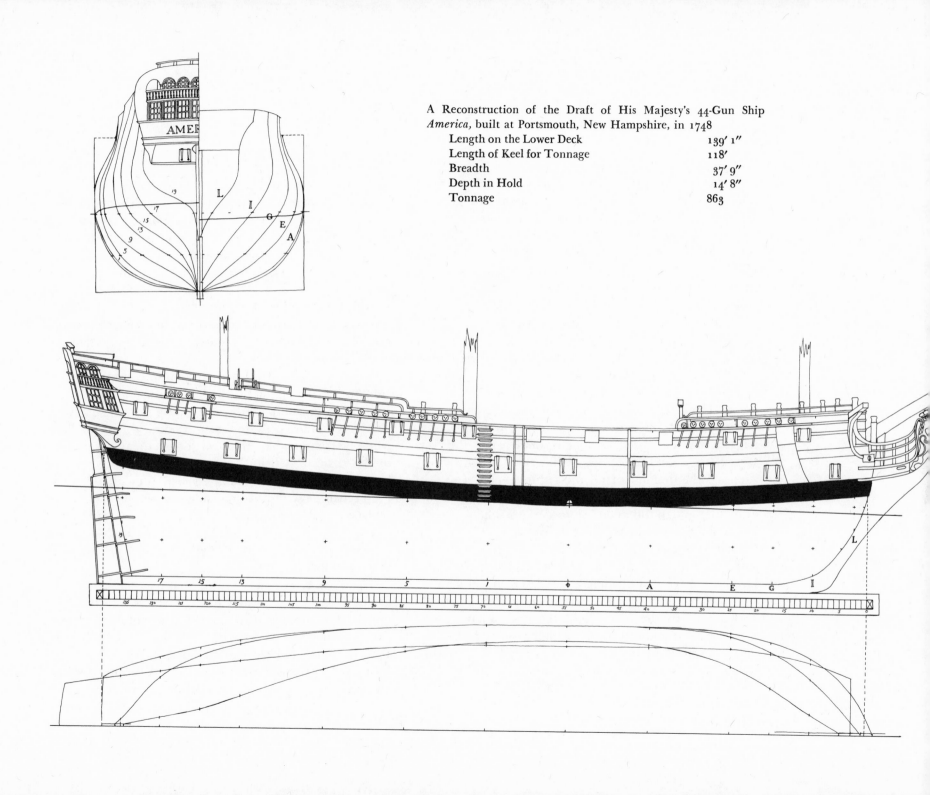

A Reconstruction of the Draft of His Majesty's 44-Gun Ship
America, built at Portsmouth, New Hampshire, in 1748

Length on the Lower Deck	139′ 1″
Length of Keel for Tonnage	118′
Breadth	37′ 9″
Depth in Hold	14′ 8″
Tonnage	863

AMERICA

At the time of the American Revolution, all the major navies of the world had battleships of 74 guns and more. The infant United States had nothing larger than a 32-gun frigate in 1776, so Congress set about rectifying the situation and on 9 November 1776 ordered three 74s built. Shortly thereafter, on 15 January 1777, the New York Committee of Safety also ordered that the timbers be cut to build a 74 far up the Hudson River. Shortages of funds forced the cancellation of the New York ship and of two of the national 74s, but the other was built at Portsmouth, New Hampshire, by the Hackett family of shipbuilders. She was laid down in May 1777.

The Hacketts were responsible for building many of the major ships used in the Revolution, including the frigates *Raleigh, Alliance,* and *Alexander,* and the corvettes *Ranger* and *Hampden.* As far as we can tell, they supplied the designs for all these ships themselves, not making use of the designs supplied by Congress. However, they did build their 74 to designs sent up from Philadelphia (which were modified as building progressed). An early form of the design is preserved in a half-model that can be seen at Independence National Historical Park in Philadelphia, and the official design, as approved by Congress, is preserved in the National Archives. Both the model and the design have been attributed to young Joshua Humphreys, and the design is certainly by the same hand as the design for the frigate *Randolph,* but what the connection with Humphreys was we will leave for others to debate.

Construction was delayed by lack of money, and there were even schemes to cut her down to a ship of 60 guns or smaller from time to time, but happily these came to nought. In 1781, John Paul Jones was appointed her commander and the resident inspector in the hope that construction would be speeded up. Jones found her to be well behind schedule but he had little luck in speeding up the construction. He also apparently ordered some changes made in the upper works, some of which are not reflected in our drawing, which is based on the official draft. Finally, *America* was launched on 5 November 1782. Jones had put all his efforts into completing the ship for so long because he looked forward to commanding such a fine ship, and also because he was sure that Congress would create the post of admiral just for him while he commanded *America.* Jones's dreams were not to be realized; already on 3 September, two months before her launching, Congress had presented her to the French navy out of gratitude for past favors and to replace *Le Magnifique,* a French 74 that had been wrecked in Boston Harbor. The chevalier de Martigne, former captain of *Le Magnifique,* was given command of her immediately after launching.

The French, probably noting that her sharp bow did not have enough buoyancy to support the forward cannons as it should, reported that she did not combine all the qualities that a vessel of her class should have. In 1786 she was surveyed and found to be totally rotten. Minister Castries ordered that she be broken up at Brest and another ship of 74 guns be built and given her

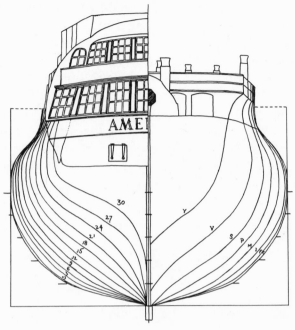

A Draft of the 74-Gun Continental Ship *America,* built at Portsmouth, New Hampshire, in 1778–82

Length between Perpendiculars	180'
Length of Keel for Tonnage	147'
Breadth	49'
Depth in Hold	19'
Tonnage	1,982

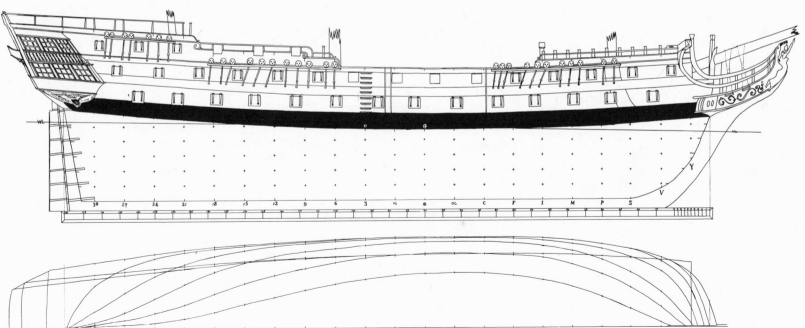

name. Many historians have been misled into believing that the original *America* somehow survived in the French navy until being captured by the British in 1794, but an examination of the lines of this ship show her to be totally French in design; just to confuse matters further, the British also had a 64-gun ship called *America*, which was burned at Portsmouth, England, by accident.

There is a painting of *America* at Mystic Seaport in Connecticut. It was painted by John S. Blunt in 1834 and shows her under American colors, which she never flew under sail. The painting, while attractive, is merely fanciful; Blunt wasn't even born until 1798.

If the official draft is correct, then these were *America*'s measurements: length overall, 221'; length on the deck, 181'; length on the keel, 147'; beam, 50'; depth in hold, 19'; draft, 24'; tonnage, 1,982. Except for Spanish ships, such as *Fenix,* built at Havana, Cuba, in the eighteenth century, *America* was the largest ship yet built in North America, and she was not to be exceeded by any United States ship until the end of the War of 1812.

AMERICAN

In the fall of 1775, American forces launched a two-pronged invasion of Canada; one force under Benedict Arnold marched through Maine to Quebec, while another marched up to Montreal, using the Lake Champlain route. The American troops captured Montreal and Trois Rivières, but were badly defeated in front of Quebec. Arnold built a number of small warships on the St. Lawrence River to assist with the land operations, and probably all of these were gondolas or "gundalows."

Gondolas were easily, quickly, and cheaply built, for they had flat bottoms, nearly flat sides, and were double-ended. They were powered by oars, but could sail when the wind was fair. When Arnold had to evacuate the St. Lawrence area in the face of British reinforcements, at least one of his gondolas fell into British hands. Her name has been variously given as *American, American Convert,* and *Convert.* When the British found her, they called her *Loyal Convert.*

The British reassembled their gondola at St. John's on the Richelieu River at the northern end of Lake Champlain and used her against Arnold's naval forces on the lake. Presumably she was dismantled at the end of the war. The British kept the American rig of a square topsail and course with one jib, and they added a gaff mizzen. There are a few pictures of her sailing with the new rig, one in the Public Archives of Canada and the other in the Royal Collection at Windsor Castle in England. In addition, her plans survive at the Na-

tional Maritime Museum at Greenwich, England. She mounted ten guns. In 1777, this large gondola capsized in a strong wind, and was only righted by cutting away all her spars and rigging.

Dimensions: length overall, 69′ 10″; length on the deck, 62′ 6″; length of keel, 58′ 6″; beam, 20′ 3″; depth, 3′ 7″; draft, 3′ 8″; tonnage, 109.

Gondola *Loyal Convert (American)*
From a watercolor painting, 1776
The Royal Collection, Windsor Castle

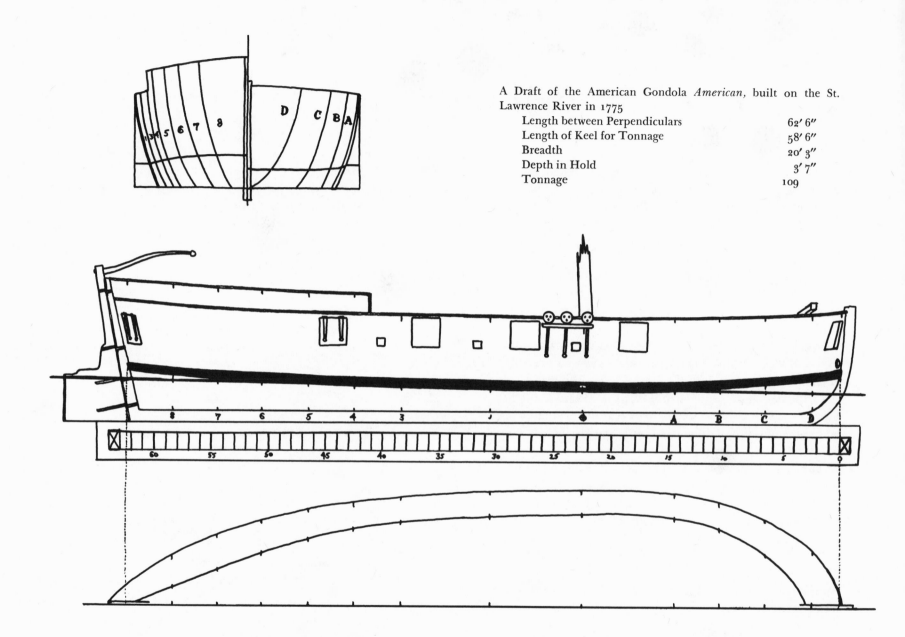

A Draft of the American Gondola *American,* built on the St. Lawrence River in 1775

Length between Perpendiculars	62′ 6″
Length of Keel for Tonnage	58′ 6″
Breadth	20′ 3″
Depth in Hold	3′ 7″
Tonnage	109

AMERICA OF CHARLESTON

THE Peabody Museum at Salem, Massachusetts, has in its collection two pictures by Michel Cornè of an American merchant ship called *America of Charleston*. The pictures are dated 1789 (which is likely a mistake), and must be almost the earliest dated pictures to show the use of a dolphin striker under the bowsprit. One picture shows her in a terrible storm, with the legend "8 days from Grand Bank to the Channel of England," which is an exceedingly fast passage. The other shows her on the Grand Banks, more or less hove-to in a light breeze with all her fishing lines out, not that she was a fishing boat. Both paintings are by Michel Felice Cornè, in the Mediterranean style that was made popular by Caglieri and the Roux family.

Very little is known about *America of Charleston* except that she was a British ship called *Pompey* that was captured toward the end of the American Revolution. She looks the epitome of speed, with an exceptionally low freeboard for her length, a long head, and a raked sternpost. There was apparently no provision for carrying cannons.

Her dimensions, as we have reconstructed her, were about as follows: length overall, 115' 6"; length on the deck, 96'; tonnage, 330.

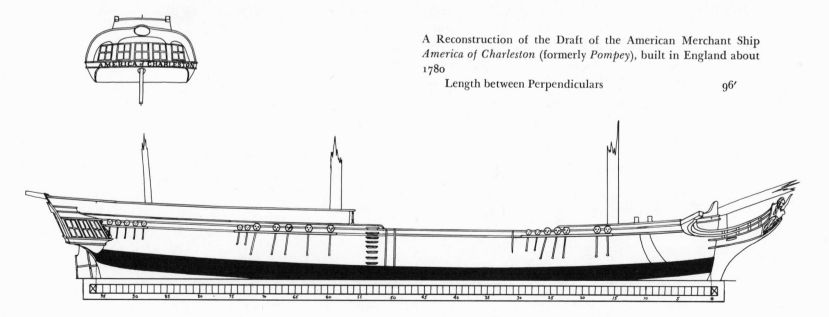

A Reconstruction of the Draft of the American Merchant Ship *America of Charleston* (formerly *Pompey*), built in England about 1780

Length between Perpendiculars   96'

AMSTERDAM

THE appearance of the brig *Amsterdam* is known to us only through a painting by Thomas Dodd. The painting shows her (after she was captured by the British frigate *Amphitrite* on 19 October 1780 and subsequently renamed *Observer*) doing battle with the Salem privateer *Jack* on 29 May 1782. Although *Jack* was the larger vessel, *Observer* captured her and took her into Halifax. Her commander during the battle was Lieutenant Crymes. She was sold on 21 October 1784.

Amsterdam was built in Massachusetts and named after one of the principal cities of Holland, which had become one of the allies of the United States toward the end of the war. Basically, she was a typical 14-gun brig that could be used as a privateer or a merchant ship, and could have passed for practically any nationality. Her dimensions, as we have reconstructed them, were: length overall, 88′ 6″; length on the deck, 75′; beam, 24′; tonnage, 170.

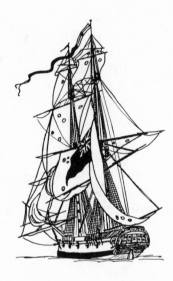

Brig *Amsterdam*
From an engraving after a painting by Robert Dodd, 1782

A Reconstruction of the Draft of the 12-Gun American Brig
Amsterdam, built in Massachusetts about 1777
Length between Perpendiculars   75′
Tonnage   170

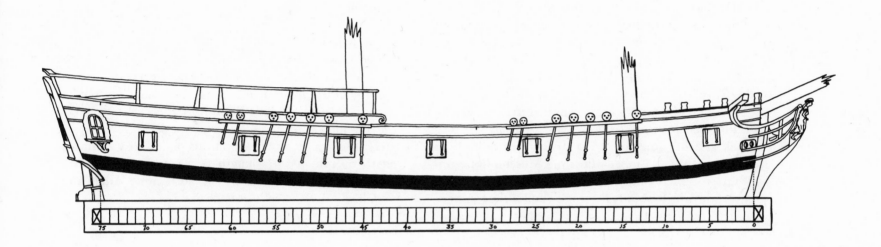

ANT

SCHOONERS and sloops built in Bermuda had the reputation of being very fast, which is confirmed by a look at their sharp lines. *Ant* was an 8-gun schooner built in Bermuda in about 1788, and her lines appear to owe something to the developments in design that occurred not far away on the Chesapeake Bay at the end of the Revolution. She was taken into the Royal Navy, one source says by purchase and another says by capture from the French in 1797. In any case, she was put into drydock and her lines recorded in that year; the lines are on file at the National Maritime Museum. She was sold out of the navy in 1815. Since one of the most frequent complaints about Bermuda and other American fast schooners of the period was that they were so lightly built (for speed) that they fell apart after only a short period of use, it is surprising to see this schooner last perhaps thirty years.

The most noticeable features about her design are the sharp deadrise and the taper of the keel; the fact that the lines are drawn, as was the usual custom in those days, parallel with the top of the keel makes the drawing look a little strange to the modern eye.

Her dimensions as drawn on this plan were as follows: length overall, 69′ 6″; length between perpendiculars, 59′ 4″; length of keel, 42′ 6″; breadth, 18′ 7″; depth in hold, 8′ 7″; draft, 8′ 3″; tonnage, 90.

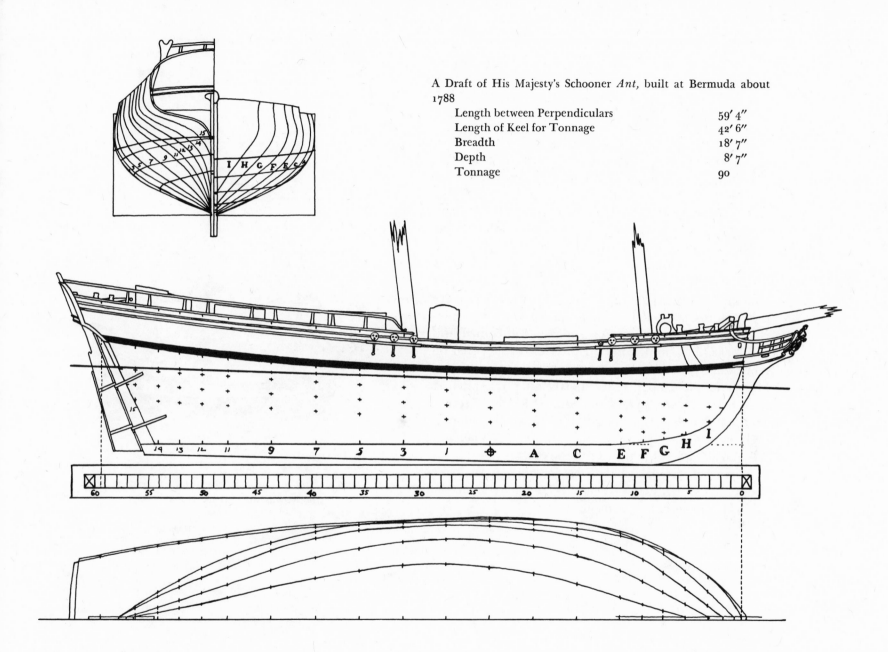

A Draft of His Majesty's Schooner *Ant*, built at Bermuda about 1788

Length between Perpendiculars	59′ 4″
Length of Keel for Tonnage	42′ 6″
Breadth	18′ 7″
Depth	8′ 7″
Tonnage	90

ARGO

About 1780 a syndicate of businessmen from Marblehead, Massachusetts, ordered the construction of an 18-gun privateer to be called *Argo*. She was probably built in Salem. From the two rather crude contemporary paintings of her at the Peabody Museum in Salem (these watercolors were by a seaman called Ashley Bowen, who lived in Marblehead; one shows *Argo* under full sail returning from France in 1782, and the other shows her scudding before a gale in a snowstorm with only three reefed sails set) she looks equally suited to being a merchant ship or a privateer, for she has a full-bodied hull and looks like a miniature frigate. Her career lasted no more than two years, for she was wrecked near York, Maine, in November 1782, shortly after the pictures were painted. Her captain was Samuel Russell Trevett, who fortunately escaped death in the wreck; interestingly enough, her previous captain, John Williamson, was also aboard at the time of the wreck.

As we have reconstructed her, her dimensions were about as follows: length overall, 112'; length on the deck, 92'; breadth, 27'; tonnage, 370.

Ship *Argo*
From a watercolor painting by Ashley Bowen, 1782
Peabody Museum, Salem, Massachusetts

A Reconstruction of the Draft of the 18-Gun American Privateer
Argo of Marblehead, Massachusetts, built about 1780

Length between Perpendiculars	92'
Breadth	27'
Tonnage	300

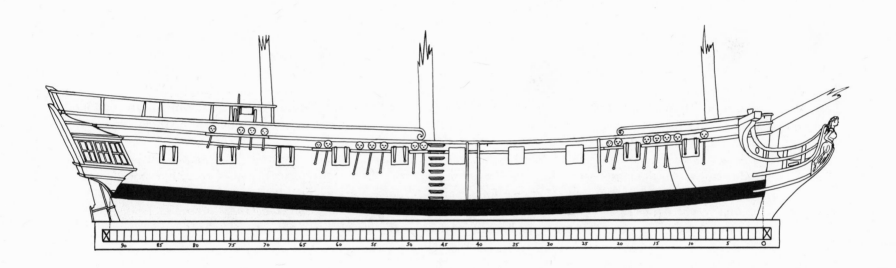

ARIEL

IN 1780, when John Paul Jones lost his command of the frigate *Alliance* to mad Captain Pierre Landais, he was presented with a much smaller frigate called *Ariel*, which he found was quite inadequate to do the job he had been asked to do: to ferry across to the United States over 300 tons of military equipment, including 11,000 muskets, 10,000 uniforms, and 800 barrels of powder. *Ariel*'s French armament of 26 guns was reduced to 16 to make more room, but it was not enough. After many delays (some caused by Jones's having affairs with ladies on shore) and a false start, *Ariel* finally got to sea on 7 October, just in time to run into a terrible storm. All the masts had to be cut away to avoid going on the rocks. She returned to France for repairs and finally sailed on 18 December. As he neared the American shore Jones nearly captured the loyalist privateer *Triumph* (formerly the Massachusetts privateer *Tracy*); this was his last battle under American colors.

Ariel arrived at Philadelphia on 18 February and was handed back to the French, who sailed her back to France in the summer.

Ariel was built at the Perry yard at Blackwall on the Thames (a private contractor rather than a Royal Navy yard) in 1777. She mounted 24 guns, and was captured in September 1779 by the French frigate *L'Amazone* (*L'Amazone* was at one point commanded by the great explorer de la Pérouse, but whether he was in command at this instant has not been determined). She was lost at sea in 1793.

Ariel's plans have been lost, but we have drawn here the lines of a typical British ship of her size, type, and date. This would give her a length overall of 129' 6"; length on the deck, 108'; length on the keel, 89' 5"; beam, 30'; depth in hold, 9' 7"; draft, 13' 8"; and tonnage, 429.

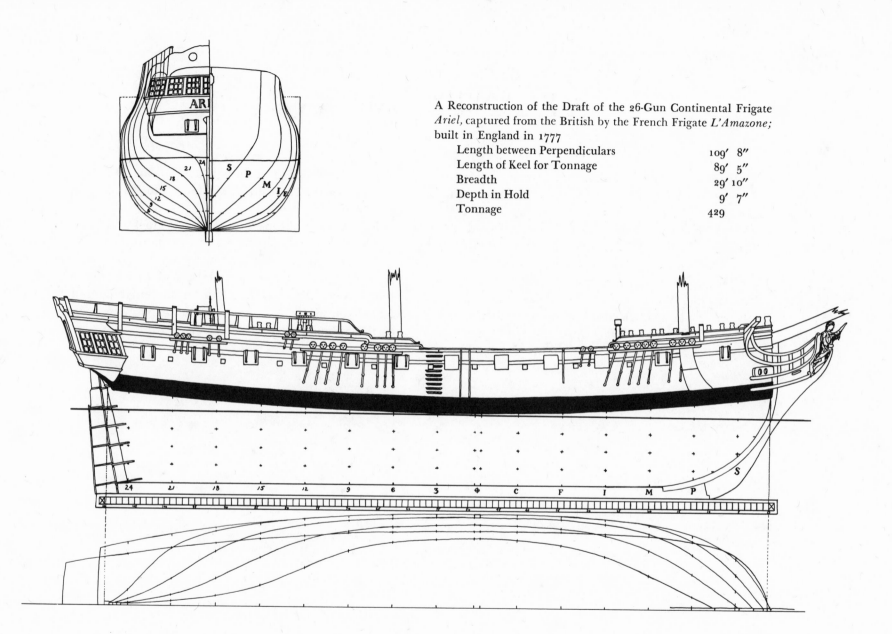

A Reconstruction of the Draft of the 26-Gun Continental Frigate
Ariel, captured from the British by the French Frigate *L'Amazone;*
built in England in 1777

Length between Perpendiculars	109′ 8″
Length of Keel for Tonnage	89′ 5″
Breadth	29′ 10″
Depth in Hold	9′ 7″
Tonnage	429

ATLANTIC *and* PATTY

THE Marblehead seaman Ashley Bowen, who left us a splendid record of his life and times in the form of several illustrated journals, painted crude watercolor sketches of many of the ships he either sailed on or encountered in his travels. Two of these were the merchant ships *Atlantic* and *Patty*. Both were Portsmouth, New Hampshire, ships, but although we have drawn them as identical, because of the apparent similarity between them evidenced by Bowen's drawings, they may not have been sister ships. Bowen says he had charge of *Atlantic* for a brief while in 1763, loading her at the Isle of Shoals, although he also says that George Dimon was the "master Chief Mate" and William Temple the owner.

Bowen then shipped on *Patty* as chief mate under Captain Monsieur Bunbury to Grenada in the West Indies, expecting to continue with her to London, but she was sold at Grenada and he had to find his way home some other way. We believe the length overall to have been about 102′ and the length between perpendiculars about 80′.

A Reconstruction of the Draft of the American Merchant Ships
Atlantic and *Patty* of Portsmouth, New Hampshire, built about
1760

Length between Perpendiculars   80′

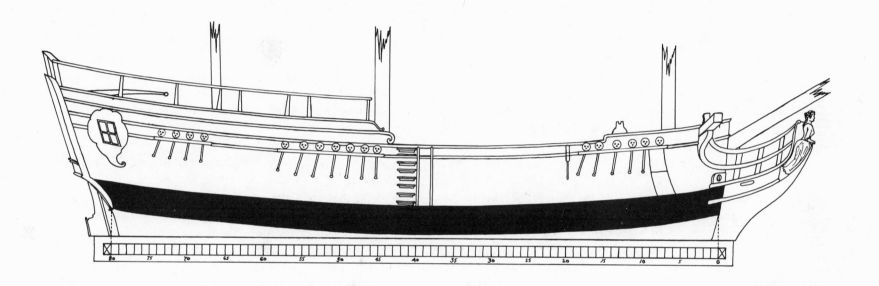

BEDFORD GALLEY

I N 1697, flushed with his recent success in having built the 44-gun ship *Falkland* and sold her to the Royal Navy, a shipbuilder by the name of Holland at Portsmouth, New Hampshire (actually New Castle, a neighboring village), built a second ship for the navy on speculation. This was the 34-gun *Bedford Galley* (not to be confused with the 70-gun ship *Bedford* that was in the Royal Navy at the same time). The Royal Navy purchased her the same year.

Unfortunately, she quickly showed areas of rot that caused her to need rebuilding in 1709, and at the time she was enlarged slightly to 410 tons although we are not told what was done that would increase the tonnage measurement by only 38 tons. She fought in the Mediterranean early in the century, and was converted into a fireship in 1716. No occasion was found to use her as a fireship, so she was sunk in either 1722 or 1725 to be a foundation for a new building at the Sheerness dockyard.

No plans of her have survived, nor any portraits. However, we do know her length, breadth, and tonnage, and we know the typical appearance of ships of her day; we also have plans of the earlier *Falkland* that was built by the same builder. It is on that basis that we present this reconstruction of her plans. She was a two-decker, with nine ports per side on each deck. On the lower deck there were fourteen oarports per side, arranged in pairs between the guns, hence the word *Galley* as part of her name; the oars must have been helpful when she was fighting in the Mediterranean. She was overmasted at first, and her spars were later reduced.

Dimensions: length overall, 121'; length on the deck, 103' 4"; length of keel, 85' 2"; breadth, 28' 8"; depth in hold, 10' 8"; draft, 13' 8"; tonnage, 372 tons.

Another ship that must have looked much the same as *Bedford Galley* was the 32-gun warship *Boston,* about which we unfortunately know very little. She was built in America in 1692, possibly by Holland at Portsmouth, and presented to the Royal Navy by the citizens of Boston in 1694. She did not remain long in the Royal Navy, for she was captured by the French in the Atlantic in January 1695. No trace of her has been found in French records.

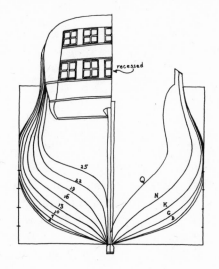

recessed

A Reconstruction of the Draft of His Majesty's 34-Gun Ship *Bedford Galley,* built at New Castle, New Hampshire, in 1697

Length on the Lower Deck	103′ 4″
Length of Keel for Tonnage	85′ 2″
Breadth	28′ 8″
Depth	10′ 8″
Tonnage	372

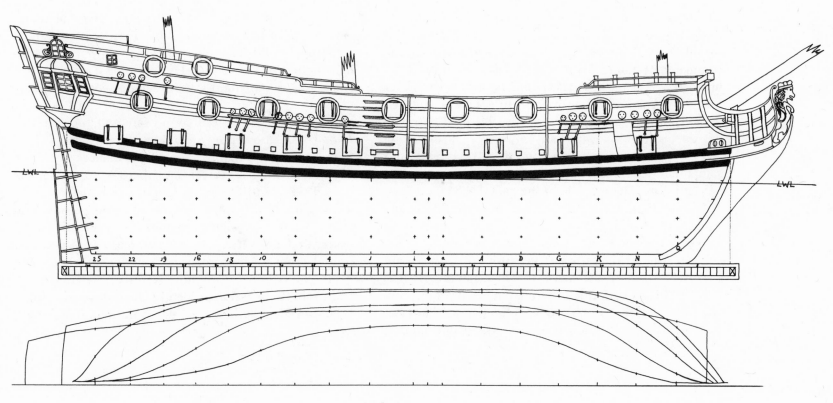

BELISARIUS

ONE of the larger American privateers in the Revolution was an unusual ship called *Belisarius*. She was built at Paul's shipyard in Boston about 1780 to plans by a maverick designer named John Peck, who was apparently also responsible for the privateer *Rattlesnake* and the East Indiaman *Empress of China*. Very little is known about her. An advertisement appeared in the *Gazette* at Providence, Rhode Island, in April 1781 announcing that she was ready for sea at Boston and would cruise for five months as a privateer under the command of James Munro, who had previously commanded the *General Washington*. However, she never finished her five-month cruise, because she was captured in a flat calm in August 1781 by the British frigate *Medea* because someone had forgotten to bring along any sweeps. She was taken into the Royal Navy and sometimes described as a 20-gun ship and sometimes as a 24-gun ship. She was sold at the end of 1783.

Joshua Humphreys, the well-known builder from Philadelphia, visited Peck after she was built and he wrote down her measurements and the notation that she was "one of the fastest sailing ships that ever swam the seas." He also sketched a few of her frame designs and we have used this information to try to reconstruct her lines for this book. The British, however, were not as enthusiastic as Humphreys, for one admiral said that she "did not answer all that was expected," although he did not enumerate her faults. He described her as a good sailer and stiff in a moderate breeze. He also said that she had a sharp entrance but with no hollow in the waterlines, and that she had a great deal of deadwood and a large gripe or forefoot. Some of the British dimensions do not agree with Humphreys; the British measurements could have been taken at different stations or taken carelessly, but Peck, scatter-brained as he was, could have given Humphreys only approximate figures. We have used Humphreys's figures.

Various commentators have made much of the supposed French influence in Peck's designs, but it seems that Peck was influenced by no one and the fact that *Belisarius*'s midsection resembles the typical French midsection is probably mere coincidence. If Humphreys's drawing is correct, and there is no saying that it is, Peck continued the pronounced knuckle of the lower bilge all the way aft, which is a most peculiar and un-French design, slightly reminiscent of the after lines of the 12-meter yacht *Mariner* that was an unsuccessful candidate for the defense of the America's Cup in 1974.

Her dimensions, as we show her, were: length overall, 128'; length between perpendiculars, 111'; length of keel, 93' 8"; breadth, 30' 6"; depth in hold, 9' 6"; draft, 13' 2"; tonnage, 514.

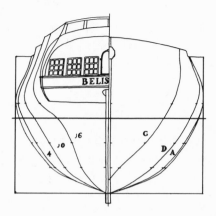

A Reconstruction of the Draft of the American Privateer Ship
Belisarius, built in Massachusetts about 1780

Length between Perpendiculars	111'
Length of Keel for Tonnage	93' 8"
Breadth	30' 6"
Depth in Hold	9'
Tonnage	514

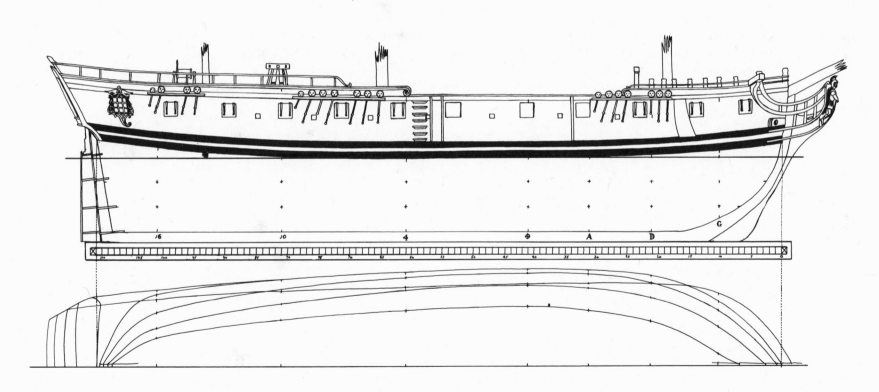

BERBICE

THE 8-gun schooner *Berbice* was built in America, probably in the Chesapeake Bay area, about 1780. She was captured in the West Indies, and was purchased for the Royal Navy under orders of Admiral Rodney. Rodney used her as a tender, and we may assume that this included carrying messages back and forth between the islands, since she was very fast for her size. She was, according to one record, condemned and sold out of the navy at Antigua in September 1788, but another record says that she was (again?) purchased in 1793 by the Royal Navy when war broke out against France, and that she was wrecked on the island of Dominica in the West Indies at the end of 1796. If this is so, she lived a long life for such a lightly built boat. Her design should be compared to the schooner *Ant*.

Two copies of her lines survive, one at the National Maritime Museum at Greenwich and the other in private hands; however, they do not agree. Howard Chapelle synthesized the two designs, and we have followed his lead: length overall, 78′ 8″; length between perpendiculars, 72′ 9″; length on the keel, 54′; breadth, 20′ 8″; depth in hold, 7′ 6″; draft, 9′; tonnage, 121.

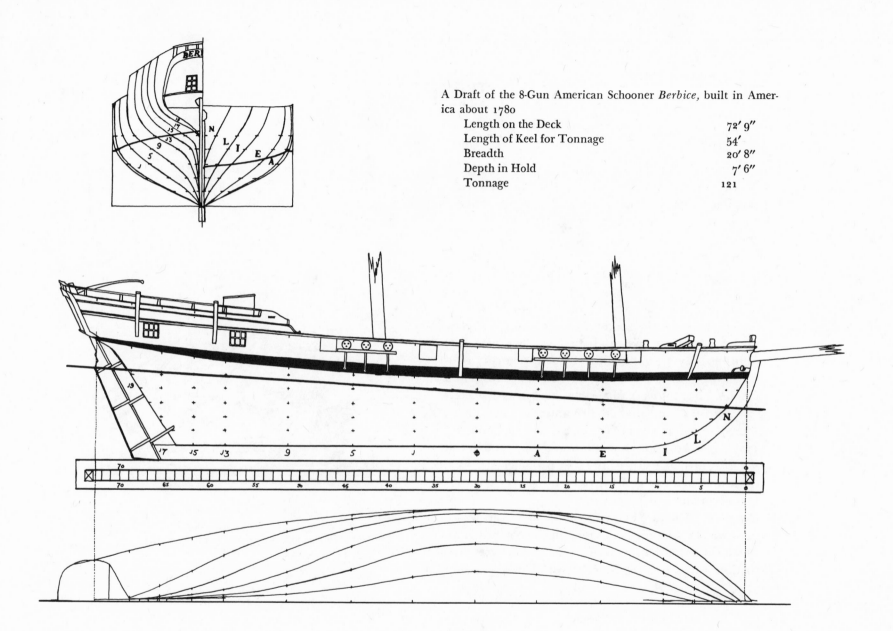

A Draft of the 8-Gun American Schooner *Berbice,* built in America about 1780

Length on the Deck	72′ 9″
Length of Keel for Tonnage	54′
Breadth	20′ 8″
Depth in Hold	7′ 6″
Tonnage	121

BETHEL

A FINE contemporary oil painting exists of the Massachusetts privateer *Bethel*. The picture, true to a popular convention of the day, shows her under sail in two different poses as if there were actually two ships in the picture. It is said to be the earliest portrait of an identified American ship, and was painted in 1748. *Bethel* belonged to the Quincy family of Boston, and may have been built only a few years earlier by the well-known Boston builder Benjamin Hallowell.

In 1748, she had the good fortune to capture a Spanish treasure ship of 24 guns and 110 men. She herself was mounting only 14 guns with 38 men, so many of the guns showing in the portrait must have been dummies. Such dummy guns were sometimes known as "Quakers," to rhyme with the Elizabethan name for a certain class of guns known as sakers. Theoretically, she could have carried over 20 guns, but 16 would be usual for her size. An unusual feature for a ship of her size is the double-decked stern gallery, resembling the stern of an East Indiaman.

No plans of her are known to exist. However, we have reconstructed lines for her, based on the portrait and on other ships of her period. The dimensions of our reconstruction are as follows: length overall, 100′ 9″; length on the deck, 84′; length on the keel, 68′ 3″; breadth, 26′; depth in hold, 12′ 3″; draft, 12′ 10″; tonnage, 240. We have been unable to find any record of her later history.

Privateer Ship *Bethel*
From an anonymous oil painting dated 1748
Peabody Museum, Salem, Massachusetts

A Reconstruction of the Draft of the 16-Gun American Privateer
Ship *Bethel,* built at Boston about 1746

Length on the Range of the Deck	84'
Length of Keel for Tonnage	68' 3"
Breadth	26'
Depth in Hold	12' 3"
Tonnage	240

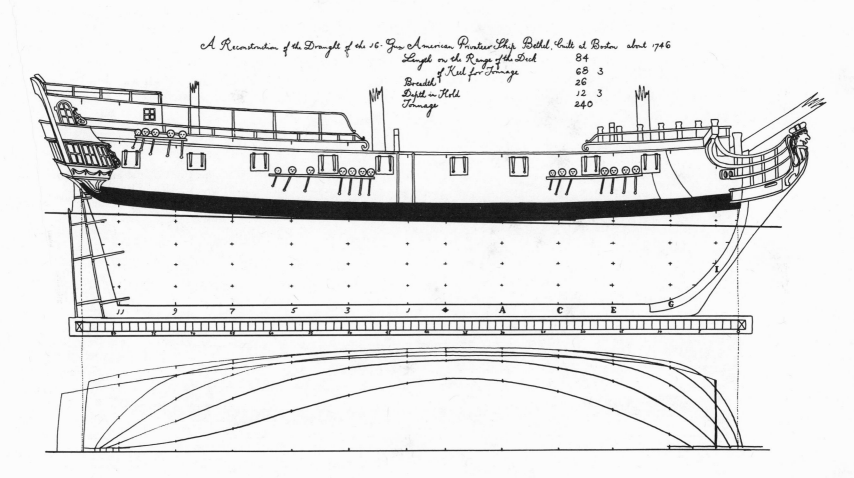

A Reconstruction of the Draught of the 16-Gun American Privateer Ship Bethel, built at Boston about 1746
Length on the Range of the Deck 84
of Keel for Tonnage 68 3
Breadth 26
Depth in Hold 12 3
Tonnage 240

BLACK PRINCESS

ONE of the many merchant ships that were fitted out with a few cannons and issued a letter of marque by a state governor in the Revolutionary War was the Connecticut brig or snow *Black Princess*. She mounted eight or ten guns, and sailed under the command of Humphrey Crary in 1781, although she looks as if she were built considerably before that date. She belonged to Dudley Woodbridge & Co., and cruised to St. Maarten in the West Indies with a crew of only twelve men. On her return voyage she was chased into Stonington, Connecticut, by a frigate. There is no record of any captures made by her.

A crude sketch of her exists at the Connecticut Historical Society and we have based our simple plan on that sketch. Her length overall was about 79′ 7″, and her length between perpendiculars was about 66′.

A Reconstruction of the Draft of the 10-Gun Connecticut Brig *Black Princess,* built about 1776

Length between Perpendiculars   65′

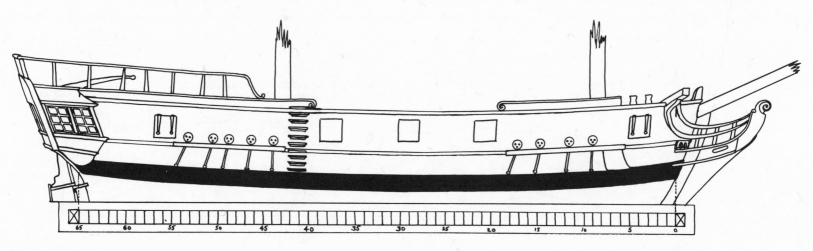

BONHOMME RICHARD

JOHN PAUL JONES spent a good deal of time in France in the hope that the French might outfit him with a fleet of heavily armed ships to do battle with the British; he was convinced that he would never get such a fleet if he waited around Philadelphia for Congress to present it to him. When he got his fleet, it was not exactly what he had wanted in terms of the quantity and quality of men and ships under him, but he used it to good advantage so that the favorable publicity that he gained from the fleet's single major (but insignificant) engagement with the enemy far outstripped the reputation of more important naval combats.

Jones's flagship was a tired French East Indiaman by the name of *Le Duc de Duras,* equipped with 36 guns. Carpenters made a number of gunports on the lower deck, filling them with obsolete eighteen-pounders (that exploded in the battle), bringing her strength up to 42 guns. The little fleet left France in June 1779 to go clockwise around the British Isles. In all of Jones's efforts with the fleet, he was not supported at all by Pierre Landais in the *Alliance,* and hardly supported by any of the other captains. Time after time he was frustrated in his plans to raid a section of British coast and hold a town for ransom. Finally, off Flamborough Head, Yorkshire, he spotted a large convoy arriving from the Baltic, guarded by only a 44 and a 20. As good convoy guards should, the two British ships sheered off to do battle with Jones so that the convoy would have time to escape. One of Jones's 20s engaged and captured the 20-gun guardship, and Jones himself did battle with the larger ship, whose same was *Serapis.*

In deference to his patron, Benjamin Franklin, the author of *Poor Richard's Almanac,* Jones had named his ship *Bonhomme Richard* (i.e., *Poor Richard*). The contest was unequal, but Jones fought with such determination that he carried the day (or actually night), in

Ship *Bonhomme Richard*
After an oil painting by William Elliott, 1789
U.S. Naval Academy Museum, Annapolis, Maryland

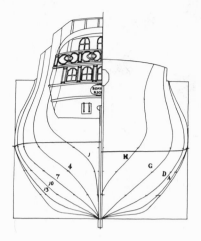

A Reconstruction of the Draft of the 42-Gun Continental Ship
Bonhomme Richard, built in France in 1765

Length between Perpendiculars	152'
Length of Keel for Tonnage	124' 5"
Breadth	40'
Depth in Hold	19'
Tonnage	1,050

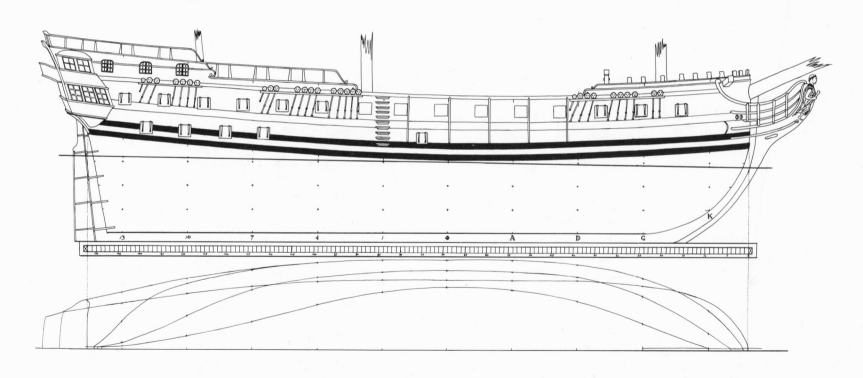

spite of having to put down mutinies and in spite of the fact that his ship was not only leaking faster than the pumps could handle but was also on fire. It was in this battle that Jones is reported to have uttered his immortal words "I have only just begun to fight." After the victory, Jones put his own crew and the crew of *Serapis* to work at plugging the leaks, pumping her, and putting out the fires, but after a while he realized it was hopeless and gave the order to abandon her. This must be one of the strangest outcomes to a sea battle, for the winner was the ship that was sunk.

This battle so close to British shores struck terror into the British population, who fully expected a large invasion at any moment. Nevertheless, the *Serapis* had done her job, for the convoy arrived in Britain unscathed, and any ordinary captain would have surrendered *Bonhomme Richard* long before the actual end of the battle, so much damage had she sustained.

There are a great many portraits of *Bonhomme Richard* in this battle, either from the bow or the stern, but none full on from the side. There are no surviving plans of the ship, and even her dimensions are unknown. However, we have based our reconstruction of this important ship on other French East Indiamen of the period and on what can be seen in the contemporary paintings and prints of the battle. She may have looked a bit like the South Carolina Navy 44-gun ship *La Bricole,* which had been loaned to them by the French.

Her dimensions as we see her were: length overall, 186′ 10″; length on the deck, 152′; length of keel, 124′ 5″; beam, 40′; depth, 19′; draft, 19′; tonnage, 1,050.

BOSTON

AFTER the New England troops and ships had played such a major part in the capture of the French fortress of Louisbourg in Nova Scotia in 1745, pressure was exerted on the Royal Navy to build some of its ships in America. The navy initially agreed rather reluctantly to build four, which they then scaled down to two. The 44-gun ship *America* was built at Portsmouth, New Hampshire, and the 24-gun ship *Boston* was built by Benjamin Hallowell in Boston. She was soon found to be rotten and in 1752 was ordered broken up after only four years. Although the British and Americans thought of her as a Sixth Rate, and although she had one port on the lower deck (probably used only as a loading port and not as a gunport), she approached very close to the concept of a frigate. As such, she may have been the first frigate-type ship built in America, as far as we know. She was very similar to other ships of her type built in England, except that she followed the American custom of making a ship of a given rate a few feet larger than other ships of her rate. Her plans survive at the National Maritime Museum, Greenwich.

Dimensions: length overall, 142′; length on the deck, 118′; length of keel, 97′ 8″; breadth, 32′ 8″; depth in hold, 7′; draft, 15′; tonnage, 555.

[75]

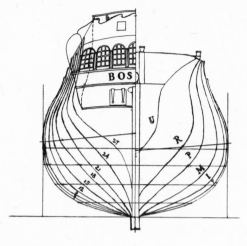

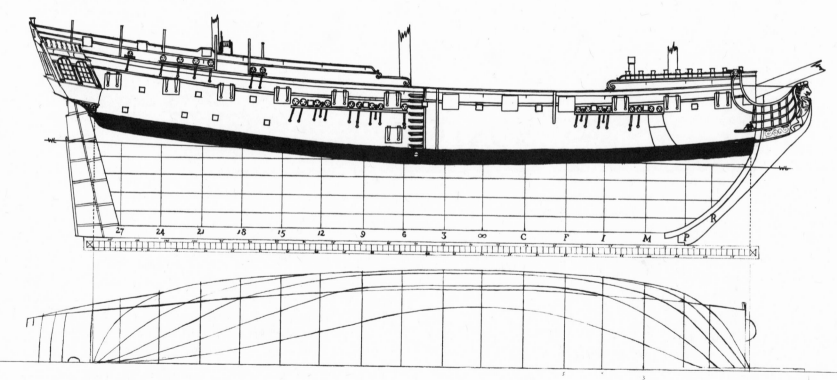

A Draft of His Majesty's 24-Gun Ship *Boston*, built at Boston in 1748

Length on the Lower Deck	118′
Length of Keel for Tonnage	97′ 8″
Breadth	33′
Depth in Hold	7′
Draft	16′ 6″
Tonnage	555

BOSTON *and* PROTECTOR

Of the initial thirteen frigates ordered by Congress in 1775, *Boston,* one of the three 24-gun ships, was built at Newburyport, Massachusetts, by Greenleaf & Cross. She was an exceptionally pretty ship, judging from the set of contemporary oil paintings of her by Francis Holman. Her rig was unusual in that she set a lateen sail on the ensign staff, thus giving her a fourth mast. Her armament was nominally that for a 24-gun ship, but her builders made her a scaled-down copy of the 32-gun frigate *Hancock,* which they were building at the same time, so that she could actually carry 32 guns if necessary. When the British captured her, they rated her as a 28-gun ship. Due to shortages of nine-pounder cannons, some of her initial cannons were twelve-pounders.

Under Captain Hector McNeill, she departed from Boston in May 1777 on her first cruise, in company with *Hancock.* The two of them had the good fortune to take a British frigate of 28 guns, the *Fox.* A good deal of chivalry was displayed in this battle as each side ceased fire to allow the other to put out fires caused by hot wadding lodged in awkward places. *Fox* was soon retaken by *Flora,* 32 guns, and *Hancock* was taken by *Rainbow,* 32 guns, in a disgraceful episode in which *Boston* deserted her companions in flight. McNeill was dismissed as a result. There is no doubt that the three frigates together had the strength, if not the determination, to defeat the two British ships. After this, *Boston* lay in Boston, nominally under command of Samuel

Tucker, but with no crew. He got her to sea on 15 February 1778 with John Adams as a passenger. Five days out, lightning broke the mainmast. Then she narrowly escaped from a 36-gun frigate, but captured the 16-gun brig *Martha* before arriving in the Garonne River at the end of March.

In May, she set out on a cruise in the Bay of Biscay with a troublesome crew of Frenchmen, but returned to St. Nazaire to get rid of her crew in August. In Sep-

Frigate *Boston*
From one of a set of four oil paintings by Francis Holman, 1779
Peabody Museum, Salem, Massachusetts

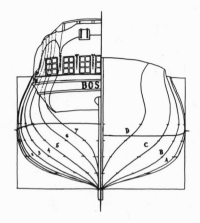

A Reconstruction of the 24-Gun Continental Frigate *Boston* and the similar 26-Gun Massachusetts Frigate *Protector,* built at Newburyport, Massachusetts, in 1776 and 1779, respectively

Length on the Lower Deck	114′ 3″
Length of Keel for Tonnage	93′
Breadth	32′
Depth in Hold	10′ 3″
Tonnage	514

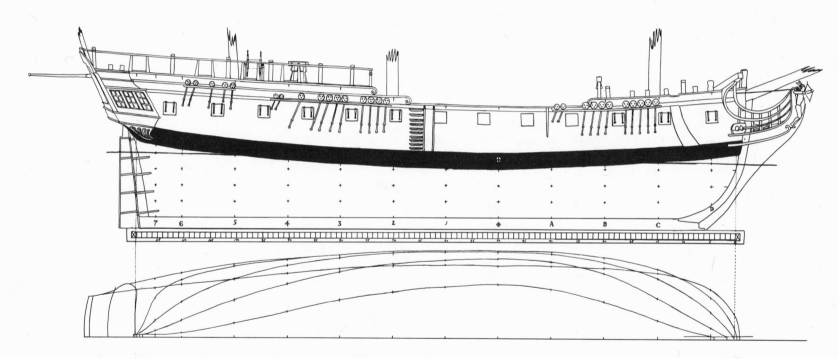

tember she set sail for home in company with *Providence* and *Ranger,* arriving at Portsmouth, New Hampshire, in October 1778. She lay mostly idle until the following July, when she took eight prizes on a short cruise with the frigate *Deane.* In September 1779 she was ordered to Charleston, South Carolina.

She was still in Charleston the following May when the British captured the city. Under the terms of the city's capitulation the ships had to be surrendered intact, so *Boston* entered the Royal Navy but with a new name: *Charleston* or *Charlestown.* She was sold out of the navy in 1783.

The Massachusetts State Navy undertook an ambitious project in 1779: the frigate *Protector* was built in Newburyport, Massachusetts. Little is known about her appearance, for neither her lines nor her measurements nor even a portrait of her survive. We do know that she rated 26 guns and that her tonnage was 586, a bit more than *Boston*'s 514, but not enough more to mean that the two measurements were of a different design (tonnage measurements of the same ship varied widely, depending on who was the measurer). It is our suspicion that the two ships were built in the same shipyard to essentially the same design, and that is how we have drawn them.

Protector did not get rigged until 1780, so she missed being a part of the disastrous Penobscot Bay expedition that had been organized by Massachusetts state forces. On her first cruise, under Captain John Foster Williams, she ran into heavy fighting. On 9 June 1780 she fought the 32-gun Liverpool privateer *Admiral Duff.* *Admiral Duff* was weak from old age and from the fact that she was once a merchant ship (an East Indiaman), but

her crew fought like wildcats and her high sides must have seemed terrifying to those on *Protector;* one of the *Protector*'s crew wrote that she was "large as a 74." After a long period of furious fighting *Admiral Duff* sank, and there were only 55 survivors. *Protector* herself was badly cut up and so headed back to port. On the way she encountered the 32-gun British frigate *Thames,* and fortunately escaped from her after a long, running fight.

In May 1781 *Protector* encountered two British ships, the 44-gun *Roebuck* and the 28-gun *Medea,* and this time there was no escape. She was taken into the Royal Navy and given the name of *Hussar.* She participated in the capture of a number of American vessels in the twenty months of the war that remained, and was sold out of the navy in August 1783. Edward Preble, later a famous captain in the U.S. Navy, had been a midshipman on *Protector,* but was fortunately exchanged before he could get a taste of British prisons; this is mentioned here because Congress, not wishing the individual states to continue to maintain their own navies, normally refused to allow crewmen of state vessels to be figured into national prisoner exchanges. Captain Williams had to wait seven months to be exchanged, and he was lucky compared to his men.

Our drawing of *Boston* and *Protector* is based on paintings of *Boston* (at the Peabody Museum, Salem), on the recorded dimensions of *Boston,* and on the lines of *Hancock* that are preserved at Greenwich. No dimensions survive for *Protector.* Length overall, 138′ 7″; length on the deck, 114′ 3″; length of keel, 93′; breadth, 32′; depth in hold, 10′ 3″; draft, 14′; tonnage, 514 (*Boston*) and 586 (*Protector*).

BRILLIANT

WE know quite a bit about the larger ships that were built in New England and the Middle Colonies, but very little about those built in the South. The merchant ship *Brilliant* was built in Virginia about 1775. She mounted 14 guns, so she could defend herself. Although there is no sign of it on the Admiralty plans of the ship, one writer says that she was fitted with a timber port in the bow, presumably for loading cargos of long-leaf yellow pine, a southern wood. She was actually used principally for transporting tobacco. She was purchased for the Royal Navy in 1776 and renamed *Druid*. She was used as a convoy guard, and in that capacity in September 1777 she frightened off *Alfred* and *Raleigh,* although she suffered considerable damage herself.

In September 1779 she was fitted out as a fireship and renamed *Blast* (a suitable name), but was never used as a fireship so she was sold out of the navy in September 1783.

Her lines are on file at the National Maritime Museum at Greenwich: length overall, 108′ 7″; length on the desk, 89′; length on the keel, 74′ 3″; breadth, 27′; depth in hold, 11′ 10″; draft, 13′ 3″; tonnage, 288.

A large model of *Brilliant* is on display at the Smithsonian Institution, and a small booklet about her was published by the Tobacco Institute.

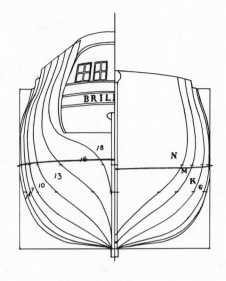

A Draft of the 16-Gun American Merchant Ship *Brilliant,* built
in Virginia about 1775

Length of the Lower Deck	89'
Length of Keel for Tonnage	74' 3"
Breadth	27'
Depth in Hold	11' 10"
Tonnage	288

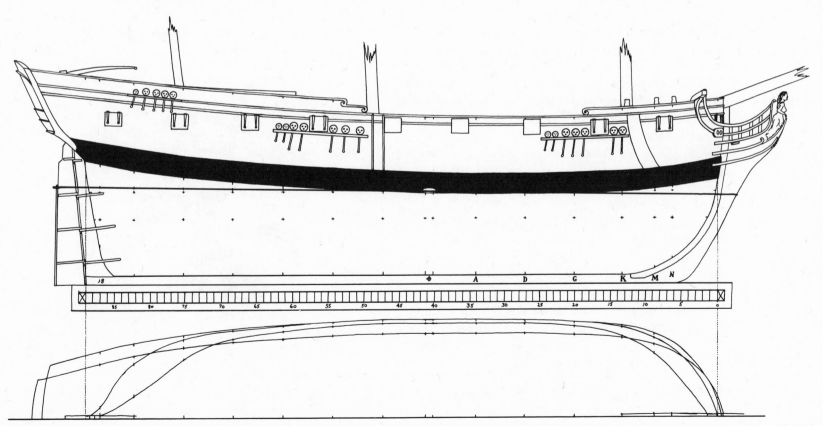

CABOT

T HE 14-gun brig *Cabot* was one of the first ships to be purchased by the Continental Navy in 1775, although she was not part of the 13 October bill that created the navy, as so many writers have claimed (according to Silas Deane, who seconded the bill, the first two vessels authorized were the sloop *Katy* and the brig *Minerva*). We don't know what her original name was, but she was renamed *Cabot* by Congress, in honor of the fifteenth-century explorer.

Commanded by John B. Hopkins, the son of the commodore, *Cabot* got to sea with the rest of the Continental fleet early in 1776, took part in the raid on Nassau, and was the first to get into action against the frigate *Glasgow;* Hopkins was wounded in the latter battle, and four of his men were killed on the second broadside. A few months later her command passed to another Rhode Islander, Joseph Olney. Olney was chased ashore in Nova Scotia by the frigate *Milford;* after he had abandoned his brig, the *Milford*'s crew got her off the rocks and took her into the Royal Navy under the same name. The date was 26 March 1777, so *Cabot* was the first vessel of the Continental Navy to be captured. She took part in the battle of Dogger Bank in the North Sea against the Dutch in 1781 and was sold out of the Royal Navy in June 1783.

There are no known portraits or lines existing of this ship, but a full set of dimensions was recorded. In addition, we have a few details of her appearance furnished by a spy: she had a small white head, all her gunports had lids, and she mounted an additional 12 swivel guns. She probably looked quite different from the commercial model kit of her that is on the market. For our reconstruction of this significant ship, we have relied on what is known of her, plus the appearance of other brigs of her size and date, especially as drawn by Chapman. The brig *Andrew Doria* probably resembled her closely.

Her dimensions were: length overall, 88′ 3″; length on deck, 74′ 9″; length of keel, 63′ 7″; beam, 24′ 8″; depth, 11′ 4″; draft, 10′ 2″; tonnage, 189.

Brig *Cato,* an armed brig similar to *Cabot*
From an oil painting, probably by Thomas Luny, ca. 1778
Sold on the London art market, ca. 1970

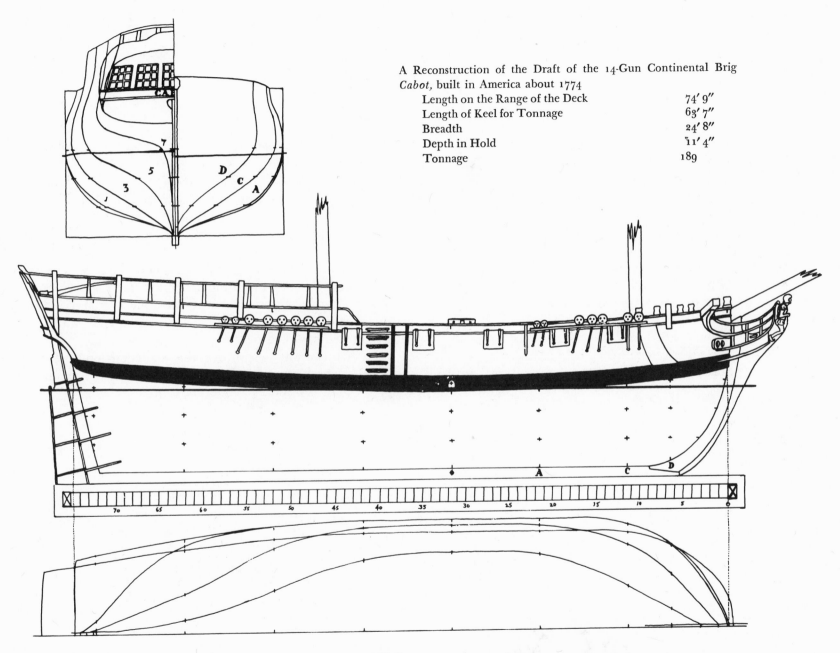

A Reconstruction of the Draft of the 14-Gun Continental Brig
Cabot, built in America about 1774

Length on the Range of the Deck	74' 9"
Length of Keel for Tonnage	63' 7"
Breadth	24' 8"
Depth in Hold	11' 4"
Tonnage	189

CARLETON

WHEN Sir Guy Carleton's Forces chased Benedict Arnold's troops out of Canada in 1776 the British decided to establish a fleet on Lake Champlain. One of these vessels was the little schooner *Carleton*. She mounted 12 guns and had the shallow draft necessary for navigating Lake Champlain. She was placed under the command of Lieutenant J. R. Dacres (we were unable to determine what relation he may have been to Captain Richard Dacres of the frigate *Guerrière* in the War of 1812). She seemed to sail rather better than the other British vessels on the lake, and that got her into trouble. She was the first British vessel to arrive at the American position behind Valcour Island, so she bore the full brunt of the American fire until she was disabled and most of her crew wounded or killed.

Finally, to avoid further slaughter, Midshipman Edward Pellew (later Lord Exmouth, the celebrated British admiral), aged nineteen, bravely crawled out on the bowsprit to hold the jib aback in order to turn her away from the battle. She escaped with heavy damage.

No record of her later career has appeared to date; we can assume that she was repaired and used on the lake until the end of the war. There are a number of portraits of her, including several in the Public Archives of Canada and one in the Royal Collection at Windsor Castle. Her lines are on file at the National Maritime Museum, Greenwich.

Dimensions: length overall, 66'; length on deck, 59' 2"; length on the keel, 46' 10"; breadth, 20'; depth in hold, 6' 6"; draft, 7' 4"; tonnage, 99.

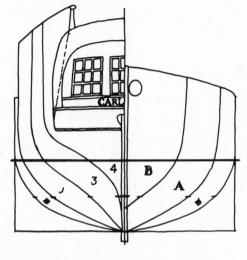

A Draft of His Majesty's 12-Gun Schooner *Carleton,* built on Lake
Champlain in 1776

Length on the Range of the Deck	59' 2"
Length of Keel for Tonnage	46' 10"
Breadth	20'
Depth in Hold	6' 6"
Tonnage	99

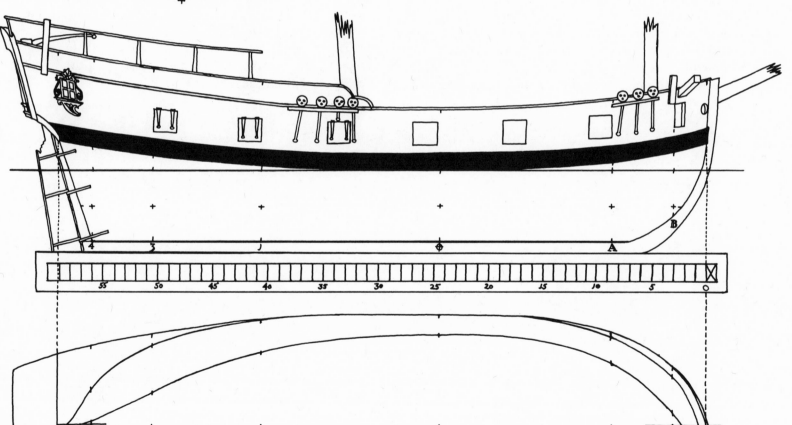

CHALEUR

THE schooner *Chaleur* was built in the 1760s in either New England or Canada. She was purchased for the Royal Navy in 1764 and was thus one of its first schooners. Her purpose was to attempt to curb some of the smuggling that had for long been carried on with impunity by the New England Colonies, particularly Rhode Island. It was thought that a fast hull with a schooner rig would be more likely to catch the smugglers, which were themselves for the most part fast hulls with schooner or sloop rigs. There must have been something wrong with her, perhaps rotten timbers, for she was sold out of the navy at the end of 1768, when the navy had more need of schooners than ever before.

She is variously referred to as a 4-gun, 8-gun, or 12-gun schooner. Her lines show ports for a total of six carriage guns, but there was plenty of room for more ports to be cut later. One account says that she was captured from the French near the American coast by the corvette *Favourite*, but it is unsubstantiated. She was probably built as a merchantman, since she was so burdensome. Her lines are on file at the National Maritime Museum, Greenwich.

Dimensions: length overall, 76′ 4″; length on deck, 69′; length of keel, 50′; beam, 20′ 4″; depth, 7′ 9″; draft, 9′ 2″; tonnage, 121.

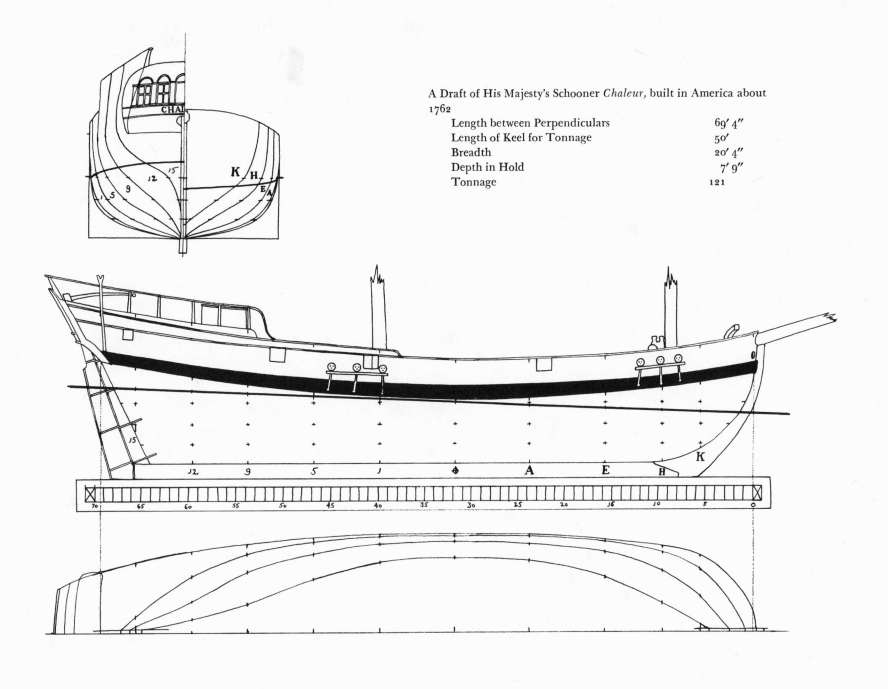

A Draft of His Majesty's Schooner *Chaleur,* built in America about 1762

Length between Perpendiculars	69′ 4″
Length of Keel for Tonnage	50′
Breadth	20′ 4″
Depth in Hold	7′ 9″
Tonnage	121

CHARMING JENNY

It is thought that something like a third of all the ships in the world flying the British flag in the 1770s were American built or owned. Such ships were commonly known as "plantation built." These ships were frequently built on speculation and sailed over to England (with a cargo, of course) and sold at auction. This kind of sale was often called "sale by the candle," because whoever's bid was on the floor at the time a particular candle went out was the winning bid.

A handbill advertising the "sale by the candle" of the 14-gun plantation-built, square-sterned ship *Charming Jenny* of 170 tons in London in August 1761 has recently been found in London. A fairly detailed portrait of the ship is engraved at the top of the paper, which is something of a rarity. We learn from the advertisement that she was regarded as suitable for trade with Virginia or the West Indies or in the North Sea, and that her captain was Joseph Todd. Since Britain was at war with France and Spain in 1761 the 14 guns that she carried were a necessary part of her, although one suspects that the buyer would have to buy the guns separately, because they are not listed in the accompanying inventory of her gear.

Dimensions: length overall, 99' 6"; length between perpendiculars, 77'; tonnage, 170.

A Reconstruction of the Draft of the 14-Gun Merchant Ship
Charming Jenny, built in America in 1761
Length between Perpendiculars   77′

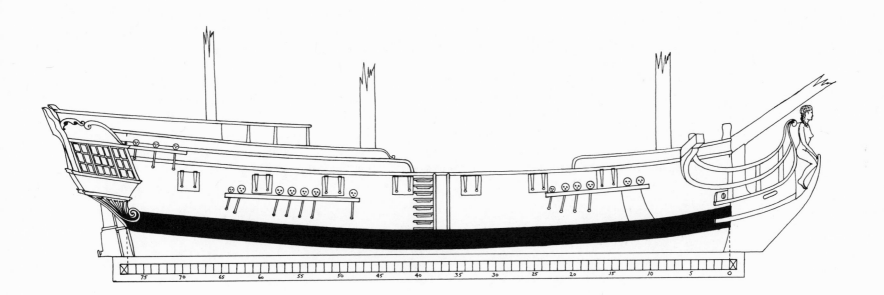

CODRINGTON

A FINE merchant ship was built at Newburyport, Massachusetts, in 1773, possibly by Greenleaf or Cross. She was unarmed and was named *Codrington*, probably after the wealthy family of that name in Barbados. A large number of British-owned ships were built in North America, so it was not unusual for this ship to be purchased by the Royal Navy in September 1774. She was renamed *Cherokee* and fitted out with six three-pounder carriage guns, eight swivel guns, and 30 men for service in the southern part of North America doing survey work. After the Revolutionary War broke out in earnest, she was converted into a transport and renamed *Despatch* in April 1777. She was well suited to being a transport, having about as much carrying capacity as it is possible to build into a ship of her length, and she sailed well after the mainmast had been nudged forward a little. Nothing is known about her after this date. Her lines are on file at the National Maritime Museum, Greenwich.

Dimensions: length overall, 87′ 8″; length between perpendiculars, 77′; length of keel, 60′ 2″; beam, 24′; depth in hold, 17′; draft, 14′ 2″; tonnage, 178.

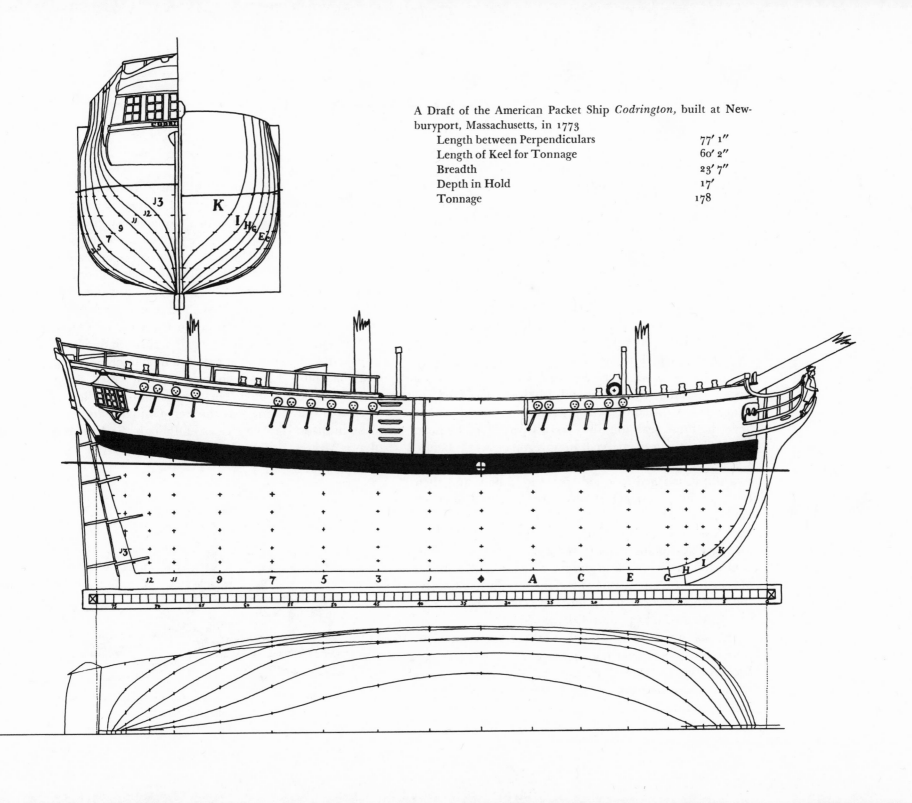

A Draft of the American Packet Ship *Codrington*, built at Newburyport, Massachusetts, in 1773

Length between Perpendiculars	77′ 1″
Length of Keel for Tonnage	60′ 2″
Breadth	23′ 7″
Depth in Hold	17′
Tonnage	178

COLUMBIA

THE little merchant ship *Columbia* is the subject of much disagreement among maritime historians. One side says that she was built in 1773 in Scituate, Massachusetts, on the same slipway that had launched the Boston Tea Party brig *Beaver* the previous year, and another says that she was built after the Revolution and that her name in any case was *Columbia Rediviva*. The Latin word *rediviva* means "brought back to life," so our suggestion is that *Columbia* was indeed built in 1773 but required rebuilding in 1787, at which time the rejuvenated ship had her name altered. Regardless of her background, there is no denying that she made history. Under the command of John Kendrick of Wareham, Massachusetts, she left Boston in September 1787 to hunt seals on the West Coast. Her consort, *Lady Washington,* arrived in Oregon a week before *Columbia* and was viciously attacked by Indians. The two ships managed to trade with the Indians and then took the furs they had obtained to Canton, China. In China, Kendrick took command of *Lady Washington* and Robert Gray of Tiverton, Rhode Island, gave up his place as captain of *Lady Washington* to move up to command of *Columbia*. *Columbia* then sailed home to Massachusetts, having exchanged the furs for tea. *Columbia* reached Boston in August 1790, the first ship to fly the American flag around the world.

She was received in Boston with great celebration, made the more exciting because she had brought back Attoo, a young chief from the Sandwich Islands (Hawaii) who marched in the welcoming parade in his full regalia. In spite of the fanfare, however, the voyage was a financial flop for her backers, who had put up the then-large sum of $50,000. But some of the backers were undaunted and they sent Gray and *Columbia* out again in the autumn of 1790. On this voyage Gray discovered the Columbia River (which he named after the ship), a fact that gave the United States a stronger claim to the land on the West Coast than Spain, Great Britain, or Russia, all of whom said that they had been there first. While there he met the British explorer George Vancouver. Gray returned in 1793 to learn that the second voyage had also been a financial failure and that the ship had to be sold at auction immediately. In 1792, Gray had built a small sloop in Oregon called *Adventure*. He had brought her frames out with him in *Columbia*'s hold. She was the first United States vessel to be built on the West Coast, although the British explorer Meares had built one there as early as 1788,

Ship *Columbia Rediviva,* being attacked by Indian war canoes
in the Pacific Northwest
From a painting by a sailor in her crew, dated 1792

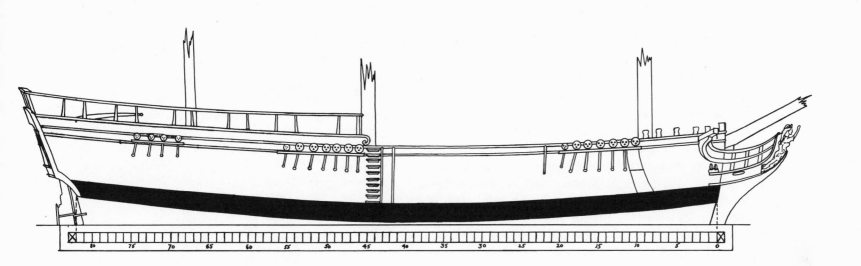

and the Russians built their *Feniks* there in 1794. *Columbia* was broken up about 1801.

No plans of *Columbia* have survived, but we do know some of her dimensions and there are a number of well-executed contemporary portraits of her; we have based our drawing on these. Disneyland in California has an operational, full-size copy of her on display, and it appears to be accurate, which is more than one can usually say for Hollywood's excursions into history. If *Columbia*

and *Beaver* were indeed built one year apart in the same yard, one would expect them to look somewhat alike, which means that the exhibit on the Boston waterfront that is supposed to represent the Boston Tea Party ship *Beaver* should be considerably altered before she can be called accurate.

Columbia's dimensions: length overall, 99′ 2″; length on deck, 82′; tonnage, 212.

COLUMBUS

ONE of the members of the first fleet of the Continental Navy in 1775 was the ship *Columbus*. She had formerly been the Philadelphia merchant ship *Sally*, and must have looked a lot like *Alfred* except for the fact that she had no head. According to the report of a British spy, she was painted all black. She mounted anywhere from 20 to 28 guns at various times, arranged with 18 on the gun deck and as many as required on the quarterdeck, and even on the waist. She had been built by Wharton & Humphreys.

Her first navy captain was Abraham Whipple, and she took part in the expedition to Nassau. She was blanketed by the other ships in the battle against the frigate *Glasgow*, and so did not actually take part in that action, apart from having one man hurt. After a brief stint at anchor in Providence, Rhode Island, Whipple took *Columbus* to sea on 16 June, only to run into the 28-gun British frigate *Cerberus*, which managed to pour three broadsides into *Columbus*, killing one man and cutting up her rigging rather badly; *Columbus* hit *Cerberus* with one answering broadside before escaping. She returned to Providence and found herself trapped there when a British fleet occupied Narragansett Bay in December 1776. She did not get to sea at all in 1777.

In the meantime Hoysted Hacker had been made her captain. He tried to get her to sea on a black night in March 1778; he had unloaded all her guns and stores first, so as to make her faster and so that the British would not get much if they captured her. The British ships stumbled onto her by accident and forced Hacker to run her aground at Point Judith, where he stripped her of everything valuable. In the morning of 28 March the British burned her.

There are no surviving plans of *Columbus*, nor even dimensions, although there is a crude picture of her scratched on a powderhorn engraving of Providence in February 1777. The dimensions of our reconstruction of her: length overall, 98'; length on deck, 89'; length of keel, 72' 10"; breadth, 27'; depth, 12'; draft, 13' 6"; tonnage, 270.

Ship *Columbus*
From a powderhorn engraving made for Charles Hewitt, 1777
Private collection, New Jersey

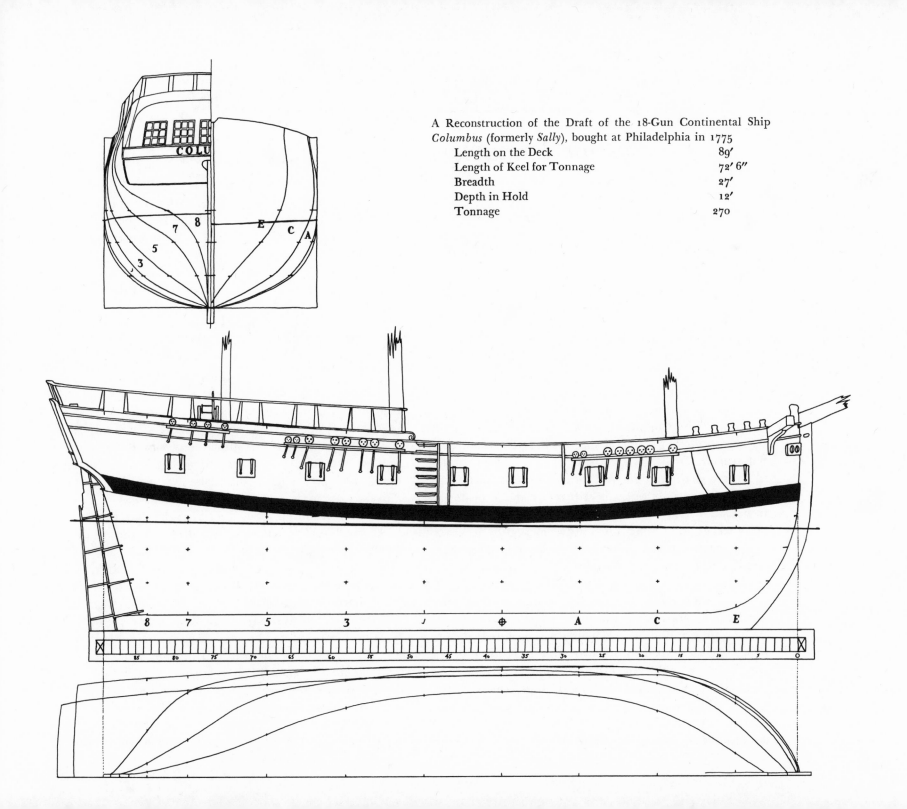

A Reconstruction of the Draft of the 18-Gun Continental Ship
Columbus (formerly *Sally*), bought at Philadelphia in 1775

Length on the Deck	89′
Length of Keel for Tonnage	72′ 6″
Breadth	27′
Depth in Hold	12′
Tonnage	270

CONFEDERACY, BOURBON,
and an Unnamed Frigate in Virginia

Among the ships authorized by Congress on 20 November 1776 were five frigates of 36 guns. Of these, *Alliance* was built in New Hampshire to local designs, an unnamed ship being built in Virginia was burned on the stocks by a British raiding party, and *Confederacy* and *Bourbon* were both built in Connecticut. Funds were lacking, which delayed construction of those that were built, and quite likely the fifth authorized frigate was never even begun for that reason.

Confederacy was launched in 1778, having been built on the Thames River at Norwich, Connecticut, by Jedediah Willets. The design was furnished by Congress, and is obviously related to the designs of the frigate *Randolph* and the 74-gun *America*. She was an unusually large ship for her rate and she was heavily ornamented with carving, which is surprising in view of the shortage of money. Although the hull form was quite sharp, making her potentially fast, she still retained the beakhead bulkhead which had been discarded by other frigate designers a long time previously. Her gun deck was pierced with fourteen ports per side, and it was high enough out of the water to allow for a complete deck of oarports, plus a loading port below the gun deck but above the wale. Her keel was slightly rockered forward, for no apparent reason.

In 1779, Captain Seth Harding was assigned to *Confederacy*, but he had so much trouble recruiting a crew that he impressed some French prisoners as they were released by the British on an exchange; this got him into trouble, so he was obliged to release the Frenchmen. On her first voyage *Confederacy* was ordered to take John Jay, U.S. ambassador to Spain, to his post, and

Monsieur Gérard, French ambassador to the United States, back to France. To avoid the likelihood of contact with enemy ships, they took a circuitous route and on 7 November 1779 *Confederacy* was savaged by a hurricane, which neatly removed the bowsprit, all three masts, and the rudder. She put into Martinique for a few months of temporary repairs while the ambassadors continued to Europe on a French ship. Then she returned to Philadelphia for complete repairs in May 1780. She cruised in the Delaware River in company with the frigate *Boston*. In the spring of 1781 she went to the West Indies to escort home a large convoy, in company with the frigate *Deane* and the corvette *Saratoga,* and she herself was heavily laden with goods. She was fallen upon by the 44-gun *Roebuck,* and the brand-new 32-gun frigate *Orpheus,* so Seth Harding surrendered without firing a shot. She was taken into the Royal Navy under the name of *Confederate,* but was broken up in March 1782. She was probably rotten.

As for *Bourbon,* she was not even laid down until early 1780 (at Middletown, Connecticut) and was launched in July 1783 into the Connecticut River. Still incomplete, she was sold in September 1783 by a Congress that had no further use for her. She would have been well suited to service as an East Indiaman, but we have no information as to whether she was so used. We are not even sure if she was built to the same design as *Confederacy;* it seems likely that she was, although perhaps a round bow was substituted for the vulnerable beakhead bulkhead.

The other frigate, built at Gosport, Virginia (near Portsmouth and Norfolk), was nowhere near finished

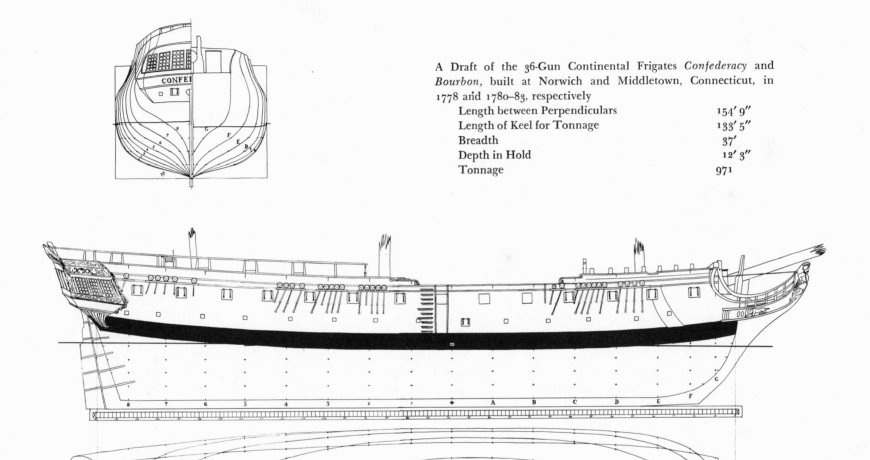

A Draft of the 36-Gun Continental Frigates *Confederacy* and *Bourbon,* built at Norwich and Middletown, Connecticut, in 1778 and 1780–83, respectively

Length between Perpendiculars	154′ 9″
Length of Keel for Tonnage	133′ 5″
Breadth	37′
Depth in Hold	12′ 3″
Tonnage	971

when a British force occupied the area. The frigate, according to Sir George Collier, commander of the 44-gun *Rainbow,* was burned along with over 130 other ships in the area. It is likely that this frigate was identical to *Confederacy.*

No contemporary portraits survive of any of these three ships, but the British thoughtfully took off *Con-* *federacy*'s lines, and these are the source for our plans: Length overall, 185′ 3″; length on deck, 154′ 9″; length of keel, 133′ 5″; breadth, 37′; depth in hold, 12′ 3″; draft, 16′; tonnage, 971. It is possible that experience with a large frigate like *Confederacy* helped pave the way for the *Constitution* and her class in the 1790s.

CONGRESS, *a Privateer*

Aᶠᵗᵉʳ only one of the initial four frigates built at Philadelphia managed to get to sea under American colors, Congress was understandably reluctant to order any more major warships built at Philadelphia. However, the shipyards were still there, and one of them turned out a fine frigate of 32 guns to be used as a privateer by Philadelphia merchants. She was named *Congress* and placed under the command of George Geddes as soon as she was finished in 1781. She took part in a bloody battle in September 1781 off Charleston against the 14-gun British corvette *Savage*. *Savage* was captured, but *Congress* suffered 8 killed and 30 wounded out of her crew of 215, and had to put into port for repairs. *Savage* was later retaken by the British frigate *Solebay* and sent into Charleston for repairs. *Congress* herself was captured not long after that, but she was not taken into the Royal Navy. (Chapelle errs when he says that the Philadelphia privateer *Congress* was captured and taken into the Royal Navy as *General Monk; General Monk* was formerly the Rhode Island privateer *General Washington*.)

There are no surviving portraits of *Congress,* nor any plans. However, the British did record some of her dimensions, and these show, as might be expected, that she was nearly identical to the Philadelphia-built frigate *Randolph*. Accordingly, our plan shows a version of the *Randolph* plan, minus the outmoded beakhead bulkhead.

Dimensions: length overall, 154'; length on the deck, 130' 9"; breadth, 32' 9"; about 685 tons. (There is a report that the famous Captain Thomas Truxtun served on her as a young lieutenant, but it could easily have been another ship called *Congress,* as there were naturally many of that name.)

A Reconstruction of the Draft of the 32-Gun American Privateer
Ship *Congress,* built at Philadelphia about 1781

Length between Perpendiculars	130′ 9″
Breadth	32′ 8″
Tonnage	685

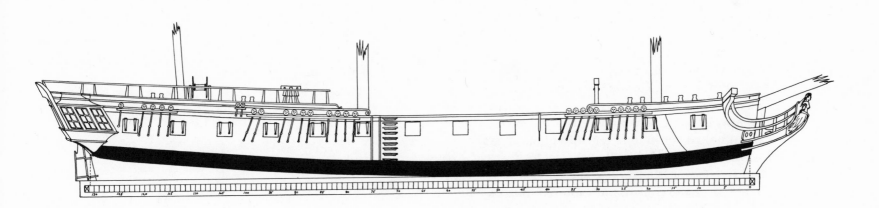

LA COUREUSE

WHEN the American Revolution was over and there was therefore no further need at the moment for fast privateer schooners, designers who knew the secrets of building fast schooners set their hands at building pilot schooners. With a fast schooner, a pilot could get aboard an incoming ship much sooner, and theoretically could thus pilot more ships in a given day and so derive a greater profit. One of these schooners was built at New York around 1785. When the French Revolution got under way she was purchased by some French Republicans, who renamed her *La Coureuse* and installed her in the French Republican Navy.

She was sighted by the British frigates *Pomone, Artois,* and *Galatea* off Isle Groix as she was guarding a convoy. The rest of the convoy was captured, but *La Coureuse* was not taken until the end of a nineteen-hour chase on 27 February 1795, which means that she was very fast if she could stay ahead of large and fast frigates. She carried eight two-pounder cannons, plus six swivels, but since these were added by the French we have omitted them from the drawing. Her crew numbered 23. Her lines were taken off at Plymouth Dockyard, and they are on file at the National Maritime Museum, Greenwich. After that, she was sent to the Mediterranean as a dispatch vessel for the Royal Navy, with a crew of 36. She was paid off in September 1796 and probably sold, but no record of her survives after this date.

This little schooner had a square-tuck stern, considerable drag to the keel, moderate deadrise, and slack bilges with quite a flair to the topsides. She had a trunk cabin aft, and her masts were apparently unstayed except for a forestay. She had a simple rig of only three sails. She would not be far out of place if used today as a yacht.

Dimensions: length overall, 57'; length between perpendiculars, 53' 2"; length of keel, 39' 5"; breadth, 16'; depth, 6' 5"; draft, 8'; tonnage, 55.

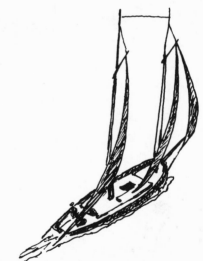

American Schooner similar to a Pilot Schooner like *La Coureuse*
From a grisaille by Pierre Ozanne, 1778
Le Musée de la Marine, Paris

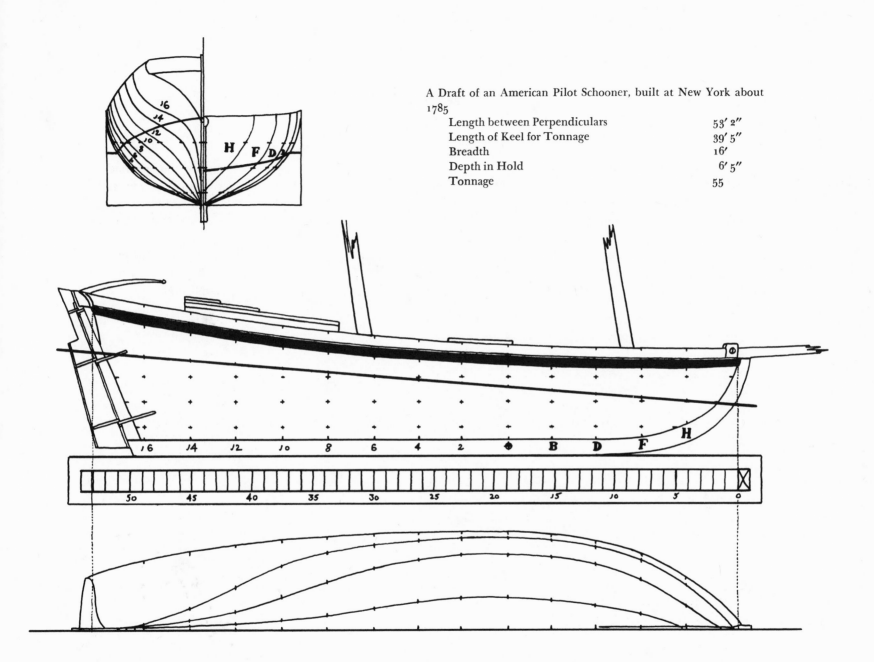

A Draft of an American Pilot Schooner, built at New York about
1785

Length between Perpendiculars	53′ 2″
Length of Keel for Tonnage	39′ 5″
Breadth	16′
Depth in Hold	6′ 5″
Tonnage	55

CUPID

THE 14-gun armed merchant ship *Cupid* was purchased by the Royal Navy in 1777. She was presumably used as a convoy guard, but little is known of her. She foundered in a bad storm off the coast of Newfoundland on 28 December 1778. Judging from stylistic similarities to *Oliver Cromwell,* which was probably built in Rhode Island, we believe that *Cupid* was built in Rhode Island about 1774. From a quick glance at her profile, she looked quite similar to merchant ships from many different places, including Philadelphia, but she had an open waist that was not found on most Philadelphia ships of her type. Her original name is not known. Her plans are on file at the National Maritime Museum, Greenwich.

Dimensions: length overall, 111'; length on the deck, 93' 2"; length on the keel, 74' 10"; breadth, 27'; depth in hold, 12' 2"; draft, 15' 8"; tonnage, 290.

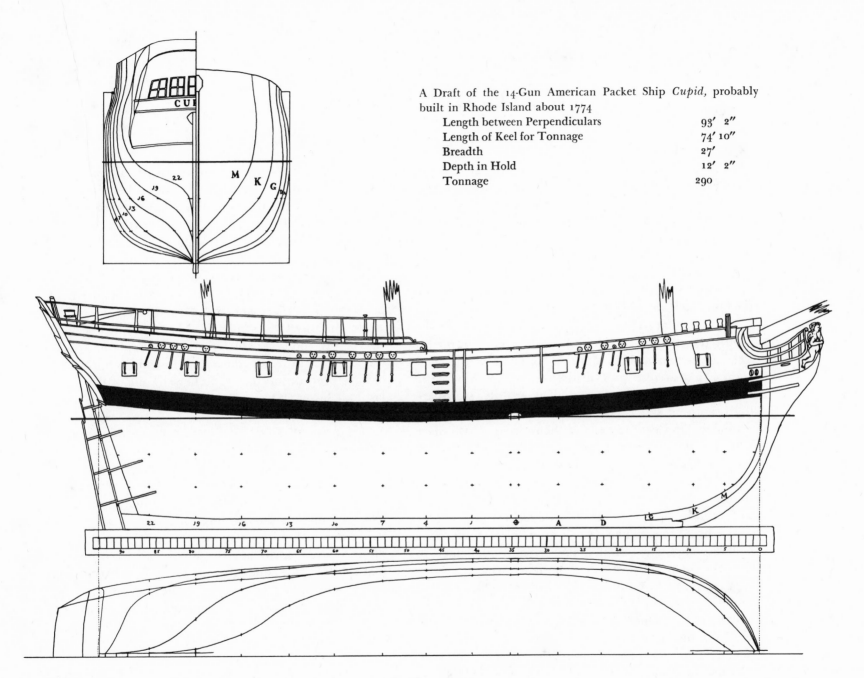

A Draft of the 14-Gun American Packet Ship *Cupid*, probably built in Rhode Island about 1774

Length between Perpendiculars	93′ 2″
Length of Keel for Tonnage	74′ 10″
Breadth	27′
Depth in Hold	12′ 2″
Tonnage	290

DEANE/HAGUE

THE 32-gun frigate *Deane* was built at Nantes, France, in 1777 to the order of the American commissioners in Paris. She was a very small ship for her rate, partly so as not to attract the attention of British spies and partly because the commissioners had little money to spend. With Samuel Nicholson in command, she arrived in Boston in May 1778, where she had to stay for several months because of a shortage of crew and the severity of the British blockade.

On 14 January 1779 she left on a cruise on which she captured a 16-gun British ship called *Viper*, burned a London merchant ship, captured six prizes in the West Indies, and arrived at Philadelphia on 17 April. She left Philadelphia on 1 July, and by 27 July, so we are told, captured sixteen enemy vessels between the Delaware and the Chesapeake, and then captured two more while she was in company with *Boston*. She returned to New England where she was idled for want of a crew. In March 1781 she sailed with *Confederacy* and *Saratoga* to escort a rich convoy from the West Indies, returning to Boston where she was once more left without a crew.

She had been named *Deane* after Silas Deane, who had seconded the bill that had founded the navy in October 1775. However, in 1782 Silas Deane had publicly advocated reunion with Britain, so he was branded a traitor and forced into exile. In 1782 the frigate was renamed *Hague*, after the capital city of Holland, the latest ally of the United States. In September 1782 her original captain was replaced by John Manley who took her immediately to Martinique, making a number of captures on the way. After she left

Martinique once more, she captured a rich prize called *Baille* about 7 January 1783, the last significant prize of the war. On 9 January she was chased for thirty-six hours by five larger British warships until she ran aground on a reef off Guadeloupe. She remained aground for two days while the British kept up a long-range bombardment. Finally she got off and escaped to the protection of a French fort. She had completed repairs by 26 January and sailed for Boston, where she arrived in May 1783, some time after peace had been declared. As soon as *Hague* arrived, Captain Manley was arrested on trumped-up charges which appear later to have been dropped. *Hague* herself, one of the navy's last four ships, was left idle until she was sold at auction on 2 October 1783.

One account says that *Deane*'s plans were sent to Congress for approval before she was built, but the plans have never been found. We do know her dimensions, and we do know that she carried 24 twelve-pounder cannons, eight four-pounders on the quarterdeck, and two six-pounders on the forecastle; she therefore had the configuration of a standard French frigate, even if she was on the small size. Some writers have contended that she had two complete gun decks of 16 guns each, but this is clearly nonsense. We have taken the lines of a number of smaller French warships and combined features from them with what we already knew about *Deane* to produce the reconstruction of her lines shown here.

As we have reconstructed her, her dimensions are as follows: length overall, 135′ 6″; length on the deck,

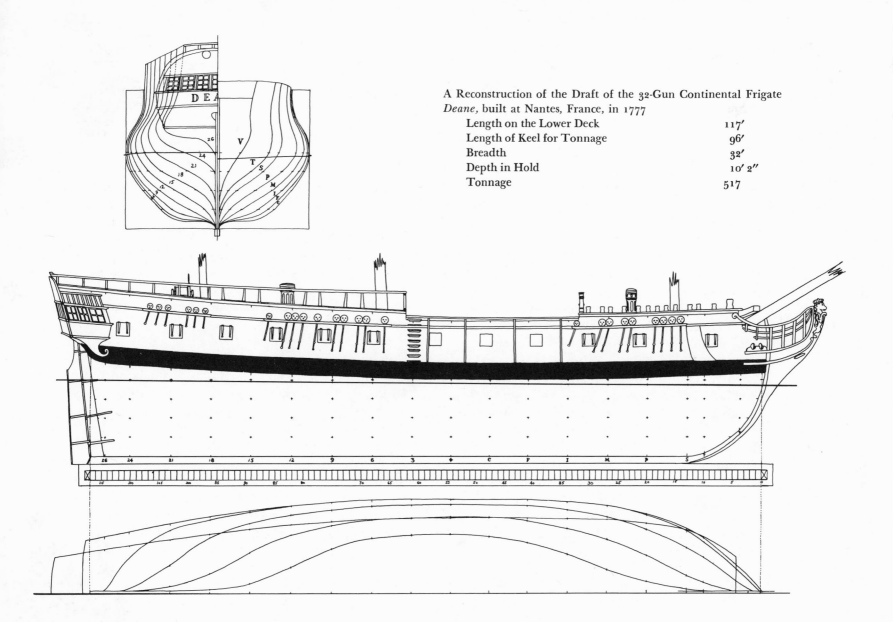

A Reconstruction of the Draft of the 32-Gun Continental Frigate
Deane, built at Nantes, France, in 1777

Length on the Lower Deck	117'
Length of Keel for Tonnage	96'
Breadth	32'
Depth in Hold	10' 2''
Tonnage	517

117'; length of keel, 96'; beam, 32'; depth in hold 10' 2''; draft, 14' 6''; tonnage, 517. It will be seen that although she carried more and heavier guns she was approximately the same size as the 24-gun frigates *Boston* and *Delaware.*

DEFENCE

ONE of the most extraordinary warships of the American Revolution was the Connecticut State Navy ship *Defence*. She started life in 1775 as the brig *Lily Ann* owned by John Griggs of Greenwich, but the General Assembly purchased her in December 1775 after she had completed only one voyage to the West Indies. She was armed with 16 six-pounders and 24 swivels, and she was commissioned under Captain Seth Harding in February 1776. She cruised a bit in 1776, but on her next cruise in the spring of 1777 she was placed under command of Samuel Smedley, who was only twenty-four years old.

Smedley complained that she was a clumsy ship and should be enlarged. Amazingly enough Governor Trumbull agreed, so she was taken to Boston and hauled out at Hancock's dock. Her keel was allegedly lengthened from 62 feet to 80 feet; her breadth was increased from 23 feet to about 25 feet; her bulwarks were enlarged, as was her quarterdeck; and she was converted from a brig to a ship, measuring about 230 tons. These are the figures given in Louis F. Middlebrook's *History of Maritime Connecticut During the American Revolution,* but they seem a bit suspect. For one thing, it would have been practically impossible to increase her beam without starting from scratch, which they did not do;

for another, even after the alterations her armament was exactly the same as before. Our guess is that her beam stayed the same and that her length increased only two or four feet. Therefore, her *gun deck*, not her keel, would have been increased to about 80 feet. Middlebrook shows a crude picture of the ship after she was lengthened, but he does not say where he found it, and there is therefore a chance that it is not contemporary. Nonetheless, we have used it to draw our reconstruction of the ship.

After her enlargement, *Defence* sailed in company with the Connecticut ship *Oliver Cromwell* and was much hampered by an outbreak of smallpox on board. However, she managed to capture the privateer *Cyrus* of 16 guns, and with a crew numbering just over 100 she cruised between Newfoundland and the West Indies. On 10 March 1779 she was chased by a British ship of far superior force, and in trying to escape by a shortcut she was wrecked on Goshen Reef in Long Island Sound. Only her spars and some of her gear could be salvaged.

As we have reconstructed her, her dimensions were as follows: length overall, 99′ 2″; length on the deck, 80′; length of keel, 66′; breadth, 25′; depth in hold, 11′; draft, about 8′; tonnage, about 145.

A Reconstruction of the Draft of the 16-Gun Connecticut Navy
Corvette *Defence,* as rebuilt at Boston in 1777

Length between Perpendiculars	80'
Breadth	25'
Tonnage	145

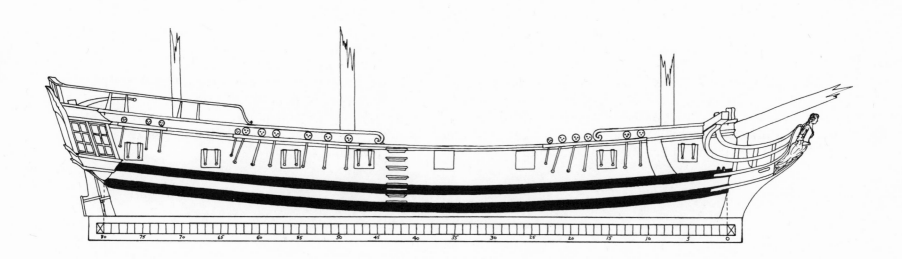

DEFENCE

A FINE brig that had been built in the Chesapeake Bay area around 1775 found her way into the Royal Navy in 1776 and became the 14-gun brig *Badger*. Horatio Nelson was given command of her at one time. The British records indicate that her previous name had been *Pitt,* named after an earlier prime minister, but Chapelle believes that she had earlier been the privateer *Defence.*

Typical of Chesapeake boats, she had a coach roof aft for her captain's cabin, but unlike others she had a small billet head on her stem. Her keel had plenty of drag and was built with an intentional hog in it, which makes taking off her lines rather difficult.

Vice Admiral Clark Gayton wrote praiseworthy accounts of *Badger*'s performance, saying that she had captured twenty-two American ships in two cruises. He sent her to England in the summer of 1777, where she was put in Portsmouth drydock for cleaning, repairs, and drawing her lines. She returned to the West Indies in September 1777 with 90 crewmen, but arrived in such bad condition that she had to be replaced.

Her lines are preserved at the National Maritime Museum at Greenwich. Her dimensions: length overall, 78'; length between perpendiculars, 68' 6"; length of keel, 54' 3"; beam, 21' 10"; depth in hold, 9' 4"; draft, 11' 8"; tonnage, 138.

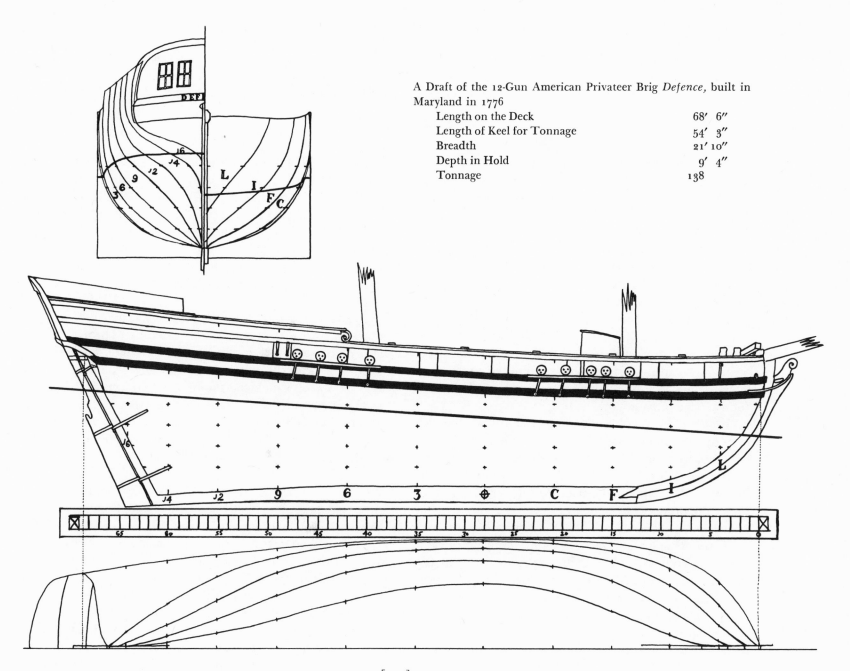

A Draft of the 12-Gun American Privateer Brig *Defence,* built in
Maryland in 1776

Length on the Deck	68' 6"
Length of Keel for Tonnage	54' 3"
Breadth	21' 10"
Depth in Hold	9' 4"
Tonnage	138

DELAWARE *and* MONTGOMERY

Two of the original thirteen frigates authorized by Congress in 1775 were *Montgomery* and *Delaware,* both of 24 guns and both apparently built from the plans approved by Congress. *Montgomery* was built in 1776 by Lancaster Burling at Poughkeepsie, New York, on the Hudson. Since the British occupied New York City and Lake Champlain, it was decided in October 1777 to burn and sink both the *Montgomery* and the 28-gun frigate *Congress,* which was built in the same town at the same time. Some historians think that the wrecks of these two frigates still lie undiscovered in the Hudson ten miles downriver from where they were built, just waiting for a concerted effort of underwater archaeology. *Montgomery*'s captain was to have been John Hodge of New York.

Delaware, on the other hand, was built at Philadelphia by Warwick Coates, and was completed in time to be employed on the Delaware River in operations against the British fleet that advanced up the Delaware in 1777. Her captain, Charles Alexander, was placed under the orders of Commodore John Hazelwood of the Pennsylvania State Navy. *Delaware,* in company with the Pennsylvania State Navy corvette *Montgomery,* came down the river on 27 September 1777 to attack British gun emplacements. Alexander anchored 500 yards away from the guns, but when the tide went out *Delaware* was hard aground. British gunners, having stepped up their shooting, soon had her on fire, and Alexander reluctantly had to surrender the most powerful ship then on the river.

The British got her off the mud and incorporated her into the Royal Navy. She remained for a time with the fleet that was proceeding up the river to Philadelphia. A tiny sketch of her, marked "frégate," appears on a French map of the British operations on the Delaware that is in the possession of the Musée de la Marine in Paris. On 9 March 1779, she took part in the capture of the Connecticut State Navy ship *Oliver Cromwell* of about 20 guns.

Delaware was sold by the Royal Navy at the end of the war on 14 April 1783. She was acquired by Mary Hayley, an English widow living in Boston, Massachusetts. Mrs. Hayley amused herself by immediately renaming her *United States,* which she thought would annoy British authorities, and she used the ship for whaling, sealing, and trading. *United States* had to visit such out-of-the-way places as the Falkland Islands to do her mistress's bidding. The ship was then sold to French owners, who renamed her *Le Dauphin,* and there is a suggestion that they used her for whaling. In 1794 she was sold at auction in Charleston, South Carolina, and bought by a French privateer captain with the improbable name of Jean Bouteille. British consular officials were alarmed at this turn of events, and they combined with American officials to try to prevent Bouteille from doing anything with his new acquisition. Nevertheless, he fitted her out once more as a warship, and removed her quarter galleries and "upper deck," and painted her all black. The desired result was that she should look like an innocent merchant ship, so that she could blend in

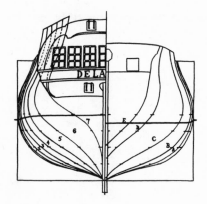

A Reconstruction of the Draft for Building the 24-Gun Continental Frigates *Delaware,* built at Philapelphia in 1776, and *Montgomery,* built on the Hudson River, New York, in 1776

Length between Perpendiculars	119'
Length of Keel for Tonnage	96'
Breadth	32' 4"
Depth in Hold	10'
Tonnage	563

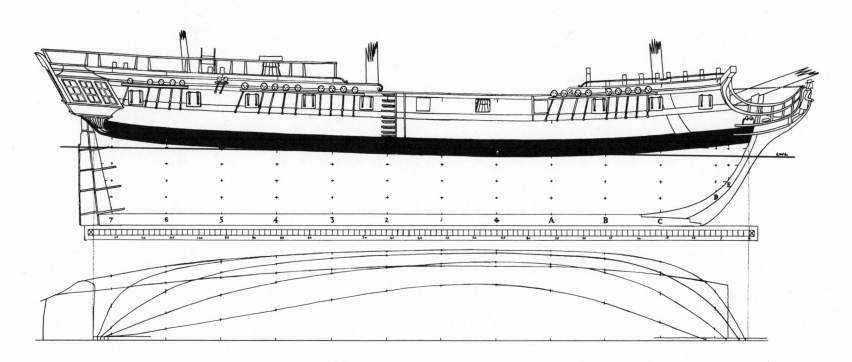

with British convoys unnoticed. The last record of her was her departure from Charleston for Port de Paix in 1795. It is quite likely that the tired old ship foundered in a gale in the West Indies soon after that date. In any event, she was clearly the last survivor of the original thirteen frigates authorized by Congress in 1775.

Her design, as approved by Congress, is said to have been modeled closely on a Philadelphia privateer frigate called *Hero* that fought successfully in the Seven Years' War in the 1760s, and this may explain the out-of-date beakhead bulkhead that appears to have been used in so many of the Philadelphia-designed warships of the Revolution. The official designs of the 28-gun frigates and the 32-gun frigates are said to have been merely scaled-up versions of *Delaware*'s plans. Since the plans of one each of the 28- and 32-gun frigates survive, we have scaled them down to the dimensions of *Delaware*, as recorded by the British, for the British apparently did not see fit to record her actual lines. The British used her as a 28-gun frigate, so we have made sure that her design had enough room for 28 guns.

Dimensions: length overall, 141′ 9″; length on the deck, 119′; length of keel, 96′; breadth, 32′ 10″; depth in hold, 9′ 9″; draft, 13′ 10″; tonnage, 563.

Frigate *Delaware*
Detail from a French map of the Delaware, 1778
Le Musée de la Marine, Paris

DILIGENCE

THE pink-sterned (not the color, but the shape!) snow *Diligence* was built in Boston in 1739, designed to be an all-purpose trading and fishing vessel. She was loaded with fish bound for Bilbao Spain, but news of the outbreak of hostilities between Britain and Spain (the War of Jenkins' Ear) arrived before she could set sail. Her cargo was taken off again and she was sent empty to the Cape Fear River, North Carolina, to load with tar for Bristol, England. At Bristol many of her crew were impressed into the Royal Navy. She then moved further down the Severn estuary to Swansea, Wales, where she took a load of coal back to Boston. That is about all we know of her history.

The Marblehead seaman Ashley Bowen, then aged eleven years, sailed on her during this time, and he recorded not only what happened but the appearance of the vessel. He even painted a watercolor picture of her before she was launched, which has served as the basis for our profile drawing. One useful feature that is prominent in her design is the loadng port in the stern, which would permit her to load large pieces of timber, some of which might be used for spars by a ship in some faraway port.

Her dimensions, as we reconstruct her: length overall, 79'; length between perpendiculars, 66'.

A Reconstruction of the Draft of the American Pink *Diligence*, built at Boston in 1739
Length between Perpendiculars   66'

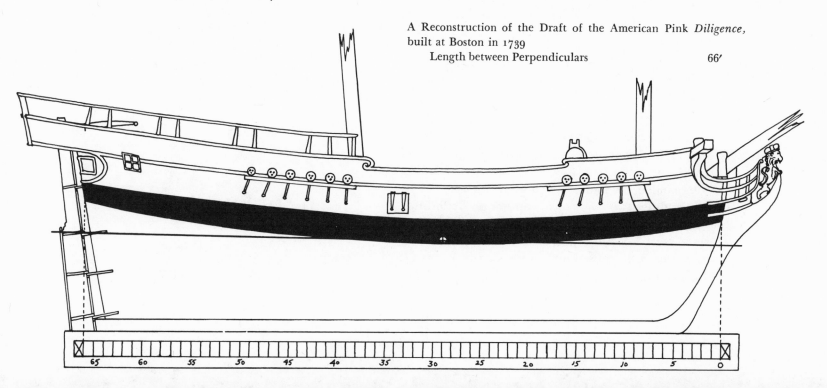

65 60 55 50 45 40 35 30 25 20 15 10 5 0

DOLPHIN

An oil painting of a cutter flying a red-and-white-striped flag was executed on the revolving part of the dial of a tall-case clock that was made in Dublin, Ireland, about 1777. The clock is now in a private collection in the United States. Although the cutter appears to have 16 guns on its gun deck, the artist probably had heard exaggerated tales of the Yankee ship's strength. Her real strength was 10 carriage guns and 12 swivels, but she cruised brazenly off Dublin in 1777, and her name was *Dolphin*.

While Benjamin Franklin was American commissioner in Paris, he tried to stir up trouble between Britain and France and capture some British shipping at the same time by fitting out ships under American captains to raid British shipping from French ports. One of the vessels so fitted out was *Dolphin,* described as a Folkstone or Dunkirk cutter, and she had fallen into Franklin's hands courtesy of the British Secret Service. The Secret Service had donated her to the Americans through an intermediary in the hope that they could catch her at sea with a precious cargo of Franklin's secret dispatches. But Franklin sent the dispatches another way and armed the cutter to sail with his little fleet. *Dolphin* was commanded by Samuel Nicholson. An attempt by *Dolphin* and her two consorts to capture the Irish linen fleet failed, but they did take about twenty British ships in a short period of time off the Irish coast. There is no record of *Dolphin*'s subsequent career, nor of her plans nor dimensions. Being an old vessel at the start of her American career, she was probably sold after a short time.

If the artist's conception is at all accurate, *Dolphin* was a most unusual cutter, for she had raised quarterdeck, quarter galleries, and a square-tuck stern. It is possible that the quarterdeck and quarter galleries were alterations made by the Americans.

Dimensions: length overall, 62' 10"; length between perpendiculars, 56'.

Cutter *Dolphin*
From a Dublin clock dial
Private collection, Bristol, Rhode Island

A Reconstruction of the Draft of the 10-Gun Continental Cutter
Dolphin, built about 1770 at Folkestone or Dunkirk
Length between Perpendiculars   56′

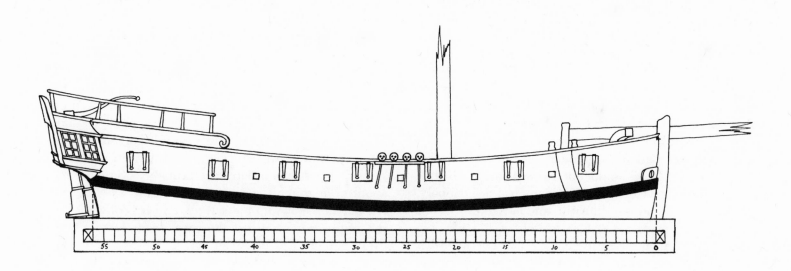

EMPRESS OF CHINA

Before the Revolution, the only legal way for Americans to buy goods from China, India, and the East Indies was to purchase them through the East India Company in London, which had a monoply for British subjects. This was both slow and expensive (East India Company tea with a British tax on it was the cause of the Boston Tea Party), and even more so after the Revolution when the British could rightfully place high tariffs on some of their exports to America.

The answer was to send American ships to the Far East directly. They would not be welcome in British India, where the East India Company had a monopoly, but they could trade at Mauritius and at Canton, as well as a few other places. Robert Morris of Philadelphia and a few others resolved to give it a try. The first such try was with a new 360-ton ship built at Boston for the purpose of privateering and designed by John Peck. She was the *Empress of China,* and she left New York in February 1784, arriving in Canton 28 August with a cargo that included thirty tons of ginseng. Her captain, John Green, was not much of a navigator for he missed the Sunda Strait by miles, but eventually he arrived at Whampoa by trial and error and saluted the town with thirteen guns. They were received warmly by British, French, and Danish captains already there.

The ginseng was surprisingly not a success, but other items in her cargo sold well so that she was able to buy 200 tons of tea. She arrived in New York on 11 May 1785. The tea, spices, silks, and chinaware that she had brought home realized Morris a thirty percent profit, which was not regarded as terribly good, but good enough to encourage other merchants to try the China trade.

There is only one known authentic portrait of *Empress of China,* and this is a painting on a Chinese fan brought home by Captain Green, and now the property of the Historical Society of Philadelphia. We have based our reconstruction mostly on this portrait, and on the known appearance of other American merchant ships of her size and date. She probably originally had about nine gunports per side on her gun deck, but the fan portrait shows no ports at all, and it is obvious that she would not have had the capacity to carry all her cargo if there had been cannons in the way. The thirteen-gun salute at Whampoa could easily have been fired by the four guns on the quarterdeck, whose position is indicated on our drawing. There is a punchbowl at the New Jersey State Museum that belonged to Captain Green which shows a picture of a ship flying the American flag and the caption *Empress of China;* this ship shows a number of guns. Experts are convinced that it is a portrait of a British ship called *Hall,* whose portrait was used for any ship that visited Whampoa with only the flag and name changed; *Grand Turk* of Salem is among the ships awarded a portrait of *Hall.*

In any case, the gunports were probably planked over before she left for China to make the ship better able to withstand the heavy weather likely to be encountered

A Reconstruction of the Draft of the American East India Ship
Empress of China, built in Massachusetts in 1783

Length between Perpendiculars	96′
Tonnage	360

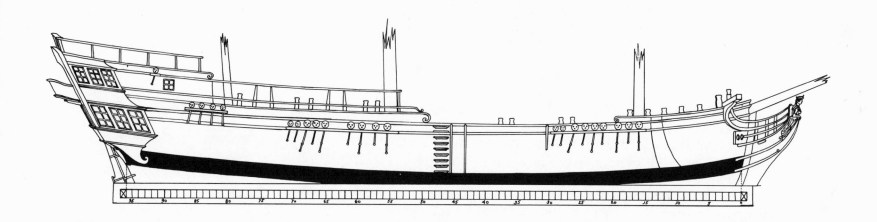

on a long voyage. At the same time, the high poop was probably fitted to make her a more comfortable ship for her officers and supercargo for traveling in the tropics.

As we have reconstructed her, her dimensions were: length overall, 117′ 8″; length on the deck, 96′; tonnage, 360.

EXPERIMENT

THE 360-ton ship *Empress of China* was the first American ship to arrive in China, but she was not the first to leave for China. The first to leave for China was the tiny 55-ton sloop *Harriet,* of Hingham, Massachusetts, which left in December 1783 under the command of Captain Hallet. However, *Harriet* never reached China, for she found a ready market for her goods at Capetown, South Africa, and returned home.

Another sloop that entered the China trade was the New York sloop *Experiment,* built in 1783 on the Hudson near Albany. She left New York for Canton on 15 December 1785 with a crew of seven men and two boys under Captain Stewart Dean.

The wide, shallow-draft sloop was a Dutch legacy to New York that has continued in one form or another up to the twentieth century. More than a few people have seen the Hudson River sloop *Clearwater,* a 1960s recreation of the typical nineteenth-century Hudson River sloop; although *Clearwater* has a clipper bow, wider beam, shallower draft, and a centerboard, her family resemblance to *Experiment* is unmistakable.

Our drawings of *Experiment* are loosely based on plans that appeared in the September 1932 *Yachting* in an article by C. G. Davis about Hudson River sloops. There is no statement in the article as to whether these are copies of original plans that are now lost or whether Davis used his own imagination. Many models have been built from the Davis plans, including one that is exhibited at Mystic Seaport, Connecticut.

Approximate dimensions: length overall, 65′ 8″; length between perpendiculars, 58′; length of keel, 49′ 6″; breadth, 19′; depth in hold, 8′ 6″; draft, 8′ 8″; tonnage, 80 to 85.

Eighteenth-century Hudson River Sloop similar to *Experiment*
From a contemporary woodcut

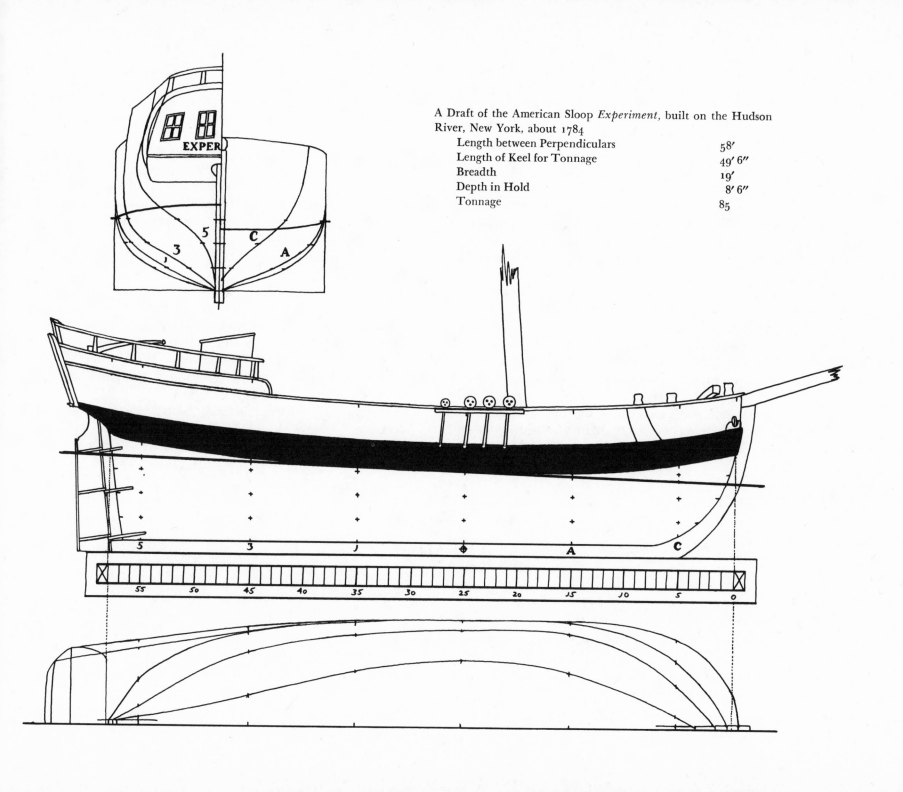

A Draft of the American Sloop *Experiment,* built on the Hudson
River, New York, about 1784

Length between Perpendiculars	58′
Length of Keel for Tonnage	49′ 6″
Breadth	19′
Depth in Hold	8′ 6″
Tonnage	85

FAIR AMERICAN

A T the museum of the U.S. Naval Academy at Annapolis, Maryland, is a contemporary, large-scale model of a brig, complete with sails. Tradition says that she represents the 14-gun American brig *Fair American* which was captured by the British in the Revolutionary War, and that an admiring new owner commissioned the model so that he would have a reminder of the sleek lines of the ship long after the actual vessel had been broken up. Since there were many American ships of that name, it is difficult to identify which one is represented by the model: one was a privateer temporarily on duty with the South Carolina State Navy in 1778, cruising with the frigate *Randolph* on her last fateful cruise; one was captured by the British frigate *Vestal* in 1780; one was owned by Blair McClenahan of Philadelphia, and accompanied the celebrated privateer *Holker* on cruises in 1781; and one was captured by the British and used in their blockade squadron in the mouth of the Delaware in 1782. This last one appears in the painting of the *General Monk* and *Hyder Ali* engagement that hangs at the U.S. Naval Academy, and she could well be the one whose model is also at the Academy.

Notable features about the ship represented by the model are her steep, straight deadrise and her large beam, both typical of faster American designs for smaller ships. The deadrise is similar to that of the frigate *Loyal American* (never built) designed by Loyalist scientist Benjamin Thompson.

Her dimensions: length overall, 80' 8"; length on the deck, 68'; length on the keel, 55' 3"; breadth, 24'; depth in hold, 9'; draft, 11' 8"; tonnage, about 120.

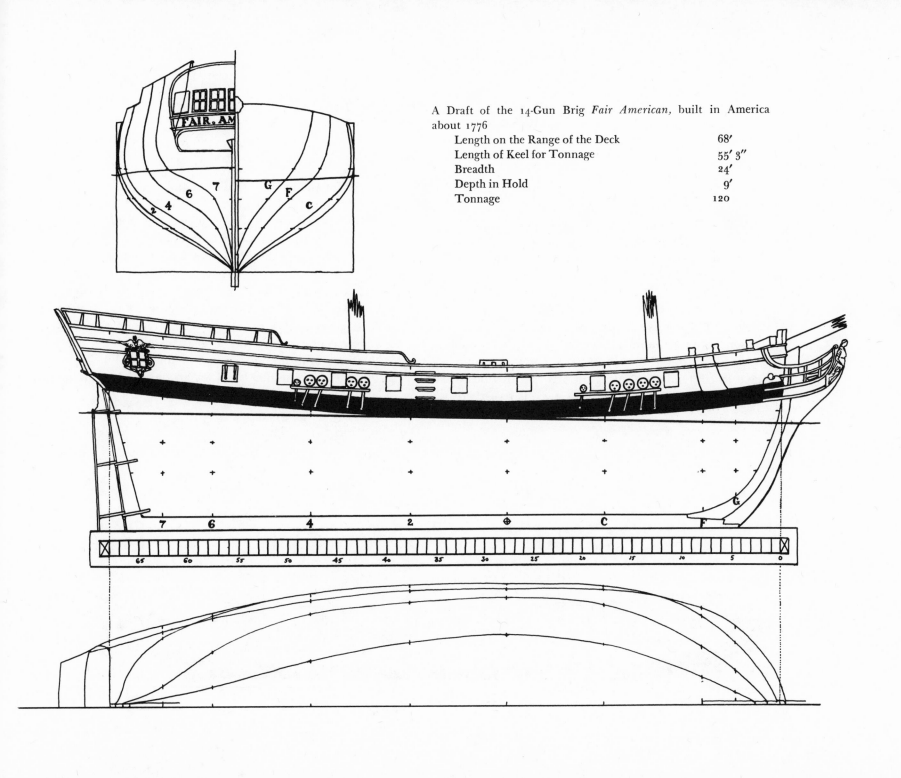

A Draft of the 14-Gun Brig *Fair American,* built in America about 1776

Length on the Range of the Deck	68′
Length of Keel for Tonnage	55′ 3″
Breadth	24′
Depth in Hold	9′
Tonnage	120

FAIR AMERICAN

ONE of the many vessels in the Revolution with the name of *Fair American* was a privateer brig from Connecticut, built about 1780, and mounting 12 or 14 guns. Judging from the sketch of her that is preserved at the Connecticut Historical Society she was a very fast ship, and she carried all her guns on a spar deck, rather like the Salem privateers *Mohawk* and *Jack* (although they also had gun decks under their spar decks). The unusual arrangement may have been chosen because the owner wished to use her as a merchant ship after the war and he therefore would not have to contend with any gunports. An obvious disadvantage to this arrangement, however, is that there was no cover for the men working the guns. It could be that the owner intended for her to fight only with unarmed or lightly armed vessels, trusting that she would be fast enough to escape from a ship of equal or superior force. She was owned by Jabez Perkins & Co. of Norwich, Connecticut, and was commanded first by Samuel Champlin and later by Peleg Eldred. She was commissioned on 18 July 1781, and had 90 men in her crew. She captured at least eight enemy ships before the end of the year, but there is no record of her after that time.

No lines or dimensions survive for her, but as we reconstruct her she measured 87′ in overall length and 69′ in length between perpendiculars.

A Reconstruction of the Draft of the 12-Gun Connecticut Brig *Fair American,* built about 1780

Length between Perpendiculars   69′

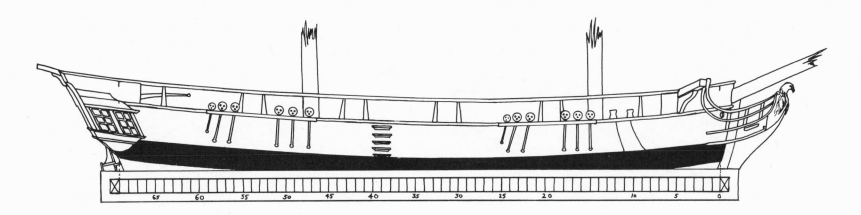

FALKLAND

THE first large ship built on the North American continent, and the first American-built ship to be taken into the Royal Navy, was the 44-gun ship *Falkland*. She was built at Holland's shipyard at New Castle (a section of Portsmouth), New Hampshire, about 1690. She had been ordered by John Taylor, a London mast and lumber merchant, as a speculation; he hoped to sell her to the Royal Navy if she could pass their rigid inspection standards, and if she failed he could still use her profitably to transport masts from Maine and New Hampshire to England. For some reason or other, she was not actually taken into the navy until 1696. By 1701, it was noticed that she was rotten in places, and thirty-three frames had to be replaced. After service with out incident, mostly in the English Channel, she had to be extensively rebuilt in 1720.

At the time of this rebuilding her lines were taken off and recorded, and these lines are preserved at the National Maritime Museum at Greenwich. These lines, however, reflect the way she was rebuilt in 1720, not the way she looked when she arrived at the dockyard. In this rebuilding, the stern appears to have been altered to bring it up to date with the current styles, and the elaborate carving that was typical of late seventeenth-century ships, such as wreaths around the gunports, was removed. In our drawing we have attempted to reconstruct the stern and the wreaths, based on other ships of the period. Apart from these details, it is believed by experts that very little change was made to the overall shape and size of the ship in 1720.

Falkland appears to have lasted for a long time after this, for the records say that she was not transferred out of active service until as late as 1768. This is actually misleading, for she was rebuilt in 1744 at Bursledon, Hampshire, so extensively that she had increased her tonnage from 638 to 974; in other words, she was almost completely replaced at that time, but in order to get the necessary funds for a new ship from Parliament the navy had to pretend that they were only repairing an older ship. The new ship took part in the first battle of Finisterre in 1747, the battle of Quiberon Bay in 1759, and the capture of Martinique in 1762. In 1768 she was turned into a victualing hulk, one of those infamous purveyors of rotten and maggot-infested salt beef and pork. There is no record of her after that.

The purchase of *Falkland* by the navy was enough of a success for Taylor that he immediately ordered another ship, *Bedford Galley*, of 34 guns, to be built at Holland's shipyard.

There is a beautiful Admiralty-type model of *Falkland*, built by Robert V. Bruckshaw of Toledo, Ohio, on display at the Smithsonian in Washington, D.C., but it looks a little strange in that it combines the *Falkland*'s original seventeenth-century rig with the simplified hull design of the 1720 rebuilding. The ship appears in various oil paintings and prints of the battles she took part in after the 1744 replacement, but these pictures would be of absolutely no use to anyone studying the American *Falkland*.

Dimensions: length overall, 146'; length on deck, 128' 6"; length of keel, 109'; breadth, 33' 2"; depth in hold, 13' 9"; draft, 16'; tonnage, 638.

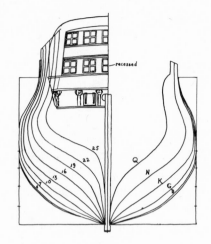

A Reconstruction of the Draft of His Majesty's 44-Gun Ship
Falkland, built at New Castle, New Hampshire, in 1690

Length on the Lower Deck	128′ 6″
Length of Keel for Tonnage	109′
Breadth	33′ 2″
Tonnage	638

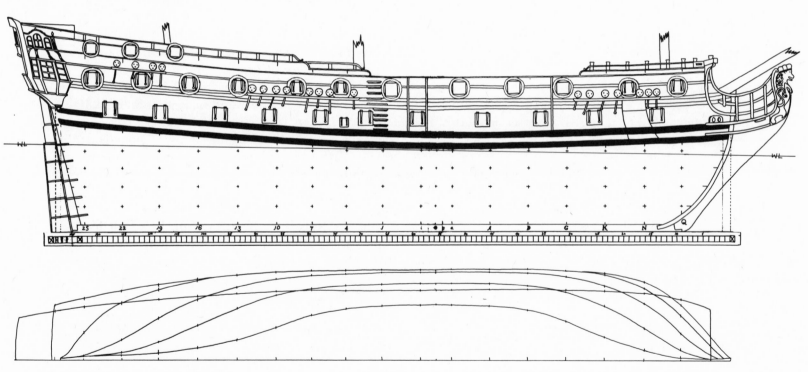

FANCY

IN the celebrated engraving by Burgis of New York Harbor in 1717 is a little yacht under sail. Her name was *Fancy,* and she belonged to Colonel Morris. We know little about her except what can be seen in the picture. There had been other yachts in New York at an earlier date, but they were all Dutch in style while the lineage of this little sloop is clearly English. By our estimate, her length overall was 38′, and her length between perpendiculars was 35′.

A Reconstruction of the Draft of Colonel Morris's Yacht *Fancy,* built in New York about 1715

Length between Perpendiculars   35′

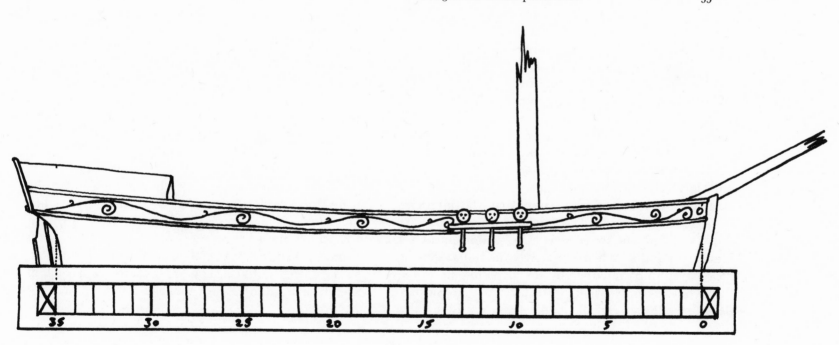

FENIX

IT is tantalizing to think that a number of large warships were built out of Cuban mahogany at Havana in the eighteenth century, but it is practically impossible to find out anything about them because of the total lack of cooperation accorded to researchers in this field both by the Spanish and Cuban authorities. Perhaps some enterprising scholar will break through the red tape in the next few years.

The 80-gun ship *Fenix* (Spanish for "Phoenix") was built at Havana in 1749 for the Spanish navy. She was probably the largest ship built in the Americas up to this date. We can find nothing about her career until January 1780, when we learn that she was the flagship of a fleet under Admiral Don Juan de Langara, and her captain was Don Francisco Melgareso. She was then captured by Admiral Sir George Rodney's fleet that had been sent to relieve Gibraltar. She was taken into the Royal Navy and renamed *Gibraltar*.

She was sent to the West Indies and served as Rear Admiral F. S. Drake's flagship, under Captain C. Knatchbull, in Hood's fleet in the unsuccessful attempt to dislodge de Grasse's fleet from its hold on Martinique in April 1781. She returned to England shortly afterward and was fitted out to be sent as a reinforcement for Hughes in India. When she arrived in India, she was the largest ship in either of the opposing fleets out there, but she only had time to take part in one battle before the war ended, Cuddalore, on 20 June 1783.

In the French wars that began a few years later she was again in the thick of the fighting, taking part in the so-called Glorious First of June, 1794, the battles of Basque Roads in 1801 and Aboukir Bay (Egypt) in 1801. As the naval side of the war diminished she was converted into a powder hulk at the end of 1813, and later into a lazaretto in 1824. She was finally broken up at the end of 1836 at Pembroke Dock. She had a career of eighty-seven years and apparently required no major rebuilding in her whole career. Not only is this a tribute to her construction, and particularly to the Cuban mahogany, but also to her design, for it is hard to believe that a ship designed at the end of the War of Jenkins' Ear could still have been a useful and competitive ship for Nelson at the Nile in 1801.

Gibraltar appears in a number of oil paintings and prints of the various battles in which she took part. Her lines, as taken off by the British, are on file at the National Maritime Museum at Greenwich, where there is also a half-model of her. Her design looks very English, a fact that is probably explained by the presence in the Spanish dockyards of a number of British shipwrights. Whether the design was sent out from Spain or drawn in Havana is not known.

Dimensions: length overall, 211′ length on the deck, 178′ 11″; length of keel, 144′ 6″; breadth, 53′ 4″; depth in hold, 22′ 2″; draft, 25′ 8″; tonnage, 2,157.

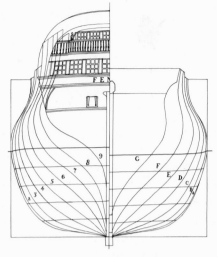

A Draft of the 80-Gun Spanish Ship *Fenix,* built at Havana, Cuba,
in 1749

Length on the Gun Deck	178′ 11″
Length of Keel for Tonnage	144′ 6″
Breadth	53′ 4″
Depth in Hold	22′ 2″
Tonnage	2,157

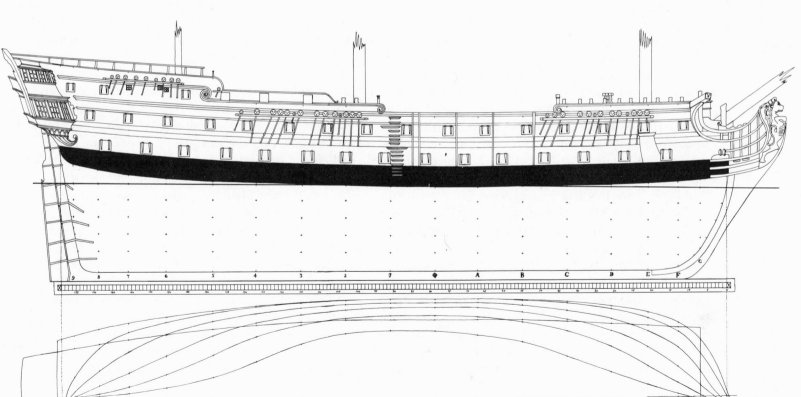

FLORA

HARDLY any ship that fought on the American side in the Revolution had a more interesting career than the frigate *Flora,* and yet few people have ever heard of her. She was built in France in 1756 with the name of *La Vestale,* and was intended to carry 26 eight-pounder cannons. She took part in the battle of Quiberon Bay in 1759, where a British observer said she carried 34 guns. She was captured by the British frigate *Unicorn* in January 1761, and was recorded as carrying 32 guns. Since there was already a *Vestal* in the Royal Navy, her name was changed to *Flora,* and her eight-pounders were replaced by twelve-pounders. In the American Revolution, she was still described as a 32-gun frigate, and under Captain John Brisbane she was responsible for the recapture from the Americans of the British frigate *Fox* in June 1777. In August 1778, Brisbane, then commodore of a small British fleet at Newport, Rhode Island, found himself surrounded and trapped by d'Estaing's powerful fleet and ordered the destruction of all his ships. Either because he was fond of her, or because she was anchored next to the town and he wished the town no harm, he merely scuttled *Flora* while all the other British frigates were blown up.

The British continued to occupy Newport for another year, but no attempt was made to raise *Flora* from the bottom of the harbor. In July 1780 the Americans raised her, made temporary repairs at a Newport wharf, and then towed her to Providence where she would be safer from possible British raids while repairs were made (apparently the Americans still did not trust the French, who had just occupied Newport with a large force of both army and navy). She must have been exceptionally well built in order to have withstood, after twelve years of regular service, two years on the bottom of the harbor and then be so easily made serviceable once more. One might assume that the Providence merchant John Brown was involved in the resurrection of the ship, for he was the kind of man who could not resist the idea of owning one of the most powerful privateers of the Revolution. The records of this period are very spotty, but it seems that she was owned by Jacob and Griffin Greene of Providence in August 1781 and commanded by Captain Henry Johnston, and campaigned as an American privateer of anywhere from 26 to 32 guns, that she captured a London merchant ship called *Industry* on 28 June 1782, and that she was based in Boston in August 1782. At the end of the war her owners decided that they might make more of a profit on her if they sold her back to the French. The French navy, probably embarrassed by the blunt proposition, agreed to purchase her subject to survey. She evidently passed the survey and she was briefly called *La Flore* until it was found that there was already another ship of that name in the French navy. She was renamed *La Reconnaissance,* and armed with 26 cannons of eight-pounder size. She was employed in cruising off Africa from 1787 to 1789, and her captain reported that she steered well and heeled less than any warship in Europe

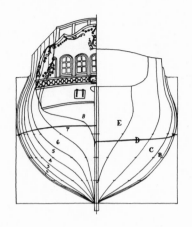

A Reconstruction of the Draft of the 28-Gun French Frigate *La Flore,* said to have been employed in American service, built in France about 1770

Length between Perpendiculars	136′ 8″
Length of Keel for Tonnage	124′
Breadth	33′ 8″
Depth in Hold	11′ 8″
Tonnage	740

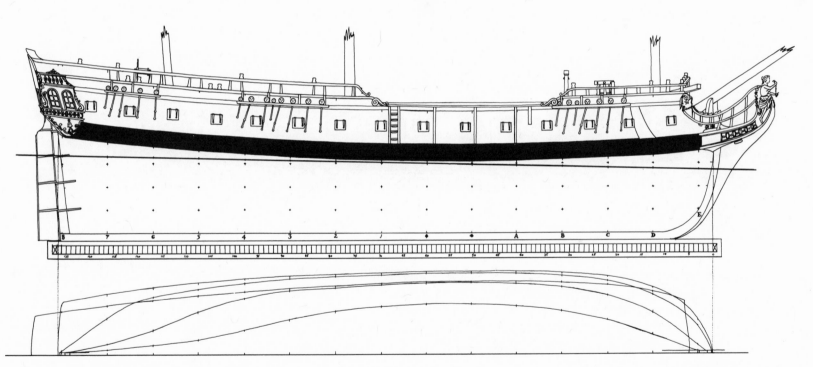

[129]

A Reconstruction of the Draft of His Majesty's 32-Gun Frigate
Flora, captured from the French in 1761
Length between perpendiculars   136′ 8″

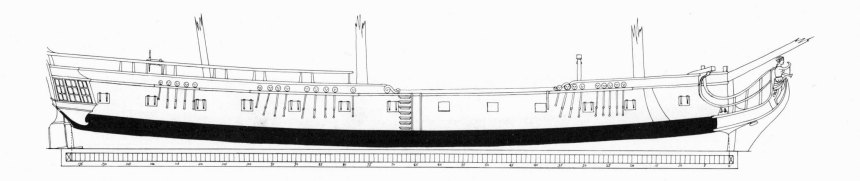

in a breeze, although she did not go so well to windward in light airs.

In 1792 the French navy had no further use for her, even though a war had just begun. However, there was still life in the old ship, for she was purchased by the Sieur Fauré de Rochefort for use as a privateer. What success she had as a privateer we do not know, but she was not captured by the British until 1798 when she encountered the 38-gun British frigate *Phaeton*. She was sold immediately.

Her dimensions are known to us from the first time she was captured, and there are four oil paintings of her engaging the *Fox* in 1777, all done by Francis Holman. There is a lovely contemporary model of a frigate at the Musée de la Marine in Paris entitled *"La Flore," dite Americaine.* Certainly, the model represents no other French ship called *La Flore,* for their lines and dimensions were quite different. However, the model does not agree with Holman's paintings (which do accurately portray the other ships in the battle), and the model also differs from typical French frigate design (although it is definitely a French design in other respects) by the number of gunports; the model has fifteen ports on a side, while the paintings of *Flora* and the designs of other French frigates all show only thirteen ports. The conclusion is that the model represents an experimental design that may never have been built, and it was named *La Flore* perhaps as a salute to the French captain who commanded her on her voyage back

to France in 1784. Strangely enough, her dimensions agree very well with the model, although the model seems to have had a foot less beam than the actual ship.

Our drawings are taken from the model, but we also show a waterline drawing that is scaled from the Holman paintings. Her dimensions: length overall, 156′ 6″; length on the deck, 136′ 8″ (British records say 132′); length of keel, 124′; breadth, 33′ 8″ (British records say 35′); depth in hold, 11′ 8″; draft, 17′; tonnage, 698.

Frigate *Flora*
From one of a set of four oil paintings by Francis Holman, 1779
Peabody Museum, Salem, Massachusetts

FOX

Fox seems to have been an unlucky ship; she was captured three times in her short career. The 28-gun frigate was built at Calhoun's shipyard at Northam, Hampshire, and taken into the Royal Navy in 1773. While she was cruising under Captain Fotheringham not far from the New England coast she was captured by the American frigates *Hancock* and *Boston* on 7 June 1777 in a battle that was characterized by the appearance of considerable chivalry; whenever hot wadding could be seen to have set the opposing ship on fire, the respective captains ordered a cease-fire until the fires had been extinguished, and then recommenced hammering away at each other. *Fox* cruised for a while with *Hancock* and *Boston* until the British ships *Rainbow*, 44 guns, and *Flora*, 32 guns, attacked them. *Boston* turned and fled, leaving *Hancock* to be taken by the aged *Rainbow* and *Fox* to be retaken by *Flora*. This was on 8 July 1777. Late in 1778 (one record says it was 17 September and another 11 November) *Fox* hauled down her colors once more. *Fox* had been cruising near Ushant off the French coast under the command of Captain Windsor when she encountered the 32-gun French frigate *Junon*. After having her main and mizzen masts shattered in several places she surrendered, having apparently done her adversary little harm. What happened after that is not recorded.

The lines of *Fox* do not survive, although she appears in four contemporary oil paintings by Francis Holman of the action with *Flora* and in a French engraving of the fight with *Junon*. Based on these five pictures and on her known dimensions we have reconstructed her. She appears to have an unusually long waist and a short quarterdeck. We think that her figurehead may have represented the politician Charles James Fox, who had been active in the administration of the British Admiralty starting in 1770 (at age 21).

Dimensions: length overall, 140′ length on the deck, 120′ 6″; breadth, 34′; tonnage, 585.

A Reconstruction of the Draft of His Majesty's 28-Gun Frigate
Fox, built at Northam, Hampshire, in 1773

Length on the Lower Deck	120' 6"
Breadth	34'
Tonnage	585

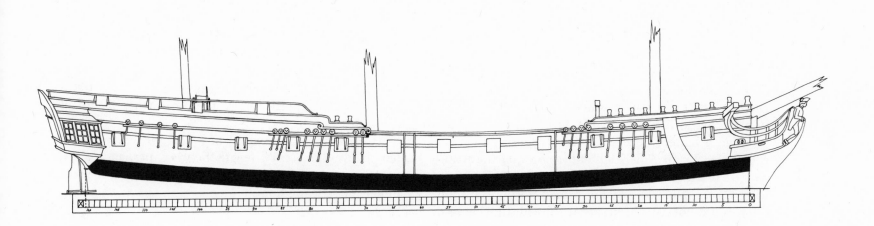

FURY

When the British were trying to force their way up the Delaware River to build a supply line for their garrison in Philadelphia, they encountered difficulties from a number of forts built by the Americans in the mud banks and on islands in the river. The waters around these positions were frequently quite shoal, so the British fitted out two ships to deal with the batteries. They took a retired East Indiaman called *Grand Duchess of Russia,* renamed her *Vigilant,* cut her down to make her as light as possible, fitted her for oars, and gave her a battery of 24-pounder cannons. She was accompanied by an American-built sloop that the British had been using to transport horses, which they fitted with three 24-pounders and named *Fury.* Naturally, *Fury* would not have been safe at sea with three guns of

such large size, but anchored on spring cables in the river she would be an effective floating battery. Both ships were used in the attack on Fort Mifflin in November 1777, and a wash drawing of them in this operation was made by John Hunter in an inset on his map of the Delaware that is now at the Library of Congress. After the river was cleared all the way to Philadelphia one assumes that *Fury* was either converted back to a transport or was scrapped, for we find no further record of her.

As we have reconstructed her, her dimensions were: length overall, 61' 6"; length between perpendiculars, 54'; tonnage, 76. Obviously, there was not much room in her for carrying horses.

A Reconstruction of the Draft of His Majesty's 6-Gun Sloop *Fury,* built in America about 1775
Length between Perpendiculars   54'

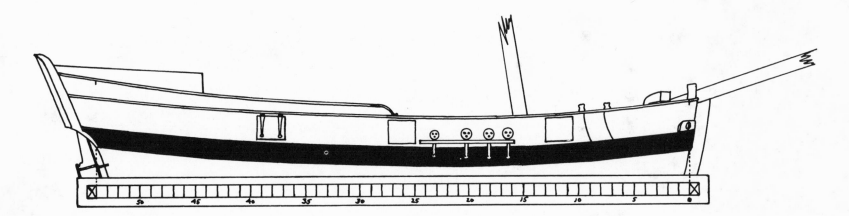

GASPÉE *and* ST. JOHN

THE 8-gun schooner *Gaspée* played an important part in the excitement that led to the American Revolution, but there are no contemporary pictures of her, nor do her lines survive. She was probably built in Canada about 1763 (her name is French for "Girl from the Gaspé Peninsula"), and she was purchased by the Royal Navy in North America in 1770 for use in the enforcement of Customs duties. Under the command of Lieutenant William Dudingston she was assigned to eliminate smuggling in Rhode Island. Since smuggling was Rhode Island's major industry (they had previously fired on and burned three other Customs vessels from 1764 to 1769), Rhode Islanders looked for a chance to destroy *Gaspée*. The chance came when she ran aground off Warwick, Rhode Island, on 9 June 1772 on a falling tide. Several open boats from Providence and Bristol converged on her in the middle of the night and set her on fire, wounding Dudingston. The Royal Enquiry into this incident trampled so severely on Rhode Island's charter and on other Colonial rights that the Committees of Correspondence were formed between the various Colonies; this was an important step on the road to independence.

The lines that we show here are similar to those drawn up by naval architect and historian William A. Baker when a Rhode Island group was considering building a full-sized copy of the *Gaspée*. Baker based his lines of those of the similar schooner *Chaleur,* using the known dimensions of *Gaspée*.

Dimensions: length overall, 68′; length between perpendiculars, 62′ 10″; length on the keel, 49′; breadth, 19′ 10″; depth in hold, 7′ 10″; draft, 9′; tonnage, 102.

Another schooner almost exactly the same size as *Gaspée* was purchased for the Royal Navy in 1763 at the same time as *Gaspée* and for the same purpose; her name was *St. John*. Some Rhode Islanders link the name of *St. John* with "the first shots of the American Revolution." The incident in question, which occurred on 9 July 1764, almost exactly twelve years before independence, happened as follows: Newport, Rhode Island, then the second most prosperous city in America, had

Schooner, thought to be *St. John*
From a contemporary engraving

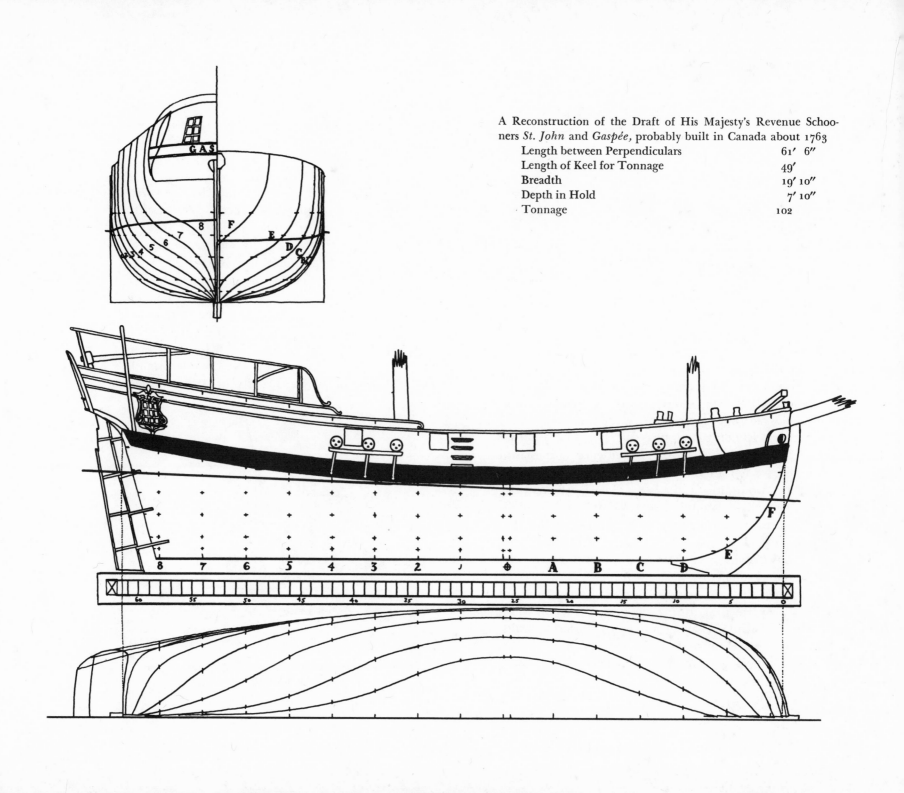

A Reconstruction of the Draft of His Majesty's Revenue Schooners *St. John* and *Gaspée,* probably built in Canada about 1763

Length between Perpendiculars	61' 6"
Length of Keel for Tonnage	49'
Breadth	19' 10"
Depth in Hold	7' 10"
Tonnage	102

gained her wealth by smuggling French and Spanish goods, especially molasses, from the West Indies and then reexporting them duty free to other British colonies in North America. *St. John*'s job, under the command of Lieutenant Thomas Hill, was to stop this, and she did such a good job that the elected governor, Stephen Hopkins, and members of the General Assembly or-dered the chief gunner at Fort George in Newport Harbor to fire his eighteen-pounder cannons at *St. John* until she pulled up her anchor and left. Fortunately, his aim was not as good as it might have been, and *St. John* fled from Newport after suffering only moderate damage. She was apparently sold out of the navy in 1771 or earlier.

GENERAL GATES

LATE in 1776, Congress authorized the construction of a number of new ships for the Continental Navy, including three corvettes of 18 guns apiece (although the actual bill has not been found). These were subsequently named *Ranger* (built at Portsmouth, New Hampshire), *Saratoga* (built at Philadelphia), and *General Gates* (built at Boston). *General Gates* was launched in 1777 and taken into the navy in 1778 and named after the supposed hero of the great victory at Saratoga the previous year, General Horatio Gates; one record says she was formerly a brig called *Industrious Bee,* but this is apparently an error.

She departed Boston under Captain John Skimmer in the summer of 1778. At the end of July she captured a brig laden with fish, and then a schooner and a letter-of-marque brig called *Montague.* Skimmer was killed in the *Montague* action, so the ship returned to Boston at the end of August. Her command shifted to Captain Daniel Waters, and she departed in the middle of November in company with the sloop *Providence.* They captured a Quebec schooner that was bound for New York, and then they got separated in a gale. *General Gates* continued alone to Martinique, where she repaired some leaks, and captured a British privateer on her way home to Boston. She reached Boston on 13 April 1779 and was immediately sold as unserviceable. Whether she was then broken up or repaired for use as a privateer is not recorded. There were a number of privateers of the same name (including one belonging to John Grush in 1779 and one—the same?—captured by the British later that year) and the records are confusing, to say the least. Another was captured in the West Indies with a cargo of flour in 1781.

For our reconstruction of *General Gates,* we have assumed that she was designed by the same man as were *Hancock* and *Boston,* although there were plenty of other capable designers in Massachusetts at the time.

Dimensions: length overall, 111'; length on the deck, 94'; breadth, 29'; tonnage, 300.

A Reconstruction of the Draft of the 18-Gun Continental Corvette
General Gates, built in Massachusetts in 1777

Length between Perpendiculars 94'
Breadth 29'
Tonnage 300

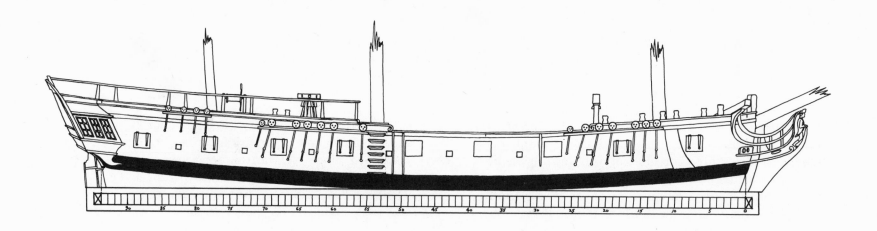

GENERAL PICKERING

CAPTAIN Jonathan Haraden of Salem, Massachusetts, had established a good reputation for himself as captain of the ship *Tyrannicide* by the time he was given command of the 16-gun Salem letter-of-marque ship *General Pickering* in 1780; she had been named after Timothy Pickering of Massachusetts, who was adjutant general and later quartermaster general of the Continental Army. On her way to Spain laden with sugar, she fended off a Royal Navy cutter of 16 guns and captured the 14-gun schooner *Golden Eagle*. On her arrival off Bilbao, Spain, she was attacked by the armed British merchant ship *Achilles* of 40 guns and 130 men, which was either a former East Indiaman or a former two-decker warship. When Haraden ran out of cannonballs he ordered the guns loaded with crowbars, and eventually *Achilles*, much damaged, broke off the engagement. Haraden had his ship repaired and set off for home again. After a three-day chase she escaped from a fleet of pursuers and arrived back in Salem on 14 September 1780, followed by two brigs she had captured. Haraden took *General Pickering* on a number of trading voyages to France before the end of the war and his luck continued. He had a narrow escape from a large British battleship and then captured three British ships at the same time, armed with a total of 42 guns. At another time he captured three more British ships within sight of each other with a total of 44 guns. This kind of capturing must have been hard on his crew, which numbered a scant 45 men and boys, hardly enough to man

one additional ship, let alone three. At still another time he disguised his ship so as to lure two British privateers within range and then captured them. All this time he was ferrying munitions and supplies from France back to the United States, and the privateering was merely incidental. Presumably *General Pickering* returned to being a regular merchant ship at the end of the war.

No lines or dimensions survive for *General Pickering*, which is not surprising for she was built as an ordinary armed merchant ship. However, after her exploits had made her famous, her owners presented a silver tankard and two silver canns to Haraden, each piece carefully

Ship *General Pickering*
From a silver tankard, ca. 1780
Peabody Museum, Salem, Massachusetts

A Reconstruction of the Draft of the 16-Gun American Letter-of-Marque *General Pickering*, built at Salem, Massachusetts, about 1780

Length between Perpendiculars	83'
Tonnage	180

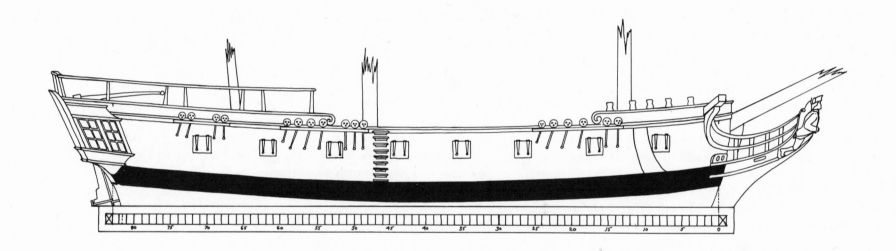

engraved with a picture of the *General Pickering* under sail, and from these engravings we have managed to reconstruct her appearance. The silverware is now at the Peabody Museum at Salem. Unusual features of her design were the especially long head, and the position of the mizzenmast, which looks as if it had been added to a brig rig as an afterthought (perhaps it had).

As we see her, her dimensions were: length overall, 106'; length on the deck, 83'; tonnage, 180.

[140]

GENERAL PUTNAM
and OLIVER CROMWELL

THE 16-gun privateer ship *General Putnam* was built in Connecticut in 1778. She was named after the unflappable Connecticut farmer Israel Putnam, who left his plough in midfurrow to walk to the aid of Massachusetts as soon as he heard the news about the battles of Concord and Lexington in 1775.

She was built at Winthrop's Neck, New London, at the shipyard belonging to Nathaniel Shaw, who also became the owner of the ship. Her first captain was Thomas Allen, and she was reported ready to sail on 13 May 1778. On 18 September she returned to New London, after taking six brigs. Early in 1779 she went out under the command of Nathaniel Saltonstall and captured at least three enemy vessels. By June 1779 she had put into Boston and changed commanders once more, this time taking on John Harmon. Harmon took her on a cruise off the coast of Maine in which she took about four prizes, and narrowly missed being taken herself by a British frigate off Saco. When she returned to Boston she changed captains again.

In 1779 the Continental Navy sold the corvette *General Gates* because she had become unserviceable. This left her captain, Daniel Waters, without a ship, so he returned to privateering. The first job offered to him was as captain of *General Putnam*. She became part of the fleet that Massachusetts was sending to the Penobscot Bay to dislodge the weak British garrison at Castine, Maine. The whole operation was bungled by the land and sea forces alike, resulting in the loss of 13 August of the whole fleet of ships that had sailed there with such high hopes. *General Putnam* was blown up along with the other ships. At that time, she was reported to have mounted 20 guns, and no doubt some of these were mounted on the quarterdeck, whose rail would have had to be altered to accommodate them.

A contemporary sketch of the ship can be seen at the Connecticut Historical Society, and it is from this that we have reconstructed our drawing of her. Dimensions, as scaled from the drawing, are: length overall, 107′ 3″; length on the deck, 90′; tonnage, about 275. One document from the Penobscot expedition claims that this ship measured about 350 tons; if this is so, then her length could have been up to five feet greater, but it is possible for her to have measured 350 tons with the length we have drawn, given the widely differing measurement practices of the day. Unusual features of her design include the double wale and the marked lack of sheer.

From all the existing information, it seems that the Connecticut State Navy ship *Oliver Cromwell* (not to be confused with other ships of that name) was similar in size and appearance to *General Putnam*. She was built at Uriah Hayden's shipyard at Essex, Connecticut. She was ordered by the General Assembly in January 1776, launched on 13 June, damaged by lightning on 1 August, and away at sea under Captain William Coit (formerly of Washington's little fleet) by 18 August. She measured 80′ on the keel, 27′ beam, and 12′ depth in hold, and her tonnage was about 300. Her first cruise was only to New London, where she was finished under the direction of Nathaniel Shaw (the owner and builder of *General Putnam* in 1778). She mounted 18 nine-pounders, plus two two-pounders and six swivels.

A Reconstruction of the Draft of the 16-Gun Connecticut Privateer *General Putnam* and Connecticut State Ship *Oliver Cromwell,*
built in Connecticut about 1777

    Length between Perpendiculars   90′

    Tonnage   275

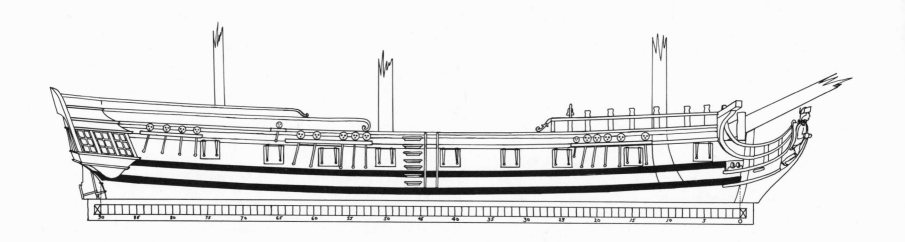

Coit was fired in April 1777 and replaced by Captain
Seth Harding, later captain of the frigate *Confederacy*.
Harding got her to sea immediately and soon captured
a number of prizes. He put his prisoners ashore at the
Kennebec River in Maine, but being ill himself, he
proceeded over land to Boston and Lieutenant Timothy Parker took over command. Parker was later confirmed as captain. On 15 April 1778, while cruising with
the Connecticut state ship *Defence*, *Oliver Cromwell*
fought a fierce battle with the 18-gun privateer *Admiral
Keppel* and captured her just as *Defence* captured the
16-gun *Cyrus;* aboard the *Keppel* was Governor Henry
Shirley of Jamaica. The prizes went to Boston while

Defence and *Oliver Cromwell* went to Charleston, South
Carolina, for repairs. Then Parker sailed for Nantes,
France, although he seems to have changed his plans en
route and *Oliver Cromwell* stayed on this side of the
Atlantic. In the spring of 1779 she left New London for
the last time, captured a few more prizes, and was then
herself caught by the 24-gun British frigates *Daphne*
and *Delaware* (formerly the Continental frigate *Delaware*) and the privateer *Union*. *Oliver Cromwell* was
taken into New York and sold. One source says that she
was bought by a New York Loyalist as a privateer,
and was renamed *Restoration*.

GENERAL WASHINGTON

IN 1779, John Brown, a rich merchant of Providence, Rhode Island, had a 20-gun privateer ship constructed which he called *General Washington*. She was almost exactly equivalent in size and type to the three Continental corvettes *Ranger, General Gates,* and *Saratoga*. Her first captain was James Munro, who made some moderately successful cruises on her including capturing a ship called *John Barrington*, before he left her to be captain of the larger ship *Belisarius*. In the summer of 1780 the command of *General Washington* was given to Silas Talbot, who held commissions as a captain in the Continental Navy and a colonel in the Continental Army at the same time. Soon after Talbot got her to sea, she captured a valuable British merchant ship that was on her way from Charleston, South Carolina, to London. Not long after, *General Washington* captured another British ship bound from the West Indies to Ireland, but she was retaken before she could reach port. Talbot's luck had changed.

Just as a fierce storm descended on him, Talbot was chased by several British warships. In the strong winds, the larger ships could sail faster than the little *General Washington*, so Talbot reluctantly had to surrender. The date of this action differs wildly, depending on the source, and some sources claim that she was captured by *Culloden*, 74 guns, while others say by *Chatham*, 50 guns. In any event, Talbot was shamefully treated on his way to prison in England, and his old ship, renamed *General Monk*, was taken into the Royal Navy.

Under Captain Rogers, *General Monk* inflicted considerable damage to American shipping. In August 1781, she assisted the 32-gun frigate *Iris* (formerly the American frigate *Hancock*) in capturing the 28-gun Continental frigate *Trumbull*. On 8 April 1782 she was patrolling the mouth of the Delaware with the frigate *Québec* when she captured one or two ships of an American convoy. The convoy guard ship, a converted merchant ship called *Hyder Ali* (named after the prince who was fighting the British in India at that time), was

Corvettes *Hyder Ali* and *General Washington*
From an oil painting by Louis-Philippe Crépin, ca. 1800
U.S. Naval Academy Museum, Annapolis, Maryland

A Reconstruction of the Draft of the 20-Gun Rhode Island Privateer *General Washington,* built at Providence, Rhode Island, in 1779

Length between Perpendiculars	98'
Tonnage	340

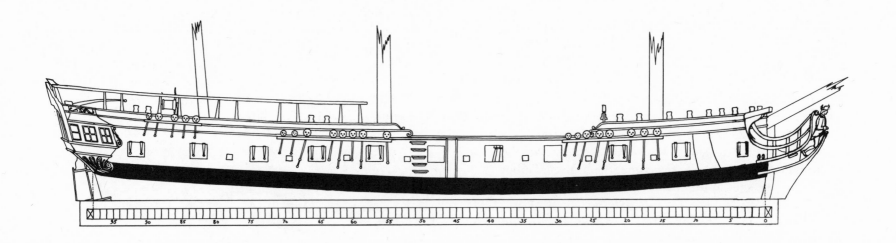

her next target. Although they were almost evenly matched in terms of cannons, *Hyder Ali*'s young captain, Joshua Barney, was sure he would be captured because of the weakness of his ship. Nonetheless, he tried a trick that enabled him to board *General Monk* and capture her.

She was immediately given back her old name, *General Washington,* and was chartered by Robert Morris, who was more or less in charge of the Continental Navy at that time. He sent her to the West Indies and she fought a sharp action with a British privateer off Cap François (now Cap Haitien in Haiti), and captured an-

[144]

other ship before arriving in Havana, Cuba. In Cuba she loaded a large shipment of gold to bring back to Philadelphia. She returned to Philadelphia on 17 July 1782, after clearing the Delaware of some small British craft.

In September she was purchased by the Continental Navy, and departed for France on 7 October with letters for Franklin. She made a very fast passage (she was regarded as a particularly fast ship anyway), arriving at l'Orient in under three weeks. She left l'Orient in January 1783, returning to Philadelphia on 12 March, only a few days before news arrived from Britain announcing the end of hostilities. She left once more for France on 10 November 1783 with Joshua Barney still her captain and with John Paul Jones as a passenger. Jones wished to go ashore in England for some business, so *General Washington* put him ashore at or near Plymouth, making her the first ship of the American navy to visit Britain in peacetime. Barney took the occasion to give a sumptuous dinner party for all the people in the area who had assisted him in his escape from the dreaded Mill Prison two years earlier. Then he took the ship on to France and thence back to Philadelphia. By summer 1784, all the ships of the Continental Navy had been sold except *General Washington* and *Alliance,* and then the *General Washington* was put up for auction in midsummer. The successful bidder was none other than John Brown, the Providence merchant who had had her built five years earlier. Brown fitted her out as an East Indiaman and she left for China in 1787, the first Rhode Island ship to do so. She apparently made several successful voyages to the Orient before the end of her life, but the records are lacking.

Chapelle gives her dimensions as those of a large ship, but evidently he was confusing her with the privateer *Congress;* the British never recorded her dimensions, as they had put her into service before she could be measured and drawn. There are two portraits of the ship, one a contemporary oil painting of her at anchor in the background of a portrait of a Rhode Island black sailor, and the other a postwar picture painted at Barney's direction of *General Monk* being taken by *Hyder Ali;* the former is in a private collection, while the latter is at the U.S. Naval Academy at Annapolis.

We feel that *General Washington* was probably built by the same builder as the privateer *Oliver Cromwell* whose draft is preserved at the National Maritime Museum at Greenwich. Hence, we have simply enlarged the Greenwich draft for our drawing, with few alterations. Her dimensions, according to our drawing, were: length overall, 114' 3"; length on the deck, 98'; breadth, 30'; tonnage, 340.

Corvette *General Washington*
From an anonymous oil painting, ca. 1780
Private collection, Kingston, Rhode Island

GEORGE/ENTERPRISE

THE British had long understood the strategic importance of Lake Champlain, for it could be used as an invasion route in either direction between Canada and what is now the United States. Therefore, they began a program of building some small warships to protect their interests on the lake. Their base and shipyards were at St. John on the Richelieu River at the northern end of the lake. Benedict Arnold arrived there with the armed ketch *Liberty* on 18 May 1775 and the base surrendered without a shot. Already built and ready for launching was the schooner *Royal Savage,* and already launched was the sloop *George,* capable of mounting ten guns.

Arnold renamed her *Enterprise* and took her into his growing naval force on the lake. She was involved in the battle of Valcour Island in October 1776, and appears to have been among the ships that Arnold burned in 1777 to avoid their capture by the powerful British fleet that had miraculously materialized on the lake.

She had a shallow draft and almost a flat bottom, which was ideally suited to navigating the shallower parts of the lake, but she was a dull sailer. She was equipped with oars or sweeps for rowing when the wind was either unfavorable or dead.

Her lines and dimensions are unrecorded, although there are a few contemporary paintings of her, and we have drawn her lines based on the pictures and on an enlargement of the lines of the cutter *Lee,* which

was being built at St. John's at the same time. Although she was pierced for ten guns she is reported to have carried 12 four-pounders, so the other two must have been mounted on the quarterdeck. Her crew numbered 50 men.

As we see her, her dimensions were: length overall, 50′ 11″; length between perpendiculars, 46′ 4″; length on the keel, 39′ 10″; breadth, 17′ 6″; depth, 5′ 9″; draft 5′ 9″; tonnage, 55. It is possible that she was two or three feet longer than this, but not likely.

Sloop *Enterprise*
From a watercolor painting by C. Randle, 1776
The Public Archives of Canada, Ottawa

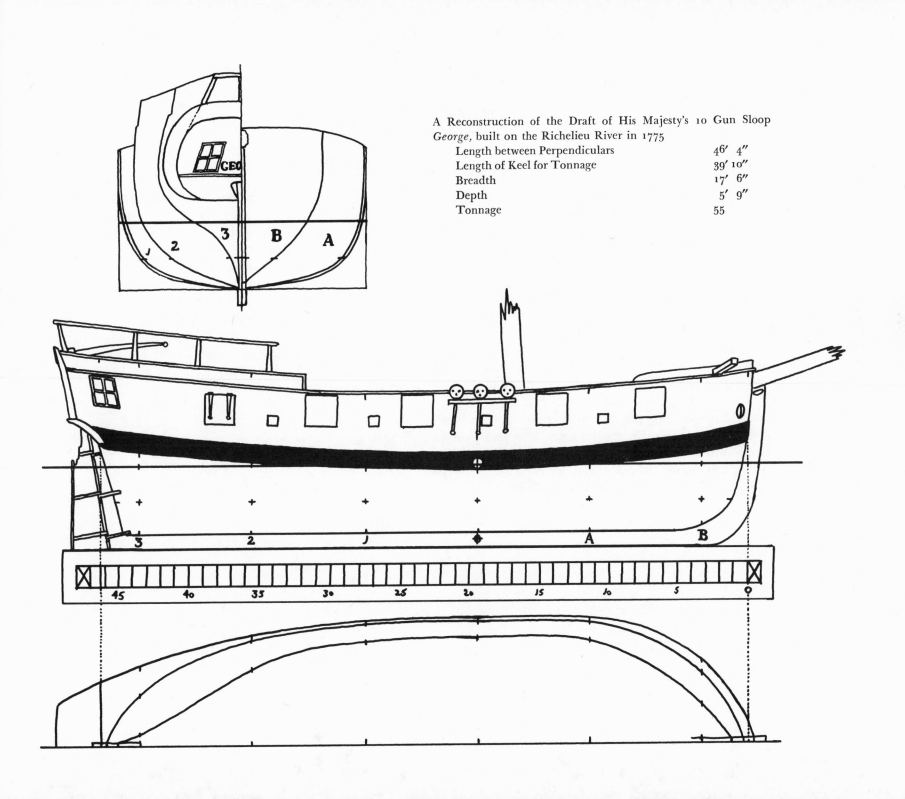

A Reconstruction of the Draft of His Majesty's 10 Gun Sloop
George, built on the Richelieu River in 1775

Length between Perpendiculars	46′ 4″
Length of Keel for Tonnage	39′ 10″
Breadth	17′ 6″
Depth	5′ 9″
Tonnage	55

HALIFAX

THE best eighteenth-century route, either for trade or for military invasion, between the Hudson River and the St. Lawrence River was along Lake George and Lake Champlain, and the shores of both these lakes were heavily fortified. We have included a number of Lake Champlain vessels in this book, but we have only found enough information on one vessel from Lake George to include her. This was the sloop *Halifax,* apparently built in 1759.

During the Seven Years' War, Captain Joshua Loring * of the Royal Navy was sent into the mountains of New York to put together and operate a naval force on Lake George. This force, which was assembled around Fort William Henry and Fort George, consisted of the sloop *Halifax,* the radeau *Invincible,* and a number of "whaleboats" and bateaux. Loring is said to have maintained good discipline and morale, but little is known of the ships themselves or their histories.

According to an engraving on display at Fort Ticonderoga Museum on Lake Champlain, the sloop *Halifax* looked like any saltwater sloop. She was armed with about ten carriage guns and a few swivels. The big (and successful) French offensive down Lake George had taken place in 1757, so the sloop *Halifax* saw little action, and it seems likely that she was either broken up or sold as a merchant vessel as soon as the British took possession of Canada from the French, thus eliminating any military threat along Lake Champlain. As we see her, she measured 69 feet in overall length and about 60 feet in length between perpendiculars.

---

* Loring's son of the same name was married to the lady who became General Sir William Howe's mistress during the Revolution, giving many satirical poets the golden opportunity of rhyming "snoring" with "Mrs. Loring."

A Reconstruction of the Draft of His Majesty's 10-Gun Sloop
Halifax, built on Lake George about 1759

| Length between Perpendiculars | 60′ 2″ |
| Tonnage | 90 |

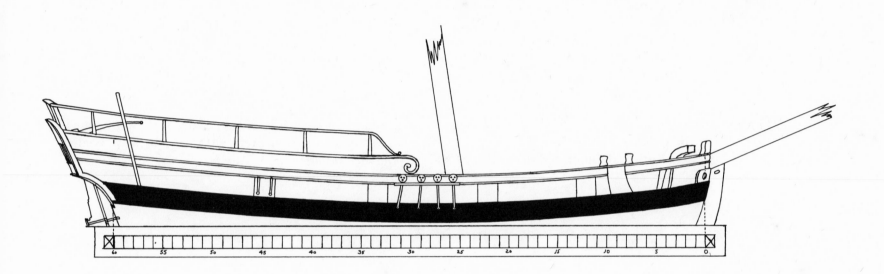

HALLIFAX

THE schooner *Hallifax* [sic] was purchased in New England by the Royal Navy in 1768, presumably to assist with enforcement of the Customs laws. Although her full hull lines indicate that she would have been too slow to catch the smugglers, she was fitted out with a few small carriage guns. She may have been employed briefly as a troop transport. She seems to have visited England at one time, for two sets of lines (one showing "improvements" made by the navy) survive at the National Maritime Museum at Greenwich. She was wrecked on the coast of Maine in February 1775; Cha-pelle says that she took part in the infamous raid on Falmouth (now Portland), Maine, in October 1775, but that was another vessel of the same name. Her figurehead is not recorded, but the lines do show a finely carved mermaid on the headrails; we have drawn a woman for the figurehead.

Dimensions: length overall, 67′ 8″; length between perpendiculars, 57′; length on the keel, 46′ 10″; breadth, 18′ 3″; depth, 8′ 10″; draft, 8′ 5″; tonnage, 83. She should be compared with the slightly smaller schooner *Sultana*.

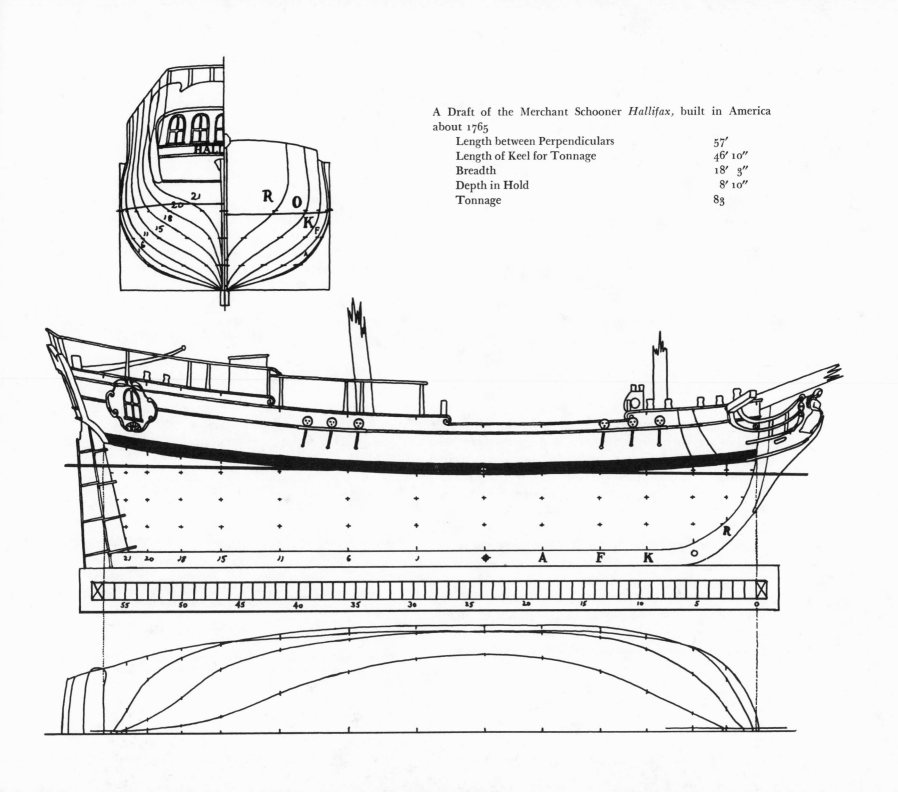

A Draft of the Merchant Schooner *Hallifax,* built in America
about 1765

Length between Perpendiculars	57′
Length of Keel for Tonnage	46′ 10″
Breadth	18′ 3″
Depth in Hold	8′ 10″
Tonnage	83

HANCOCK

IN December 1775, Congress passed the second half of the Rhode Island Navy Bill; this called for the construction of thirteen frigates, including five of 32 guns. One of these, later known as the *Hancock,* was to be built at the yard of Greenleaf & Cross at Newburyport, Massachusetts. Congress approved a design for the 32-gun ships, but it was so long in getting to New England that the builders had the ship half built to their own design when it arrived. Their own design resulted in a ship slightly bigger than the other 32s, and much prettier. When she was captured by the British she was described as the "finest and fastest frigate in the world."

She was launched in July 1776, but did not set sail until the spring of 1777. She left Boston on 21 May in company with the 24-gun frigate *Boston,* which had been built in the same shipyard. Early in June they captured the 28-gun British frigate *Fox* in an action characterized by chivalry on both sides. Early in July the three frigates were cruising in company when they were chased by the 44-gun ship *Rainbow* and the 32-gun frigate *Flora.* If they had stood and fought they would quite likely have taken both their adversaries, but they split in three directions. *Boston* escaped, her captain much criticized for having deserted the others; *Fox* was quickly recaptured by *Flora;* and *Hancock* was taken by *Rainbow* after a long chase. She should have been fast enough to escape from the aging *Rainbow,* but for some reason her captain, John Manley, had shifted her ballast so that she was trimmed heavily down by the head.

Hancock was taken into the Royal Navy and was renamed *Iris,* her previous name not being exactly popular with the British. She was taken to England, where her lines were recorded in drydock, and they survive today at the National Maritime Museum at Greenwich. She was sent back to the American station and captured her share of Allied shipping. In 1780, she fought a duel with the French frigate *La Hermione* and was on the point of capturing her when another French warship appeared on the scene. *Iris* escaped. In August 1781,

Frigate *Hancock*
From one of a set of four oil paintings by Francis Holman, 1779
Peabody Museum, Salem, Massachusetts

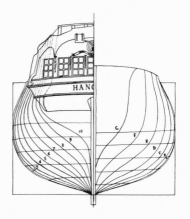

A Draft of the 32-Gun Continental Frigate *Hancock*, built at Newburyport, Massachusetts, in 1776

Length on the Lower Deck	136′ 7″
Length of Keel for Tonnage	115′ 10⅞″
Breadth, moulded	35′ 2″
Depth in Hold	11′ 1/2″
Tonnage	762

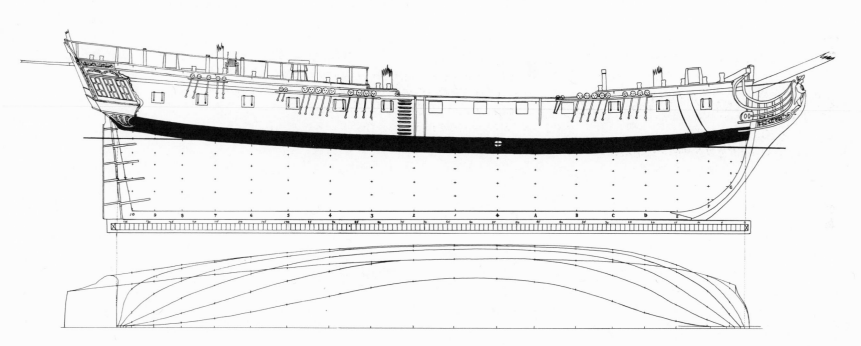

she and the 20-gun *General Monk* (formerly the Rhode Island privateer *General Washington*) captured the already-disabled 28-gun Continental frigate *Trumbull* in an "all-American" battle.

But *Iris*'s days as a British ship were coming to an end. De Grasse's powerful French fleet left their mooring in the Chesapeake early in September 1781 to do battle with a British fleet off the coast. Almost like naughty schoolboys, *Iris* and another frigate went around the anchorage cutting all the moorings of the French ships, but the French came back from the battle before the frigates could escape, so they were taken into the French navy on 11 September. Iris remained in the French navy until 1793, when the French Royalists asked the British to occupy Toulon as a base against the Republicans. When the Republican artillery under Napoleon forced its way through the British lines, the British and French Royalists evacuated Toulon on 18 December 1793, taking thousands of refugees with them on ships formerly of the French navy, and blowing up other French ships. One of these latter was *Iris,* which was then being used as a gunpowder storage hulk; she was the next-to-last survivor of the original frigates of the Continental Navy, the last being *Delaware.*

An unusual feature about *Hancock* was her rig. Like *Boston* and *Raleigh,* she used her ensign staff as a fourth mast, setting on it a small lateen sail for balance. This clearly shows up in the four oil paintings (at the Peabody Museum of Salem) by Francis Holman of the engagement with *Rainbow* and *Flora.* In addition to these four pictures, there is a possibility that she can be identified in one or more of the pictures of the evacuation of Toulon.

Dimensions: length overall, 161' 7"; length on the deck, 136' 7"; length of keel, 115' 11"; breadth, 35' 6"; depth, 11' 1"; draft, 17'; tonnage, 750.

HANNAH, BALTICK, *and* FRANKLIN

At the Peabody Museum in Salem, Massachusetts, are two interesting contemporary paintings of the Salem merchant schooner *Baltick,* built in the late 1760s. She was fairly typical of schooners of her size from New England, there being many like her among the sketches of Ashley Bowen.

When George Washington decided to commission a naval force in his Continental Army in 1775, it was to vessels like these that he turned. The first to be commissioned was the fishing schooner *Hannah,* on 2 September 1775. She was exactly the same tonnage (and therefore the other dimensions would have been almost identical) and date as the schooner *Baltick.* Washington chartered *Hannah* from Nicholas Broughton and hired Broughton as captain. For crew, he used soldiers from John Glover's Marblehead regiment, and he armed *Hannah* with four small carriage guns poked through hastily cut gunports in her waist. She set sail on 5 September and returned on the seventh after capturing a vessel called *Unity.* The crew was mutinous, Broughton was surly, and the vessel did not sail very well, so the first ship chartered by Washington was quickly dropped and replaced by others of the same type, called *Lynch, Franklin, Lee, Warren, Washington,* and *Harrison.*

The Peabody Museum also has a modern sketch of the *Franklin,* which, it is hopefully suggested, is based on an original that is now lost. Allowing for obvious distortion in the sketch, *Franklin* looks much the same as *Baltick* and *Hannah,* although she was a little smaller. She had been the 60-ton schooner *Eliza,* and was chartered from Archibald Selman of Marblehead. Under the command of Selman, she disobeyed orders and raided Charlottetown, Prince Edward Island, much to Washington's disgust. Her next captain, Samuel Tucker, was relieved by James Mugford in April 1776. A few days after Mugford had captured a rich British transport, *Franklin* ran aground in Boston Harbor and was attacked by the British. The schooner was saved, but Mugford was killed. *Franklin* continued in army serv-

Schooner *Lady Washington,* similar to the Schooner *Hannah*
From a powderhorn engraving, 1777
Private collection, Kingston, New York

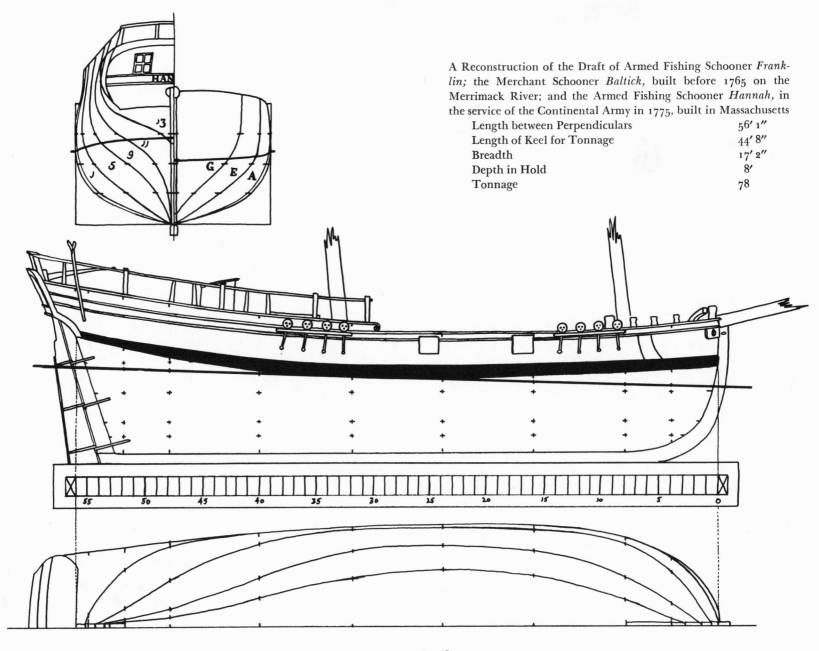

A Reconstruction of the Draft of Armed Fishing Schooner *Franklin;* the Merchant Schooner *Baltick,* built before 1765 on the Merrimack River; and the Armed Fishing Schooner *Hannah,* in the service of the Continental Army in 1775, built in Massachusetts

Length between Perpendiculars	56' 1"
Length of Keel for Tonnage	44' 8"
Breadth	17' 2"
Depth in Hold	8'
Tonnage	78

ice for a few more months until Congress ordered Washington's little fleet disbanded.

Dimensions of *Hannah* and *Baltick,* as we have reconstructed them from the paintings (and with advice from Howard Chapelle), were as follows: length overall, 61′ 3″; length on the deck, 56′ 1″; length on the keel, 44′ 8″; breadth, 17′; depth, 8″; draft, 8′ 1″; tonnage, 78.

Schooner *Franklin*
From a watercolor painting of uncertain date
Peabody Museum, Salem, Massachusetts

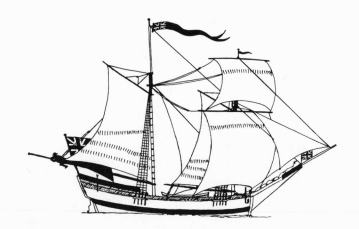

Schooner *Baltick*
From a watercolor painting, 1766
Peabody Museum, Salem, Massachusetts

HARLEQUIN

THE 12-gun ship *Harlequin* was built in America about 1778, and was purchased by the French for use as a fast mail packet in the West Indies. She was captured by the brand-new 32-gun British frigate *Cerberus* off Martinique on 6 June 1780. Commodore George Johnston wrote to his superiors in July, praising his new acquisition and saying that she was extremely swift. However, her shape was such that she could easily be overloaded, and when that was coupled with the unusual square-tuck stern with its high drag she was a disaster. Naval officials not being noted for a keen eye for the finer points of a ship, *Harlequin* was overloaded and Johnston's superiors reprimanded him for his poor choice of a purchase; they ordered her sold on 19 June 1782. While in British service she was named *Porto* because Johnston expected she would be used on the coast of Portugal. One of the most unusual features about this pretty design was her small amount of freeboard even when she was light.

Dimensions: length overall, 90′ 6″; length on the deck, 80′; length of keel, 66′ 10″; breadth, 20′ 5″; depth in hold, 9′ 3″; draft, 10′ 7″; tonnage, 142.

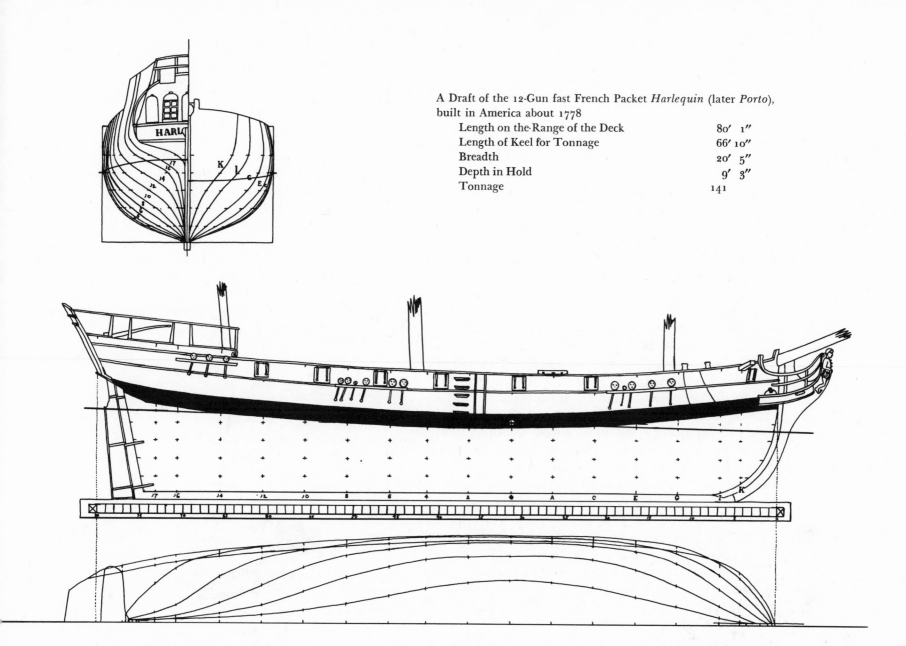

A Draft of the 12-Gun fast French Packet *Harlequin* (later *Porto*),
built in America about 1778

Length on the Range of the Deck	80′ 1″
Length of Keel for Tonnage	66′ 10″
Breadth	20′ 5″
Depth in Hold	9′ 3″
Tonnage	141

HORNET

ONE of the members of the first fleet of the Continental Navy was the little 10-gun sloop *Hornet* from Maryland. Originally named *Falcon*, she was purchased in the autumn of 1775 from William Stone and he was then made her captain. She sailed with the fleet for Nassau in February 1776, but got separated from them in a storm and collided with the sloop *Fly*. *Hornet*'s damage was far greater than *Fly*'s, and she limped back to Philadelphia by early April, having carried away her boom and the top of her mast.

Several months later she was given a new captain, John Nicholson, the younger brother of James Nicholson. He attempted to get her to sea in company with the frigate *Randolph* around Christmas 1776, but British patrols at the mouth of the Delaware thwarted their plans. They did get out in February, guarding a tobacco convoy that was bound for France, but once the convoy was a safe distance from the coast *Hornet* teamed up with *Fly* and headed for Martinique.

They returned from Martinique with some valuable military supplies, but soon found themselves trapped in the Delaware by the British fleet that was forcing its way upriver to open a supply line to Philadelphia. There being no longer any hope of escape, *Hornet* was burned to avoid capture, along with *Andrew Doria*, *Wasp*, and the frigates *Washington* and *Effingham* in November 1777.

We have reconstructed *Hornet*'s lines from an existing picture of the sloop (in the background of a portrait of William Stone, painted by Peale) and from knowledge of other Chesapeake Bay sloops. As we see her, her dimensions were: length overall, 64'; length between perpendiculars, 56'; length of keel, 39'; breadth, 17' 6"; depth, 7' 4"; draft, 10'; tonnage, 75. Her rig, according to the painting, included a gaff topsail, very rare on sloops of this period; this may have been an invention from the Chesapeake Bay, as there are gaff topsails in a primitive painting of a Maryland shipyard from before the Revolution.

Sloop *Hornet*
From an oil painting by Charles Willson Peale, 1774/5
Maryland Historical Society, Baltimore

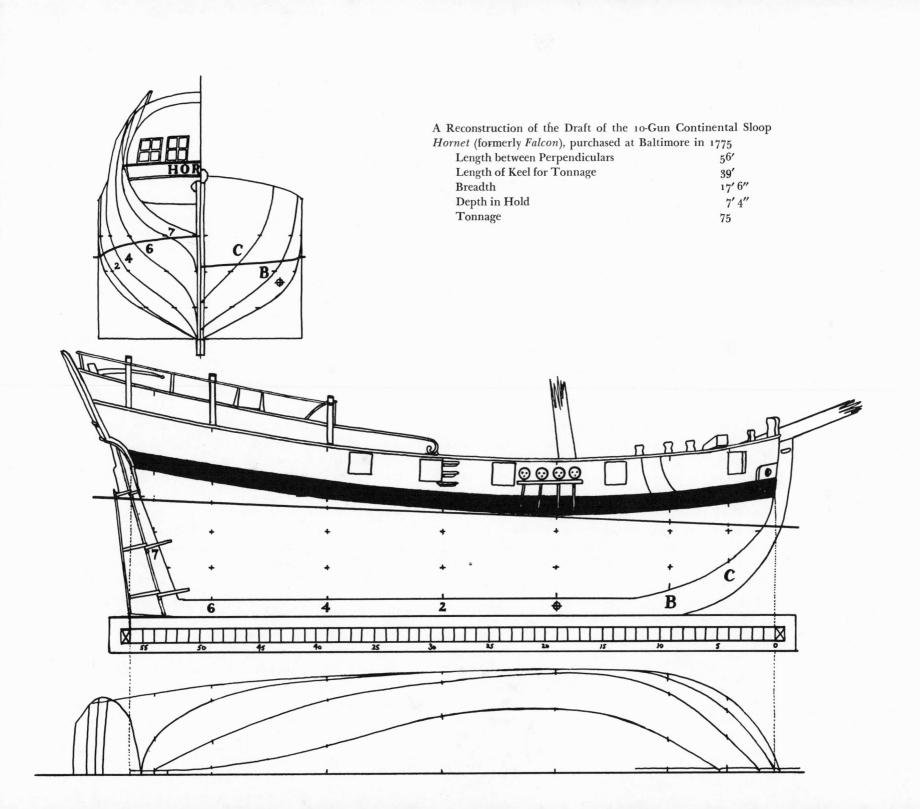

A Reconstruction of the Draft of the 10-Gun Continental Sloop
Hornet (formerly *Falcon*), purchased at Baltimore in 1775

Length between Perpendiculars	56'
Length of Keel for Tonnage	39'
Breadth	17' 6"
Depth in Hold	7' 4"
Tonnage	75

INFLEXIBLE

In the summer of 1776, British forces in Canada were building an 18-gun corvette on the St. Lawrence near Quebec City. They had been stung by the American expedition to Quebec the previous year (led by Montgomery and Arnold) and had decided to build this powerful rivercraft with ship rig and shallow draft to make sure Arnold did not show himself on the St. Lawrence again. Suddenly Sir Guy Carleton, the British commander, realized where the real danger lay; Arnold was not planning to come to Quebec, but he was building a fleet on Lake Champlain to prevent Carleton from making a fast attack along the lake into the heart of the infant United States. The corvette would thus be much more useful, in fact almost vital, on the lake.

Carleton immediately ordered the corvette dismantled and the pieces dragged overland to St. John's. There the ship was reassembled in only twenty-eight days by a team working day and night under the direction of Lieutenant John Schank of the Royal Navy; Schank had recently invented the drop-keel or centerboard, but his superiors refused to allow him to use it on the lake even though it would have given the British vessels a marked superiority with the shoal-draft flat-bottomed boats on the lake.

The ship was named *Inflexible* and mounted 18 twelve-pounders on her gun deck, which made her one of the most powerful warships yet built on America's inland waters. Unfortunately, she was quite unable to work to windward, a handicap that Arnold soon perceived. She was placed in commission on 1 October 1776 and immediately set sail with the British fleet toward the south. Arnold's fleet was hiding behind Valcour Island, and the British had gone two miles past him before they saw him. This meant that they would have to tack to windward, and it caused them to be strung out. The schooner *Carleton,* the most weatherly of the British fleet, was able to exchange fire with the Americans as early as noon, but *Inflexible* did not get to the scene of the battle until sunset, at which time the firing ceased. Arnold's fleet slipped away in the foggy night and was a few miles to windward toward Crown Point by the time the British saw them. *Inflexible* and the other British ships were able to catch up to Arnold's rearguard after several hours. They captured the galley *Washington,* and *Inflexible*'s fire so heavily damaged the galley *Congress* (Arnold's flagship) that Arnold was forced to run her ashore and burn her. When he saw that he had destroyed the bulk of the American fleet Carleton withdrew his fleet to St. John for the winter, but that extra winter of time was exactly what Arnold had been trying to buy. Carleton figured that he could have crushed American forces in New York if only he had had an extra four weeks of good weather; four weeks was the time it took to build *Inflexible,* which the British needed to have clear superiority over Arnold's fleet, and four weeks was all Arnold needed to ensure American independence.

Inflexible was used on the lake the following year, but she had no opposition. Presumably she was broken up at the end of the war. She appears in a number of contemporary paintings and prints of the activities on Lake Champlain, and we have used these as the basis for

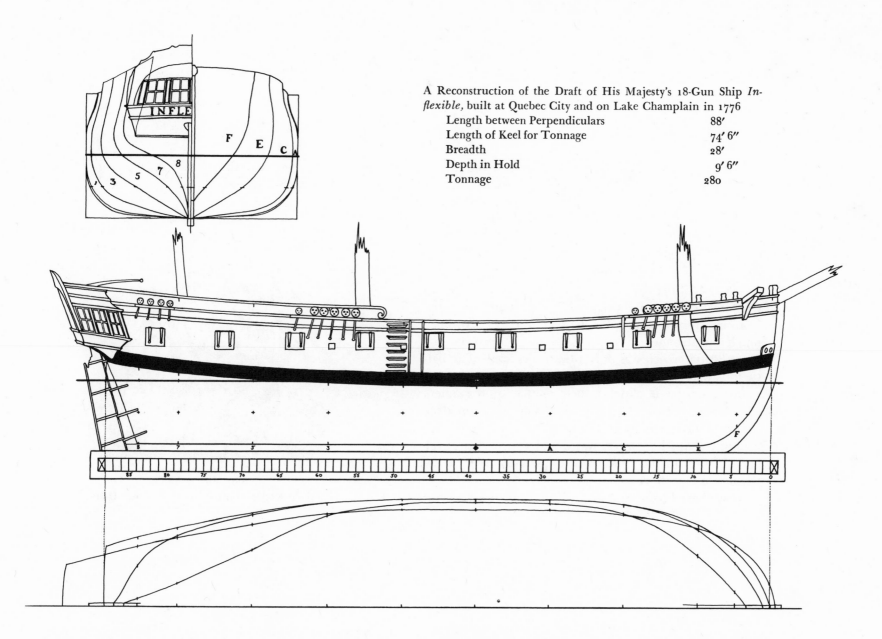

A Reconstruction of the Draft of His Majesty's 18-Gun Ship *Inflexible,* built at Quebec City and on Lake Champlain in 1776

Length between Perpendiculars	88'
Length of Keel for Tonnage	74' 6"
Breadth	28'
Depth in Hold	9' 6"
Tonnage	280

our reconstruction of her. The only measurement recorded was that she was 180 tons. She had quarter galleries but no head.

Dimensions: length overall, 97'; length on the deck, 88'; length on the keel, 74' 6"; breadth, 28'; depth, 9' 6"; draft, 8' 10"; tonnage, 180.

JACK

THERE is a painting by Robert Dodd, from which prints were made, of a battle between the British brig *Observer* and the Salem privateer *Jack*. Both ships were precisely drawn in the picture, which helps in reconstructing them. *Observer* herself had previously served as the Salem privateer *Amsterdam*. During the battle, *Jack*'s captain, listed variously as David or John Ropes, was killed by a shot from *Observer*, and so all resistance crumbled shortly afterward. This was quite fortunate for *Observer*, for *Jack* appears to have been much the stronger ship. *Jack* was taken into Halifax, Nova Scotia, which was only a few miles away. The battle took place on 28 May 1782.

Jack's design is closely allied to that of the Salem privateer *Mohawk*. The idea of having the gun deck completely covered by a flush spar deck on which more cannons could be placed was an idea that was developed further in the 1790s with the construction of the frigate *Constitution*.

As we have reconstructed *Jack*, her dimensions were: length overall, 98'; length on the deck, 85'; breadth, 23' 6"; tonnage, 185.

Ship *Jack*
From an engraving after an oil painting by Robert Dodd, 1782

A Reconstruction of the Draft of the 14-Gun American Privateer
Ship *Jack,* built at Salem, Massachusetts, about 1781

Length between Perpendiculars	85′
Breadth	23′ 6″
Tonnage	195

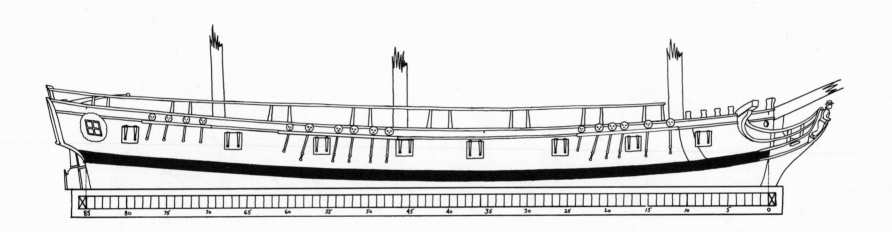

KATY

KATY seems to have been a relatively common name for American ships in the eighteenth century, with the result that it is often difficult to find reliable information about the history of any specific vessel of that name. One of these was the merchant brig from Boston that is shown in a fine watercolor painting belonging to the Bostonian Society at the Old State House, Boston. Its owners know no more about the ship than is written on the painting, that her captain was Martin Pease and that she is shown in the painting sailing out of the French port Havre de Grâce. She has no dolphin striker and she is flying an American ensign with thirteen stars and thirteen stripes, so one might date the picture slightly before 1790. Her head was unusually long, and the planking of the bow was reinforced in the manner of some French ships just below the hause hole.

A few words about her color scheme might be helpful, not that it was unusual. Her off-white bottom extended past the waterline to the bottom of the wale. The black paint of the wale itself was extended a few inches above and below the wale. The sheer planks above the ochre of the topsides were painted a light bluish-green, while the planks under the forecastle and quarterdeck rails were bright red, and the canvas or light planks that formed a bulwark around the quarter-deck were painted plain black. Her length overall was about 89′ and her length between perpendiculars was about 72′.

Brig *Katy*
From an anonymous French watercolor painting in the style of
Antoine Roux, ca. 1790
The Bostonian Society, Boston

A Reconstruction of the Draft of the American Merchant Brig
Katy of Boston, about 1788
Length between Perpendiculars   72′ 0″

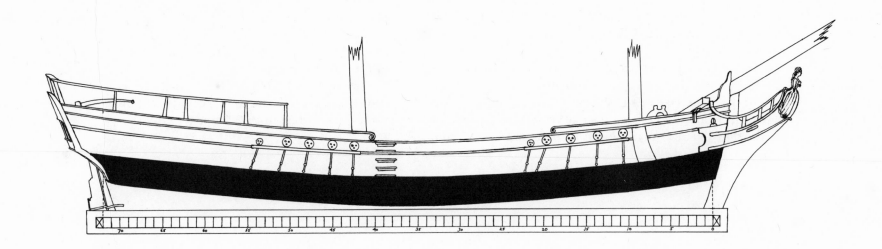

LADY HAMOND

THE 10-gun sloop *Lady Hamond* was built in Bermuda about 1788. She was measured in Britain and her lines taken off in both 1792 and 1804, and one of these drafts is now on file at the Science Museum in London. The scale is badly drawn, but the drawing is good enough to be interpreted reasonably accurately. At one time or another she was rigged as a schooner, or at least such a change was contemplated. In 1804, the Admiralty ordered twelve sloops or cutters built to her design in Bermuda, but for some reason the Bermudans thought her design to be out of date and used a completely different design, which was probably nowhere near as fast.

She had a flush deck, somewhat like some European cutters and luggers. She had a double wale, which was unusual for this late date, and a fairly sharp deadrise. Her keel, which was rockered at the forward end, had quite a bit of drag.

Dimensions: length overall, 70'; length between perpendiculars, 63' 8"; length of keel, 51' 2"; breadth, 20'; depth, 9' 11"; draft, 10' 1"; tonnage, 119.

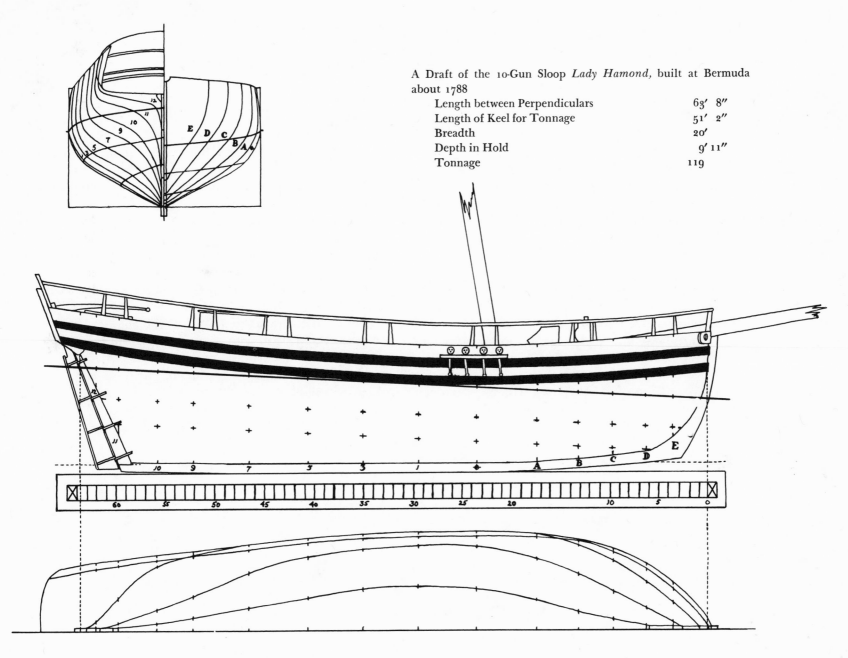

A Draft of the 10-Gun Sloop *Lady Hamond,* built at Bermuda
about 1788

Length between Perpendiculars	63' 8"
Length of Keel for Tonnage	51' 2"
Breadth	20'
Depth in Hold	9' 11"
Tonnage	119

LADY WASHINGTON

Wᴴᴇɴ the ship *Columbia* departed on her epic voyage around the world in 1787, she was accompanied by a tiny 90-ton sloop. The sloop is sometimes known as *Washington* in the records, but more often called *Lady Washington* (the new republic frowned on titles, but Martha Washington seems to have been called Lady Washington on many occasions), just as the ship *Columbia* is also known as *Columbia Rediviva*.

The sloop's captain was Robert Gray of Tiverton, Rhode Island, who was an enterprising man. When the two vessels were parted from each other in a storm off Cape Horn, Gray managed to get his sloop to the rendezvous at Nootka Sound before Kendrick could get *Columbia* there, so *Lady Washington* became the first American vessel to reach the West Coast. Gray explored and traded (mostly for sea otter skins, which he would sell in China for a high price) along the coast from Oregon to a point far up in Alaska. He then amicably arranged with Kendrick that they should swap commands.

Gray took *Columbia* back home, via China, and Kendrick took *Lady Washington* to China. Then he sold the sloop to himself, never actually sending the money back to the owners, and wandered around the Pacific. In December 1794 he was killed on her deck by an accidentally loaded saluting cannon at Honolulu, and what happened to the sloop after that is not recorded. At some point she was apparently rerigged as a brig.

The only record of the sloop's appearance is a watercolor on the title page of Robert Haswell's log of *Columbia*'s first voyage around the world. She was a simple New England sloop with a square topsail to be set only downwind, and, curiously enough, she had a long head, which is most unusual for a sloop, but probably necessary for long voyages.

According to our reconstruction, she measured 74′ in overall length, 58′ in length between perpendiculars, and 90 tons.

A Reconstruction of the Draft of the Sloop *Lady Washington,*
built in America about 1780
      Length between Perpendiculars   58′
      Tonnage   90

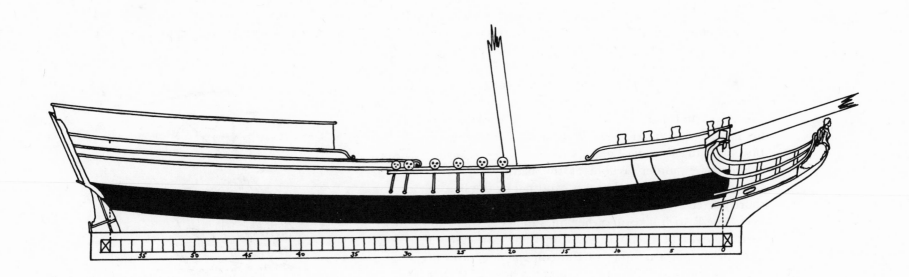

LEE

WHEN Benedict Arnold captured St. John's at the northern end of Lake Champlain in May 1775, he took possession of two vessels that had recently been built by the British: the sloop *George* (which he renamed *Enterprise*) and the schooner *Royal Savage*. The British had also begun construction of a cutter, but all they had built to that date was the frames. Arnold took these over and had his men complete the vessel, which he named *Lee* (after General Charles Lee, or possibly one of the Virginia Lees).

She served under Arnold at the battle of Valcour Island in October 1776, but was captured by the British shortly after the battle and was incorporated into their fleet. The British take-off of her lines following her capture survives at the National Maritime Museum at Greenwich and a number of contemporary pictures of the fleets on Lake Champlain portray her. With her blunt lines and flat bottom she seems not to have been a good sailer, but she had ports for three large oars or sweeps per side so as to be able to row when the wind was foul or calm.

Dimensions: length overall, 48′ 4″; length between perpendiculars, 43′ 9″; length on the keel, 34′; breadth, 16′ 4″; depth, 4′ 8″; draft, 4′; tonnage, 48.

Cutter *Lee*
From an engraving published by R. Sayer & J. Bennett, 1776
National Maritime Museum, Greenwich, England

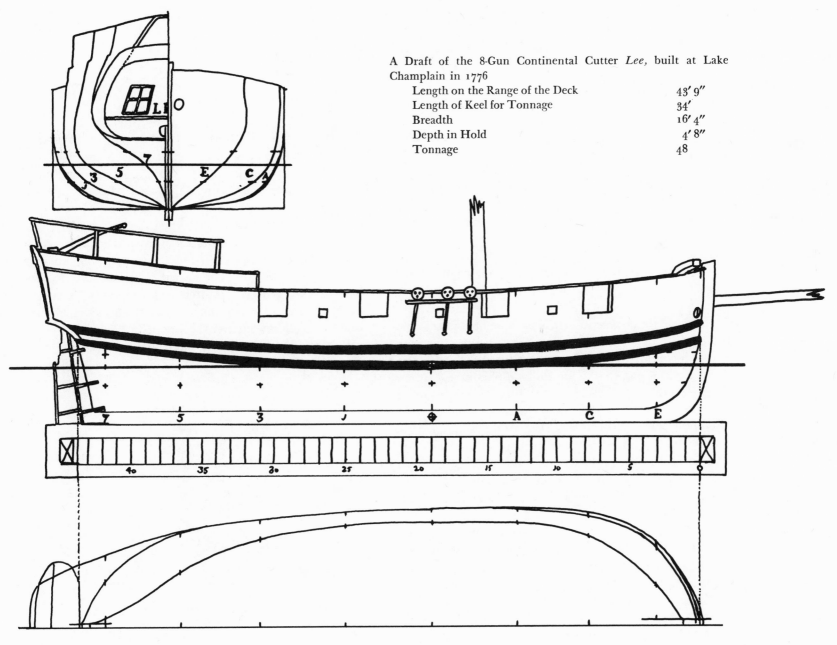

A Draft of the 8-Gun Continental Cutter *Lee,* built at Lake Champlain in 1776

Length on the Range of the Deck	43' 9"
Length of Keel for Tonnage	34'
Breadth	16' 4"
Depth in Hold	4' 8"
Tonnage	48

LEXINGTON

A LARGE merchant brig called *Wild Duck,* probably built in Philadelphia, was purchased in the Caribbean by the Maryland Committee of Safety in 1775, fitted with guns, and then sold to the Continental Navy in the fall. She was fitted with 14 four-pounders, 2 six-pounders, and 12 swivels, and given the name of *Lexington.* Joshua Humphreys was given the job of converting her into a warship, and John Barry was made captain. On 7 April 1776 she captured the small armed sloop *Edward* (tender to the frigate *Liverpool*) which was the first capture of the war by a Continental Navy ship in a single-ship action (it is because of this capture, and because of the fact that Barry was the first officer to receive a commission in the reconstituted United States Navy in the 1790s, that many Philadelphians and Americans of Irish descent consider John Barry to have been the "founder of the Navy," whatever that means). *Lexington* was careful to stay close to the coast to avoid capture by British patrols, which could not match her shallow draft. On 29 June she helped the gunpowder brig *Nancy* escape from six enemy ships off Cape May. Then Barry was relieved by William Hallock of Maryland.

Hallock took her to the West Indies and back, but was captured at the mouth of the Delaware by the 32-gun British frigate *Pearl.* Hallock and his officers were taken onto the frigate, but the rest of the crew stayed on the brig under her prize crew of six men. In the night the 70 Americans rose up, overpowered the prize crew, and brought the brig back to Philadelphia.

Her next captain was Henry Johnson, a Massachusetts privateersman who had already been captured and had escaped from a British prison. He set sail for France on 27 February 1777 from Baltimore. After taking two prizes he arrived at Bordeaux on 3 April and delivered some important dispatches from Congress to Paris. He was ordered to take *Lexington* a few miles up the coast to Nantes, and narrowly escaped from the 80-gun ship *Foudroyant.* At Nantes he joined the squadron of Lambert Wickes with the cutter *Reprisal* and the lugger *Surprise,* and together they set out to attack the Irish linen fleet. They missed the linen fleet, but took eighteen prizes between them. Then they were chased by a

Brig *Lexington*
From an oil painting, probably by Francis Holman, 1777
Private collection, New Haven, Connecticut

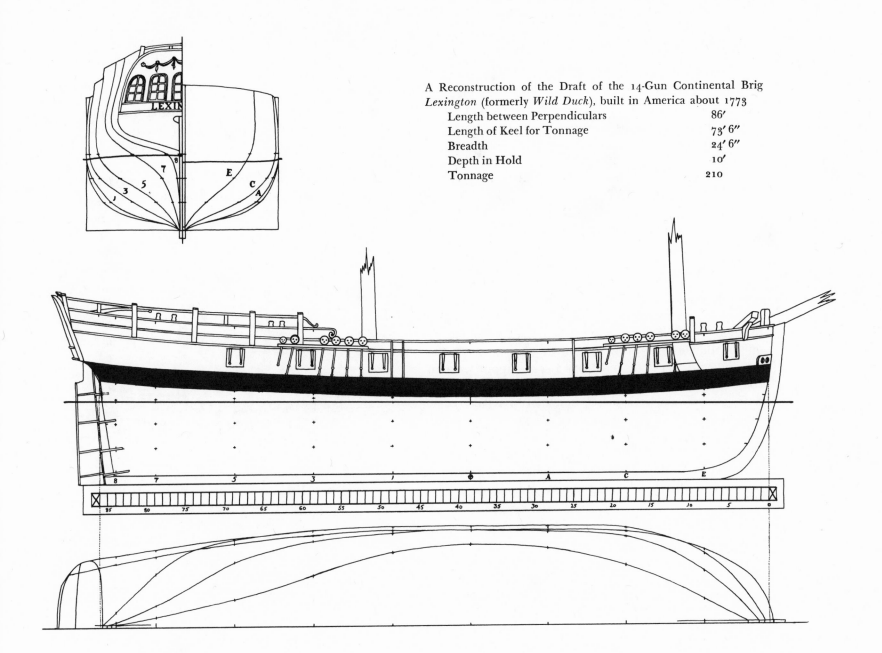

A Reconstruction of the Draft of the 14-Gun Continental Brig
Lexington (formerly *Wild Duck*), built in America about 1773

Length between Perpendiculars	86'
Length of Keel for Tonnage	73' 6"
Breadth	24' 6"
Depth in Hold	10'
Tonnage	210

British squadron and sought sanctuary in different French ports on 27 June.

Lexington left France with dispatches for Congress on 17 September 1777, but two days later she met the British cutter *Alert. Alert,* under Lieutenant John Bazely, had only ten guns, but they were ten-pounders (far more effective than *Lexington*'s four-pounders), and she had a copper bottom, which made her the faster boat. They fought each other for a few hours, doing considerable damage to the rigging on both sides. Finally, Johnson decided to surrender (some say it was because he had run out of ammunition and others say it was because the French members of the crew had refused to man the guns any more). Fortunately, Johnson had the presence of mind to throw the dispatches overboard in a weighted bag first.

The appearance of the *Lexington* is known to us through a fine oil painting by either Francis Holman or one of the Cleveley brothers, showing her in the act of surrendering to *Alert,* and from a contemporary watercolor of the same scene. At that time, she was apparently setting royals on both masts, and two spritsails. From British records after her capture we know her length and breadth, and from the report of a British spy in Philadelphia we know that she had a "square-tuck stern painted yellow, and a low, rounded stem painted lead colour, black sides and yellow mouldings." From the watercolor we know that she had no head (the stem is hidden in the oil painting), and we can see from the painting that her foremast was stepped very far forward. (The real *Lexington* clearly bears no resemblance at all to the model plans bearing her name that have been in wide circulation for many years. The model plans appear to represent a vessel of the 1815 period.)

As we see her, the dimensions were: length overall, 94'; length between perpendiculars, 86'; length of keel, 73' 6"; breadth, 24' 6"; depth, 10'; draft, 10' 6"; tonnage, 210.

Brig *Lexington*
From an anonymous watercolor painting, 1777
National Maritime Museum, Greenwich, England

LIBERTY

ON 9 May 1768 John Hancock's little sloop *Liberty* arrived in Boston with a cargo of wine and other goods. The amount of wine that was declared to the Customs was considerably less than such a vessel could carry, so the Customs officials suspected that she had actually carried far more wine and had smuggled it off during the night. When they found a witness to the smuggling, they seized the hapless sloop, using seamen and marines from the 50-gun ship *Romney* for protection. Boston radicals rioted, seriously injuring some of the Customs commissioners and publicly burning a yacht that belonged to one of the commissioners. Although the seizure took place on 10 June, the court procedure lasted all the following winter. Hancock eventually lost the sloop, and she was given to the Customs Service to assist them with their patroling.

Under the command of Lieutenant Reid, *Liberty* (what a bizarre name for a Customs vessel!) was sent to Newport, Rhode Island. Presumably she was outfitted with a handful of carriage guns, and she did such a good job at interfering with the smugglers (smuggling was Rhode Island's major industry at that time) that the local mob found a slim pretext and boarded the sloop when she came alongside the dock. They forced the crew ashore, pillaged the sloop of all her contents, cut down her spars with axes, and set her adrift in the harbor, whereupon she grounded less than a mile away at Goat Island. In the meantime, they took her longboat and dragged it to a prominent spot and publicly burned it. The next night, "persons unknown" boarded the sloop and finished the destruction by burning her to the waterline. This was 19 July 1769, five years before independence.

Liberty's appearance is known to us through watercolors by Christian Remick, showing her in Boston Harbor protected by British warships from being retaken by the Boston mob.

Dimensions: length overall, 64′; length between perpendiculars, 55′.

Sloop *Liberty*
From a watercolor painting by Christian Remick, 1768
Massachusetts Historical Society, Boston

A Reconstruction of the Draft of the Boston Sloop *Liberty*, built about 1765
    Length between Perpendiculars   55'

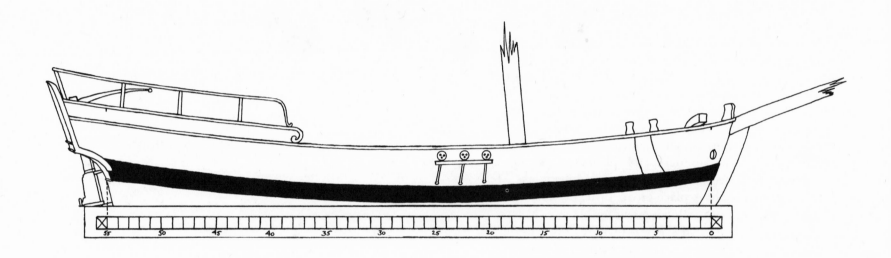

LIBERTY (*formerly* KATHARINE)

PHILIP Skene was a prosperous gentleman who lived at the southern end of Lake Champlain in New York, at a place he immodestly called Skenesborough (most atlases call the place Whitehall today, but local inhabitants renamed it Skenesborough at least for the period of the Bicentennial). Skene had a yacht built for him, and he named her *Katharine* after his wife. This yacht had two masts, and some accounts called her a schooner while others said she was a ketch. Based on the pictorial evidence (it has been suggested that even this one picture of her, entitled *God Bless Our Armes,* is actually a forgery dating only from the 1930s) she seems to have been a ketch, with a single yard on the mainmast on which could be set a square sail when the wind was fair. The rail of the quarterdeck projected out over the stern in the manner of a pink.

In May 1775 Ethan Allen and his Green Mountain Boys captured Fort Ticonderoga on the shores of Lake Champlain. A few days earlier, another group of New England troops seized the yacht *Katharine,* armed her with eight small carriage guns, and set sail for St. John's at the other end of the lake, with Benedict Arnold at the tiller. St. John's put up no resistance and Arnold was able to add the sloop *George* and the schooner *Royal Savage* to his fleet; both had been recently built at St. John's. The date was 18 May 1775, and some enthusi-

asts claim that this was the first naval battle of the Revolution, even if there was no actual resistance by the British. *Liberty* missed the battle of Valcour Island since she had been sent on a mission elsewhere, but she was burned to avoid capture in 1777.

Dimensions: length overall, 48′ 4″; length between perpendiculars, 41′; tonnage, 40.

Ketch *Liberty*
From the sketch "God Bless Our Armes," 1776
Fort Ticonderoga Museum, Fort Ticonderoga, New York

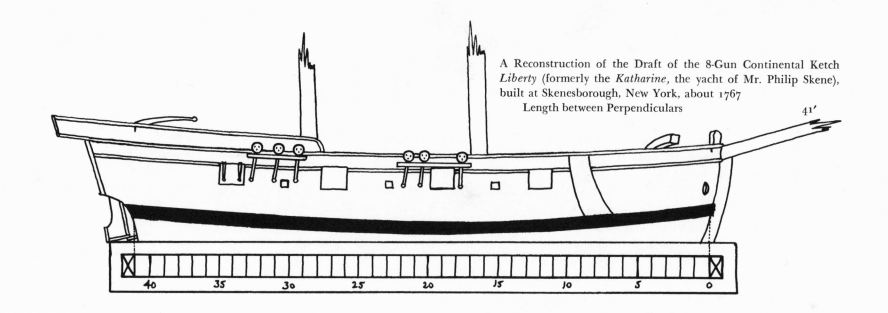

A Reconstruction of the Draft of the 8-Gun Continental Ketch *Liberty* (formerly the *Katharine,* the yacht of Mr. Philip Skene), built at Skenesborough, New York, about 1767
Length between Perpendiculars   41'

LONDON

THE merchant ship *London* was built in New York in 1770 or 1771, and was presumably used in the transatlantic trade. About 1775 she was chartered by the Admiralty for use in transporting troops to America, and in 1776 she was surveyed at Deptford with a view to purchasing her for the navy. She was purchased in 1777 and fitted with 14 guns; there is no existing plan of the location of her gunports, but they must have been very close to the water. Her new name was *Grasshopper,* and she was used as a guard for the convoy that was unsuccessfully attacked by the Continental ships *Alfred* and *Raleigh* on 3 September 1777.

On 27 August 1779 she was renamed *Basilisk* and was fitted out as a fireship; this entailed, among other things, rehinging the gunport lids so that they opened downward instead of upward in order to prevent them from closing and snuffing out the fire. She was never used as a fireship, and was finally sold at Plymouth (England) in April 1783. Her plans survive at the National Maritime Museum at Greenwich. She appears to have carried an unusually large sail area.

Dimensions: length overall, 111' 10"; length between perpendiculars, 92' 6"; length of keel, 69' 2"; breadth, 26' 9"; depth in hold, 10' 10"; draft, 15' 8"; tonnage, given variously as 276 or 282.

[180]

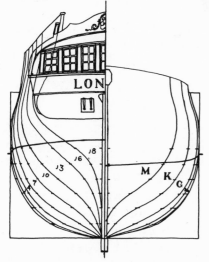

A **Draft** of the American Packet Ship *London,* built at New York
in 1771

Length between Perpendiculars	92′ 6″
Length of Keel for Tonnage	69′ 2″
Breadth	26′ 9″
Depth in Hold	10′ 10″
Tonnage	282

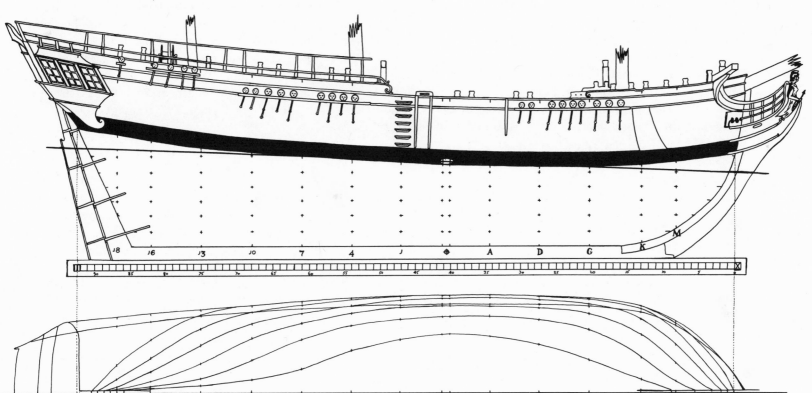

LORD CAMDEN

THE merchant ship *Lord Camden* (this ship and the city of Camden, New Jersey, were both named after the lord Chancellor of Britain in the 1760s) was built in Philadelphia and registered there in March 1775. She was purchased for the Royal Navy not long after and was fitted to be a fireship under the name of *Vulcan*. For this, several ports with hinges at the bottoms of the lids had to be cut in her side, and her plans, together with these alterations, survive at the National Maritime Museum at Greenwich. Unfortunately, the records of the many ships called *Vulcan* and *Volcano* have been much confused over the years so it is not presently possible to know exactly what happened to this ship during the first half of the Revolution. However, it is fairly certain that she was one of the four fireships used by the British against the French fleet in the Chesapeake just as the siege of Yorktown began in 1781. According to one source, she was the last to catch fire and, while the other three went wide of their marks, she very nearly set a French battleship on fire. The Royal Navy used quite a number of American-built ships as fireships in the various wars of the eighteenth century.

As far as we know, *Lord Camden*'s appearance was almost identical to the two other Philadelphia merchant ships of the same date that were later converted into the warships *Alfred* and *Drake*, and it is from her plans that we have reconstructed the plans of those other two ships. Their dimensions were almost exactly the same.

Dimensions: length overall, 110′ 1″; length between perpendiculars, 91′ 6″; length of keel, 72′ 4″; breadth, 27′ 9″; depth, 12′ 3″; draft, 14′ 7″; tonnage, 296.

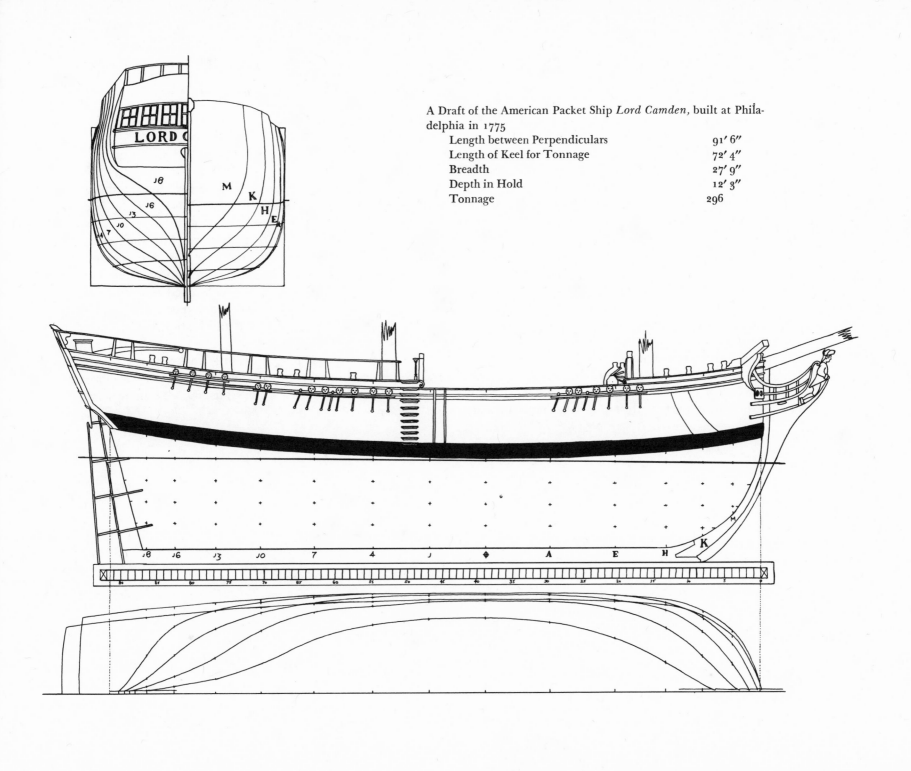

A Draft of the American Packet Ship *Lord Camden,* built at Philadelphia in 1775

Length between Perpendiculars	91′ 6″
Length of Keel for Tonnage	72′ 4″
Breadth	27′ 9″
Depth in Hold	12′ 3″
Tonnage	296

LOVELY LASS

ONE of the many American merchant ships purchased for use in the Royal Navy at the time of the Revolution was built in Philadelphia in 1774 and named *Lovely Lass*. She had the standard Philadelphia pattern of decks and otherwise her shape was fairly similar to *Lord Camden,* except that she was a few feet shorter in length and she had quarter galleries in the stern. The British purchased her in 1776 and renamed her *Sylph.* They outfitted her with 14 carriage guns and perhaps 12 swivels, and fitted her for use as a convoy guard. Experts disagree as to whether all these guns were mounted on the weather deck or whether ports were cut in her sides to receive them; if the former, she would have been quite top-heavy, and if the latter, the ports would have been dangerously close to the waterline, as on *Alfred, Drake,* and others. If she had not been fitted with ports for her guns in 1776, she was definitely fitted with them in 1779, with the lids hinged to open downward, because her new job was to serve as a fireship with the new (and appropriate) name of *Lightning.* She was not actually used as a fireship, and was sold out of the navy when peace came in 1783. Her lines are preserved at the National Maritime Museum at Greenwich.

Dimensions: length overall, 101' 8"; length between perpendiculars, 85' 2"; length of keel, 68'; breadth, 27' 6"; depth in hold, 11' 8"; draft, 14'; tonnage, 274.

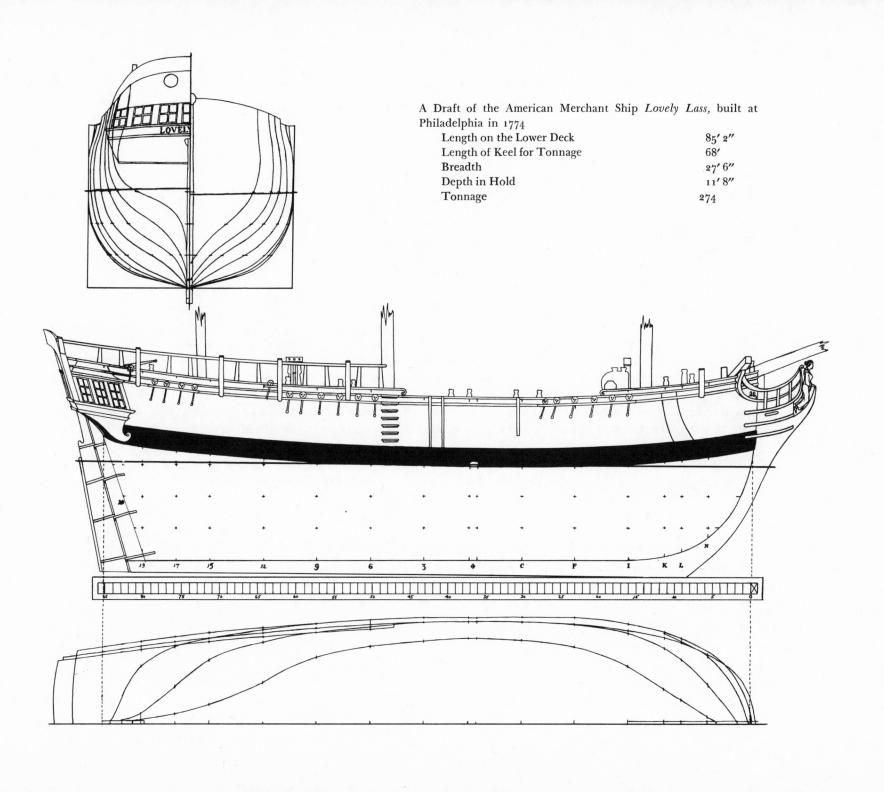

A Draft of the American Merchant Ship *Lovely Lass*, built at
Philadelphia in 1774

Length on the Lower Deck	85′ 2″
Length of Keel for Tonnage	68′
Breadth	27′ 6″
Depth in Hold	11′ 8″
Tonnage	274

LOYAL AMERICAN

I⊤ has been customary to compare scientists of the Colonial period with Benjamin Franklin, and to say something like "He was almost another Benjamin Franklin." If the British had won the War of Independence, we might have found ourselves saying "Franklin was almost another Benjamin Thompson." Thompson, who was raised in Massachusetts, was not popular with his contemporaries, who did not care for his undisguised ambition ("He never lost an opportunity to kick an underdog," said one of his biographers). He applied for a commission in the Continental Army, but was turned down when some of his personal enemies spoke out against him. He therefore, with little conviction, became a Loyalist, working first as a spy, then in the government in Britain, and, late in the war, as a cavalry officer in the South.

In 1781, to amuse himself he drew designs for a 38-gun frigate that he hoped the Royal Navy would build for service in American waters, and he won the approval of many senior officials of the navy. However, the war was almost over, so the frigate was never built. Above the water she looked much the same as any other British frigate of her size and date, but below the water she was very sharp, with straight floors and steep deadrise, almost like a Chesapeake Bay privateer schooner. There never had been a design for a large vessel with such deadrise, and it would have been interesting to see how she performed. Chapelle says that she would have been very fast with the right rig, but one suspects that she would have been restricted to carrying only small caliber guns (or carronades?) and stores for only short cruises. Whether or not her specific design influenced Humphreys when he conceived the *Constitution* almost fifteen years later, the *Constitution* had significantly more deadrise than earlier frigates had; this has often been attributed to a French influence of some sort, but although French theory influenced some American frigates (such as *New York* of 1799, for example) no real French connection can be traced to *Constitution*.

Thompson had the design for his frigate printed in Marmaduke Stalkaart's *Naval Architecture,* published in 1784, and it is from that source that we have obtained her lines. Thompson gave no name for the frigate—that, after all, would have been the province of the navy—but it has been suggested that he intended that she be called *Loyal American,* so that is what we have called her.

Dimensions: length overall, 169'; length on the deck, 148' 2"; length of keel, 120' 6"; breadth, 39' 6"; depth, 11' 4"; draft, 16' 7"; tonnage, 1,000.

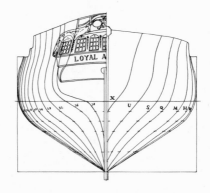

A Draft of the 38-Gun Frigate *Loyal American,* proposed to be built for the Royal Navy in 1782

Length between Perpendiculars	145′ 4″
Length of Keel for Tonnage	120′ 6″
Breadth	39′ 6″
Depth in Hold	11′ 4″
Tonnage	1,000

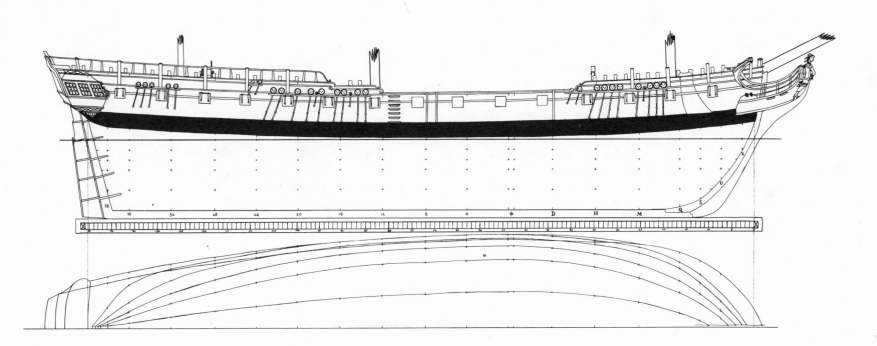

MARIA

WHEN the British decided to launch an invasion into New York from Canada in 1776 there was one small obstacle: Benedict Arnold had hastily built and assembled a fleet of warships on Lake Champlain on the main route southward. The British countered by building an even larger fleet, but the time it took them to do this was just long enough to force them to postpone the invasion until 1777, when the Americans would be readier for them. One of the vessels in the British fleet on the lake was the schooner *Maria,* armed with 14 six-pounders. She had been built in Quebec out of a kit that had been sent over from England in the hold of a large merchant ship, and she was named after Guy Carleton's wife. The plan was to sail her to the Richelieu River and roll her ten miles over logs until she had by-passed the rapids, all the way to St. John's on Lake Champlain. Unfortunately, it rained and rained, which rendered the rollers useless. Lieutenant Schank, the inventor of the centerboard, was directed to dismantle her once more and cart the pieces to St. John's, where they were assembled again.

As soon as the fleet was ready in October 1776, Carleton and Pringle boarded *Maria* and led the way south to Valcour Island. *Maria* somehow totally failed to get into the action, but redeemed herself in the next action when she outstripped all the other British ships in catching up to the American rearguard and helping capture the galley *Washington.* Her design, which is preserved at the National Maritime Museum at Greenwich, shows that she would have been faster than most of the other vessels on the lake. A number of paintings of her also survive. Presumably she was broken up at the end of the war in 1783.

Dimensions: length overall, 79'; length on the deck, 66'; length of keel, 52' 2"; breadth, 21' 6"; depth, 8' 2"; draft, 7' 2"; tonnage, 128.

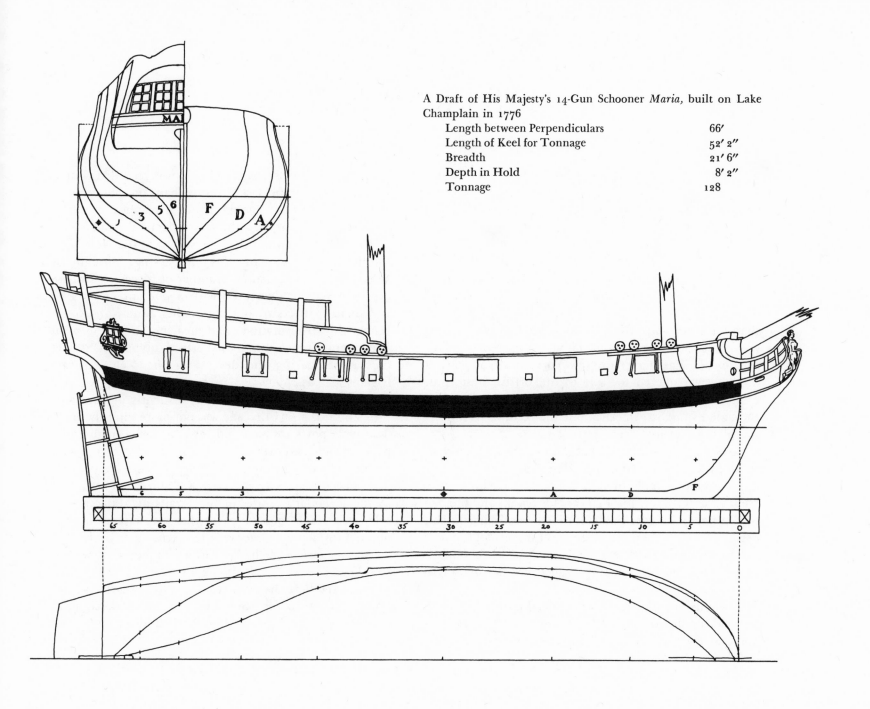

A Draft of His Majesty's 14-Gun Schooner *Maria,* built on Lake
Champlain in 1776

Length between Perpendiculars	66'
Length of Keel for Tonnage	52' 2"
Breadth	21' 6"
Depth in Hold	8' 2"
Tonnage	128

MASSACHUSETTS

IN 1786, Major Shaw of Massachusetts was sent to China to become America's first consul ever sent there, because it was thought that trade with China would increase considerably in the next few years. In 1788, Shaw ordered a fine ship to be built in Quincy, Massachusetts, by the same Hackett family who had previously built the warships *America, Alliance, Raleigh, Ranger,* and *Hampden.* Named *Massachusetts,* she was launched in 1789, possibly America's first true East Indiaman. (A slightly larger ship, *Maria Wilhelmina,* of 1,000 tons, was launched in 1774 from Thomas Cheeseman's shipyard on the East River in New York, and it is possible that she was offered for sale to the British East India Company; it is also possible that there were other East Indiamen built in America, but the records are too incomplete to say for sure.)

Local mystics declared that *Massachusetts* would be an unlucky ship, so the crew deserted. A second crew also deserted, but she departed for China with a third crew under Captain Job Prince. Her planks and the barrels in her hold were made of green wood and quickly began to rot. Consequently, the meat in her hold spoiled before she had sailed far. She carried no chronometer, so it was a miracle that she reached her destination at all.

The outward voyage was a financial failure for Shaw. He sold the ship at Canton and died himself on the way home a few months later, aged only thirty-nine. What happened to the ship after that is not recorded, but it is unlikely that she lasted more than another year or two. We know little enough about her appearance. She measured 820 tons, and there is a detailed pen-and-ink sketch of her elaborate stern preserved at the New York Public Library, showing the fine carvings wrought by S. Skillin. There are also a number of pieces of Chinese export porcelain decorated with a portrait of an East Indiaman of her size and date flying American colors. Using this information, and bearing in mind what British and French ships of her size and type looked like, plus remembering the designs of the New England frigates such as *Hancock, Alliance,* and *Raleigh,* we have reconstructed her lines. She was evidently a handsome ship, and it is a pity that she was not more soundly built. The little ports we have indicated in between the gunports are not oarports; they are for ventilating the ship in the tropics, although one assumes that they could have been used as oarports if the ship were attacked by the legendary pirates of the Straits of Malacca in a calm. Although most ships of this period had an odd number of windows across the stern, such as five or seven, *Massachusetts* had eight, a number that was to be echoed in the *Constitution* a few years later.

As we see here, her dimensions were: length overall, 159' 8"; length on the deck, 137'; length of keel, 116'; breadth, 37' 6"; depth in hold, 11'; draft, 17' 4"; tonnage, 820.

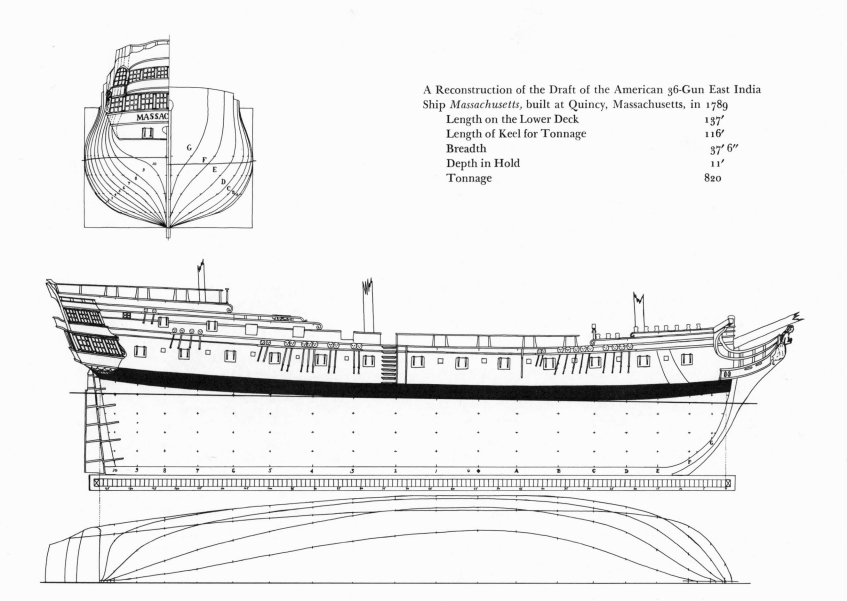

A Reconstruction of the Draft of the American 36-Gun East India
Ship *Massachusetts,* built at Quincy, Massachusetts, in 1789

Length on the Lower Deck	137′
Length of Keel for Tonnage	116′
Breadth	37′ 6″
Depth in Hold	11′
Tonnage	820

MEDIATOR

IN April 1745, the Royal Navy purchased a "Virginia-built" (meaning anywhere in the Chesapeake Bay, not necessarily Virginia) sloop in the West Indies and named her *Mediator*. She was fitted out with 10 four-pounder carriage guns and no fewer than 18 swivels. She was sent off immediately to England where her lines were taken off, and they are on file at the National Maritime Museum at Greenwich. She had been built in 1741. On 29 July 1745, she was captured by a French privateer off Ostende, and reportedly was sunk there shortly afterward.

She was built in the style of the so-called Bermuda sloop, a form that was popular in the Chesapeake and in Jamaica. These were fast vessels with fairly sharp lines, and they were useful for smuggling, among other things. The master's cabin was almost invariably in the stern under a rounded coach roof. An unusual feature of *Mediator*'s design was the backward-sloping stem. She was steered with a wheel, like most of the Bermuda sloops, while virtually all other sloops of her size were steered with a tiller.

Dimensions: length overall, 67'; length between perpendiculars, 60' 10"; length of keel, 44'; breadth, 21' 3"; depth, 9' 9"; draft, 10' 8"; tonnage, 105.

Sloop *Hope* of Rhode Island, similar to the Sloop *Mediator*
From an advertisement in the
Providence Gazette & Country Journal, 1781

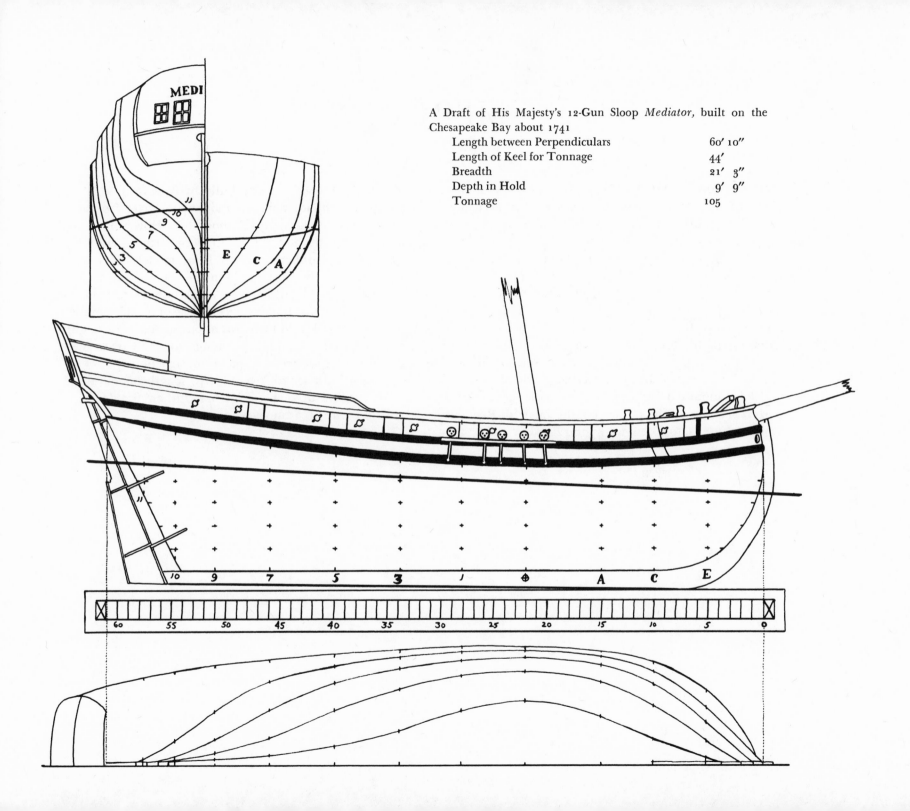

MEDI

A Draft of His Majesty's 12-Gun Sloop *Mediator,* built on the
Chesapeake Bay about 1741

Length between Perpendiculars	60' 10"
Length of Keel for Tonnage	44'
Breadth	21' 3"
Depth in Hold	9' 9"
Tonnage	105

MERCURY

THE Continental Navy commissioned a number of different ships in the Revolution with the name of *Mercury,* and it is not always clear which one was which. As might be expected from the name of the mythological messenger of the gods, all these ships were intended to be fast packets to take important messages to and from Paris for Congress. One packet *Mercury* was captured by the corvette *Fairy* and the frigate *Vestal* near the Newfoundland Banks on 10 September 1780; this packet was reported to be a ketch, but it now seems that this was a clerical error, for she was a brig. Her dimensions were recorded, and she was said to have mounted eight guns. A schooner packet called *Mercury* was built a few months later at Plymouth, Massachusetts, to a design by John Peck.

The brig *Mercury* was built by Wharton & Humphreys at Philadelphia around 1776. Apart from her dimensions we know little about her. However, it was thought worth attempting to reconstruct her, since there are a number of nicely built models (including one at Mystic Seaport in Connecticut) that purport to represent her, but which were actually built to plans of a British ketch of the *Speedwell* class of a much earlier period, and it would be useful to put the record straight. The Wharton & Humphreys design for the frigate *Randolph* was an influence on our reconstruction.

Dimensions: length overall, 84′; length on the deck, 72′ 6″; length of keel, 60′ 2″; breadth, 20′ 6″; depth, 8′ 10″; draft, 10′ 4″; tonnage, 135.

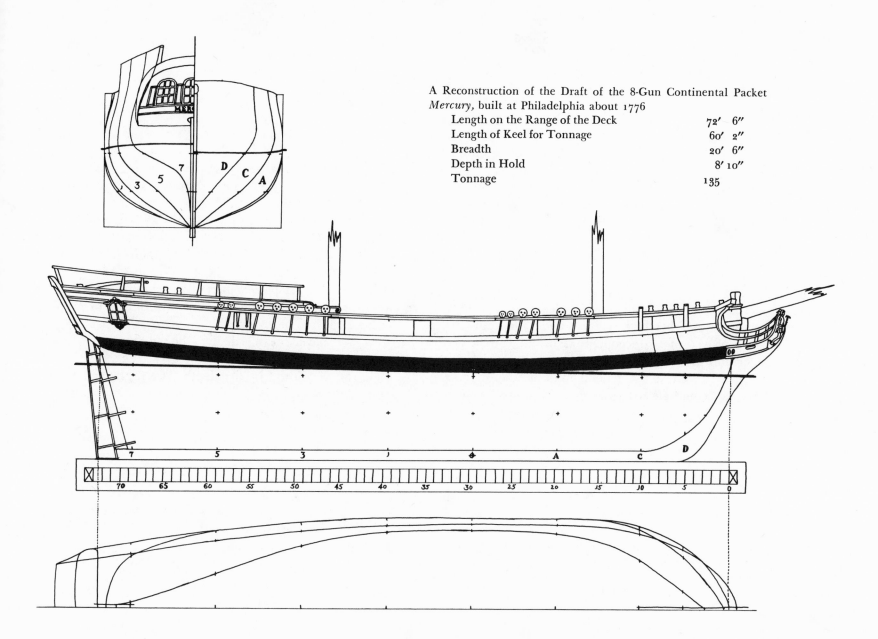

A Reconstruction of the Draft of the 8-Gun Continental Packet
Mercury, built at Philadelphia about 1776

Length on the Range of the Deck	72' 6"
Length of Keel for Tonnage	60' 2"
Breadth	20' 6"
Depth in Hold	8' 10"
Tonnage	135

MEXICO

THERE is a beautiful model at the National Maritime Museum at Greenwich of a 60-gun Spanish ship of the period of about 1730. She bears on her stern the arms of the province of Mexico, so we have decided to call her *Mexico*. She is thought to have been built out of local mahogany at Havana, Cuba, but the chaotic state of Spanish records makes it virtually impossible to conduct further research into this ship in particular, or Cuban shipbuilding in general. In fact, it is worth pointing out that both Spanish and Cuban authorities have proved most uncooperative in our search for further information.

Mexico follows the general lines of Spanish ships of her day, complete with several vertical boat fenders on her topsides, but she was obviously the result of an English shipwright working in her shipyard, as so often happened with Spanish vessels. Her figurehead had the head and upper body of a horse with the scaly lower body of a fish. Her channels were set low, after the custom of the day, and this caused considerable damage to many ships in serious storms. Her lower gun deck had a row of oarports interspersed between the gunports; one wonders how much good a few oars would be to move such a large and heavy ship.

As we have measured her, her dimensions are: length overall, 167'; length on the deck, 142'; length of keel, 115'; breadth, 40' 6"; depth, 16'; draft, 19'; tonnage, 1,000.

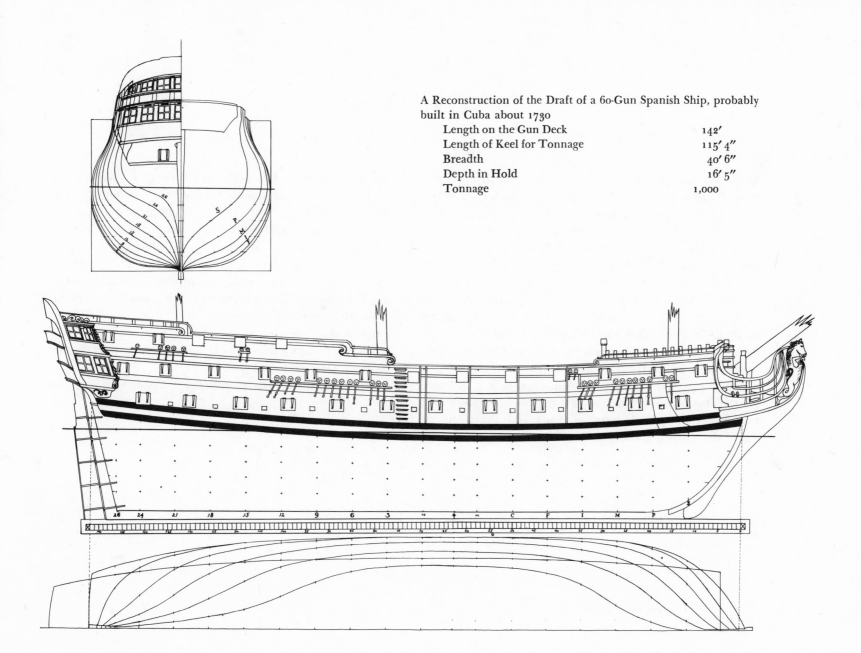

A Reconstruction of the Draft of a 60-Gun Spanish Ship, probably built in Cuba about 1730

Length on the Gun Deck	142'
Length of Keel for Tonnage	115' 4"
Breadth	40' 6"
Depth in Hold	16' 5"
Tonnage	1,000

MOHAWK

URING the Seven Years' War from 1756 to 1763, the British and the French built a number of small and medium-size warships on the Great Lakes. The first group of British vessels was built in 1756, including a 16-gun brig and a 22-gun snow that were sent out from England as kits; all were captured by the French that same year. The next group of three included the 22-gun snow *Onondaga* and the 18-gun snow *Mohawk;* these were built in 1759–60, and both were lost in an accident in 1764 after the war ended. There is a wash drawing of these two vessels in front of Oswego, New York, on Lake Ontario with Fort Ontario in the background, but the picture of *Onondaga* is not distinct enough for a reconstruction. Five more schooners and two snows were built between 1763 and 1771, and of these, the 18-gun snow *Seneca* was still going strong in 1788.

Judging from what little we know of her, the snow *Mohawk* had a fairly shallow draft with a bottom that was nearly flat. Naturally, this configuration assisted navigation in shallower or uncharted sections of the lake, but it was also adopted for another good reason: ships in the ocean had to carry several tons of drinking water, which in turn made the ships more burdensome; ships on lakes did not have to carry water because the water they were sailing in was drinkable then (will the Great Lakes ever be that pure again?), and they did not have to carry much food because they were never far from land and wild game.

Dimensions: length overall, 95' 2"; length on the deck, 77'.

A Reconstruction of the Draft of His Majesty's 18-Gun Snow
Mohawk, built at Oswego, New York, in 1759
Length on the Deck   77′

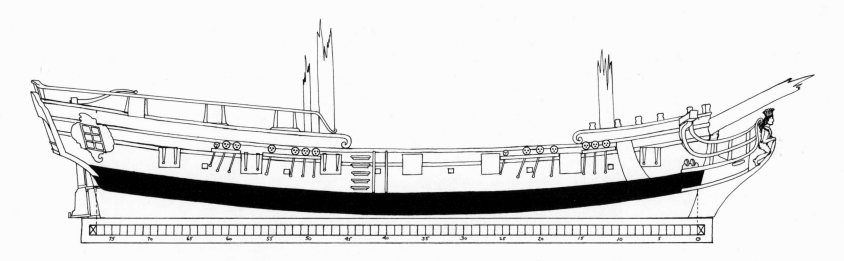

MOHAWK

In 1779 a neat little privateer ship was built at Salem, Massachusetts, to a design that was most unusual for her early date. She was placed under the command of John Carnes, but he lost her to a British ship that was not much larger. A much later picture of the engagement can be seen in the background of a portrait of Carnes in the 1790s at the Peabody Museum at Salem. The British used her in the New York area for wages and sea victualing "in conformity with Admiral Pigot's establishment" of 18 October 1782. In September 1783 she was measured at Deptford Dockyard and her lines recorded (they can be seen at the National Maritime Museum at Greenwich), and she was then prepared for sale.

She mounted up to 18 guns, probably six-pounders, on her gun deck, with provision for another 18 guns (they must have been small if fitted at all) on a flush spar deck. This is an arrangement that looks forward several years to the design of the frigate *Constitution*, and is only seen in one or two other ships in the Revolution. She had relatively steep deadrise, and was presumably a fast ship. Her bottom is known to have been copper sheathed.

Dimensions: length overall, 112′ 4″; length on the deck, 95′ 8″; length of keel, 78′ 9″; breadth, 27′; depth, 10′ 2″; draft, 12′ 3″; tonnage, 285.

Ship *Mohawk*
From an oil painting, ca. 1800
Peabody Museum, Salem, Massachusetts

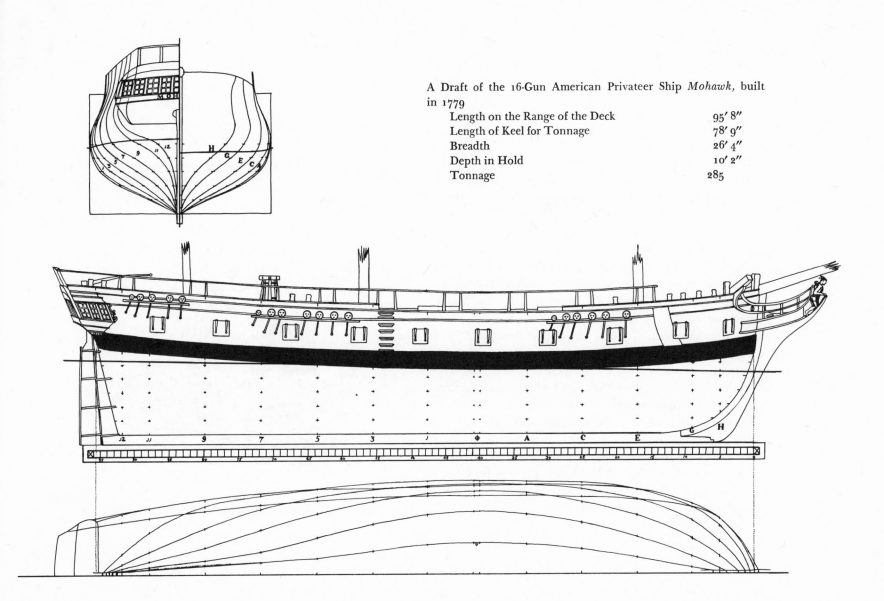

A Draft of the 16-Gun American Privateer Ship *Mohawk,* built
in 1779

Length on the Range of the Deck	95′ 8″
Length of Keel for Tonnage	78′ 9″
Breadth	26′ 4″
Depth in Hold	10′ 2″
Tonnage	285

NASSAU

THE story of the dashing pirates who operated in the Caribbean and the Indian Ocean in the period 1680–1725 is an exciting one, and has been told often. Many Americans were among the early pirates. The first Americans to enter the Indian Ocean were two pirates from Newport, Rhode Island, Thomas Tew and William Mayes, Jr. (probably no relation to the baseball player!). They were soon followed by others from New York and elsewhere, and they found that life on Madagascar was most congenial. A New York ship of some size, the 30-gun ship *Nassau*, was one of those fitted out to go to Madagascar. She left New York in 1697 under Captain Giles Shelley. One may well imagine what happened to her men when they arrived at their destination, but we can leave that for another book.

All we know about the appearance of *Nassau* is from a fine portrait of her that was engraved on the lid of a silver tankard. Judging from the shape of her quarter galleries and the design of her head, she was built to a Dutch design, but whether she was built at New York or in Holland is unknown.

As we have reconstructed her, her dimensions were: length overall, 117′; length on the deck, 96′; breadth, 28′; tonnage, 350.

Ship *Nassau*
From an engraving on the lid of a silver tankard, ca. 1700

A Reconstruction of the Draft of the 30-Gun New York Ship
Nassau, built about 1695

Length on the Range of the Deck	96′
Breadth	28′
Tonnage	350

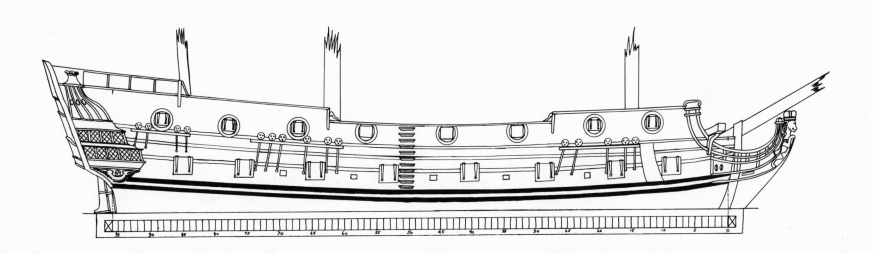

NORTHWEST AMERICA

THE first vessel constructed on the West Coast by English-speaking people was the little schooner (she was called a schooner, but she was actually a lugger) *Northwest America*. She was built in British Columbia in 1788 by the British explorer John Meares to aid him in exploring and charting the coast. Such a small vessel would be much safer for poking into uncharted bays and estuaries. Meares's regular ship was called *Felice,* and he used her as much for trading in sea otter skins as for exploring; it was already his second voyage to British Columbia.

When *Northwest America* was launched, she shot down the ways at high speed and, since no one had thought to tie a line to her, she continued some distance out into the Pacific before longboats could catch up to her. On her deck, Kaiana, a Hawaiian prince who had been traveling with Meares, danced excitedly as she slid through the water. Meares left four days later, but *Northwest America* stayed on with the other ship of Meares's expedition, *Iphigenia,* under Captain Douglas. *Northwest America* remained in the general area of her birth for a few years, experiencing a period of difficulty when Spanish authorities captured her, along with three other British vessels, in July 1789. In Spanish hands, she was renamed *Santa Gertrudis la Magna.* The matter of Spanish sovereignty in the area was not settled (it was finally resolved in Britain's favor) for another sixteen months, but the Spanish released their captives after just over a year. What happened to *Northwest America* after that is not recorded. *Adventure,* the first United States vessel to be built on the West Coast, followed in 1792, and the first Russian ship built on that coast, the *Feniks,* appeared in 1794.

As we reconstruct her, her dimensions were: length overall, 56'; length between perpendiculars, 50'; tonnage, 40.

Lugger *Northwest America*
From an anonymous watercolor painting, 1788

A Reconstruction of the Draft of the Schooner *Northwest America,*
built in British Columbia in 1788

Length between Perpendiculars	50′
Tonnage	40

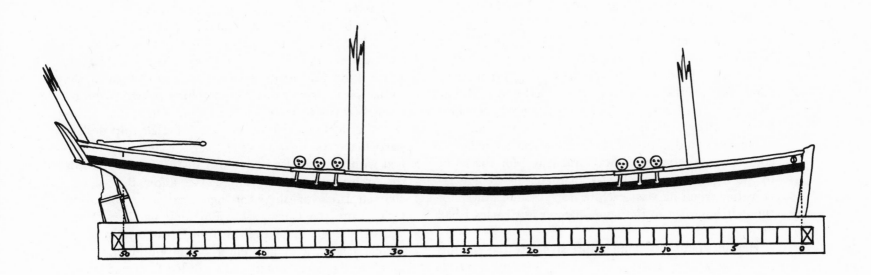

OLIVER CROMWELL

A CONSIDERABLE amount of oratory has been expended over the years concerning various ships in the American Revolution with the name of *Oliver Cromwell*. The most famous of these ships is undoubtedly the Connecticut State Navy ship, while another came from Beverly, Massachusetts, and still another, which belonged to Nicholas Brown and William Russell of Providence, was destroyed in August 1777. The ship shown here, however, was a smart-looking privateer of about 16 guns that was captured by the British corvette *Beaver* on 19 May 1777. She was subsequently renamed *Beaver's Prize,* which was not a terribly imaginative name; she could not have retained her earlier name, of course, while serving in the Royal Navy, for the name of the regicide Cromwell was anathema to George III at a time when he was reaching for absolute power for the British crown in the same manner as Charles I had done.

Harold Hahn has done impressive research on this ship, published in both *Model Shipwright* and *Nautical Research Journal.* The earliest record he has found of her shows that she was bonded as a Philadelphia privateer on 7 February 1777. Her principal owners were John Bayard and James Caldwell; her captain was Harmon Courter, and she carried 150 men in her crew. The late Marion Brewington has suggested that she had previously been a Philadelphia merchant ship called *Juno,* while V. R. Grimwood suggests that she was formerly a Rhode Island ship by the name of *Ye Terri-*

ble Creture. The figurehead of a lady could represent either of those former names, the latter being of course the first owner's wife, a joke entirely in keeping with humor of the Colonial period.

Our own opinion, and it is no more than that, is that she was built at Providence about 1774. At the end of 1776, Narragansett Bay was occupied by a powerful British garrison and fleet at Newport which would have made it too difficult to sail her in or out of Providence, so she was transferred to Philadelphia ownership and renamed *Oliver Cromwell* at that time. One piece of circumstantial support for this theory is that ship design, particularly for major vessels, can be as easily identified with a particular region as can furniture design or the architecture of buildings. We know the general characteristics of ships of her size and type from Charleston, the Chesapeake, Philadelphia, New York, and New England, as well as from Great Britain. Only Rhode Island, a major center of shipbuilding, is left blank in the documented and recorded designs of ships. This *Oliver Cromwell* is completely different in many ways from ships of all the areas mentioned above. It seems very likely that she represents the Rhode Island type, as might *Cupid,* which is more closely related to her than to any other ship (*Cupid* has no documented association with any geographical area). It is because of this that we have gone out on a limb and reconstructed the appearance of three other important Rhode Island ships (the frigates *Warren* and *Providence,* and

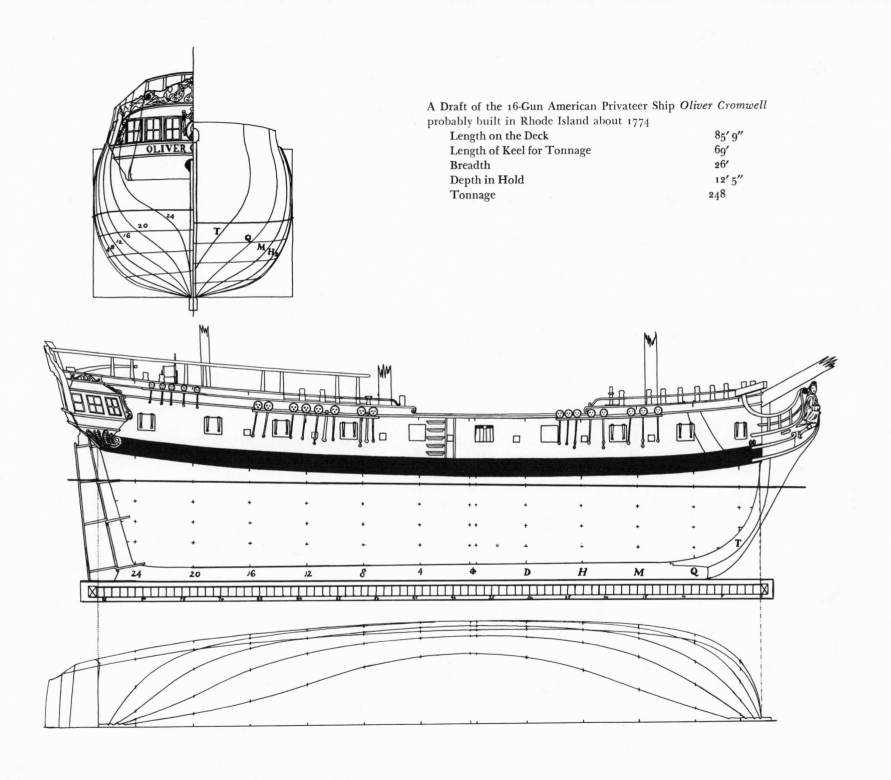

A Draft of the 16-Gun American Privateer Ship *Oliver Cromwell*
probably built in Rhode Island about 1774

Length on the Deck	85′ 9″
Length of Keel for Tonnage	69′
Breadth	26′
Depth in Hold	12′ 5″
Tonnage	248

the corvette *General Washington*) with no more than their recorded dimensions and some crude pictures to go by, other than the lines of *Oliver Cromwell*.

Oliver Cromwell's lines, among the handsomest ever recorded by the British Admiralty, are on file at the National Maritime Museum at Greenwich. We have reconstructed portions of her rail that we believe was shot away and never replaced after her capture. She was probably originally steered only with a tiller, but a wheel was added later, which we show. Her rudder post was so close to her tafferel that the center window of the stern was omitted, and a bust, possibly of Cromwell, was placed there in its stead. Her capstan was located in the waist, so the British added a second one (a two-decker) in their favorite place on the quarter-deck. She was fitted with port lids for all her gunports, even in the waist. She had a full-bodied hull for carrying a lot of cargo or supplies, but her ends were fine enough to give her a moderate turn of speed (British records say that she was slow, but she also had a foul bottom at that time). An unusual feature was the extra decorative rail in the head, also found on *Cupid* and a few others. At the time of her capture she was obviously overloaded, for she is reported to have been mounting a total of 24 carriage guns in addition to a number of swivels and cohorns; the carriage guns were 12 nine-pounders, 6 six-pounders, and 6 four-pounders. The British, who stated that her guns were worthless, refitted her with first 12 six-pounders and eventually 16 six-pounders.

This miniature frigate, for so she was, sailed from Philadelphia in 1777 to cruise in the West Indies. She captured a number of prizes there, but was herself captured off the island of St. Lucia a few weeks later. Her unruly crew, composed largely of foreigners, was blamed for her capture. She was taken to England where she served as a convoy guard, and was temporarily assigned to the convoy guarded by *Serapis* and *Countess of Scarborough* that was so notably attacked by John Paul Jones, but she had been reassigned just before that incident. She was sent to Goree, Senegal, in Africa, with a convoy, and then found her way back to the West Indies where she was wrecked in a terrible hurricane on 11 October 1780. The location of her wreck, recently discovered by an underwater archaeological team, is close to Vieux-Fort, St. Lucia, less than ten miles from the scene of her capture some three years earlier.

Dimensions: length overall, 101' 7"; length on the deck, 85' 9"; length of keel, 69'; breadth, 26'; depth, 12' 5"; draft, 12' 8"; tonnage, 248.

ONTARIO

DURING the American Revolution the British felt it necessary to strengthen their forces on the Great Lakes by building a 16-gun brig called *Ontario*. She was launched at Carleton Island on the Canadian side of Lake Ontario on 10 May 1780. She did not last long, for she foundered on 1 November 1780 in one of those sudden Great Lakes winter storms. She had the shallow draft common to all lake vessels. Her stern was unusual for such a small vessel in having quarter galleries, and her bow was unusual for the period in that it had only a billet head instead of a figurehead. Her lines are preserved at the National Maritime Museum, Greenwich.

Dimensions: length overall, 95′ 3″; length on the deck, 79′ 9″; length of keel, 68′; breadth, 24′ 4″; depth, 7′ 9″; draft, 7′ 8″; tonnage, 187.

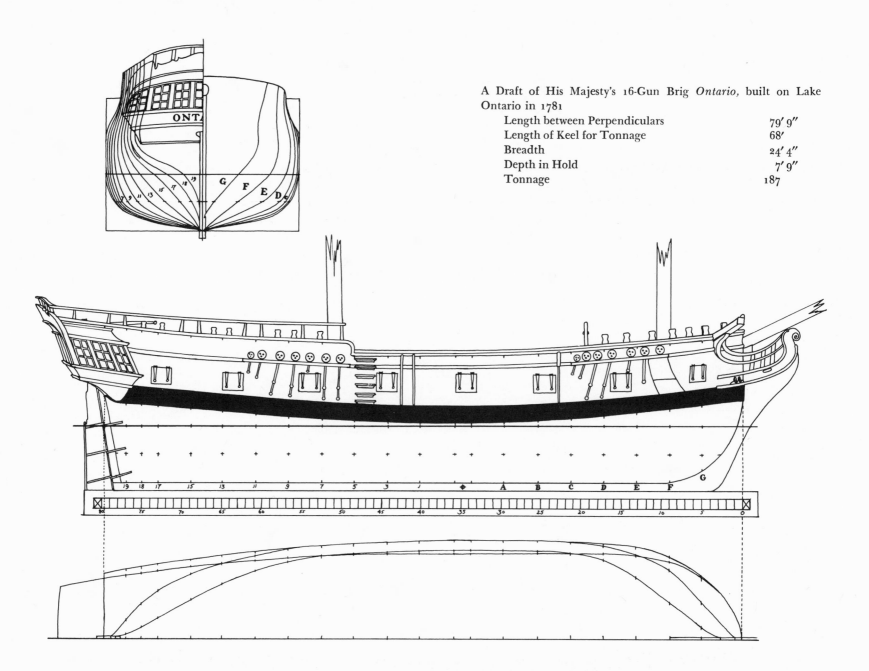

A Draft of His Majesty's 16-Gun Brig *Ontario,* built on Lake
Ontario in 1781

Length between Perpendiculars	79' 9"
Length of Keel for Tonnage	68'
Breadth	24' 4"
Depth in Hold	7' 9"
Tonnage	187

L'ORIGINAL

IT is not generally known that the French built some substantial warships in Quebec in the 1740s and 1750s (for a complete list of these ships, see the description of the frigate *L'Abenakise*). Of all these ships, however, very little in the way of descriptive records remains: a partial drawing of the lines of *L'Abenakise* at the National Maritime Museum at Greenwich, England, and a list of the names and types of the other ships. Monsieur Jean Boudriot of Paris, the world's leading authority on eighteenth-century French ships, writes "I am very embarrassed to have to say that information on these warships constructed in Canada is non-existent, at least as far as my research in the French Archives is concerned."

We know that *L'Original* was built at Quebèc in 1750 and that she mounted 70 guns, but we know nothing more. Accordingly, because this ship is so important to the history of American ships of this period, we have reconstructed her appearance by taking the dimensions and designs of other French 70-gun ships of this period and crossing them with various "local" features from the design of *L'Abenakise,* and we have done the same thing with two other French-Canadian ships, *Le Saint-Laurent* and *Le Québec.* As we see her: length overall, 196' 8"; length on the lower deck, 166'; tonnage, about 1,600.

Notice that the upper gun deck has no gunport lids; this was a typical French feature, and one wonders what they did in the winter. Also, notice the row of windows just forward of the Great Cabin; the French were very particular about the comfort of their officers, and these windows, which were never used as gunports, represent the location of "l'État Major" or "officers' country."

A Reconstruction of the Draft of the 70-Gun Ship *L'Original,* built at Quebec for the French Navy in 1750

Length on the Gun Deck	166'
Tonnage	1,600

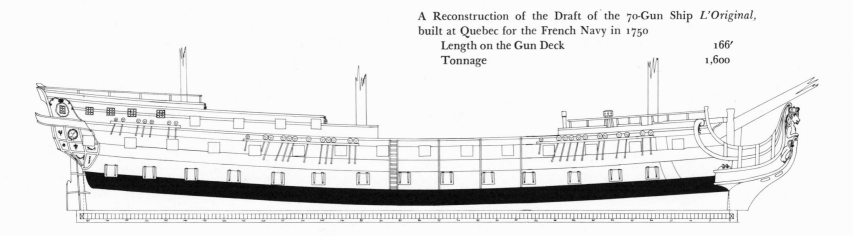

L'OUTAOUAISE

THE French and the British both built a number of small warships for service on the Great Lakes, Lake Champlain, and the St. Lawrence River in the mid-eighteenth century. One such craft was presumably built at Quebec shortly before 1760 and fitted with 18 carriage guns, probably four-pounders or six-pounders. Her name was *L'Outaouaise,* which means "girl from the Ottawa tribe," one of the lesser Algonquin tribes. She was rigged as a brig, or possibly as a snow, and was stationed in the St. Lawrence about a third of the way from Lake Ontario to Montreal near Fort La Galette (now Ogdensburg, New York) in 1760 in an effort to block Major General Jeffery Amherst's advance toward Montreal from the west. Amherst had cleverly built at least four galleys each armed with a twelve-pounder, and he used their superior mobility to capture the French warship, thus leaving the way open to Montreal. A painting of the battle by British military artist Thomas Davies can be seen at the National Gallery of Canada in Ottawa. No record of what happened to the brig after her capture seems to have survived, nor do we know her dimensions. However, judging from the painting, she appears to have been about 98' 6" in length overall and 84' in length between perpendiculars. Her shallow draft and flat bottom would have made her suited for only inland waters such as the St. Lawrence, so she may have continued on guard duty in the Montreal area under a new nationality.

French Brig *l'Outaouaise* being captured by British galleys
in the St. Lawrence River in 1760
From a watercolor by Thomas Davies
National Gallery of Canada, Ottawa

A Reconstruction of the 18-Gun French Brig *L'Outaouaise,* built
in Quebec about 1757
    Length between Perpendiculars   84'

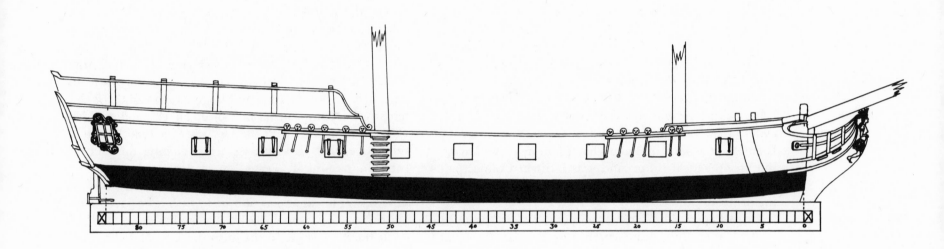

PERSEVERANCE

Surprising as it may seem, the period covered by this book contains a great many of the advances in maritime affairs that were not actually to bear fruit until much later. For example, fast sailing vessels, with sharp lines were being produced in the 1770s and 1780s, long before the clipper ships; one of the greatest improvements in gunnery, the carronade, was introduced in 1779; the first American ship to circumnavigate the globe was *Columbia;* the first vessel to be built by English-speaking people on the West Coast was the *Northwest America* of 1788; centerboards were invented by Lieutenant Schank on Lake Champlain in 1776; *Turtle,* the first practical submarine, was built in Connecticut in 1775. Another advance of the period was the harnessing of steam power.

Denis Papin of France first proposed a steam-powered boat in 1700, but steam engines of the day were not powerful enough to use, and jealous contemporaries destroyed his boat before he could try it out. John Hull in England built a functional stern-wheeler powered by steam in 1732, but it had problems. After the invention of Watt's improved steam engine of 1770, the comte de Follenay and the comte d'Auxiron collaborated to build a steamboat, but it too was sabotaged and sunk in the River Seine. In 1783 Comte Jouffrey d'Abbans operated his *Pyroscaphe* on the Saône River for fifteen minutes against the current, but the Academy of Sciences, which was more interested in Montgolfier's balloon projects, forced him to drop his experiments.

But all this work in Europe had not gone unnoticed in America. As early as the 1760s industrialist William Henry tried to launch a steamboat on the Conestoga River, and in 1783 John Fitch of Philadelphia began a series of experiments that would lead to several steamboats. His first design was for a boat with twelve paddles, in two banks of three on each side of the boat; the boat, which he intended to name *Perseverance,* was to have been about 34′ long and large enough to carry passengers. It seems that he first built an 18′ model which worked satisfactorily on the Delaware in 1786, and it is this model that we show; we are stretching the point a little in naming it *Perseverance,* for it was just the model for *Perseverance. Perseverance* herself was to have been put into operation in 1791, but he gave up on her in favor of another design that he had been working on at the same time. In the meantime, he had also built a larger side-paddle boat, 45′ long and 8′ wide, begun in August 1786, but little is known about this.

His first boat of a different design was launched in 1788; this was 60′ long and 12′ wide, and had its paddles arranged like a duck's feet aft of the stern. He operated this boat as a packet between Philadelphia and Trenton for about four months in 1790, but operations were never resumed again, perhaps a reflection on the excessive maintenance required for such crude machinery. This vessel was named *Experiment.* He built still another boat in 1790 on the duck-feet principles, but it was wrecked before its trials and never repaired. Fitch

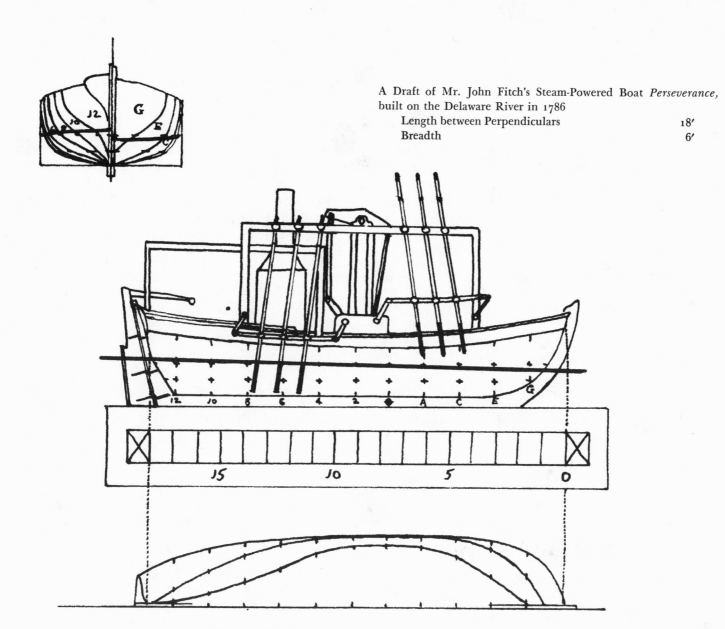

A Draft of Mr. John Fitch's Steam-Powered Boat *Perseverance,*
built on the Delaware River in 1786
     Length between Perpendiculars   18′
     Breadth   6′

was unstable and always in trouble; he committed suicide in 1798 in the midst of great poverty, but others followed after him and made the United States a leader in the development of steam. We do not show a drawing of any of Fitch's duck-paddle models.

At the same time as Fitch's experiments, James Rumsey of Berkeley Springs, Virginia, was developing his own steamboat. He began it in 1787 (some say 1784, but they are confusing it with a manual-powered vessel) and ran it in the Potomac River in 1788. It had a high-pressure "flash" boiler (very dangerous when one considers how little was known about metal strengths at that time), and the steam engine operated a water pump that sent a stream of water out of the stern—the first water-jet boat. The boat was considered a success, so Rumsey went to England to build another boat there, but he died before it was finished. His backers completed it and ran it in the Thames, but it was not impressive enough to continue the experiments. Not enough reliable information exists about either of Rumsey's boats to justify a drawing in this book.

In 1792, engineer Elijah Ormsbee took a steamboat against a strong current from Providence, Rhode Island, to Pawtucket, and he was followed by Oliver Evans, John Stevens, and Robert Fulton in Philadelphia and New York.

POLLY

NEAR the northeasternmost point of Maine is a village
(now it is larger than a village) called Machias.
The people of Machias proudly believe, as do inhabitants of many other communities, that their town was
the location of the first naval battle of the Revolution. These claims will no doubt be debated for years
to come, but here is what happened. A tiny (although
some say she was 100 tons, she was actually 35 tons)
British armed schooner called *Margaretta* had come to
Machias to escort some large sloops loaded with lumber
to Boston or Halifax. News of Concord and Lexington
had excited the inhabitants and they resolved to capture the schooner. They set off on two sloops, *Unity*
and *Polly,* after the fleeing *Margaretta;* the British
schooner was armed with some small cannons while
the American sloops had a few muskets, pitchforks,
and scythes, and a lot of courage. *Polly* ran aground,
leaving *Unity* to catch the schooner. Jeremiah O'Brien
led the boarding party, and *Margaretta* was captured
on 12 June 1775. The schooner being both small and
slow, the citizens of Machias decided to take the cannons off her and mount them on *Polly,* renaming *Polly*
for the occasion *Machias Liberty* (some accounts say
that it was *Unity* that was so used, but recent evidence
indicates that it was *Polly*).

Polly was immediately used to capture two small
British craft called *Diligent* and *Tattamagouche* that
were being used to make measurements for a new atlas
of North America. Fearing British reprisals after these
bold captures, Machias sent representatives to the Massachusetts General Court (Maine was then part of Massachusetts) to petition for support. At the end of August
the legislature voted to accept *Machias Liberty* and *Diligent* as the first commissioned ships of the Massachusetts
Navy.

Evidence as to the appearance of any of these vessels
is scant, but one contemporary portrait of *Polly* survives; the prisoners captured at Machias were taken for
arraignment at the Pownalborough Court House in

Sloop *Polly*
From a primitive carving on wood
Pownalborough Court House, Dresden, Maine

A Reconstruction of the Draft of the American Timber Sloop
Polly, built in New England about 1770

Length between Perpendiculars	58'
Tonnage	90

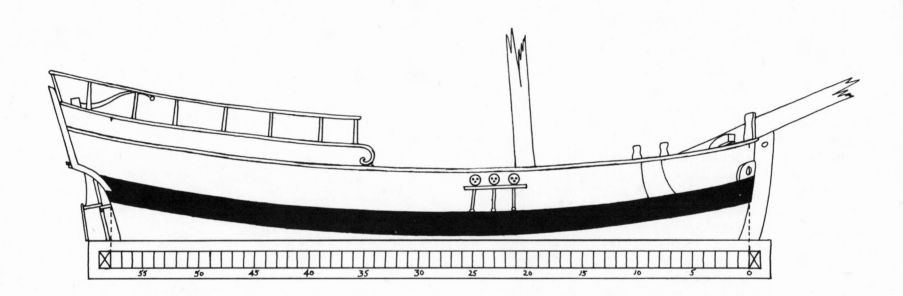

Dresden, and either one of the prisoners or one of the guards took a penknife and scratched a crude picture of *Polly* on the wall paneling. It shows that she was a standard lumber sloop, having a square-tuck stern with a large port in it to one side of the rudder for loading timber. She is shown flying a striped flag for a jack and another striped flag for an ensign at the top of the mast. She set a square topsail for going downwind. We also know that she measured 90 tons. We believe that her length overall would have been about 65' 9", and her length between perpendiculars, 58'.

POSTILLION

Among the watercolor sketches of various ships that Ashley Bowen of Marblehead executed during the course of his travels is a series showing the ship *Postillion* of Salem, Massachusetts. *Postillion* was a merchant ship built about 1780 and armed with 12 guns. We know very little about her except that on 28 January 1781 she ran into a serious storm. Her masts and rigging were cut away, but it was too late. She capsized and later sank, but her crew were fortunate and were able to row to safety. The paintings are on file at the Peabody Museum at Salem.

She seems to have been a typical armed merchant ship of the period. Our reconstruction was naturally based on the paintings, and for that reason we may have placed the main and mizzenmasts too far forward for good balance.

Dimensions: length overall, 80' 2"; length between perpendiculars, 66'; tonnage, about 125.

A Reconstruction of the Draft of the 12-Gun American Merchant Ship *Postillion* of Salem, Massachusetts, built about 1780
Length between Perpendiculars   66'

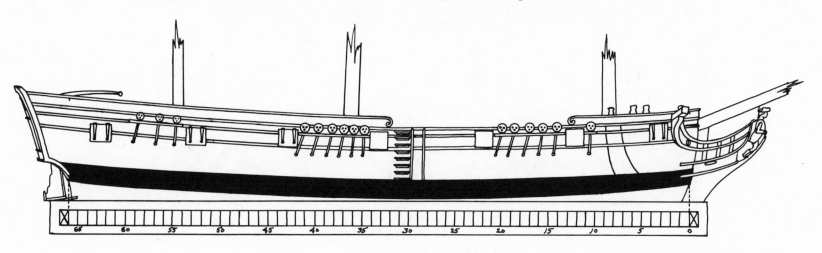

PROVIDENCE, *a Sloop*

THE sloop *Katy* was built at Providence, Rhode Island about 1768 for wealthy merchant John Brown. He used her briefly for whaling, and may have used her in the slave trade. When the Rhode Island General Assembly voted to found the first navy of any of the Colonies during the Revolution on 12 June 1775, *Katy* was chartered as the flagship of the Rhode Island Navy, and her captain, Abraham Whipple, was appointed commodore. Three days later, on 15 June, she captured the British sloop *Diana* in what must be considered the first act of war committed by any American Colony against Great Britain on the water. At this time, she was armed with 10 four-pounders, all on the main deck.

Her main job was to harass the 24-gun British frigate *Rose,* that had effectively put an end to Rhode Island's main industry of smuggling. But August, the General Assembly concluded that it needed outside help to get rid of the *Rose,* and on 26 August it voted to instruct its delegates at the Continental Congress to introduce a bill to create the Continental Navy. The bill passed on 13 October 1775, and written into the bill was authorization by Congress to purchase *Katy* and one other vessel. The other vessel was not available, so *Katy* was thus the first vessel authorized for the Continental Navy, even though she was not actually commissioned until December. In the meantime, she was sent to Bermuda on a fruitless mission to seize some gunpowder.

When she was taken into the navy, she was renamed *Providence.* (There were three vessels in Continental service in 1776 by the name of *Providence:* the sloop, the 28-gun frigate, and a gondola on Lake Champlain. No doubt this caused great confusion to friend and foe alike, as it does to historians.) *Providence* was rearmed and given 12 carriage guns, some or all of them being six-pounders, and 10 swivels; she had 8 carriage guns on the maindeck and 4 on the quarterdeck. Her new captain was John Hazard of Philadelphia. She took part in the expedition against Nassau in March 1776, and since she had a shallower draft than the rest of the fleet she was able to get close enough to the beach to land the marines in their first amphibious landing. After her

Sloop *Providence*
From an oil painting by Francis Holman, 1777
Private collection, Providence, Rhode Island

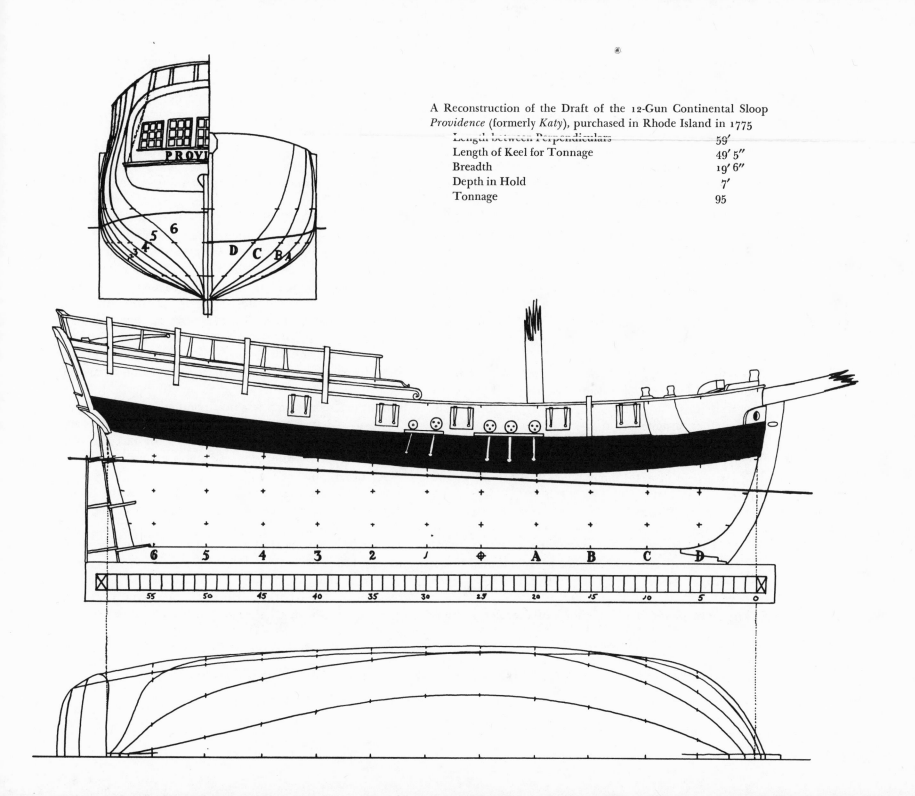

A Reconstruction of the Draft of the 12-Gun Continental Sloop
Providence (formerly *Katy*), purchased in Rhode Island in 1775

Length between Perpendiculars	59'
Length of Keel for Tonnage	49' 5"
Breadth	19' 6"
Depth in Hold	7'
Tonnage	95

return to Rhode Island she became the first command of John Paul Jones, on 10 May 1776; Hazard had been dismissed.

Jones used her aggressively, capturing over sixteen prizes in six months before he was promoted to captain of *Alfred*. Her next captain was Hoysted Hacker of Rhode Island, and he cruised for a while in company with Jones before returning to Providence just in time to be bottled up by the British occupation of Newport a few days later.

Her command then passed to John Peck Rathbun of Rhode Island, and the nimble *Providence* dodged British patrols and escaped to Charleston. From there Rathbun took her to Nassau, which the *Providence* captured once more, but this time single-handedly with 50 men in her crew. She also released American prisoners held there and captured nearly a ton of gunpowder along with five ships and a big supply of muskets; the date was 28 January 1778. In 1779 she was once more commanded by Hacker, and on 7 May she captured the 12-gun British navy brig *Diligent* off Newfoundland. She was then assigned to the expedition to the Penobscot Bay in Maine. When a British force appeared off the bay, the American vessels all fled up the bay and their crews set fire to them when they could go no further. That could be the end of the story of the "lucky" sloop *Providence,* for her crew reported that they had indeed set her on fire on 15 August, but one record of the Royal Navy states that she was captured and taken into the Royal Navy for a few months; if this is so, perhaps the fire went out without doing her much damage.

The only pictorial descriptions of the sloop *Provi-dence* are in an oil painting, dated 1777, by Francis Holman (it is from that painting, now in a private collection, that we have reconstructed her lines), and in a grisaille in the Franklin D. Roosevelt Collection at Hyde Park. New York, that purports to be *Alfred* capturing *Mellish;* the artist, who obtained his information from a primitive sketch presumably made on the scene, mistakenly transposed the flags on the two vessels, thus leading to the incorrect identification of the scene. Before World War II, a ship model club, of which Howard Chapelle was a member, developed a speculative set of plans of her from which many models were made. There is one of these models at each of the following (not a complete list): the Mariners Museum, Newport News, Virginia; the Boston Museum of Fine Arts; the Phillips Andover Academy Museum, Andover, Massachusetts; the Rhode Island Historical Society, Providence; the Bristol Historical Society, Rhode Island. The model turns out to be quite inaccurate in the stern and quarterdeck, but otherwise acceptable except for the dolphin striker, which was not invented until the 1790s. We know that she was a fast ship, which is partly attributable to her design and partly to the fact that she had a copper bottom, a rarity among American ships.

A "biography" of the sloop *Providence,* called *Valour Fore & Aft,* by Hope Rider, was published by the Naval Institute Press in 1976. This book appeared at the same time as a full-sized copy of the sloop *Providence* was launched in Newport. The new *Providence* has proved to be a fast sailer.

Her dimensions, as we reconstruct her, were: length overall, 67′ 6″; length on the deck, 59′; length of keel, 49′ 5″; breadth, 19′ 6″; depth, 7′; draft, 9′; tonnage, 95.

PROVIDENCE, *a Frigate*

THE 28-gun frigate *Providence* was built at Providence, Rhode Island, in 1776 as one of the original thirteen frigates ordered by Congress late in 1775. She was built by Talman and Bowers, and in spite of the accuracy of the charge made by Esek Hopkins that the supervisory committee had diverted supplies for the frigates *Providence* and *Warren* to equip the privateers belonging to members of the committee, the two frigates were launched before those in any of the other Colonies. *Providence* was launched second, on 18 May 1776, and the ever-generous committee voted to appropriate $50 for the entertainment of the shipwrights.

Abraham Whipple, one of Rhode Island's favorite sons, was made her captain, and she was armed with a mixture of twelve-pounders and eighteen-pounders, which made her more powerful than any other frigate of her rate in the world. Nevertheless, she did not get to sea for almost a year after her launching because a British fleet had occupied the mouth of Narragansett Bay. Whipple made a run for it on the night of 30 April 1777 with 170 men in the crew (not quite full strength), and escaped after a damaging battle with the 32-gun frigate *Lark*. Whipple arrived at Nantes, France, on 26 May, joining *Boston* and *Ranger*.

The three of them finally left St. Nazaire, France, on 26 September 1778, arriving at Boston before Christmas. There they and three other frigates sat for several months with no crew and few supplies. In the summer *Providence* left on a cruise with *Queen of France* and *Ranger*. On 18 July 1778, while in a thick fog off Newfoundland, they had the good fortune to run into a sixty-ship convoy from Jamaica bound for London, and guarded by one two-decker and some smaller ships. They carefully surprised and cut out eleven transports (of which three were later recaptured). The prize money realized from this escapade came to over $1 million, which made it the most lucrative cruise made by the Continental Navy in the whole war.

Late that year, *Providence* was ordered to Charleston, South Carolina, in company with *Boston, Ranger,* and the rotten *Queen of France* (a 28-gun frigate that had

Frigate *Providence*
From a powderhorn engraving made for Charles Hewitt, 1777
Private collection, New Jersey

[223]

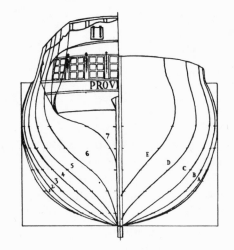

A Reconstruction of the Draft for the 28-Gun Continental Frigate
Providence, built at Providence, Rhode Island, in 1776

Length between Perpendiculars	124' 4"
Length of Keel for Tonnage	102' 8½"
Breadth	33' 10⅜"
Depth in Hold	10' 8"
Tonnage	632

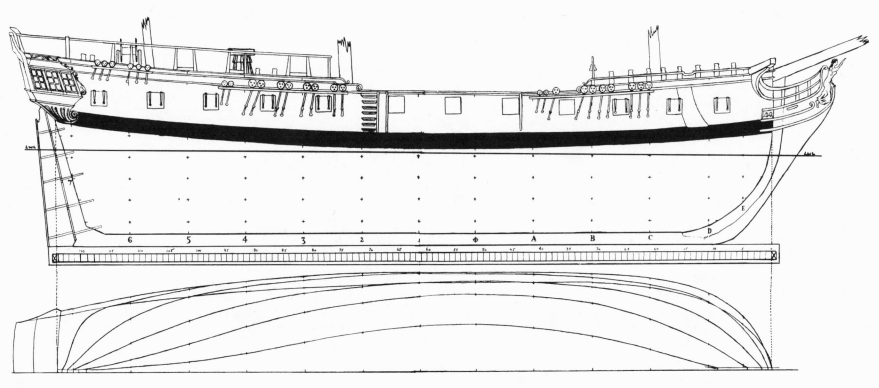

been purchased from the French in 1777 after the French navy had no further use for her; she probably looked very much like the French frigate *La Sirenne* which can be seen elsewhere in this book). Their job was to assist the South Carolina Navy ships *La Bricole,* 44 guns, and *La Truite,* 26 guns (these ships had also been obtained from the French; *La Bricole* was a retired East Indiaman very similar to *Bonhomme Richard,* and *La Truite* was almost identical to *Queen of France*), in defending Charleston against a massive British invasion. *Queen of France* was sunk in an attempt to block the entrance of the harbor, but the others were all captured when the city had to capitulate on 12 May 1780. *Providence* was taken into the Royal Navy with no change of name and was sold out of the service after the war on 11 March 1784.

The British recorded *Providence*'s dimensions, but if her lines were taken off, they have not been found. There is one crude engraving of her on a powderhorn, dated 1777, and she is also possibly the ship in the background of Savage's portrait of Whipple (dated 1786), which means little since Savage probably never saw her. Our reconstruction, then, is based on the British dimensions and on an enlargement of the plans of the privateer *Oliver Cromwell* which we believe to have been designed by the same man.

Dimensions: length overall, 144'; length on the deck, 127'; length of keel, 102' 8"; breadth, 33' 8"; depth in hold, 10' 5"; draft, 16' 5"; tonnage, 632. (She was not built to the official design that was approved by Congress because those designs did not arrive in time.)

LE QUÉBEC

A NUMBER of warships of different sizes were built in Quebec for the French navy in the 1740s and 1750s (for a list of these, see the descriptive text for the frigate *L'Abenakise*), but unfortunately Monsieur Jean Boudriot, the greatest expert on eighteenth-century French ships, can find absolutely no information about any of these ships in the French Archives.

One of them was the 32-gun frigate *Le Québec;* all we know about her is that she was built in Quebec in 1757. Because of her obvious importance to the history of American ships in the eighteenth century, we have attempted to reconstruct her appearance, based on the lines of other French frigates of the same date and based on the known appearance of the larger frigate *L'Abenakise,* which had been built in the same shipyard the previous year. *L'Abenakise* had a double-decked stern, like an East Indiaman, and although this was virtually never seen on British or American frigates it seems to have been fairly common on French frigates of this period, so we have given *Le Québec* the same kind of stern. The French were quite particular about the comfort of their officers, and this kind of stern added to their comfort.

As we see her, she measured as follows: length overall, 152′ 2″; length on the gun deck, 130′; tonnage, about 660.

A Reconstruction of the Draft of the 32-Gun Frigate *Le Québec,* built for the French Navy at Quebec in 1757

| Length on the Gun Deck | 130′ |
| Tonnage | 660 |

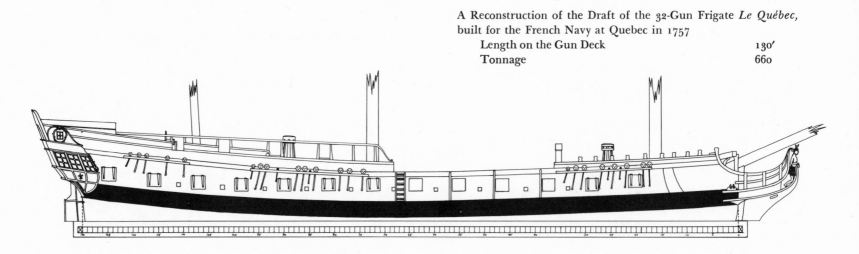

RACEHORSE

AMONG the watercolor sketches of eighteenth-century ships painted by Ashley Bowen and on file at Salem, Massachusetts, is one of the Rhode Island sloop *Racehorse*. She was probably built about 1750, and was registered at Providence. She appears to have been typical of the Rhode Island sloops that carried the bulk of illegal American trade before the Revolution and also served as the Atlantic world's tramps. Although we have no picture of the Rhode Island sloop *Fly*, which was a member of the first Continental fleet, she probably looked very much like *Racehorse*.

Dimensions: length overall, 66′ 2″; length between perpendiculars, 56′; tonnage, 80.

A Reconstruction of the Draft of the Sloop *Racehorse* of Providence, Rhode Island, built about 1750
Length between Perpendiculars   56′

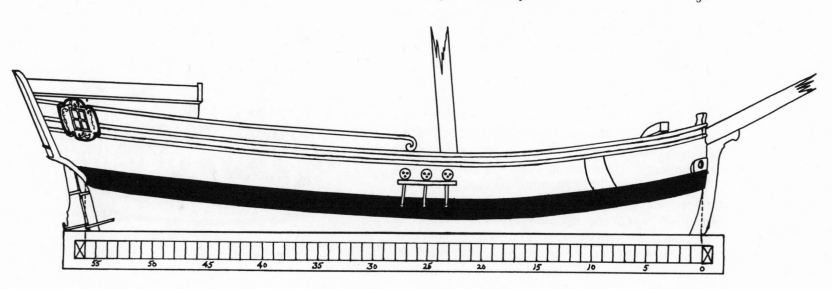

RALEIGH

THE 32-gun frigate *Raleigh* was built by the Hackett family at Portsmouth, New Hampshire. She was named after the Elizabethan sea dog and launched on 21 May 1776 after the incredibly short time of only sixty days. She was one of the original thirteen frigates authorized by Congress in 1775, but the official plans approved by Congress did not reach the wilderness of New Hampshire in time, so she was built to plans drawn by the local shipwrights. Due to shortages of men and material she did not get to sea until 1777, when she was commanded by Captain Thomas Thompson. Although short of cannons, she left in mid-August in company with *Alfred,* and they soon ran into a British convoy guarded by a group of converted merchantmen, including *Druid and Grasshopper* (both American built). *Raleigh* made a poor showing in her attack on the convoy, and the two ships arrived at Lorient, France, on 7 October.

As soon as she had acquired all the cannons she needed in France, *Raleigh* set sail for home again, still in company with *Alfred.* On 9 March 1778 they engaged two British warships of very small force near the West Indies, and *Raleigh* ignominiously fled, leaving *Alfred* to be taken. Thompson was relieved of his command as soon as he arrived in Boston in April, and John Barry was made her new captain. *Raleigh* left Boston on 25 September 1778, but only a few hours out she was chased by the 20-gun frigate *Unicorn* and the 50-gun ship *Experiment. Raleigh* quickly lost parts of her fore- and mainmasts, so Barry ran her onto the rocks of the Maine coast and escaped with a third of his men. The next day the British pulled the ship off and sent her to England. She was taken into the Royal Navy, and her plans were drawn in a royal dockyard; these plans survive today at the National Maritime Museum at Greenwich. She took part in the British expedition to Charleston, South Carolina, in 1780, and remained in the Royal Navy until the end of the war, when she was sold on 17 July 1783.

Raleigh had a round bow with no trace of a beakhead bulkhead. Her wale was unusually low, and she

Frigate *Raleigh*
From an engraving by Baugean, 18th century
Le Musée de la Marine, Paris

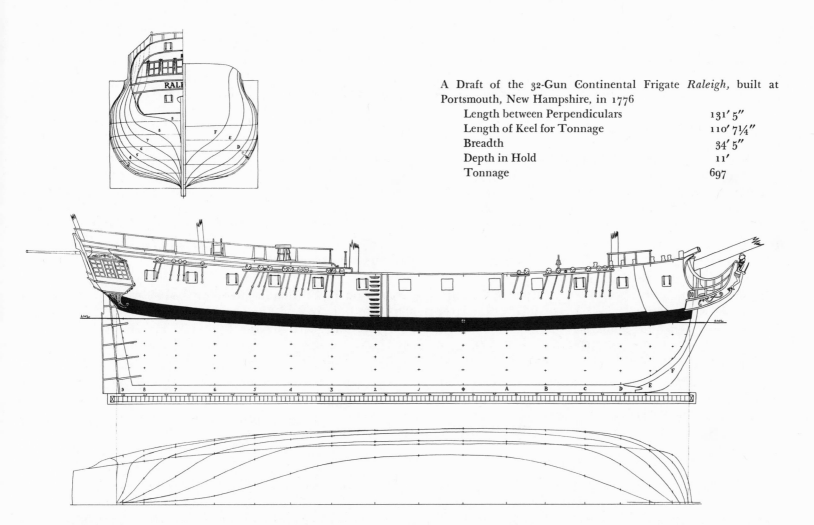

A Draft of the 32-Gun Continental Frigate *Raleigh*, built at Portsmouth, New Hampshire, in 1776

Length between Perpendiculars	131′ 5″
Length of Keel for Tonnage	110′ 7¼″
Breadth	34′ 5″
Depth in Hold	11′
Tonnage	697

had no moldings along her topsides above the gunports as other frigates usually did. Like *Hancock* and *Boston,* she had a small lateen sail set on the ensign staff for steadying her. An engraving by the French artist Baugean is one of only two known contemporary portraits of her; Baugean was only fourteen years old when *Raleigh* was in France, so he must have made his engraving later in life from a sketch made in 1778 either by him or by another artist. The other portrait is a watercolor by Nicolas Ozanne.

Dimensions: length overall, 154′ 5″; length on the deck, 131′ 5″; length of keel, 110′ 7″; breadth, 34′ 5″; depth, 11′; draft, 16′ 6″; tonnage, 697.

RANDOLPH *and* WASHINGTON

Two of the original 32-gun frigates authorized by Congress for the Continental Navy in 1775 were constructed at Philadelphia: the *Randolph* was built by Wharton & Humphreys and the *Washington* was built by the Eyre shipyard, both to the official design approved by Congress. *Washington* was launched in November 1776, and most accounts say that she was not completed before the British occupied the Delaware River area; her captain was Thomas Read of Pennsylvania. She is reported to have been scuttled in the river just above Philadelphia about 20 November 1777, without ever having been used. However, a French map of British operations on the Delaware clearly shows "*Le Washington,* frégate" at anchor just above the point where the Schuylkyll joins the Delaware, which may indicate that she was used briefly to confront a possible British breakthrough on the river early in the campaign.

She was scuttled with the 28-gun frigate *Effingham* at Bordentown Creek, but both were raised again to serve as floating barracks for 400 men. When the British made a raid up the river in May 1778, the two frigates were burned to prevent capture.

As for *Randolph,* her career was more interesting but hardly less tragic. She was launched on 16 July 1776 and assigned to Captain Nicholas Biddle of Philadelphia. On 13 January 1777, she escaped through the British blockade of the Delaware with only half her complement of crew to go on a cruise with *Fly* and *Hornet.* However, she was seriously damaged by a storm off Cape Hatteras, so she put in to Charleston, South Carolina, for repairs. In July she was ordered to sail in search of a convoy from Jamaica and returned in September with but three prizes. She was hove down for a bottom cleaning and then departed for France; she arrived at Lorient in December.

Early in 1778 she returned to Charleston, and then set sail on 12 February with a small squadron into the West Indies. Around 8:00 P.M. (after dark) on 7 March they were engaged by the 64-gun ship *Yarmouth* off Barbados. *Randolph* gave a good accounting of herself for about twenty minutes, apparently inflicting considerable damage on her much larger adversary. Suddenly, a spark got into her magazine and she blew up with a tremendous explosion. There were only four survivors, and they were miraculously picked up five days later by *Yarmouth* as she cruised through the same waters once more. One of the biggest tragedies of this incident was the loss of Nicholas Biddle, who probably had better qualifications than any other captain in the Continental Navy; among other things, he had served in the Royal Navy as a midshipman, and had been a messmate of the young Nelson.

Randolph's plans are the only original plans approved by Congress to survive of any of the first frigates. The plans were not followed exactly, for accounts were written of the alterations that were made. Our plans reflect these alterations as far as possible, as set down

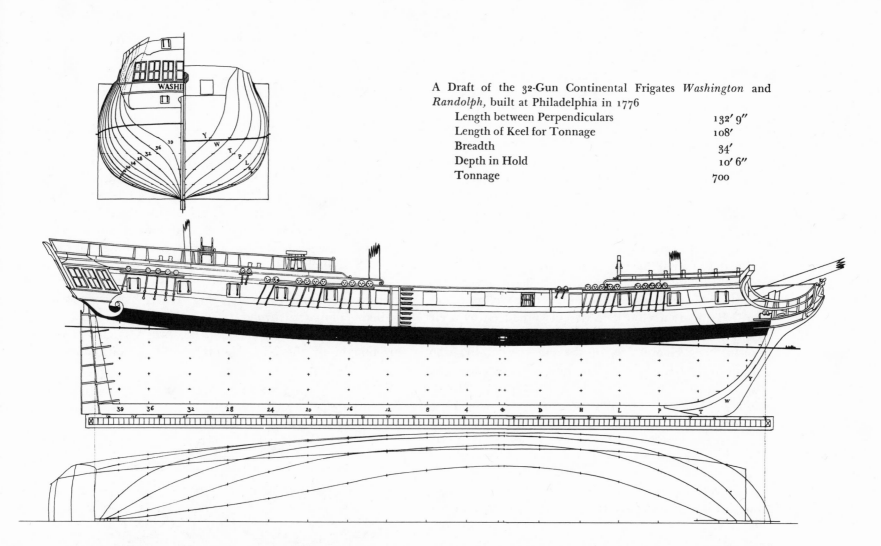

A Draft of the 32-Gun Continental Frigates *Washington* and *Randolph,* built at Philadelphia in 1776

Length between Perpendiculars	132′ 9″
Length of Keel for Tonnage	108′
Breadth	34′
Depth in Hold	10′ 6″
Tonnage	700

by the late Howard Chapelle. We have also added the upper wale to conform with what we know about the 28-gun frigates that apparently came from the same drawingboards. Interesting features about her design are the out-of-date beakhead bulkhead (probably retained from the connection of this design with that of the privateer *Hero* that had been built during the Seven Years' War), and the sharp rake to the transom.

Dimensions: length overall, 156′; length on the deck, 132′ 9″; length of keel, 108′; breadth, 35′; depth, 10′ 6″; draft, 16′; tonnage, 700.

RANGER *and* HAMPDEN

LATE in 1776, Congress authorized construction of three corvettes of 18 guns each (although the actual authorization bill has never been found). When these ships were launched in 1777 they were named after various aspects of the great victory over the British that occurred in 1777: *Saratoga,* which was built at Philadelphia; *General Gates,* which was built at Boston; and *Ranger,* named after the riflemen who had done so much toward winning that victory. They were all apparently built to designs produced by their respective local builders. *Ranger* was built at Portsmouth, New Hampshire, by the Hackett family, who had built the frigate *Raleigh* the previous year. Not long after *Ranger* was built some New Hampshire citizens ordered a brig of the same size from the same yard, and named her *Hampden* after the member of Parliament who had stood up to Charles I and his arbitrary and absolutist taxation policies (not to be confused with another vessel of the same name that served briefly in the Continental Navy at the beginning of the war). Although *Ranger* was rigged as a ship and *Hampden* was rigged as a brig we are assuming that they were to all intents and purposes identical in design; *Hampden* was about as large a vessel as was then thought practical to rig as a brig, and there were few as big as she.

Because of the extra room on the quarterdeck due to the lack of a mizzen, *Hampden* was able to carry more guns than *Ranger;* she was described as a 20-gun or even a 22-gun brig, while *Ranger* was designed to carry only 18 guns (she did carry up to 26 on occasion). Under Captain Thomas Pickering, *Hampden* had a successful cruise in European waters during the winter of 1778–79, and sent in at least four substantial prizes. On her way home in the spring, she encountered a retired East Indiaman, armed with 26 nine-pounders and 8 four-pounders; the two pounded away at each other and wrecked each other's rigging. When Pickering was killed, *Hampden* turned away and left her adversary totally disabled. In June 1779 the brig was chartered or bought by the New Hampshire State Navy under

Corvette *Ranger*
From the printed broadside
"Great Encouragement for Seamen . . ," No. 1, 1777

A Reconstruction of the Draft of the 18-Gun Continental Corvette *Ranger,* built at Portsmouth, New Hampshire, in 1777; and the 20-Gun New Hampshire State Brig *Hampden,* built at Portsmouth, New Hampshire, about 1777

Length between Perpendiculars	97′
Breadth	29′
Tonnage	308

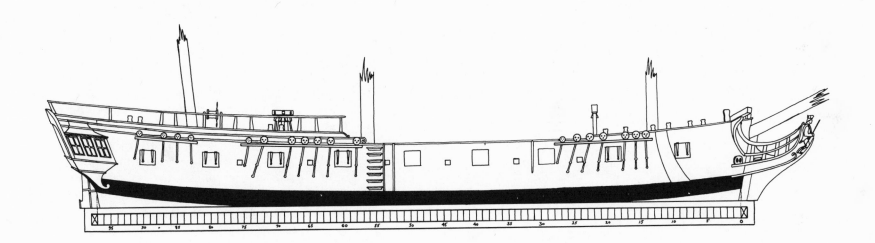

Captain Salter and was sent on the ill-fated Penobscot expedition in Maine. *Hampden* was one of the last to flee up the river, and after receiving the broadsides of three British frigates Salter was obliged to surrender; she was one of only two or three ships captured, as the rest were all burned by their crews. What happened to her in British hands is not recorded.

Ranger was given to John Paul Jones to command on 14 June 1777. He sailed for France on 1 November, capturing two brigs on the way. He arrived at Nantes on 2 December and began to have the ship rerigged and rebalasted. On 14 February 1778 he contrived to have a French warship return his salute while he was flying the new stars-and-stripes flag, and this is thought to be the first time that flag was officially recognized by a foreign government. On 10 April he left Brest on a cruise in the Irish Sea. He captured a few prizes and sank others, raided the town of Whitehaven, allowed

Corvette *Ranger*
From the printed broadside
"Great Encouragement for Seamen . . ," No. 2, 1777

his crew to plunder the mansion of the absent earl of Selkirk, and then captured the 20-gun ship *Drake* near Carrickfergus. *Drake* was not a proper warship, so the victory was not really all that it was publicized as being; she was a converted Philadelphia merchantman and a sister ship of *Alfred*. While Jones remained in France, *Ranger* was placed under command of the mutinous Lieutenant Thomas Simpson on 27 July, and on 26 September she set sail for New England from St. Nazaire, in company with the frigates *Providence* and *Boston*.

Still under the command of Simpson, the following July *Ranger* accompanied *Providence* and *Queen of France* on a cruise off the Newfoundland coast in which they captured eleven members of a British convoy; the prize money came to over $1 million, the richest cruise of the Continental Navy during the entire war. Toward the end of 1779, *Ranger* was sent to Charleston, South Carolina, along with *Providence*, *Queen of France*, and

American Brig leaving Portsmouth, N.H.;
very likely the *Hampden*
From a grisaille by Pierre Ozanne, 1778
Le Musée de la Marine, Paris

Boston. Unfortunately, the city was overwhelmed by superior British land and sea forces on 12 May 1780, and one of the terms of the surrender was that the surviving ships (*Queen of France* had been sunk) be turned over to the British intact. *Ranger* was taken into the Royal Navy and renamed *Halifax.* Unfortunately, she must have been in poor shape, for she was sold out of the service on 13 October 1781.

There are no surviving plans for either *Hampden* or *Ranger;* there are no contemporary portraits of *Hampden,* and the three portraits of *Ranger* are very crude and small. The British noted down *Ranger*'s dimensions and these have been inaccurately copied, so that Chapelle actually wrote down that she was 116' on the gun deck with a 34' beam, but measuring only 308 tons. The tonnage figure is correct, but the other dimensions were: length overall, 115' 8"; length on the gun deck, 97' 9"; breadth, 29'; tonnage, 308. We have reconstructed her appearance based primarily on the surviving drawings of the frigate *Raleigh. Ranger* was apparently a fast ship, but she was regarded as over-sparred.

RATTLESNAKE

THE 16-gun privateer ship *Rattlesnake* was built at Plymouth, Massachusetts, in 1779 or 1780 allegedly to designs by the maverick designer John Peck. She was owned by John Andrews and others of Salem, and her captain was Mark Clark. She mounted anywhere from 14 to 20 carriage guns at various times, and she usually carried about 85 men. The earliest commission found for her is dated 12 June 1781, but she may have been commissioned earlier. One privateer with the name of *Rattlesnake* is reported to have captured more than $1 million worth of British shipping on a single cruise in the Baltic, but whether it was this *Rattlesnake* or not we do not know.

Our *Rattlesnake* was captured off the American coast in 1781 by the brand-new British 44-gun ship *Assurance* and was renamed *Cormorant*. She was taken to England and her lines were drawn (her lines survive on file at the National Maritime Museum at Greenwich). It took the British bureaucracy a long time to realize that they already had a ship called *Cormorant* in the Royal Navy, so she was renamed *Rattlesnake* once more in August 1783, after the war was over. Chapelle says she was sold out of the service in 1784, but British records indicate she was not sold until 10 October 1786.

What happened next is partly conjecture, but it seems she passed into French hands during the period of the French Revolution, for there was a French privateer called *Le Tonnant* in the 1790s that had *Rattlesnake*'s exact lines. These lines have been issued as part of a European model kit of *Le Tonnant*.

Rattlesnake was extremely sharp and had moderate deadrise; she must have been very fast. For a time the British Admiralty contemplated building a corvette to her lines but to a larger scale; however, this plan was dropped.

Dimensions: length overall, 105′ 6″; length on the deck, 89′ 3″; length of keel, 74′ 11″; breadth, 22′ 4″; depth, 8′ 10″; draft, 10′ 8″; tonnage, 200.

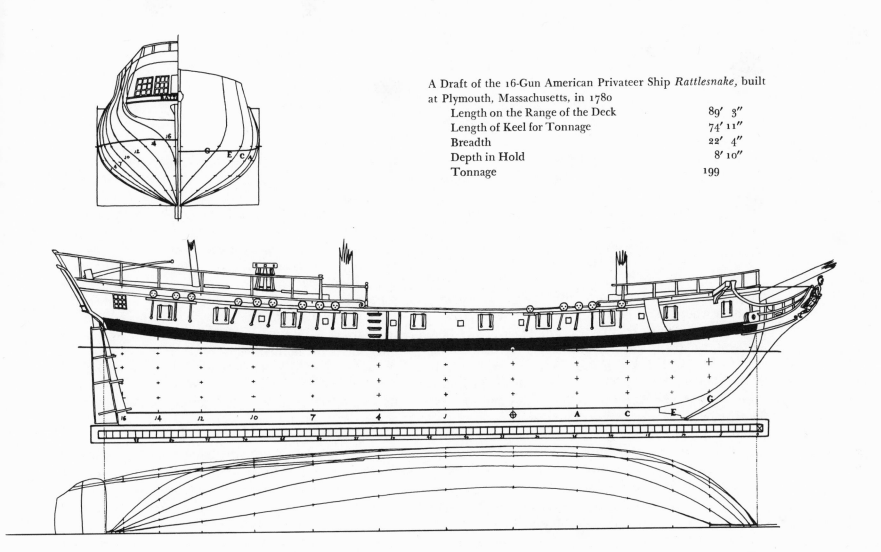

A Draft of the 16-Gun American Privateer Ship *Rattlesnake,* built
at Plymouth, Massachusetts, in 1780

Length on the Range of the Deck	89′ 3″
Length of Keel for Tonnage	74′ 11″
Breadth	22′ 4″
Depth in Hold	8′ 10″
Tonnage	199

REAL CARLOS

As far as we know, the largest ship built in the Americas before 1812 was the 114-gun (sometimes 104-gun) ship *Real Carlos* (Spanish for "Royal Charles"), which was built at Havana, Cuba, in 1787. She must have been built out of the superb local mahogany, which unfortunately no longer grows anywhere except for isolated trees in Haiti. She was built basically in the British style of design, which once more indicates the presence of British shipwrights either at Havana or in Spain where the design may have originated. Differences from a British ship of her size included her lion figurehead (British ships of this size never had a lion, which was reserved for smaller ships in the first half of the eighteenth century and mostly abandoned altogether by the time *Real Carlos* was built), and the two fender bars at the forward part of the waist.

When Spain was forced to throw in her lot with Napoleon against Britain, *Real Carlos* became an important element in the combined Franco-Spanish fleet. However, her first major test under fire was also her last. French Admiral Linois, anchored with his battered fleet in Algeciras Bay near Gibraltar, called for Spanish reinforcements from Cadiz. Six ships of the line, including *Real Carlos* (flagship of Admiral Don Juan de Moreno), and three frigates joined the French on 9 July 1801. On 12 July the combined fleet got underway and headed for Cadiz, but a British fleet of less than half the force under Saumarez came out from Gibraltar to do battle with them as the sun was setting. Saumarez detached Captain Keats in the 74-gun *Superb*

to chase the Spaniards, and Keats completely surprised *Real Carlos* in the dark. Keats got off several broadsides at the flagship from within pistol-shot range while the Spaniards were in confusion. A chance shot in the right place set the huge ship on fire. The Spaniards then began firing wildly in all directions, and particularly at another Spanish ship of over 100 guns, the *Hermenegildo*. *Hermenegildo*, mistaking *Real Carlos* for the enemy, fired back at her and then collided with her. Both ships were by then heavily on fire in a strong wind on an otherwise black night. Shortly after midnight both ships blew up as the fires reached the magazines with the loss of nearly 2,000 lives. Sir James Saumarez became a hero for his part in winning the battle of Algeciras Bay, although the Spaniards really did it all to themselves; one other French ship was captured in the action.

The source for our plans is an outstanding model of *Real Carlos* at the Museo Naval in Madrid. *Real Carlos*, once the pride of the Spanish navy, was also depicted in a number of pictures, including a horrifying scene by Breton of the two ships on fire at night. According to the model and some of the pictures, she had two spritsail yards and still had a lateen yard on the mizzen, although this had been replaced by a gaff on British ships many years before.

According to the model, she measured as follows: length overall, 231′ 6″; length on the lower deck, 188′; length of keel, 160′; breadth, 52′ 6″; depth in hold, 21′ 6″; draft, 25′; tonnage, 2,300.

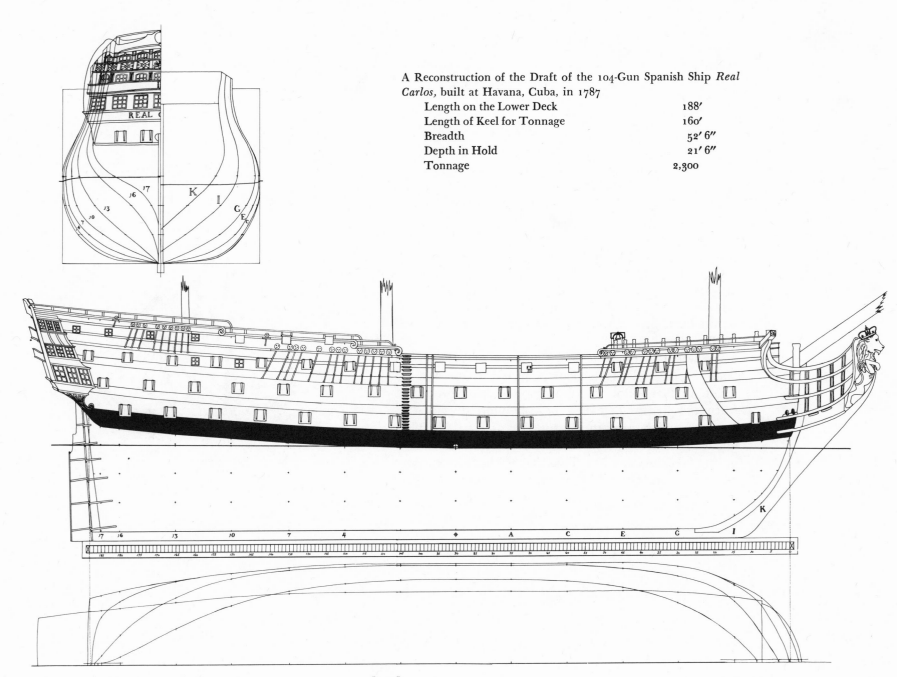

A Reconstruction of the Draft of the 104-Gun Spanish Ship *Real Carlos*, built at Havana, Cuba, in 1787

Length on the Lower Deck	188'
Length of Keel for Tonnage	160'
Breadth	52' 6"
Depth in Hold	21' 6"
Tonnage	2,300

REVENGE

WHEN Benedict Arnold set about building a fleet on Lake Champlain in the summer of 1776 to slow down the expected British attack, most of his fleet was built at Skenesborough. However, he did order one small schooner, called *Revenge*, built further along the lake at Ticonderoga. She mounted 4 four-pounders and 4 two-pounders, in addition to a few swivel guns, and carried 50 men. At her bow was a raised rail which may have been only a splashboard of sorts, but it may actually have been there to support a forecastle, which would have been an unusual feature for a vessel so small.

She was in Arnold's fleet at the battle of Valcour Island, but escaped serious damage in that action and in the flight that followed. However, the following year, when the British fleet had been reinforced, she was captured and burned in the summer of 1777. She was included in a number of pictures of the various vessels on the lake, and it is on these that we have based our reconstruction. Otherwise, we know virtually nothing about her.

As we see her, she measured as follows: length overall, 51'; length between perpendiculars, 45'.

Schooner *Revenge*
From a watercolor painting by C. Randle, 1776
The Public Archives of Canada, Ottawa

A Reconstruction of the Draft of the 8-Gun Continental Schooner
Revenge, built at Ticonderoga, New York, in 1776
Length between Perpendiculars   45'

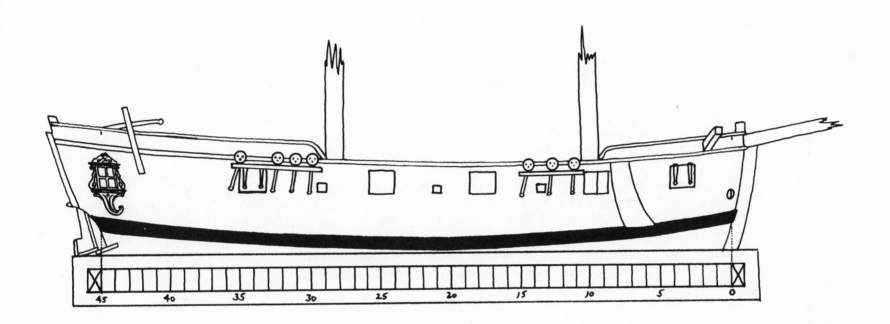

REVENGE

BENJAMIN FRANKLIN was so pleased with the results of the first ships he had commissioned to raid the British in their home waters that he tried to add more vessels to his fleet. One of these was a cutter of 14 six-pounders and 22 swivels that was lying at Dunkirk. She was named *Revenge* after Sir Richard Grenville's heroic ship from Elizabethan days, and was purchased for Continental service by William Hodge. She set off on 2 May 1777, manned by 106 men, including 66 Frenchmen. Since the French were not officially at war with Britain, the British protested loudly and caused French ports to be off-limits to *Revenge*. The restrictions were apparently unimportant to her intrepid captain, Gustavus Conyngham, who cheerfully took many British prizes within sight of their own coast, and even held the town of King's Lynn, Norfolk, for ransom (he failed to collect when the wind shifted).

Next, he made his base in a number of Spanish ports, where he was very popular. Once more the British protested to the then-neutral Spanish government, which looked the other way until Conyngham's rapacious crew insisted on capturing a Spanish-owned ship, contrary to orders. With Spanish ports closed, he took her back to Philadelphia via Martinique, arriving 21 February 1778 with a heavy load of weapons for the Continental Army. She was then sold to some Philadelphia merchants as a privateer, but Conyngham remained in command. During a cruise to the West Indies she was captured by the 20-gun frigate *Galatea*, and Conyngham was carried off in heavy chains. He had captured over seventy British ships with the sturdy cutter.

No plans, dimensions, or portraits of *Revenge* survive. However, since she was such an important vessel in the story of American ships we have reconstructed her appearance by following the lines of a number of typical cutters of her size and date.

Dimensions: length overall, 71' 4"; length between perpendiculars, 64'; length of keel, 54' 9"; breadth, 23'; draft, 12'; tonnage, 105.

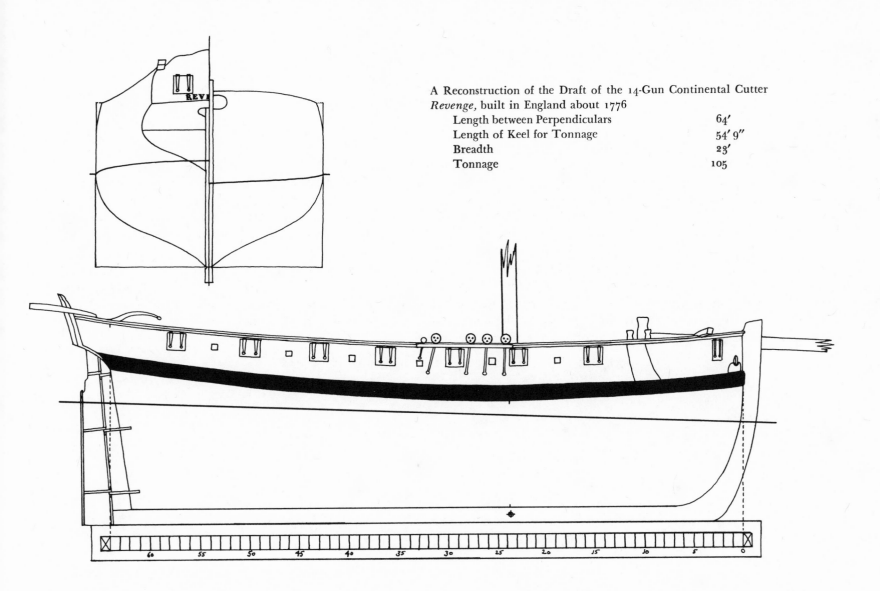

A Reconstruction of the Draft of the 14-Gun Continental Cutter
Revenge, built in England about 1776

Length between Perpendiculars	64'
Length of Keel for Tonnage	54' 9"
Breadth	23'
Tonnage	105

RHODES

THE 16-gun ship *Rhodes* was built about 1778 to 1780 in the region of Essex County, Massachusetts, and was commissioned as a privateer out of Salem. We know little of her career except that she was captured on 15 February 1782 in the West Indies by the 64-gun British ship *Prothée*. Although she is not listed in Colledge's *Ships of the Royal Navy* she was taken into the Royal Navy with the name of *Barbadoes,* and sold a few months later when the war ended. She was described as a weatherly ship, although she obviously could not carry a great deal of armament or stores be- cause of her steep deadrise. While her lines were sharp, following the trend of fast-ship design in America, she displayed the classic British balance of "cod's head & mackerel tail" with her maximum beam well forward. The British took down this ship's lines when she arrived in Britain, and these are on file at the National Maritime Museum at Greenwich.

Dimensions: length overall, 116'; length on the deck, 97' 7"; length of keel, 81' 9"; breadth, 25'; depth, 10' 7"; draft, 12' 6"; tonnage, 270.

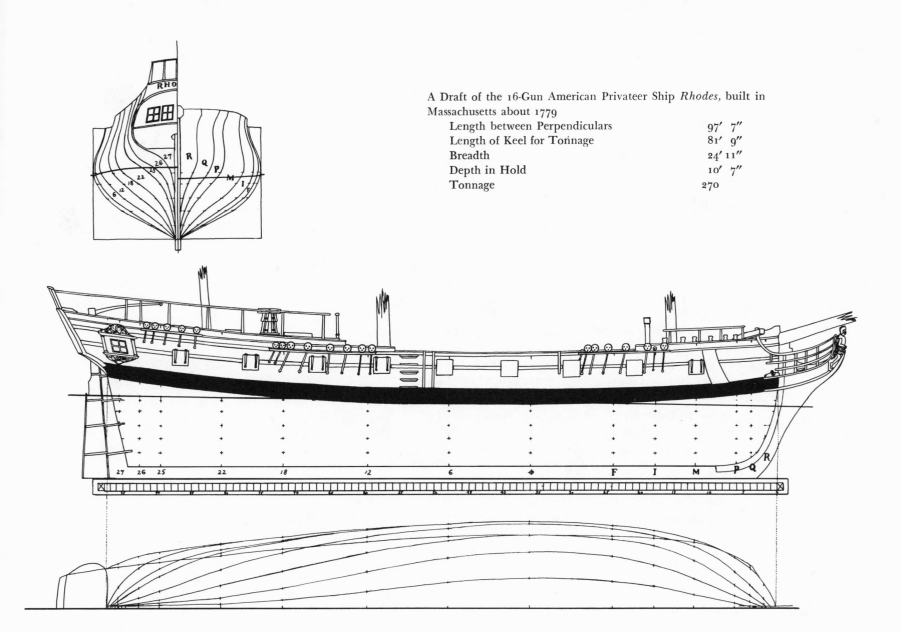

A Draft of the 16-Gun American Privateer Ship *Rhodes,* built in
Massachusetts about 1779

Length between Perpendiculars	97′ 7″
Length of Keel for Tonnage	81′ 9″
Breadth	24′ 11″
Depth in Hold	10′ 7″
Tonnage	270

ROBIN

Among the many ships drawn by Ashley Bowen in his diary was the little sloop *Robin* of Newport, Rhode Island, which he drew when he sailed on her briefly about 1750. Her stem had more rake than most sloops of her size, but otherwise she was more or less typical of American sloops. She had the little cabin with the segmental roof that was more commonly seen on southern vessels, but it must be remembered that Rhode Island sloops spent most of their lives in southern waters, for Rhode Island merchants traded more extensively with the West Indies and Africa than anywhere else. We have included her in the book (while many other Bowen sketches have been omitted for lack of clarity in the drawings or to avoid repetition) mainly because we feel that she is likely to have resembled the Continental sloop *Fly* quite closely. *Fly* was an unarmed Rhode Island sloop that was taken into the Continental Navy late in 1775 and sailed with the first fleet for Nassau after being fitted out with six guns. Contrary to some accounts, she was not a schooner and she was not destroyed in the Delaware to avoid capture in 1777 or 1778, although what actually did become of her is not clear.

As we reconstruct *Robin*, her dimensions were length overall, 65'; length between perpendiculars, 56'; tonnage, about 80.

Sloop *Eagle*
From a watercolor sketch by Ashley Bowen, ca. 1779
Peabody Museum, Salem, Massachusetts

A Reconstruction of the Draft of the Sloop *Robin* of Newport,
Rhode Island, built about 1750
        Length between Perpendiculars   56′

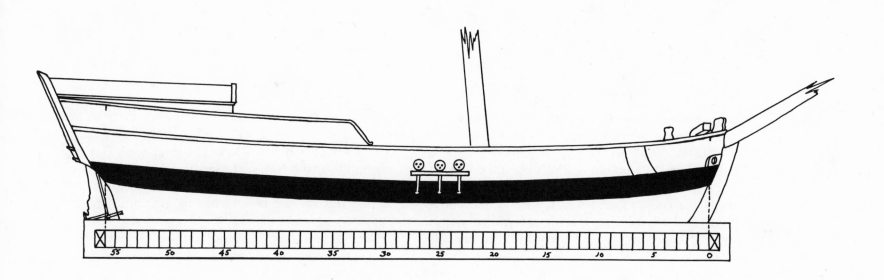

ROYAL GEORGE

LATE in 1776, the British, impressed by the usefulness of the 18-gun corvette *Inflexible* in defeating Benedict Arnold's fleet on Lake Champlain, began to build another 18-gun corvette at St. John's at the northern end of Lake Champlain. While *Inflexible* had been hastily reassembled from the pieces of a river patrol ship that had been under construction near Quebec City, *Royal George* was designed and built with care for service on Lake Champlain. She was quite a bit larger than *Inflexible* and could mount 20 nine-pounders if called on to do so. In 1777 she became the flagship of the British squadron on the lake, and the squadron had no trouble in capturing or destroying the remnants of Arnold's fleet. In fact, Arnold had not reinforced his fleet, knowing that the advantage in time that he had hoped to obtain by first building the fleet in 1776 had already been obtained, and that there was nothing further to gain by pouring more money and men into building yet another fleet on the lake. Presumably *Royal George* was broken up at the end of the war, but records about her are scanty.

(There was also another ship in the Royal Navy with the name *Royal George* at the same time; she mounted 120 guns, and she capsized and sank during cleaning operations at Portsmouth, England, on 29 August 1782 with the loss of about 800 lives.)

Royal George had the shallow draft, flat bottom, and wide beam that was characteristic of most lake vessels. It must be remembered that lake vessels did not need a huge displacement for carrying drinking water or food, for in those days one could drink the lake water and put ashore for a few hours to scrounge some food. Her plans are on file at the National Maritime Museum at Greenwich, and there are a number of distant pictures of her among the various lake scenes painted and drawn in 1777.

Dimensions: length overall, 113' 2"; length on the deck, 96' 6"; length of keel, 78'; breadth, 30' 6"; depth, 10'; draft, 9' 3"; tonnage, 386.

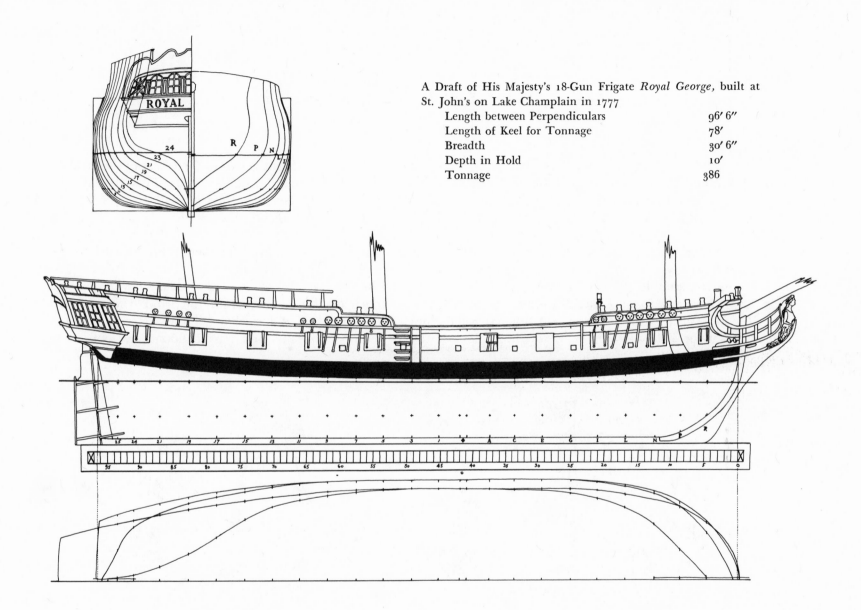

A Draft of His Majesty's 18-Gun Frigate *Royal George,* built at
St. John's on Lake Champlain in 1777

Length between Perpendiculars	96′ 6″
Length of Keel for Tonnage	78′
Breadth	30′ 6″
Depth in Hold	10′
Tonnage	386

ROYAL SAVAGE

WHEN Benedict Arnold captured St. John's, the British post at the northern end of Lake Champlain, for the Americans in May 1775, he found that the British had been busy building a few small armed vessels there. The sloop *George* was completed, the cutter *Lee* was only in frame, and the schooner *Royal Savage* had been sunk by American shore cannons. He changed *George*'s name to *Enterprise*, took *Lee*'s frames to Skenesborough for eventual completion, and raised *Royal Savage*, letting her keep her original name. She was a poor sailer, as were most of the shallow-draft, flat-bottomed, blunt vessels of the lake, but she mounted 12 guns, so Arnold made her his flagship before the battle of Valcour Island in the early fall of 1776.

At Valcour Island, the British fleet overshot the American position and had to claw their way back against the wind. To delay them a little further, *Royal Savage* went out to harass them, but soon turned back when it was realized that she would have equally as much trouble going against the wind. Unfortunately, she ran aground just short of the American position behind the island, and was abandoned as soon as the

Schooner *Royal Savage*
From a watercolor painting by C. Randle, 1776
The Public Archives of Canada, Ottawa

Schooner *Royal Savage*
From an anonymous sketch in the Schuyler Collection, ca. 1776
New York Public Library

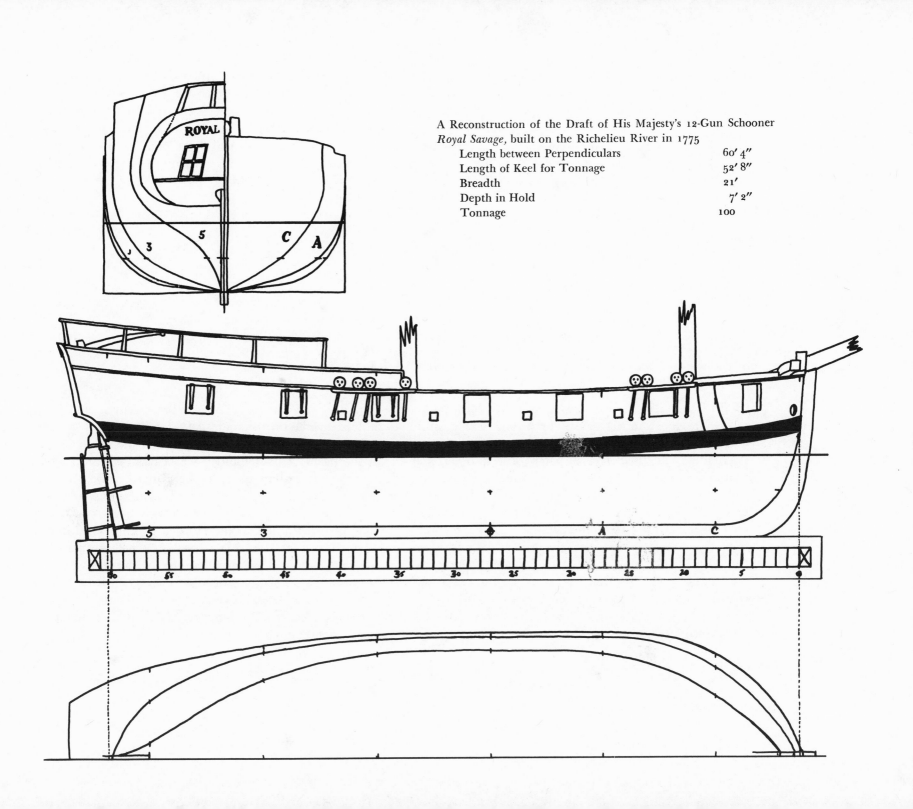

A Reconstruction of the Draft of His Majesty's 12-Gun Schooner
Royal Savage, built on the Richelieu River in 1775

Length between Perpendiculars	60′ 4″
Length of Keel for Tonnage	52′ 8″
Breadth	21′
Depth in Hold	7′ 2″
Tonnage	100

concentration of British fire made her untenable. The British boarded her and set her on fire to prevent Arnold's men from retaking her during the night.

No plans or dimensions survive of *Royal Savage,* but it is thought that in many respects she was merely a larger version of *Lee,* whose lines do survive. In addition, there are a number of portraits of *Royal Savage,* which were helpful in reconstructing her. A model at the Mariners Museum, Newport News, Virginia, that has her name bears no likeness to her at all.

Dimensions: length overall, 66′ 4″; length between perpendiculars, 60′ 5″; length of keel, 52′ 8″; breadth, 21′; depth, 7′ 2″; draft, 6′ 10″; tonnage, 100 (as we have reconstructed her).

ST. ANN

THE schooner *St. Ann* was apparently built somewhere in America before 1736, and was possibly originally intended as a yacht. She was bought by the Portuguese and used as a dispatch boat in 1736, and visited Portsmouth, England, that same year. At that time she was taken into the dock and her lines were taken off. Chapman, the great Swedish naval architect, took a copy of the lines home with him about 1753, and they can now be found at the Statens Sjohistoriska Museum in Sweden. Apart from *Falkland,* which was altered in part before her plan was drawn, this is the earliest plan of an American vessel that is known.

According to her spar and sail dimensions (tantalizingly incomplete) she had two pole masts and set a square topsail and topgallant on the foremast, and possibly the same on the mainmast, for downwind sailing only; these were furled whenever the wind came ahead of the beam. This delightful vessel was extraordinarily narrow and shallow draft for her length, which would indicate that she could not carry much sail in a blow, nor was she intended to carry cargo. However, this, combined with her relatively sharp lines (including moderately sharp deadrise), probably meant that she was very fast in a medium breeze. Nothing further is known about her history or sailing characteristics.

Dimensions: length overall, 62′ 1″; length between perpendiculars, 55′ 2″; length of keel, 46′ 9″; breadth, 12′ 1″; depth, 6′ 10″; draft, 5′ 2″; tonnage, 37.

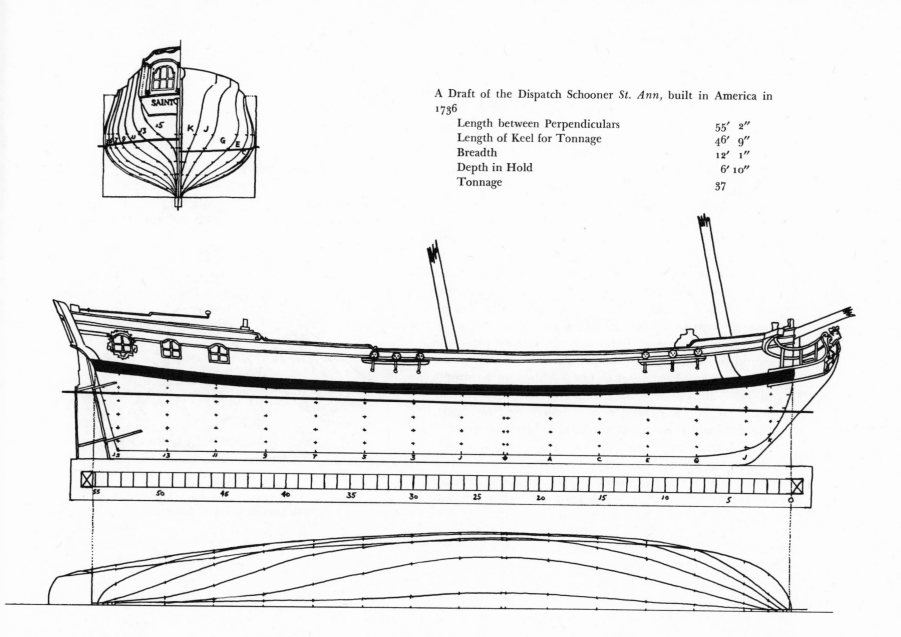

A Draft of the Dispatch Schooner *St. Ann,* built in America in
1736

Length between Perpendiculars	55′ 2″
Length of Keel for Tonnage	46′ 9″
Breadth	12′ 1″
Depth in Hold	6′ 10″
Tonnage	37

ST. HELENA

Aт the Science Museum in London is a rather fancy portrait of a ship built in Charleston, South Carolina, called *St. Helena*. The picture is one of those bombastic exaggerations that are intended to make owners happy. The ship is depicted with royals on main and fore, topgallant and top-studding sails on main and fore, two spritsails, three jibs, three staysails between each set of masts, a fore-course studding sail, and a ring-tail. An unexpected quality of this ship is that she apparently carried no armament, which gives no indication that the date of her construction was 1776; she would be fair game for any privateer or warship whose politics differed from her owner's. Although the profile of her hull gave the appearance of having a regular waist, by showing a raised quarterdeck and forecastle, the place where the waist would have been was actually decked over, thus providing more covered space for cargo. The British Navy Board employed a ship called *St. Helena* to carry ordnance supplies to the Caribbean in March 1777, but it is not known whether this was the same ship.

No plans for this ship survive, and the only dimension we know is her tonnage. As we have reconstructed her, she measured: length overall, 103′ 3″; length between perpendiculars, 86′; breadth, 26′; tonnage, 240.

Ship *St. Helena*
From an anonymous watercolor painting, 1776
The Science Museum, London

A Reconstruction of the Draft of the American Merchant Ship
St. Helena, built at Charleston, South Carolina, about 1775
    Length between Perpendiculars   86'
    Tonnage   240

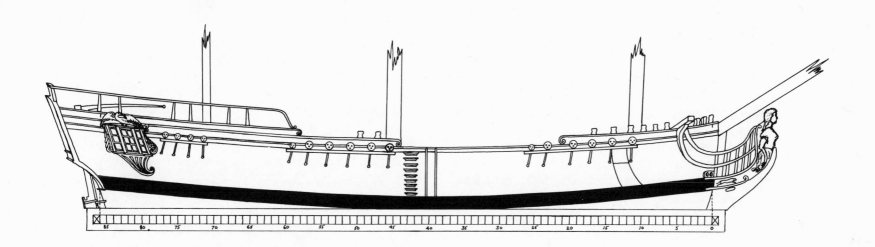

LE SAINT-LAURENT

Monsieur Jean Boudriot of Paris reports that he can find no information on ships built in Canada for the French navy before the British captured the country in 1759. A list of all these ships can be found in the text describing the frigate *L'Abenakise*. From this list, we know that a ship called *Le Saint-Laurent* was built in Quebec in 1748, and that she mounted 60 guns. Because this ship is so important to the history of American ships in the eighteenth century, we have attempted to reconstruct her appearance, based on the known lines and dimensions of French warships of the period and on certain details of *L'Abenakise*.

As we see her, she measured as follows: length overall, 182′ 8″; length on the lower deck, 154′; tonnage, about 1,100.

It is indeed a pity that we know so little about these ships, how they performed, and how long they lasted. Perhaps someday researchers will turn up information from the Canadian archives.

Two interesting features should be pointed out: the French almost never placed gunport lids on the upper gun deck, which must have made that deck very cold in winter. Also, they were very particular about the comfort of their officers, and the cabins for "l'État Major" or "officers' country" had a row of window ports leading forward from the Great Cabin; these ports never had cannons in them, and were actually situated too high off the deck for a cannon to reach anyway.

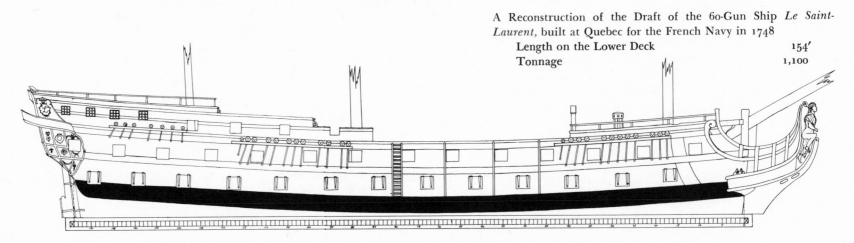

A Reconstruction of the Draft of the 60-Gun Ship *Le Saint-Laurent,* built at Quebec for the French Navy in 1748

Length on the Lower Deck 154′
Tonnage 1,100

SARATOGA *and* MONTGOMERY

Two warships were built at Philadelphia during the Revolution that were about the same size; although we have no evidence that they were identical, we have decided to give one plan for both of them. These are the Pennsylvania State Navy corvette *Montgomery* and the Continental Navy corvette *Saratoga*. Our drawing is based on the official drawing for the 32-gun frigate *Randolph*, which we know was a scaled-up version of the frigate *Delaware*, so we have made *Saratoga* a scaled-down version of *Delaware*, and we think there is more than a possibility that *Montgomery* was also a scaled-down version of *Delaware*.

Montgomery's contract was awarded to Simon Sherlock's shipyard on 7 November 1775; she was supposed to be capable of mounting 20 eighteen-pounders for river service (smoother water and calmer winds than at sea allowed a much heavier armament than this size ship would normally have carried), and John Barry, deprived of his previous ship *Black Prince* when she was taken into the Continental Navy as *Alfred*, was put in charge of the construction. In March she was given the name of *Wallace*, but this was soon changed to *Montgomery* in honor of the general who had lost his life at Quebec a few months earlier. When she was launched she was fitted with only 14 eighteen-pounders, 16 small mortars, and 8 swivels after it was found that 20 big guns would have been both too heavy and too expensive. By May 1776 she was ready with about 120 men under command of Thomas Read to lead a number of galleys in repelling the advance up the river by the 44-gun ship *Roebuck* and the 28-gun frigate *Liverpool;* after an inconclusive action, the British left the river. In June, Samuel Davidson was made her commander, and he had her armament altered to 16 twelve-pounders. He was replaced in October 1776 by Henry Dougherty, who was required by Commodore Seymour to take her up the river to Trenton to deter a possible British advance in December. Shortly thereafter, she was disarmed and her cannons given to the other forces in the area. However, when Dougherty resigned in May 1777, she was quickly rearmed with 16 nine-pounders, and command was given to William Allen; Commodore John Hazlewood made her his flagship, but it was very difficult to find more than half enough men to man her.

Montgomery came downriver at the end of September in company with the frigate *Delaware* in hopes of preventing a British fleet from proceeding up the river to meet the British army that had already taken Philadelphia. *Delaware* was captured when she ran aground and *Montgomery* was dismasted in the same action. In November, just below Philadelphia, she was destroyed to prevent capture.

Saratoga was one of the three corvettes that were ordered by Congress late in 1776 in a bill that is now lost. She mounted 16 nine-pounders plus 2 four-pounders, and was built by Wharton & Humphreys. She is sometimes referred to as a brig, but is known to have been a ship. One recent book says that she was built in time

A Reconstruction of the Draft of the 18-Gun Continental Corvette *Saratoga*, built 1777 at Philadelphia; and the Pennsylvania State Cruiser *Montgomery*, built 1775 at Philadelphia

Length between Perpendiculars	94' 2"
Breadth	29'
Tonnage	300

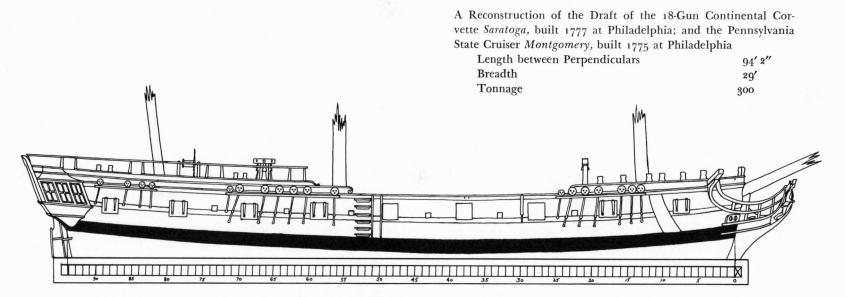

to escape from Philadelphia before the British occupied the city and was fitted out in New England, but because there is no record of her sailing anywhere before 1780 one suspects that construction was not far along when the British arrived and had to be begun all over again when they left. In May 1780 she lay at anchor in the Delaware and was put under command of Captain John Young, who picked Joshua Barney for his lieutenant. On a cruise off the New Jersey coast in October 1780 she captured three brigs and the large, heavily armed letter-of-marque *Charming Molly* which had been on its way from Bristol to New York. Barney was put in charge of the prize crew of *Charming Molly*, which was recaptured on her way to Philadelphia by *Intrepid*, 64 guns, and *Iris* (ex-Continental frigate *Hancock*), 32 guns.

Saratoga next headed south and cruised in the Caribbean until March 1781 when she was loaded with war supplies along with *Confederacy* and *Deane*, and the three ships began to escort a convoy back to the United States but the ships were separated in a storm in April. After the storm, *Confederacy* was captured and *Deane* arrived safely at Boston, but *Saratoga* had foundered with all hands during the storm; presumably she had been overloaded.

No dimensions, plans, or contemporary pictures exist of either of these two ships. Our reconstruction gives these measurements: length overall, 108' 8"; length on the deck, 94' 2"; breadth, 29'; tonnage, 300.

SERAPIS

THE 44-gun ship *Serapis* was built for the Royal Navy at Randall's shipyard at Rotherhithe on the Thames early in 1779. She was placed under the command of Captain Richard Pearson and ordered to guard a convoy returning to England from the Baltic. On 23 September 1779, the convoy was spotted by John Paul Jones, who was cruising off Flamborough Head on board the 42-gun converted East Indiaman *Bonhomme Richard*, with his small fleet. *Serapis* left her convoy to engage the intruders and the convoy escaped to safety. *Serapis* did rather more damage to *Bonhomme Richard* than she received back, but Jones was no ordinary captain. He survived a few wild broadsides fired by his supposed consort *Alliance* (the theory apparently was that if *Alliance* could sink *Bonhomme Richard*, she herself would be able to receive the surrender of the battered *Serapis*, but Jones held on). Finally, when he saw his ship was on fire, was dismasted, had been wracked by internal explosions caused by American grenades and could be attacked by the undamaged 36-gun frigate *Alliance* at any moment, Pearson surrendered to Jones. Pearson was soon exchanged and was knighted for having protected the convoy even at the expense of his own ship, to which Jones is reported to have said, "Let me fight him again and I will make him a lord."

Bonhomme Richard was too badly damaged to save, so Jones transferred his men and belongings to *Serapis* to watch his old ship sink. When he brought *Serapis* to France she was sold to the French navy, much to Jones's annoyance, for he wanted to use her himself. The French removed one deck of guns and sent her to the Indian Ocean, where she was destroyed by fire in 1781. Her dimensions but not her plans survive, but the plans of another ship of her dimensions that was built the same year do survive, so we have used them with changes indicated by the many portraits of the battle that are extant. She was unusual for her size and type in that her stern had only one deck of windows.

Dimensions: length overall, 163' 8"; length on the deck, 140'; length of keel, 116' 4"; breadth, 38'; depth, 16' 4"; draft, 19'; tonnage, 886.

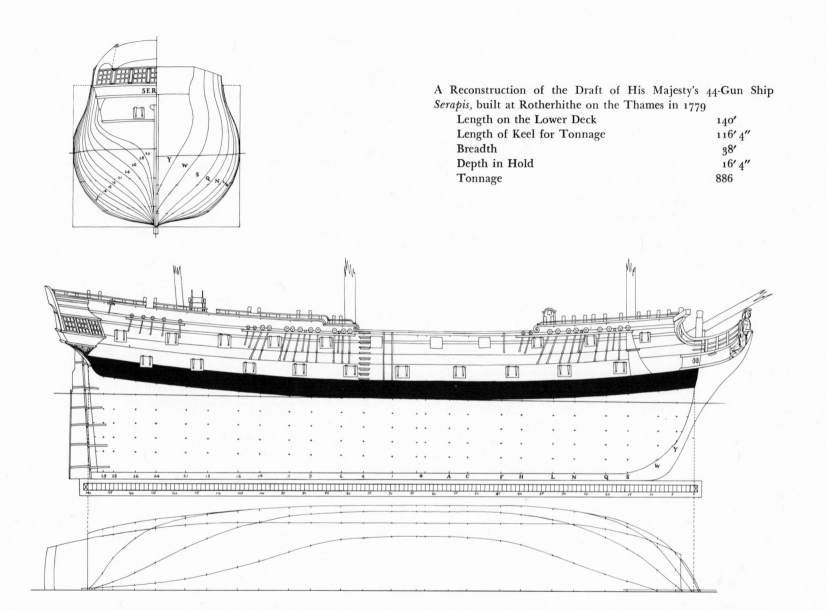

A Reconstruction of the Draft of His Majesty's 44-Gun Ship
Serapis, built at Rotherhithe on the Thames in 1779

Length on the Lower Deck	140'
Length of Keel for Tonnage	116' 4"
Breadth	38'
Depth in Hold	16' 4"
Tonnage	886

SIR EDWARD HAWKE
and EARL OF EGMONT

IN the late 1760s the British attempted to acquire a number of fast, armed schooners for the purpose of eliminating the widespread evasion of the Customs laws. Since the Americans knew how to build such schooners better than anyone else in the world, and since these schooners would be used in America, the British either had these schooners built in America or purchased already existing American schooners.

Two or three of these schooners shared the same design. They were built in New York to what was described as a Marblehead design, meaning that they were similar to the so-called heeltappers that were produced in the area of Marblehead, Massachusetts. Two were called *Sir Edward Hawke* and *Earl of Egmont*. They were commissioned on 22 May 1768 for use on the Jamaica station, and they carried eight small carriage guns apiece, in addition to a few swivels. Each carried a crew of thirty men. Their rigging plans have not been found, but it is believed that they had a square topsail on both masts in addition to the fore-and-aft sails. They were both sold out of the navy on 11 August 1773, so the *Hawke* that became the first British warship to be captured by the Continental Navy on 4 April 1776 was not one of these schooners. The lines for these schooners, drawn with slight imperfections, are on file at the National Maritime Museum at Greenwich.

Dimensions: length overall, 65′; length between perpendiculars, 57′ 7″; length of keel, 45′ 7″; breadth, 17′ 11″; depth, 7′ 4″; draft, 9′ 10″; tonnage, 100.

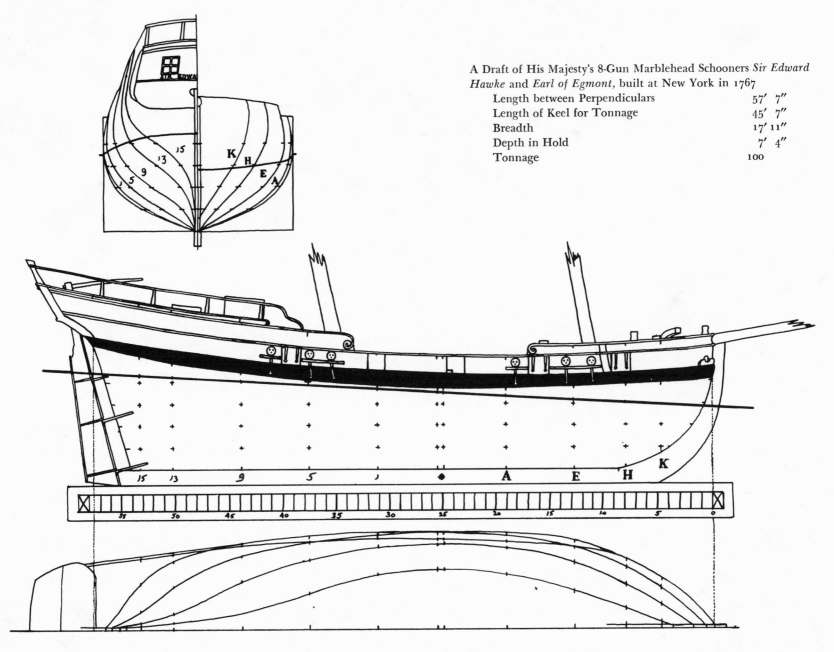

A Draft of His Majesty's 8-Gun Marblehead Schooners *Sir Edward Hawke* and *Earl of Egmont,* built at New York in 1767

Length between Perpendiculars	57′ 7″
Length of Keel for Tonnage	45′ 7″
Breadth	17′ 11″
Depth in Hold	7′ 4″
Tonnage	100

SOUTH CAROLINA

WHEN Benjamin Franklin arrived in Paris in 1776, he had authorization from Congress to buy, charter, or borrow a number of large warships from the French or from anyone else. However, since Europe, including France, was at least nominally neutral, this proved very difficult to achieve. Franklin ordered a large ship to be built at Amsterdam to French designs in 1776–77. Her name was *L'Indien*, but just as she was finished in November 1777 the British found out who the real owners were and told the Dutch to forbid the Americans to take possession of her. John Paul Jones tried to seize her, but in vain. She was then sold to the king of France.

In June 1778, Franklin wrote Jones that the way was clear to take command of *L'Indien* and Jones therefore relinquished command of *Ranger*. However, France was now at war with Britain, so the Dutch refused to allow the French king to send anyone to take possession of her. So she was sold again, this time to the duke of Luxembourg. In 1779 and 1780 the duke negotiated at great length with Commodore Alexander Gillon of the South Carolina State Navy, himself of French ancestry, and Gillon eventually chartered the ship for his state. He renamed her *South Carolina*, manned her with 250 American sailors who had recently been released from British prisons, and tried to sail out of Amsterdam in June 1780. However, the water was too shallow most of the time, and the crew was practically mutinous. He did not get her out of Amsterdam until August 1781.

She was manned with 250 sailors, some of whom had been aboard for well over a year, and no fewer than 300 French marines, who caused no end of trouble.

Her first cruise was in the North Sea, and she made her first capture on 25 August 1781. She sailed north around the Shetland Islands to Coruna, Spain, then left Spain in October and took more prizes. After a stop at Teneriffe, she headed for the West Indies. On 31 De-

Frigate *South Carolina*
From a watercolor painting by J. Phippen, 1793
Peabody Museum, Salem, Massachusetts

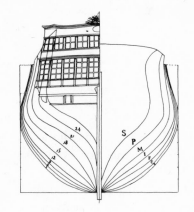

A Draft of the 40-Gun American Frigate *South Carolina* (formerly
L'Indien), built at Amsterdam in 1777

Length on the Lower Deck	154′
Length of Keel for Tonnage	138′
Breadth	40′
Depth in Hold	16′ 6″
Tonnage	1,186

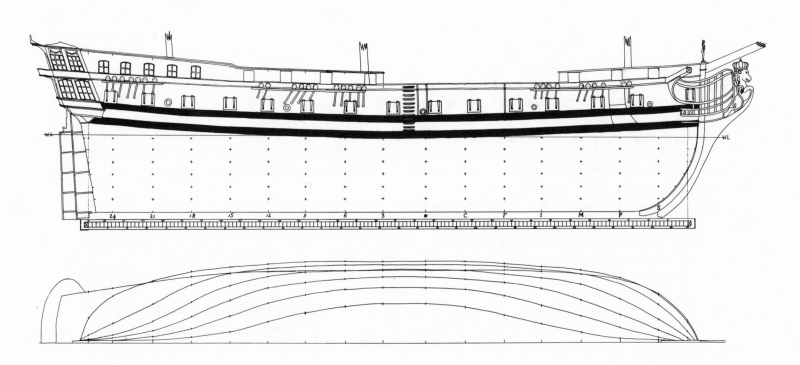

[264]

cember, she was off enemy-occupied Charleston, South Carolina, but bore away for Havana, where she arrived on 12 January 1782. On 8 May she served as flagship for the ludicrously gigantic expedition of fifty-six Spanish and American ships and thousands of troops that captured Nassau for the third time in that war; the previous time, Nassau had fallen to the sloop *Providence* and her crew of but fifty men.

South Carolina arrived at Philadelphia on 28 May, at which point a representative of the duke of Luxembourg had Gillon removed from command for no stated reason. He was replaced by Captain John Joyner of the South Carolina State Navy. *South Carolina* left Philadelphia in November as guard of a small convoy that was bound for Europe. They anchored downriver for a few weeks and set sail again on 19 December. That very night she was chased by three British ships—*Diomede,* 44 guns, and *Astrea* and *Quebec,* both 32 guns. The chase lasted eighteen hours, and *South Carolina* put up very little resistance before surrendering; this is surprising, considering the fact that her broadside's weight matched almost exactly the sum of the weights of the broadsides of her three assailants. She was taken into New York and surveyed, but was found to be too lightly built and even a bit hogged from carrying her extraordinarily heavy armament, so she was sold instead of being taken into the Royal Navy.

One crude sketch of *South Carolina* by one of her crewmembers can be seen at the Peabody Museum at Salem, and a copy of her lines was included in French Admiral Paris's book *Souvenirs de Marine,* volume 5. The dimensions on Paris's plan do not agree with those recorded by the British surveyor at New York, but Admiral Paris's are more likely to be correct. This ship was called a frigate by her contemporaries, but no frigate exactly like her had ever been built before. Her hull looked like a cross between that of a large frigate and an East Indiaman; she had two decks of stern windows. She carried 28 thirty-six-pounder cannons and 12 twelve-pounders, by far the heaviest armament to sail under the American flag during the war. However, she was built weakly like an Indiaman, which was not supposed to withstand the strains of battle like a frigate, and all that heavy armament combined with her unusual length caused her to hog (her bow and stern drooped). Experts feel that her size and her heavy armament were a direct inspiration for the large frigates that were built for the United States Navy in the 1790s, notably the *Constitution* and the *United States;* these two, although larger ships, only carried twenty-four-pounders in their main battery, but that was still more than British or French frigates were carrying at that time.

Dimensions: length overall, 186'; length on the deck, 154' (the British said 170'); length of keel, 138' (the British said 144'); breadth, 40' (the British said 43'); depth, 16' 6"; draft, 21'; tonnage, 1,186 (the British said 1,430).

SULTANA

THE handsome little schooner *Sultana* was built at Benjamin Hallowell's yard in Boston in 1766–67. Hallowell had built the 24-gun ship *Boston* for the Royal Navy, but she had become rotten in a very short space of time. He also built a pole-masted sloop for the navy that was called *Bird*.

Sultana was purchased by the navy in 1768 as a dispatch boat and as a small transport, a duty for which her full lines made her quite suitable, if a little slow. She mounted a few swivels for protection and for sig-naling, but no carriage guns. She is not mentioned in Colledge's *Ships of the Royal Navy*, and we can find no record of how or when she left the navy. Her plans are on file at the National Maritime Museum at Greenwich. An attractive wooden model kit of her is available commercially.

Dimensions: length overall, 59'; length between perpendiculars, 49' 4"; length of keel, 38' 5"; breadth, 16' 5"; depth, 8' 4"; draft, 8'; tonnage, 53.

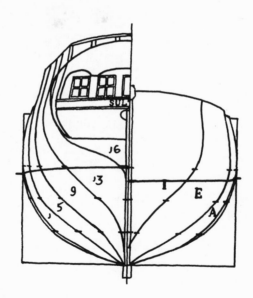

A Draft of the American Merchant Schooner *Sultana,* built at
Boston in 1776

Length between Perpendiculars	49′ 4″
Length of Keel for Tonnage	38′ 5″
Breadth	16′ 5″
Depth in Hold	8′ 4″
Tonnage	53

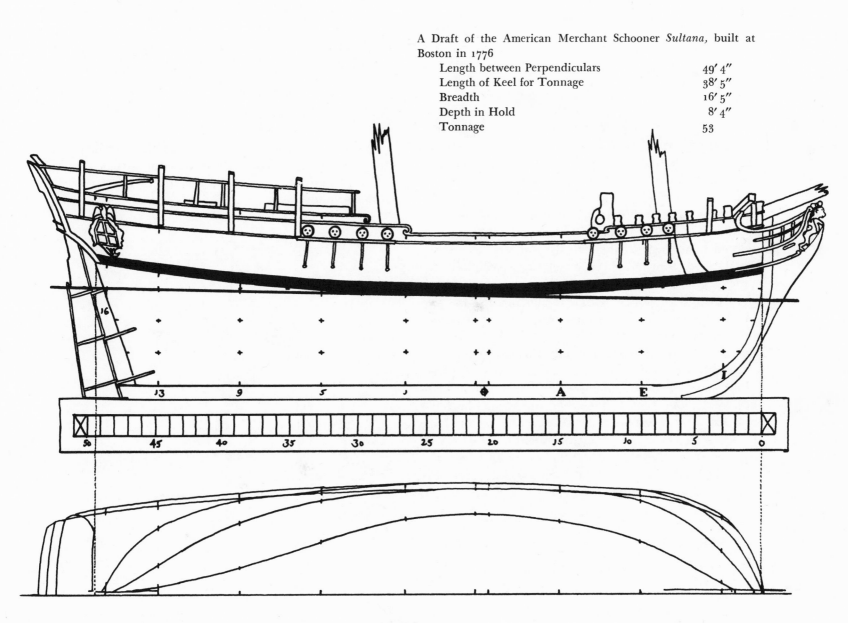

SURPRISE

A 10-GUN lugger was bought on 1 May 1777 at Dunkirk by William Hodge, the Continental agent. She was named *Surprise* and Gustavus Conyngham was put in command of her with a motley crew of Americans and Frenchmen. A few days later she returned to France, having taken two prizes. Unfortunately, one of the prizes was no ordinary merchant ship, but the Royal Mail packet *Prince of Orange;* mail packets were considered sacrosanct, so the British protested more than usual. Therefore, all three vessels were seized by the French government; the two prizes were returned to the British with effusive apologies and *Surprise* was sold to the highest bidder. As for Conyngham, the French threw him in prison to keep up appearances, but they quietly let him out again after only a short time.

No lines or dimensions of *Surprise* have survived. However, there is a contemporary Dutch engraving of her taking the *Prince of Orange,* in which she looks practically as small as a longboat next to the large packet. Luggers varied little from vessel to vessel, so we have taken the profile and section of a typical lugger of the same size and period as *Surprise* and cross-referenced it with the Dutch engraving. The typical lugger hull will be seen to have been identical to the typical cutter hull of the period.

As we have reconstructed her, her dimensions were: length overall, 65′ 10″; length between perpendiculars, 56′ 4″; length of keel, 47′ 6″; breadth, 21′; draft, 10′ 7″; tonnage, about 90.

Lugger *Surprise*
From an anonymous Dutch engraving, ca. 1777

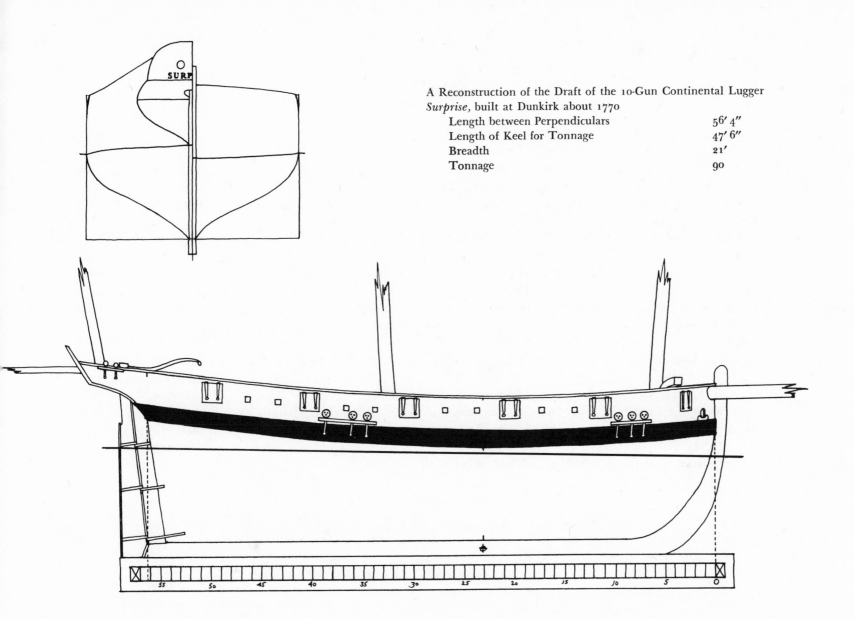

A Reconstruction of the Draft of the 10-Gun Continental Lugger
Surprise, built at Dunkirk about 1770

Length between Perpendiculars	56′ 4″
Length of Keel for Tonnage	47′ 6″
Breadth	21′
Tonnage	90

SWIFT

THE 10-gun brig Swift was built in America (probably the Chesapeake area) in 1778. Judging from her ornate finish and her sharp lines, which were designed for high speed and low carrying capacity, she was probably intended to be a mail packet between the United States and France; she had a wreath on the stern with three fleurs-de-lys in it, the French national arms. She was captured by the Royal Navy in 1779, although the records do not specify the circumstances; in fact the records are extremely confusing, for there were at least two other vessels in the Royal Navy at that time with the name *Swift,* one of 8 guns that was purchased in 1773 and sold in 1784, and another of 16 guns that was also captured from the Americans in 1779 and then captured by the French in 1782. Our *Swift* remained in the navy until her sale at the end of 1783 or the beginning of 1784.

She mounted 10 three-pounders and had a crew of forty men. When her lines were drawn at Deptford in 1783, the Admiralty surveyor noted that she was over-sparred, and he recommended that her sail area be drastically reduced, her crew brought down to thirty men and her guns reduced to six, while at the same time her ballast should be greatly increased. It is doubtful that these modifications were ever carried out. She must have been lightly built, with large frame spacing and thin planks so that her hull weight did not cause her to sink too deep into the water, thus losing the advantage of her sharp lines. Her deadrise was very steep, and continued above the waterline into flared topsides. Her plans are on file with the National Maritime Museum at Greenwich.

Dimensions: length overall, 85′ 8″; length between perpendiculars, 75′ 6″; length of keel, 52′ 4″; breadth, 20′ 6″; depth, 7′ 9″; draft, 9′ 10″; tonnage, 144.

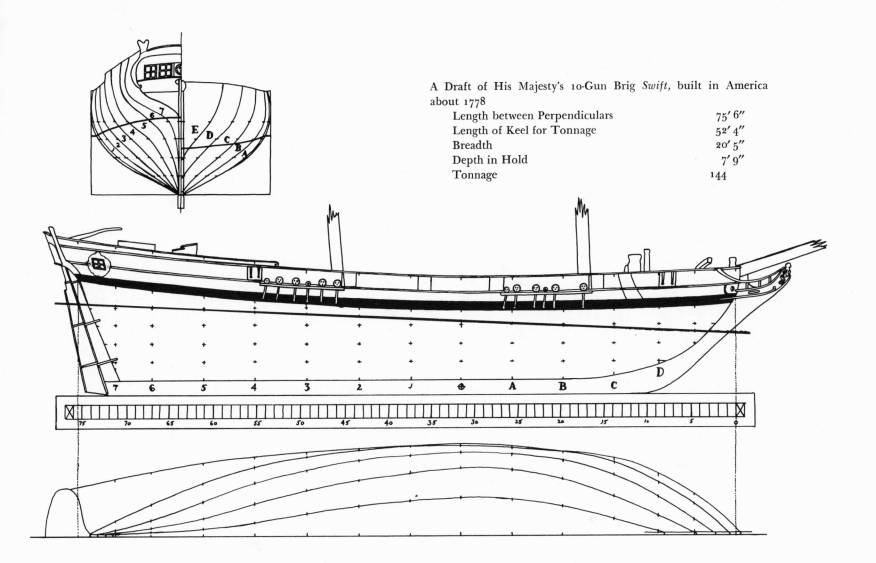

A Draft of His Majesty's 10-Gun Brig *Swift,* built in America
about 1778

Length between Perpendiculars	75′ 6″
Length of Keel for Tonnage	52′ 4″
Breadth	20′ 5″
Depth in Hold	7′ 9″
Tonnage	144

SWIFT

ONE of the delightful little pilot schooners that appeared immediately after the Revolution was *Swift*, built at Norfolk, Virginia, about 1788. She was bought in 1794 by the British consul for sending dispatches back and forth to England, but he found he did not need her for that purpose so, when a Royal Navy captain named Oakes arrived in America after the ship on which he had been a passenger home from India had been captured by a French squadron, the consul turned the schooner over to him and she carried Oakes (and other passengers and crew from the ship Oakes had been riding on) to Cork, Ireland, arriving there 30 June 1794.

The admiral of the Cork station decided to use her, first for the "impress service" and later, after some repairs, for surveying. She was then turned over to the commanding officer of the Portsmouth Dockyard for his personal use. Her lines were taken off there and are now on file at the National Maritime Museum at Greenwich. On 23 March 1803, she was formally taken into the Royal Navy and ordered fitted out and her bottom coppered. After that date, we can find no specific record of her, although the Royal Navy was obviously pleased by her performance, for they ordered twelve schooners built to her design, only to a larger scale, in Bermuda. However, the Bermudans had other ideas and refused to follow the designs that the Admiralty had sent to them.

Dimensions: length overall, 51' 10"; length between perpendiculars, 48' 3"; length of keel, 33' 7"; breadth, 15' 7"; depth, 5' 10"; draft, 6' 3"; tonnage, 46.

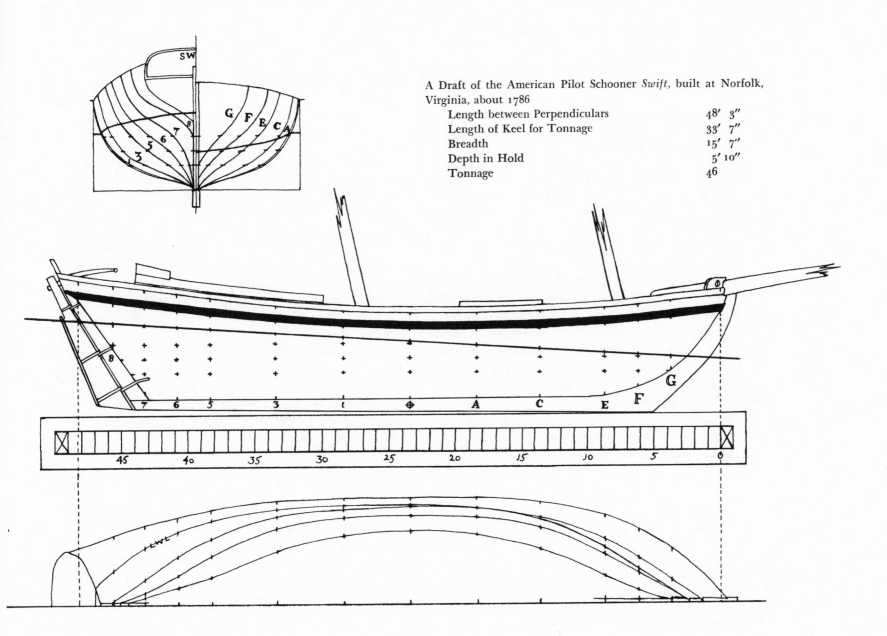

A Draft of the American Pilot Schooner *Swift,* built at Norfolk, Virginia, about 1786

Length between Perpendiculars	48′ 3″
Length of Keel for Tonnage	33′ 7″
Breadth	15′ 7″
Depth in Hold	5′ 10″
Tonnage	46

THORNTON

ASHLEY BOWEN, the wide-ranging sailor of Marblehead, Massachusetts, wrote a journal of his travels in which he included color sketches of many of the ships on which he had sailed. He served as a midshipman in the Royal Navy during the siege of Quebec, having accompanied a number of New England troops to Quebec in 1759. When the city fell the provincial troops were dismissed, and somewhere between 160 and 210 of them were crammed on a transport ship called the *Thornton. Thornton* sailed from Quebec on 8 October 1759, arriving at Boston on 9 November. She had as special passengers Colonel the Honourable William Howe and his aides and servants; Howe was to return to Boston at the beginning of the Revolution as a general in an occupying army.

Bowen drew a sketch of *Thornton,* stating that she was a transport of about 500 tons from New York under captain Exshaw. Beyond that we know little about her.

Where and when was she built? The best guess is that she was a frigate built for the Royal Navy in about 1756 and converted into a transport shortly after; with the exception of the raised poop, *Thornton* was almost identical in size and shape to frigates, such as *Rose,* that were built at the beginning of the Seven Years' War, and the poop was the sort of thing that could always be quickly added to make a transport more comfortable. She was probably built in New York on speculation and was not purchased by the navy for some reason or other. She had gunports for 11 guns per side, which is rather more than a ship of her size would have had if she had been built only for the purpose of being a transport.

As we have reconstructed her, her dimensions are: length overall, 131' 6"; length on the deck, 110'; breadth, 31'; tonnage, 510.

A Reconstruction of the Draft of the 20-Gun Ship *Thornton* of
New York, built about 1756
Length between Perpendiculars 110′
Tonnage 510

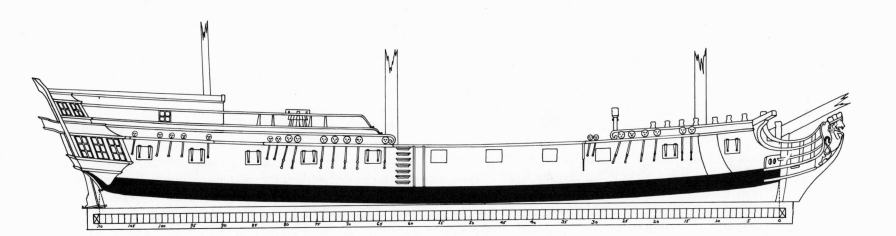

THUNDERER

WHEN the British learned in the summer of 1776 that Benedict Arnold was feverishly building an American fleet on Lake Champlain to interfere with British plans to invade New York from Canada, they began to build a fleet themselves at the other end of the lake at St. John's. Some of these craft were straightforward ship-rigged or schooner-rigged lake vessels, together with a number of ships' longboats each with a cannon in the bow. However, there was one strange craft called a radeau (radeau is the French word for "raft"). This vessel, named *Thunderer*, was ketch-rigged, but her hull was like a scow. Her bottom was nearly flat, and both her bow and stern came to a flat end about half as wide as the whole vessel. To give her longitudinal strength and rigidity the topsides were slightly curved, and she had a certain amount of sheer. She also had a small raised quarterdeck aft, with a cabin below for her officers. Her sides were pierced for a total of 18 guns, and guns could also be mounted on the bow and stern if necessary; however, in spite of her capacity, she only carried 6 twenty-four-pounders and 6 twelve-pounders, together with 2 howitzers, but even this made her about the most powerful vessel on the lake. Other radeaux had appeared on the lakes during the Seven Years' War so she was really nothing new, although she is startling to our eyes.

Her construction was supervised by Lieutenant Schank of the Royal Navy, who was the inventor of the centerboard; he is said to have asked permission to install one on *Thunderer,* but permission was denied and the wretched thing sailed very poorly as a result. In fact, she missed the fighting entirely at the battle of Valcour Island because she was unable to sail well enough upwind to get there before dark. Although there are no oarports indicated on the plan, one assumes that she was propelled by oars when the wind was not fair. Her great firepower was responsible for the destruction of a good part of Arnold's fleet not long after Valcour Island when Arnold personally set fire to many of the ships to avoid certain capture. Presumably she was broken up at the end of hostilities in 1783.

Thunderer appears in a number of contemporary pictures of the fleets on Lake Champlain, and her lines are on file at the National Maritime Museum at Greenwich.

Dimensions: length overall, 104′ 9″; length between perpendiculars, 91′ 9″; length of keel, 72′; breadth, 33′ 6″; depth, 6′ 8″; draft, 5′ 7″; tonnage, 423.

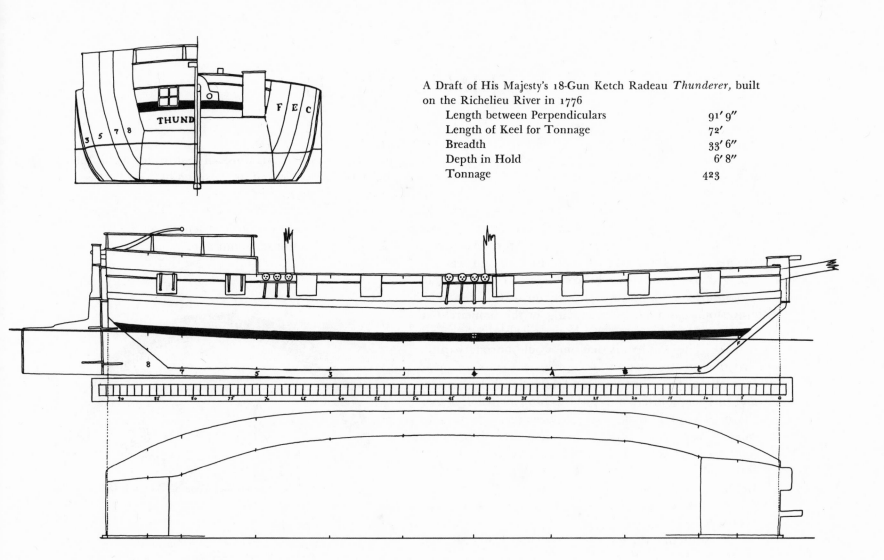

A Draft of His Majesty's 18-Gun Ketch Radeau *Thunderer,* built
on the Richelieu River in 1776

Length between Perpendiculars	91′ 9″
Length of Keel for Tonnage	72′
Breadth	33′ 6″
Depth in Hold	6′ 8″
Tonnage	423

TRUMBULL

AT the Old Granary Burying Ground in Boston is the gravestone of Lieutenant Jabez Smith, Jr., lieutenant of marines on the Continental frigate *Trumbull*, who died in June 1780. He had served in 1777 on the Connecticut State Navy ship *Oliver Cromwell* and later on the brig *Resistance*. He was captured when the frigate *Raleigh* was taken by the British, and was exchanged in 1779 so that he could serve on the frigate *Trumbull* as soon as she was ready for sea in 1780. The gravestone has a very fine carving in the semicircle at the top showing a 14-gun ship, probably a letter-of-marque. The problem is that one would normally think that this picture represents the frigate *Trumbull* or at least one of the other ships on which Smith had sailed, and this is absolutely impossible. Our conclusion is that the artist was told that Smith had been serving on a ship called *Trumbull,* and that he had then gone down to the harbor to look for such a ship. There were a great many ships by that name, for Governor Jonathan Trumbull of Connecticut was a popular man, and we believe that the artist used an armed merchant ship of that name for his model.

The ship in the engraving is flying the stars and stripes, which must be about the first representation of that flag on stone. An unusual feature for a ship of her size was the two-decked stern with a balcony between the two rows of stern windows.

As we have reconstructed her, her measurements were: length overall, 96′ 6″; length on the deck, 82′; breadth, 25′; tonnage, about 230.

Ship *Trumbull*
From the gravestone of Jabez Smith, Jr., 1780
Old Granary Burial Ground, Boston

[278]

A Reconstruction of the Draft of the 14-Gun American Armed
Merchant Ship *Trumbull,* built in Massachusetts about 1780

Length between Perpendiculars	82'
Breadth	25'
Tonnage	230

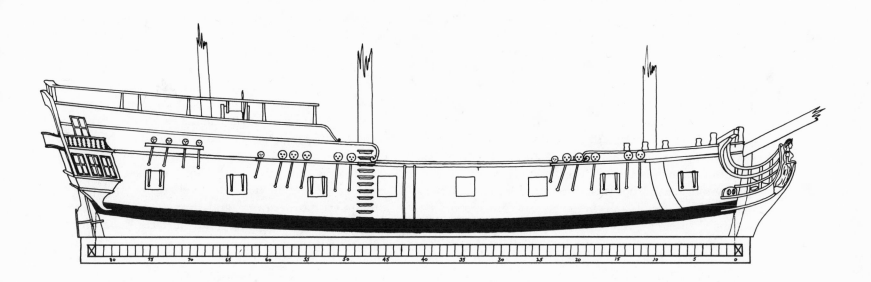

TURTLE

WHILE David Bushnell was a rather overaged student at Yale College he took time off from his studies to invent a successful underwater mine. After Lexington and Concord, while his classmates were joining the army around Boston, Bushnell went home to Saybrook, Connecticut, to build a submarine of his own invention, the *Turtle,* which would deliver the mine unseen to an enemy ship. The submarine was built in two eliptical halves made of oak staves like a barrel and well caulked with pitch. It had an entry hatch at the top that projected from a small conning tower, in which were set eight small glass windows and two schnorkels. At the bottom was a lead keel made in two pieces for ballast and neutral buoyancy; the fixed part of the keel weighed 700 pounds, and the other part, which could be jettisoned, weighed 200 pounds and could also be used as an anchor if needed. A foot-operated valve allowed water into the craft so it could submerge, and a pump could force it out again. A compass and a depth gauge were both illuminated by "foxfire" phosphorescence. The rudder was operated with a long tiller, and propulsion was effected by two hand-cranked screws, one for vertical motion and the other for horizontal motion. The mine was attached to an auger which was supposed to be able to take a bite on the bottom of a ship's hull, and the detonation system in the mine worked by clockwork and a flintlock. The vessel had only enough air for half an hour of operation submerged.

Bushnell's brother Ezra became quite proficient at operating *Turtle,* and although their original purpose of attacking a British ship in Boston had been thwarted by the British evacuation of Boston in March 1776, they were delighted to get the chance to try it out in New York when the British occupied that city in the summer of 1776. However, Ezra Bushnell became ill and David had not enough strength to operate *Turtle.* George Washington sought a replacement from his army and chose Sergeant Ezra Lee. Lee made an attack on the British 64-gun flagship *Eagle* after midnight on 7 September 1776, but the auger failed to take a bite on the bottom of the ship, for the little submarine had no way of exerting a force on the other end. Lee abandoned the attempt as dawn neared and propelled *Turtle* several miles against the current on the surface. Exhausted, he watched with glee as the British took fright at the mine blowing up harmlessly in the middle of the harbor. He made two more attempts within a few days, but with no more success.

On 9 October, the British made an attack up the Hudson, and in the fight the sloop carrying *Turtle* on her deck was sunk. *Turtle* was apparently recovered a few days later by the industrious Bushnell, but she was never used again. She is believed to have been destroyed after Washington's defeat at White Plains on 28 October 1776 to avoid capture.

A Reconstruction of the Draft of the Continental Submarine *Turtle,* built near Essex, Connecticut, in 1775

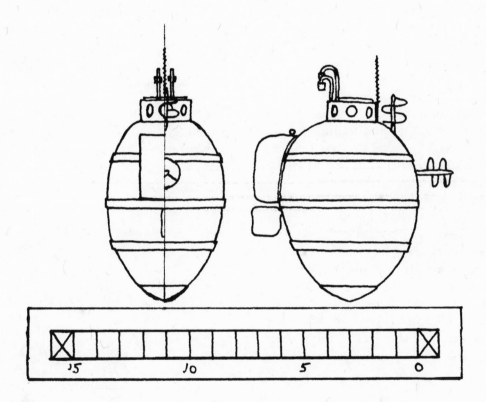

VIRGINIA

As far as we know, the first sailing vessel built by Englishmen * in the Americas was the 30-ton pinnace *Virginia*. She was constructed under the direction of Sir George Popham by a shipwright named Digby at St. George's Fort, Sagadahoc, Maine, at the mouth of the Kennebec River in 1607. The same year as another British expedition had settled Jamestown, Virginia, Popham's group of adventurers founded their fort in Maine for the purpose of fishing and trading for furs with the Indians. The settlers found that they did not care for the severe winter weather they had to face in Maine, so they built *Virginia* in order to escape, or so we are told. Since the settlement was visited by other ships from time to time, we suspect that the real reason for building her was to explore the coast.

She returned the settlers safely to England and then made several more transatlantic crossings in her life. The date and manner of her end is not recorded. A Spanish visitor to the fort drew a picture of the fort with *Virginia* moored alongside; that is the only knowledge we have of her appearance. She was a tubby boat, rigged as a sloop with a huge lateen yard or sprit on which was set the mainsail, if the picture is to be believed (some experts think the picture represents some other boat, because pinnaces often had two masts in those days). A model based on the picture and on research by William A. Baker was built by Carl Langbehn and is on display at the Bath Marine Museum at Bath, Maine.

As we see *Virginia*, her dimensions were: length overall, 56′ 1″; length between perpendiculars, 51′ 6″; length of keel, 43′ 6″; breadth, 13′; depth, 6′; draft, 6′ 2″; tonnage, 30.

Pinnace *Virginia*
From a drawing by John Hunt, 1607
The National Archives of Spain, Madrid

---

* French settlers in Florida had built a transatlantic-type vessel on the St. John's River as early as 1562–3, and the Spanish must have constructed ships in the Americas even earlier. No records of the appearance of either the French or the Spanish ships appear to have survived.

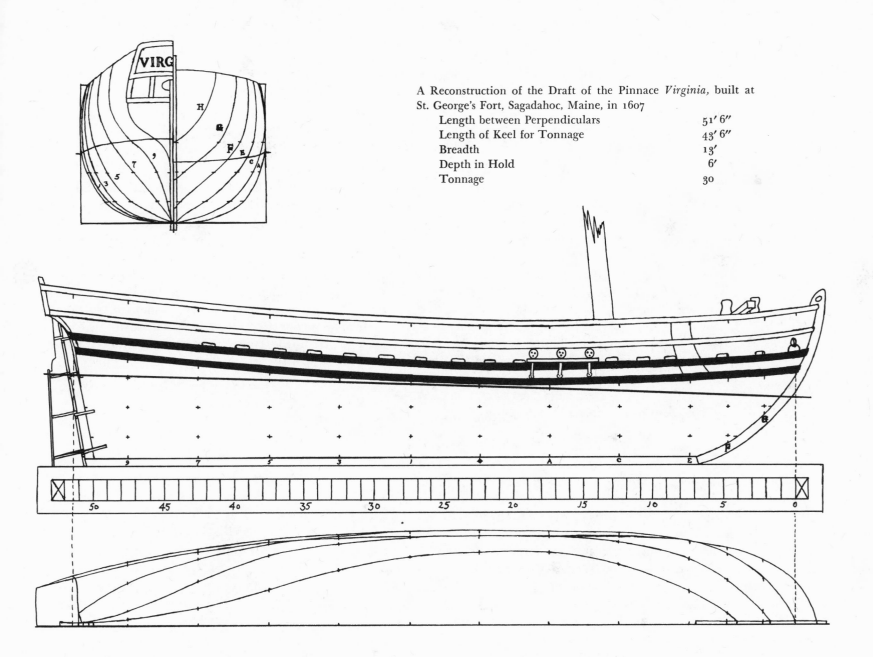

A Reconstruction of the Draft of the Pinnace *Virginia,* built at St. George's Fort, Sagadahoc, Maine, in 1607

Length between Perpendiculars	51′ 6″
Length of Keel for Tonnage	43′ 6″
Breadth	13′
Depth in Hold	6′
Tonnage	30

VIRGINIA, TRUMBULL, EFFINGHAM, *and* CONGRESS

IN December 1775 Congress passed the second half of the Rhode Island Navy Bill, which called for the construction of thirteen frigates as soon as possible. Five of these frigates were to be of 28 guns, and of these only the *Providence,* built in Rhode Island, appears to have been constructed to plans other than the official drafts supplied by Congress. The four others were *Congress,* built either by Lancaster Burling or by Lawrence & Tudor at Poughkeepsie, New York; *Effingham,* built by Grice & Company at Philadelphia; *Trumbull,* built by John Cotton at Chatham, Connecticut; and *Virginia,* built by George Wells of Baltimore, Maryland.

Construction of *Congress* and her 24-gun consort *Montgomery,* built in the same place, was slowed to allow men and material to be devoted to Benedict Arnold's fleet on Lake Champlain. Since the British had occupied New York City from midsummer 1776 onward and a powerful army was advancing along Lake Champlain toward the Hudson under General Burgoyne, it was decided to burn both ships about ten miles downriver from where they were built (they may still lie on the bottom of the river, waiting for intrepid marine archaeologists to discover them). They were burned in an unfinished condition. *Congress*'s captain was Thomas Grinnell of New York.

Effingham, named after the Elizabethan sea dog, fared little better. She had been launched at Philadelphia not long before the British occupied that city, and she was sunk upriver from there to avoid capture about 20 November 1777. She was raised shortly thereafter to serve as winter barracks for some of Washington's men, but when the British made a raid up the river in May 1778 she and her 32-gun consort *Washington* were burned to avoid capture. Her captain was John Barry.

It was announced on 24 January 1777 that *Virginia* was ready for sea, but Captain James Nicholson claimed he was short of supplies, officers, and men, so he remained at anchor. In June he ventured down the Chesapeake as far as the York River, but was quickly chased back by a British patrol. After much prodding from

Frigate *Virginia*
From an oil painting by Dominic Serres, 1780
National Maritime Museum, Greenwich, England

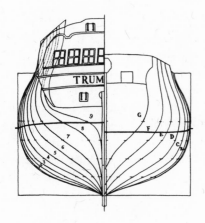

A Draft of the 28-Gun Continental Frigates *Trumbull,* built at Chatham, Connecticut; *Congress,* built on the Hudson River, New York; *Effingham,* built at Philadelphia; and *Virginia,* built at Baltimore, Maryland; all in 1776

Length between Perpendiculars	126′ 3½″
Length of Keel for Tonnage	105′ 7¼″
Breadth	34′ 4″
Depth in Hold	10′ 5½″
Tonnage	682

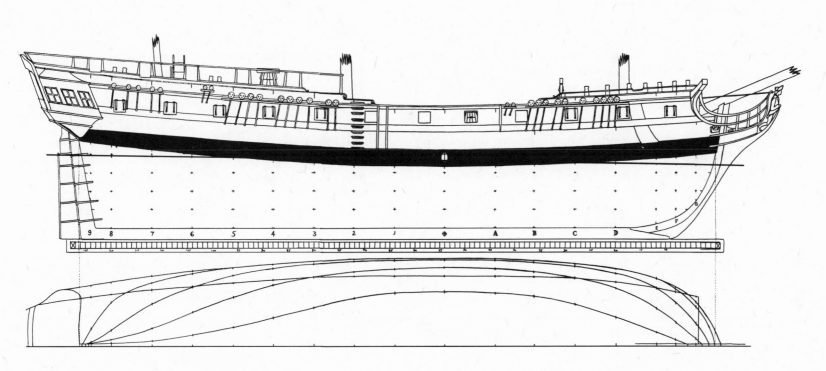

Congress, Nicholson finally got underway again with a fresh breeze at his back and an experienced pilot sailing ahead to guide him in the clear night. The British patrols failed to see him, but suddenly *Virginia* grounded on a sandbar; when she passed into deeper water on the other side, it was found that the rudder had come off, so Nicholson rowed ashore, neglecting to take or destroy his secret papers or to give orders to burn the ship. Command of the ship devolved on eighteen-year-old Lieutenant Joshua Barney, but he could do no more than surrender the ship on April Fools Day 1778 when the British spotted her the next morning, for the crew had broken into the rum supply and were drunk to a man.

Virginia was taken into the Royal Navy under her original name, but was rated as a 32-gun ship. On 3 August 1779, she left New York in Commodore Sir George Collier's squardon that was headed for the Penobscot Bay in Maine; their arrival there caused the destruction of an enormous American fleet, including the frigate *Warren,* the corvettes *Hampden* and *General Putnam,* and the sloop *Providence.* An oil painting of this incident by Dominic Serres shows a stern view of *Virginia* and can be seen at the National Maritime Museum at Greenwich. In 1780, she took part in the British capture of Charleston, South Carolina. British records state that she was then sailed to England where she was drawn in drydock (her lines are on file at the National Maritime Museum at Greenwich), and was then ordered broken up as unsound in December 1782 (although Chapelle says she was not sold until 1786).

Trumbull, named after Connecticut's popular Governor Jonathan Trumbull, was put under command of Captain Dudley Saltonstall. She turned out to draw too much water to get over the sandbar at the mouth of the Connecticut River, so she was trapped. Benedict Arnold, home briefly on leave, suggested that she be buoyed up with lighters, but he was ignored. A British raiding party nearly got close enough to burn her in April 1777. In September 1778 her crew were taken off to man the frigate *Raleigh,* and in 1779 Saltonstall was replaced by Elisha Hinman, who had just been absolved of all blame in the loss of the *Alfred.* In two months he got out of the river, tying on empty water casks to float her higher, and took her to New London for a crew. He was suddenly relieved, for no stated reason, by James Nicholson, who had earlier lost *Virginia.* He got her to sea in May 1780 and had a furious battle with the 36-gun Liverpool privateer *Watt* (ex-East Indiaman). *Trumbull* lost her main- and mizzenmasts, and *Watt* limped away in desperate condition. On 8 August 1781 she left Philadelphia as escort for twenty-eight merchant ships, but the next day a storm carried away her main and fore topmasts. While she was making repairs she was attacked by the 32-gun frigate *Iris* (formerly *Hancock*) and the 20-gun corvette *General Monk* (formerly *General Washington*) and quickly captured. She was in such bad condition that *Iris* had to tow her back to New York and there she was sold to be broken up.

The *Trumbull* that was taken into the Royal Navy as *Tobago* was a completely different ship.

Dimensions: length overall, 150′ 6″; length on the deck, 126′ 3″; length of keel, 105′ 7″; breadth, 34′ 4″; depth, 10′ 6″; draft, 18′; tonnage, 682.

WARREN

THE most powerful of all the original thirteen frigates authorized by Congress in December 1775 was the 32-gun *Warren,* for she was armed with eighteen-pounders rather than the twelve-pounders used by the others. She was the first of all the American frigates launched, on 15 May 1776 at Providence, Rhode Island, and was originally named *America,* according to the Newport *Mercury.* She was soon renamed, however, after Dr. Joseph Warren, the Massachusetts patriot who had died at Bunker Hill in 1775 and whose body had been dug up and reinterred in Boston only a short time before the launching. Some historians have thought that she might have been named for the town of Warren, Rhode Island (the Indian village where founder Roger Williams had first lived) or Commodore Peter Warren (who had coordinated the successful New England attack on Louisbourg, Nova Scotia, in 1745). Her builders were Talman & Bowers, who were also building the 28-gun *Providence* and would later build the 20-gun *General Washington.* It is our belief that they were also the builders of the 16-gun privateer *Oliver Cromwell,* whose lines are on file at the National Maritime Museum at Greenwich, and we have based our reconstruction of *Warren* on these plans.

Command of the *Warren* was given to Captain John B. Hopkins, son of Commodore Esek Hopkins. After she was rigged, she was hove down for some work on her bottom and the rotten rope that had been supplied at great personal profit by John Brown (a prominent member of the state committee that was overseeing construction of the ships) snapped, thus breaking many of her spars. An engraving of her on a powderhorn in February 1777 shows her still without her main topgallant mast. It was not until early March 1778 that Hopkins was able to get her to sea through the tight blockade imposed by British ships at Newport, and even then she was damaged in both hull and rigging by British shots. The weather being very cold and the crew only having thin clothing with them, Hopkins cruised to Bermuda, taking two prizes before returning to Boston on 23 March. Once there the crew deserted, and Hopkins spent the rest of the year looking for a crew. A year later, she still only had 70 men out of over 200 that she should have had. Finally, in late March 1779 Hopkins got her to sea with an adequate crew in company with *Queen of France,* and on 7 April they took eight out of ten ships

Frigate *Warren* (missing her topgallant mast)
From a powderhorn engraving made for Charles Hewitt, 1777
Private collection, New Jersey

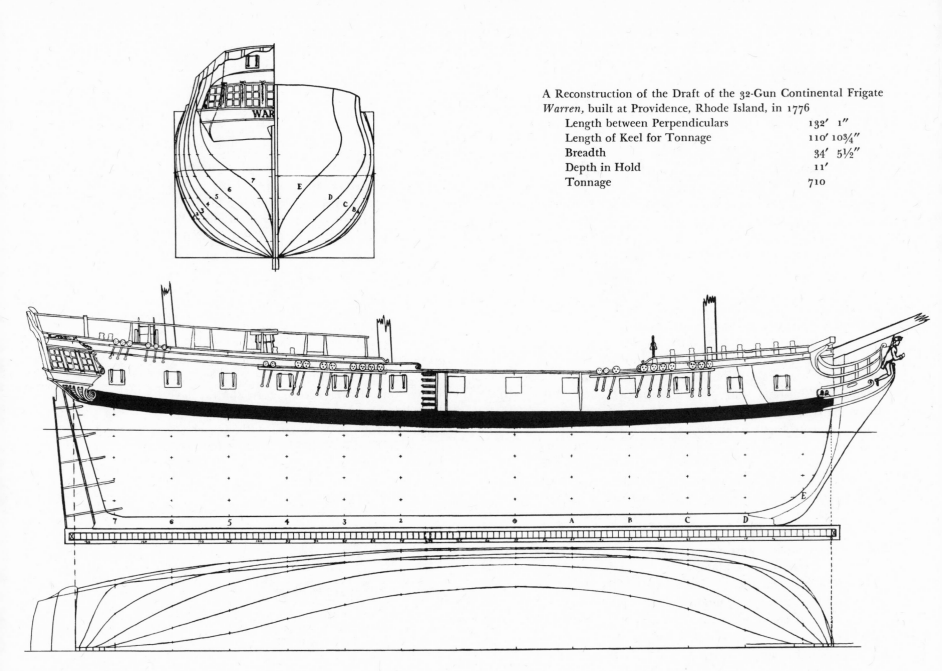

A Reconstruction of the Draft of the 32-Gun Continental Frigate *Warren*, built at Providence, Rhode Island, in 1776

Length between Perpendiculars	132′ 1″
Length of Keel for Tonnage	110′ 10¾″
Breadth	34′ 5½″
Depth in Hold	11′
Tonnage	710

in a British convoy off the Delaware, including the escort. Contrary to orders, they took all their ships back to Boston, where the crew deserted immediately and Hopkins was suspended for some irregularities in the distribution of prize money. Command of *Warren* was then given to Dudley Saltonstall, who for years had failed to get his frigate *Trumbull* out of the Connecticut River.

Saltonstall did hardly any better for *Warren*. He used her as his flagship for the huge American fleet that sailed to the Penobscot Bay in Maine. They arrived at the Penobscot in 27 July 1779, but coordination between the sea and land forces was so pathetic that they failed to dislodge the tiny British force at Castine. In the meantime, a small British fleet of seven ships, only one of them a two-decker, arrived on 13 August and the Americans fled up to the head of the bay, where they burned their ships. In this way, the whole fleet was lost, including *Warren, Hampden, General Putnam,* and the sloop *Providence,* while together they might have made a stand or escaped to sea. *Warren* appears in the background of an oil painting of the incident by Dominic Serres that can be seen at the National Maritime Museum at Greenwich.

Dimensions: length overall, 151′ 9″; length on the deck, 132′ 1″; length of keel, 110′ 11″; breadth, 34′ 5″; depth, 11′; draft, 17′; tonnage, 690.

Frigate *Warren,* on fire
From an oil painting by Dominic Serres, 1780
National Maritime Museum, Greenwich, England

WASHINGTON, TRUMBULL, GATES, *and* CONGRESS

WHEN Benedict Arnold built his little fleet on Lake Champlain in the summer of 1776 the most important elements of it were the four galleys *Washington, Gates, Trumbull,* and *Congress. Washington* was commanded by General David Waterbury; her crew numbered 110 men, and she mounted two eighteen-pounders, four twelve-pounders, two nine-pounders, and four four-pounders, plus a few swivels. After the battle of Valcour Island she and *Congress,* with the cutter *Lee,* formed the rearguard as the Americans retreated quietly toward Crown Point. Unfortunately, the British caught up with them and captured both *Washington* and *Lee.* They released Waterbury and his men on parole after only a few days, and the men praised the British for their good treatment. *Washington,* though heavily damaged, was repaired and taken into the British forces on the lake. Chapelle reports that she was rerigged as a brig, but an engraving of the British fleet in 1777 shows her rigged as she originally was: with large lateen sails on two masts.

When the schooner *Royal Savage* was put out of action at the battle of Valcour Island, Benedict Arnold made *Congress* his flagship. She håd one eighteen-pounder, one twelve-pounder, two nine-pounders, six six-pounders, and some swivels. After the battle, *Congress* formed part of the rearguard for the retreating Americans, and she was so badly damaged by the advancing British that Arnold ran her ashore at Buttonmould Bay, about ten miles north of Crown Point on the Vermont shore. Arnold personally set fire to her. Some timbers that were said to be her remains were discovered around 1900 and placed on display.

Trumbull was the only American vessel on the lake to be commanded by a genuine sailor: Seth Warner from Connecticut. He led the way out of the American position after the battle of Valcour Island, and skillfully piloted the fleet past the British ships in the foggy night

Galley *Washington*
From an engraving published by R. Sayer & J. Bennett, 1776
National Maritime Museum, Greenwich, England

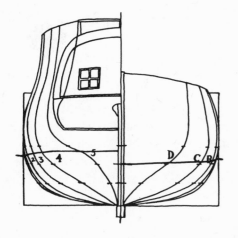

A Draft of the Continental Galley *Washington,* built at Skenesborough, New York, in 1776

Length on the Range of the Deck	72′ 4″
Length of Keel for Tonnage	60′ 6″
Breadth	19′ 7″
Depth in Hold	6′ 2″
Tonnage	123

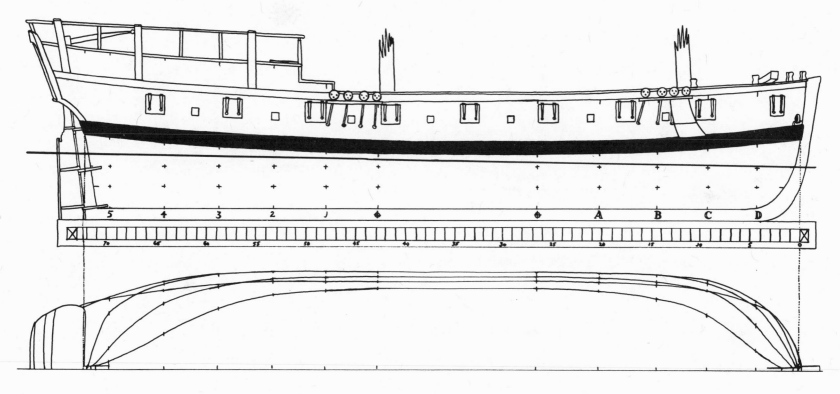

without alerting the British. *Trumbull* and most of the rest of the fleet reached Crown Point in safety, and the British turned back to St. John's because it was already so late in the year. The next year the British fleet swept south along the lake with more ships than before, so *Trumbull* was destroyed to avoid capture in the summer of 1777.

The fourth galley, named after General Horatio Gates, was not actually finished in time for the battle of Valcour Island, and when she was finished the season was over. In the summer of 1777, when the British fleet advanced along the lake, *Gates* had to be blown up to avoid capture. Thus ended her brief career without her having accomplished anything.

A plan of *Washington* was drawn after her capture, and that can be seen at the National Maritime Museum at Greenwich. There are various contemporary portraits of the galleys at the National Maritime Museum, at the Royal Collection at Windsor Castle, in the Public Archives of Canada, and at Fort Ticonderoga.

Dimensions: length overall, 80′; length on the deck, 72′ 4″; length of keel, 60′ 6″; breadth, 19′ 11″; depth, 6′ 2″; draft, 6′ 6″; tonnage, 123.

Galley *Trumbull*
From an engraving published by R. Sayer & J. Bennett, 1776
National Maritime Museum, Greenwich, England

Galley *Congress*
From a watercolor painting by C. Randle, 1776
The Public Archives of Canada, Ottawa

Bateau

A FLAT-BOTTOMED, flat-sided, double-ended craft that was used in rivers and lakes in New England and Canada was called a bateau, after the French word for boat. With the sides flaring outward, the bateau was a stable platform for the carriage of cargo on inland waters. Bateaux came in a variety of sizes, but the plans for only one have been discovered (they were so simple that they probably needed no plans for most builders to turn them out).

Dimensions: length, 30′ 4″; breadth, 6′ 6″; depth, 2′ 10″.

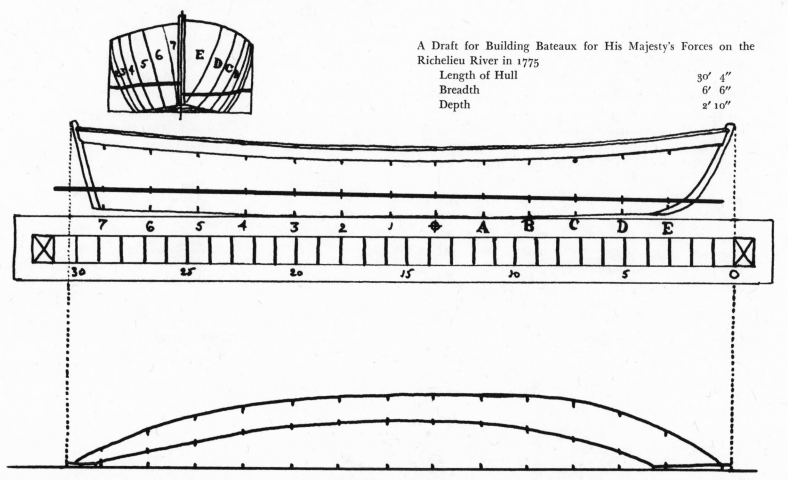

A Draft for Building Bateaux for His Majesty's Forces on the Richelieu River in 1775

Length of Hull	30′ 4″
Breadth	6′ 6″
Depth	2′ 10″

Lake Champlain Gondolas

WHEN Benedict Arnold put together an American fleet on Lake Champlain in the summer of 1776, he used sloops, schooners, cutters, ketches, and galleys. In addition to these larger craft, he also constructed gondolas or gundaloes as they were sometimes called. These had flat bottoms, flaring topsides, and double ends. They were propelled by oars except when the wind was astern, at which time they could set a square course and square topsail. They mounted three carriage guns, one twelve-pounder in the bow and one six- or nine-pounder on each side (staggered) amidships. They had a raised deck aft, under which it was possible to sleep and to stow gear, and the topsides could have their height augmented in battle by the addition of branches and other impedimenta to guard against bullets and flying splinters. The crew numbered as many as forty-five men.

It seems that all the gondolas were built at Skenesborough to the same plans, and they are said to have been painted barn-red. *Boston* was sunk in action on 12 October 1776. *Connecticut* survived the battle of Valcour Island, but no history after that is recorded. *Jersey* was captured by the British on 13 October and taken into their forces. *New Haven* was burned to avoid capture on 13 October. *New York* was probably captured by the British in October, but there is no record. *Philadelphia* was sunk at the battle of Valcour Island, and raised again in the 1930s; she has been carefully preserved and is on display at the Smithsonian Institu-

tion in Washington, D.C. *Providence* was sunk on 12 October, and *Spitfire* was burned on 13 October to avoid capture. *Success* seems not to have been present at the battle of Valcour Island, and to have had her name changed not long afterward, but there is no record of her new name nor of her ultimate fate.

Benedict Arnold is thought to have designed all the gondolas, and they are believed all to have been built from the same plans. However, Arnold's written description of them does not exactly fit *Philadelphia,* the only one presently existing. For example, Arnold called for a small keel, which no doubt would have been a help in steering, particularly when the gondola was under sail, but no keel was fitted. The dimensions are also a little different. We suspect that Arnold had to

Gondola *Philadelphia*
From a watercolor by C. Randle, 1776
The Public Archives of Canada, Ottawa

[294]

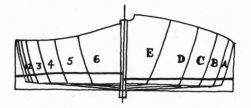

A Draft for Building Gondolas for the Continental Forces on Lake
Champlain in 1775

Length between Perpendiculars	51′ 6″
Length of Keel	48′
Breadth	16′
Depth	3′ 6″

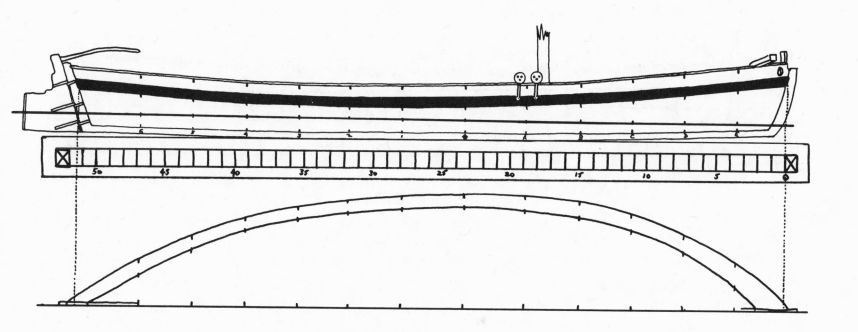

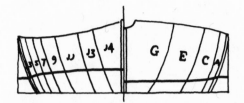

A Draft of the Continental Gondolas *Philadelphia, Jersey, New York, Connecticut, Providence, Spitfire, New Haven,* and *Boston,* built at Skenesborough, New York, in 1775

Length between Perpendiculars	51′ 6″
Length of Keel	48′ 9″
Breadth	15′ 6″
Depth	3′ 10″

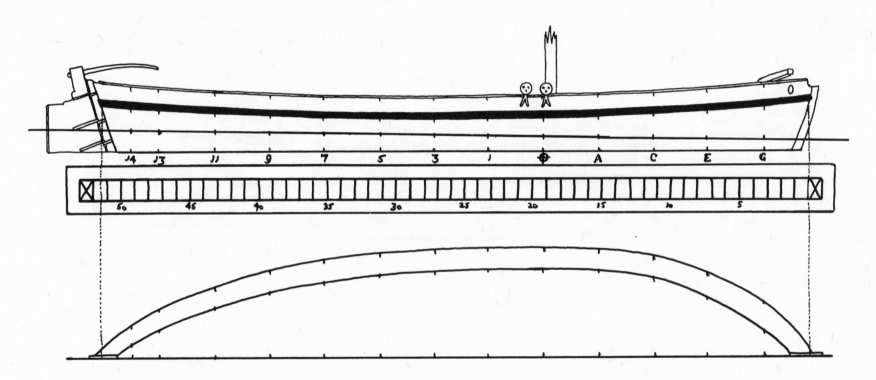

modify his original plan based on certain realities that he faced, but of which we are ignorant.

Here are the dimensions, based on Arnold's descriptions: length overall, 56′ 2″; length between perpendiculars, 51′ 6″; length of keel, 48′; breadth, 16′; depth, 3′ 6″; draft, 1′ 6″. Here are the dimensions as built (other dimensions remain the same): length of keel, 48′ 9″; breadth, 15′ 6″; depth, 3′ 10″; draft, 1′8.

Lake Champlain Gunboat

WHEN Arnold built his 56-foot, 3-gun gondolas on Lake Champlain in the summer of 1776, the British were also building smaller gun-boats at St. John's at the northern end of the lake. Some were built on the Richelieu River in 1775 and others on the lake in 1776. They had one nine-pounder gun in the bow on a raised platform, and had wide, rounded bottoms. These gun-boats were used at the battle of Valcour Island, but there is no report as to how many were disabled or sunk by American fire.

Dimensions: length overall, 38′; length between perpendiculars, 35′ 9″; length of keel, 25′ 3″; breadth, 12′; depth, 3′ 4″; draft, 2′ 6″.

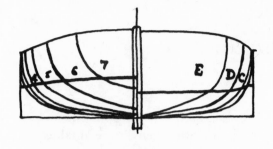

A Draft for building Gunboats for His Majesty's Forces on the
Richelieu River in 1775

Length between Perpendiculars	35' 9"
Length of Keel	25' 3"
Breadth	12'
Depth	3' 5"

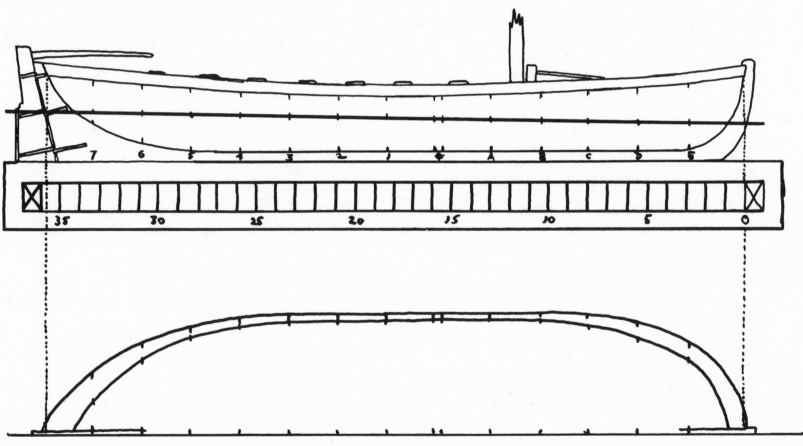

Bermuda Schooner

THERE are scores, if not hundreds, of portraits of American schooners and sloops from the period covered by our book, and it would obviously be ridiculous to try to reconstruct all of them for inclusion in the book. Many of these pictures are by the Marblehead, Massachusetts, seaman and artist Ashley Bowen. We have included this drawing of a "Bermuda" schooner (which actually could have been built at Bermuda, Jamaica, or in the Chesapeake) because we wanted to show that this type of hull was frequently driven by a schooner rig, whereas most of the other examples in the book are sloops. The picture from which our drawing was made is a semiprimitive in the style of Ashley Bowen, and it shows the schooner under sail off Curaçao flying a British ensign just after the American Revolution. She probably mounted ten small carriage guns.

As we reconstruct her: length overall, 74′ 9″; length between perpendiculars, 68′.

A Reconstruction of a Draft of a 10-Gun Schooner built at Bermuda or the Chesapeake about 1780
Length between Perpendiculars   68′

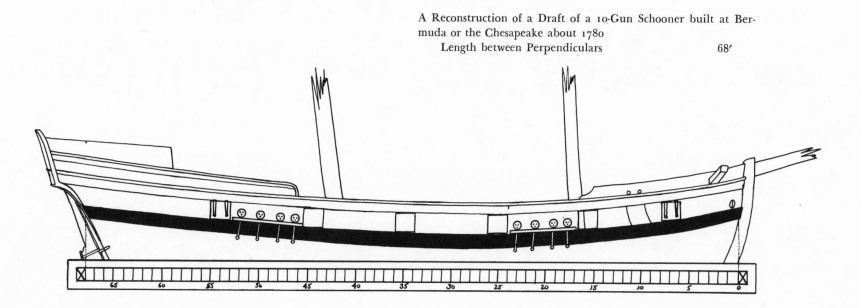

Bermuda Sloop

INCLUDED in his book *Architectura Navalis Mercatoria*, published in the 1760s, Chapman showed the plans for a 10-gun "Bermuda" sloop. This kind of vessel, although called "Bermuda," was actually produced with few variations in Bermuda, Jamaica, and the Chesapeake Bay. The earliest picture of this type so far found is dated 1707, and we know that they continued to be produced after the American Revolution. They were particularly handy for sailing to, from, and around the West Indies. They made good smugglers, too, for with their sloop or schooner rigs they could escape quickly to windward while frigates and brigs were stymied from being now so close-winded. These vessels were characterized by their sharp lines, their deadrise, and the little cabin perched high on their sterns.

Here are the dimensions of Chapman's sloop, which probably dates from about 1750: length overall, 69′; length between perpendiculars, 60′ 9″; length of keel, 41′ 9″; breadth, 21′ 3″; depth, 9′; draft, 11′ 1″; tonnage, 92.

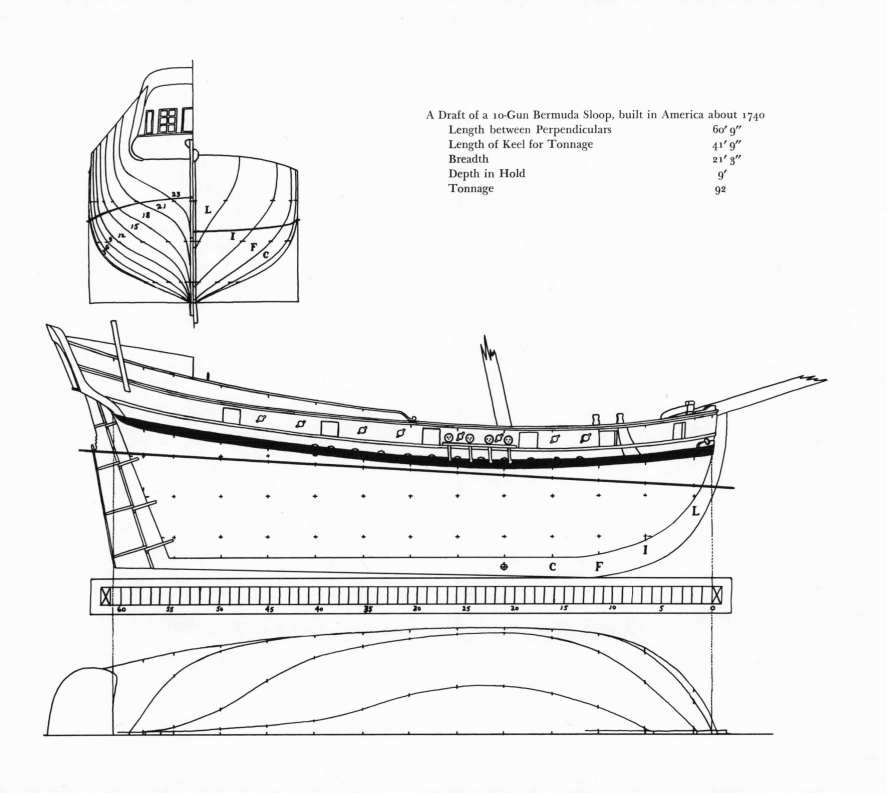

A Draft of a 10-Gun Bermuda Sloop, built in America about 1740

Length between Perpendiculars	60' 9"
Length of Keel for Tonnage	41' 9"
Breadth	21' 3"
Depth in Hold	9'
Tonnage	92

Boston Brig

IN 1769, certificates of membership as an artillery-man in Boston's South Battery were engraved and issued. On the certificate was an engraving of a Boston scene, including a 14-gun brig being built in the foreground and ready for launching. One cannot tell very much about the brig from the engraving, even though it is finely and accurately executed, so our reconstruction is no more than tentative. Her bow is completely out of the picture, hence that part is pure conjecture.

As we see her: length overall, 87′; length between perpendiculars, 72′.

American Brig captured by a British Privateer, not unlike the Boston Brig
From an oil painting by Francis Holman, ca. 1778
National Maritime Museum, Greenwich, England

A Reconstruction of the Draft of a 14-Gun Brig, built at Boston in 1769
Length between Perpendiculars   72′

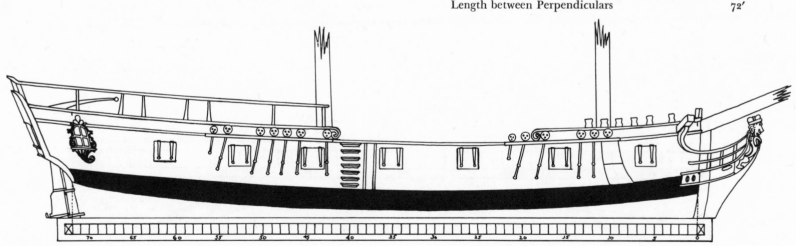

Boston Merchant Ship

A RARE Leeds mug, until recently in the Sussel Collection, bears on its back the words "Robt. H. Wilson 1784 Boston." The front of the mug shows a full-rigged merchant ship under sail, flying the United States ensign. Beyond that, we know nothing about the ship. The picture shows her to have had a raised quarter-deck and quarter gallery windows. She apparently had no raised forecastle, and the level of the waist deck is not apparent.

As we have drawn her, she measured about 97′ in overall length and 80′ in length between perpendiculars.

A Reconstruction of the Draft of a Merchant Ship owned in Boston in 1784

Length between Perpendiculars   80′

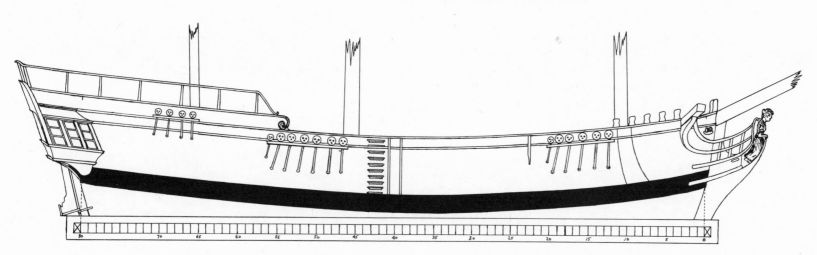

Sloop off Boston Light

ONE of the earliest American portraits of a specific ship (although we don't actually know which specific ship) is the picture known as *Sloop off Boston Light*. This was drawn by Burgis about 1729. The sloop is shown at anchor, with Boston Lighthouse in the background. She had ten carriage guns, and a small but ornate cabin aft. She was probably designed for long-distance sailing, for she had a small head projecting from the bow which is usually not seen on sloops. Judging from her rig she was an American sloop, not a British sloop. The 1720s was a period of peace, and one wonders why a supposed merchant sloop of that period would therefore waste so much carrying capacity with ten guns, but of course the guns may have simply been drawn in for the portrait; just because a sloop had gunports did not mean to say that she had to have guns mounted in them all the time. Of course, it is always possible that this sloop had been purchased for customs service, which would explain the need for guns.

As we see her: length overall, 65' 6"; length between perpendiculars, 55'; tonnage, 85.

Sloop off Boston Light
From a mezzotint dated 1717

A Reconstruction of the Draft of a 10-Gun Sloop at Boston in 1717
Length between Perpendiculars   55'

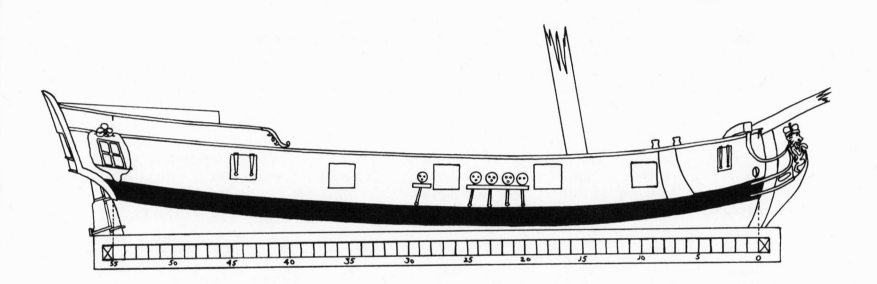

British Sloop for Lake Champlain

In the collection of Admiralty drafts at the National Maritime Museum at Greenwich is the plan for two 10-gun sloops to be built on Lake Champlain in 1776. We have been unable to find any information about whether they were actually built. They were certainly not employed at the battle of Valcour Island, but they may have been incorporated into the British fleet in 1777 and thus completed about the same time as the corvette *Royal George*. Their profile was far more like a British sloop or cutter than an American, and they had a small cabin aft that was covered by a quarterdeck raised only half a deck-height above the main deck. Although they had the usual flattish bottom found on most lake vessels, they were deeper than the normal lake boats, so they may have sailed quite well. In addition to the carriage guns, they mounted about 20 swivels.

The general concept of this design appears to have been used for the construction of a modern copy of the Great Lakes sloop *Welcome,* built in 1975. No plans or dimensions survive for the original *Welcome,* but this rather smaller sloop could not have been very different from the Lake Champlain sloops.

Dimensions: length overall, 65′; length between perpendiculars, 56′ 10″; length of keel, 44′ 3″; breadth, 19′ 7″; depth, 9′; draft, 8′ 5″; tonnage, 90.

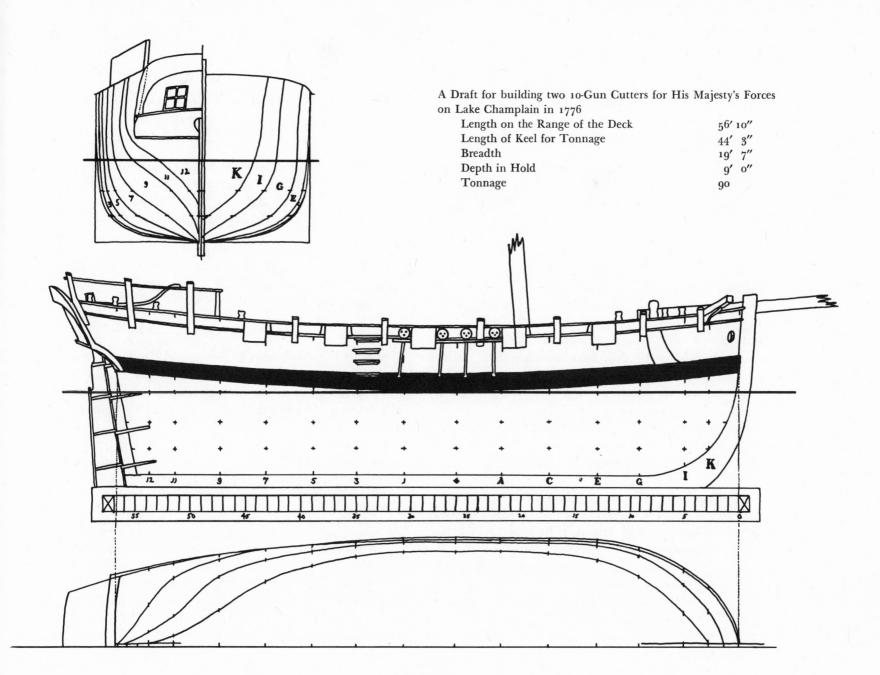

A Draft for building two 10-Gun Cutters for His Majesty's Forces
on Lake Champlain in 1776

Length on the Range of the Deck	56′ 10″
Length of Keel for Tonnage	44′ 3″
Breadth	19′ 7″
Depth in Hold	9′ 0″
Tonnage	90

Lake Champlain Radeau, Sloop, Schooner, and Corvette

ONE artistic and enthusiastic American in the Lake Champlain area, named Simon Metcalf, took the trouble to make rough plan drawings of four vessels he hoped he could get Arnold or someone else to build for use on the lake. They were. a radeau, a sloop, a schooner, and a corvette. None was ever built, but we have included the drawings anyway. The radeau (French word for "raft") had three masts, six guns, and six oars, and was steered with two long rudders. Otherwise, it had a very simple rectangular shape with a bevel in the bow and stern from the bottom to the waterline. With one of Schank's drop-keels it might have sailed on a reach, but otherwise it would only have been able to run before the wind; in that case, why the three masts?

Dimensions: length overall, 55'; length between perpendiculars, 45'; length of keel, 33'; breadth, 18'; depth, 2'; draft, 2' 8"; tonnage, 30.

The sloop, which also mounted six guns, had a raked stem with a fiddlehead, but otherwise the profile was not too far from normal. It was in its sections that this sloop was unusual. It was pinched in rather sharply to the stern, which, among other things, would have left virtually no room in the tiny cabin in the stern.

Dimensions: length overall, 55' 3"; length between perpendiculars, 45'; length of keel, 36' 2"; breadth, 18'; depth, 5'; draft, 5' 9"; tonnage, 45.

Metcalf's schooner mounted 14 carriage guns and was rather larger than most schooners of the day. She had the same raked stem and fiddlehead as the sloop, but her stern was not pinched in. She had more deadrise than the sloop.

Dimensions: length overall, 95'; length between perpendiculars, 75' 2"; length of keel, 54' 6"; breadth, 22'; depth, 6' 6"; draft, 7'; tonnage, 130.

Metcalf's corvette mounted about 18 guns (pierced for 20), and was quite a respectable design, except for its remarkable sheer: the bow and stern stick up almost like the ends of a banana. The bow, as with the sloop and schooner, was fitted with a fiddlehead.

Dimensions: length overall, 104' 6"; length between perpendiculars, 88'; length of keel, 76' 7"; breadth, 28' 6"; depth, 6' 8"; draft, 8'; tonnage, about 200.

No discussion of American ships of this period would be entirely complete without these odd vessels designed by Metcalf, but on the other hand Metcalf's work should not be taken any more seriously by us than it was by the American strategists to whom he presumably submitted these designs as proposals.

A Reconstruction of the Draft of the proposed 6-Gun Radeau to be built on Lake Champlain in 1777

Length on the Range of the Deck	40′
Length of Keel for Tonnage	33′
Breadth	18′
Depth	2′
Tonnage	30

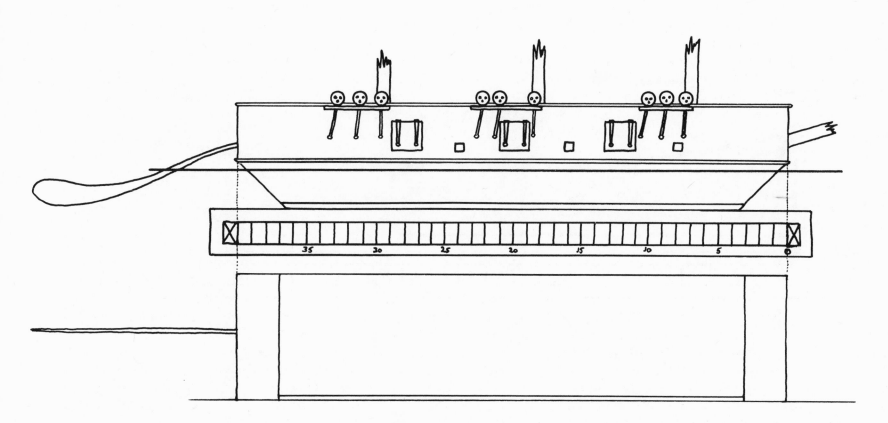

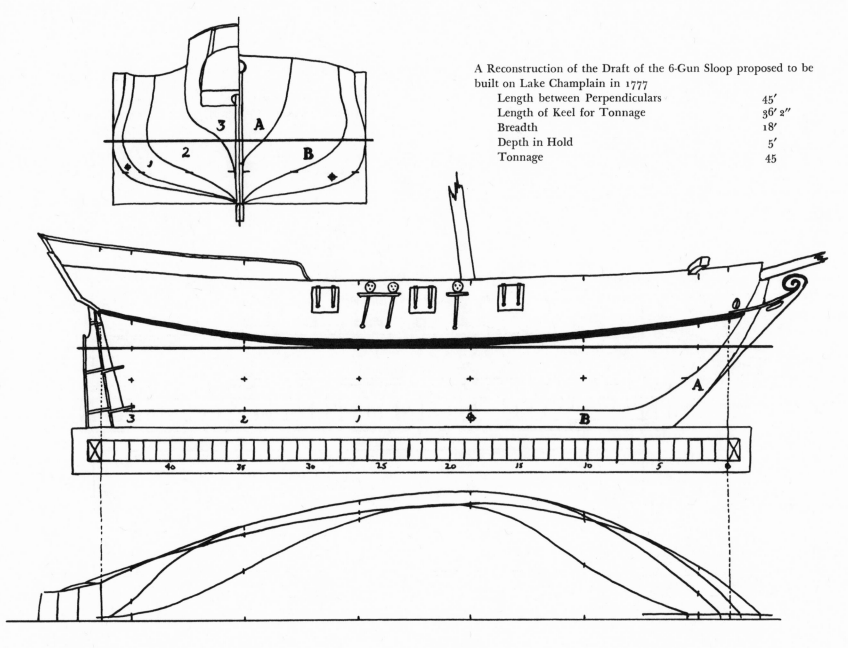

A Reconstruction of the Draft of the 6-Gun Sloop proposed to be built on Lake Champlain in 1777

Length between Perpendiculars	45'
Length of Keel for Tonnage	36' 2"
Breadth	18'
Depth in Hold	5'
Tonnage	45

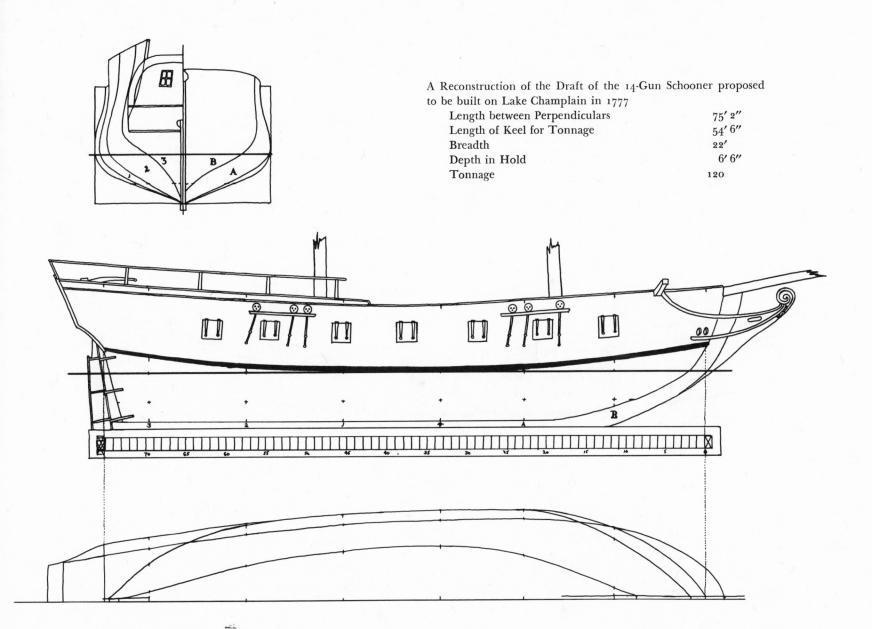

A Reconstruction of the Draft of the 14-Gun Schooner proposed
to be built on Lake Champlain in 1777

Length between Perpendiculars	75′ 2″
Length of Keel for Tonnage	54′ 6″
Breadth	22′
Depth in Hold	6′ 6″
Tonnage	120

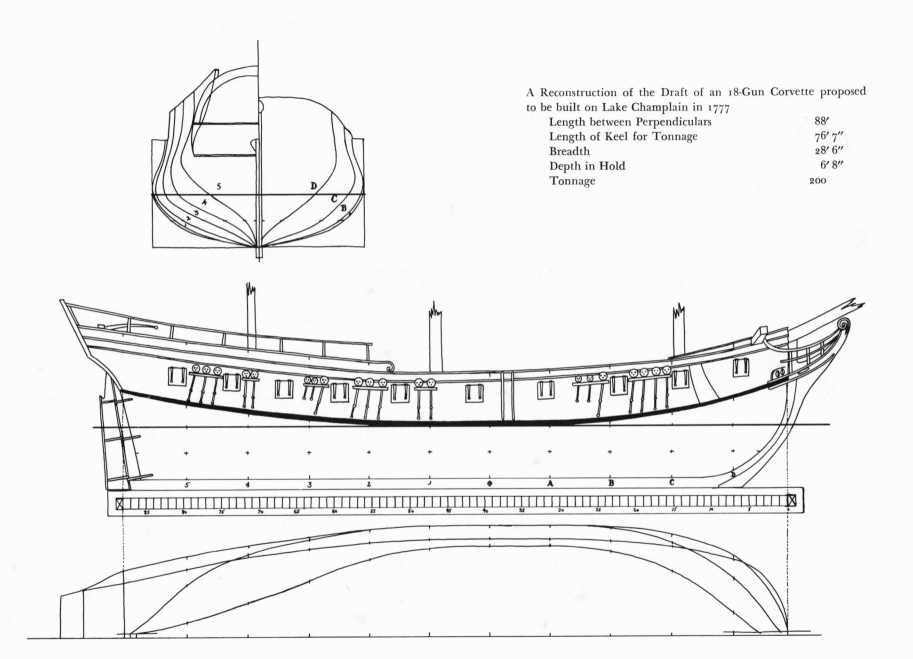

A Reconstruction of the Draft of an 18-Gun Corvette proposed
to be built on Lake Champlain in 1777

Length between Perpendiculars	88′
Length of Keel for Tonnage	76′ 7″
Breadth	28′ 6″
Depth in Hold	6′ 8″
Tonnage	200

Felucca

ONE of the smaller vessels built by the Spanish at Havana was a felucca whose plans survive, included in Admiral Paris's great work *Souvenirs de la Marine*. A felucca was a Mediterranean type of vessel, often rigged with large lateen sails, and roughly equivalent in size to a brig. This particular felucca (and there may have been dozens of them built at Havana over the years) mounted about 14 guns, although it was pierced for 16. Admiral Paris or his typesetter made serious errors with the scale, so we have had to invent our own scale, based mainly on the size and spacing of the gunports. Because of the difficulty in consulting Spanish and Cuban records we know no more about this ship than her plan and date of building, which was 1786. Research in this field would be a welcome addition to the field of eighteenth-century shipbuilding. The hull shape of this felucca was not so far different from the sketches of Simon Metcalf for vessels to be built on Lake Champlain, but of course the resemblance is only a matter of coincidence.

Dimensions: length overall, 100′ 7″; length between perpendiculars, 84′; length of keel, 70′; breadth, 27′ 3″; depth, 6′ 7″; draft, 7′ 7″; tonnage, about 200.

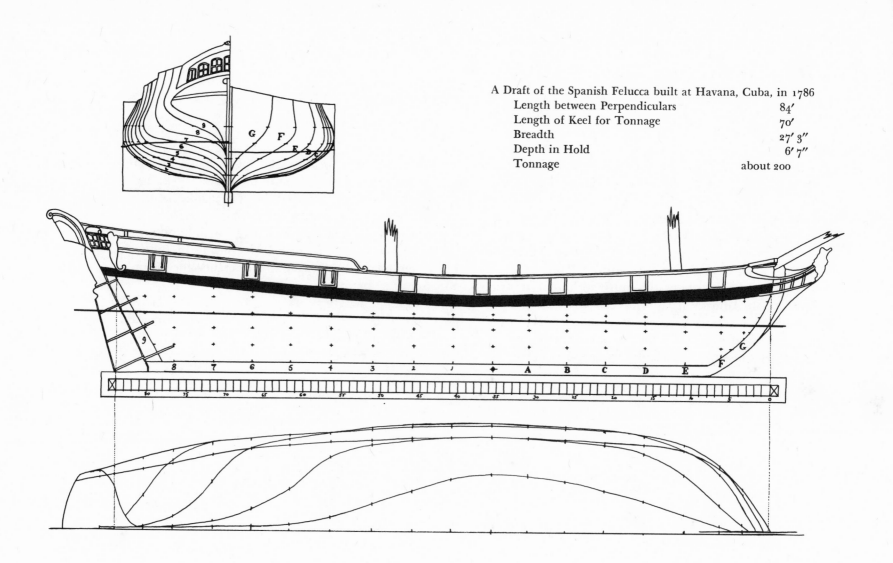

A Draft of the Spanish Felucca built at Havana, Cuba, in 1786
Length between Perpendiculars   84'
Length of Keel for Tonnage   70'
Breadth   27' 3"
Depth in Hold   6' 7"
Tonnage   about 200

Sloop at Louisbourg

THE capture of the French fortress of Louisbourg in Nova Scotia in 1745 was effected mainly by New England troops and ships, assisted by a Royal Navy squadron under Commodore Peter Warren. In 1758, Louisbourg was captured again, but this time it was by British expedition with assistance from New England troops.

However, a 1758 manuscript diagram of the second siege, drawn by a Frenchman, shows various ships in the harbor, including an armed sloop. This sloop is drawn in a primitive style and so nothing could be taken from it for the determination of relative scale, but a number of details are clear enough—and unusual enough—to warrant including a drawing of the sloop in this book. She mounted 10 guns, had a raised forecastle rail as well as a raised quarterdeck, and had a large head, similar to that shown on the exploration sloop *Lady Washington*. This sloop was rigged with a course yard and a topsail yard, which was fairly standard, but not only was there a furled topsail on its yard, but also a furled course; most courses on sloops, if fitted at all in the first place, were set flying from the deck and hoisted up to the yard, so it is most unusual to see the course furled on its yard as if it were a standard piece of equipment used every day.

No identification of this sloop has been found, but it was probably used to bring New England troops up for the siege, and anchored in Gabarus Bay.

Dimensions: length overall, 74′; length between perpendiculars, 58′.

A Reconstruction of the Draft of a 10-Gun New England Sloop seen at the Siege of Louisbourg in 1758
Length between Perpendiculars   58′

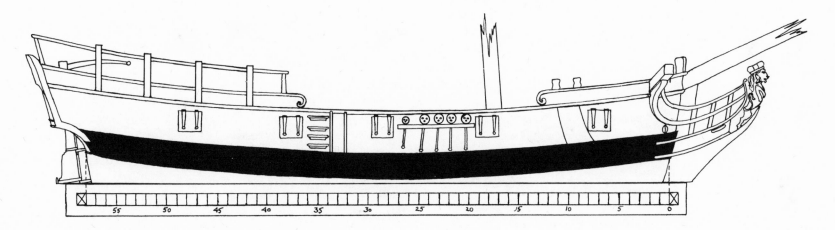

Newburyport Ship

AT the Peabody Museum at Salem, Massachusetts, is a contemporary model of an 8-gun merchant ship of about 1760. The model is rather crude, and one suspects that it is not entirely accurate, especially with regard to deadrise and sheer. However, we have drawn it as we saw it, and we are sure that it represents a ship that once existed. Of particular interest is the figurehead, which is a two-headed horse; the reason for its having two heads is quite simply that a horse sculpture always looks better if the head is slightly inclined toward the viewer, and if the ship has two sides then there have to be two heads, one to incline each way.

The scale of the model is not given, so we had to calculate our own scale, based primarily on the size and spacing of gunports: length overall, 72′; length between perpendiculars, 57′ 7″; length of keel, 45′ 6″; breadth, 25′; depth, 11′; draft, 12′; tonnage, 96. These measurements make this an extremely short ship, a hull that would be more likely to have appeared as a schooner or even a sloop than a ship, but the ship rig was apparently necessary to drive the large beam and draft of the vessel through the water.

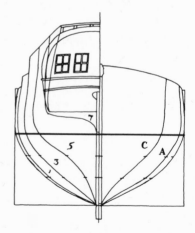

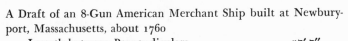

A Draft of an 8-Gun American Merchant Ship built at Newburyport, Massachusetts, about 1760

Length between Perpendiculars	57′ 7″
Length of Keel for Tonnage	45′ 6″
Breadth	25′
Depth in Hold	11′
Tonnage	96

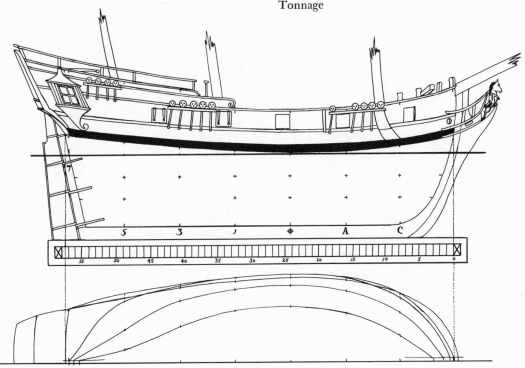

Newburyport Ship (Punchbowl)

Aᴛ the Peabody Museum at Salem is an extraordinary punchbowl, dated 1752 and titled "A Ship at Lanch [sic] Jonathan Greenleaf." It was sent by an Edinburgh, Scotland, merchant to Jonathan Greenleaf, a well-known shipwright of Newburyport, Massachusetts. It depicts a three-masted ship about to be launched, and she is pierced by fourteen gunports.

Jonathan Greenleaf (almost a quarter-century later, the Newburyport firm of Greenleaf & Cross was to build the frigates *Boston* and *Hancock* for the Continental Navy) was probably typical of American shipwrights in that they frequently built a ship with no special customer in mind, in the hopes of selling it in Britain. Occasionally, a grateful British shipowner would order another ship from the same yard, and I assume that this punchbowl represents such a second transaction. A Scottish merchant from Edinburgh presumably ordered a second ship from Greenleaf, and arranged for a sketch of the launching of that ship to be worked onto a punchbowl which he then sent to Greenleaf. Of course, it is entirely possible that the punchbowl sketch represents no more than a British artist's impression of the launching of a ship, and of no particular ship at that. However, the ship in the picture looks quite similar to other New England-built vessels of the period, so we can not be far amiss in including it in this book.

The ship has the usual lion figurehead, quarter galleries, and an unusual rail for the quarterdeck; this rail steps up partway along the quarterdeck as if it were to accommodate a poop, but it is by no means high enough for a poop. Either the Great Cabin was given a foot of extra headroom or the helmsman was given more protection against the weather.

Dimensions: length overall, 98′ 6″; length between perpendiculars, 77′; length of keel, 60′ 8″; draft, 12′ 9″; tonnage, 170.

A Reconstruction of the Draft of a 12-Gun American Ship built at
Newburyport, Massachusetts, in 1752
Length between Perpendiculars   77′
Length of Keel for Tonnage   60′ 8″

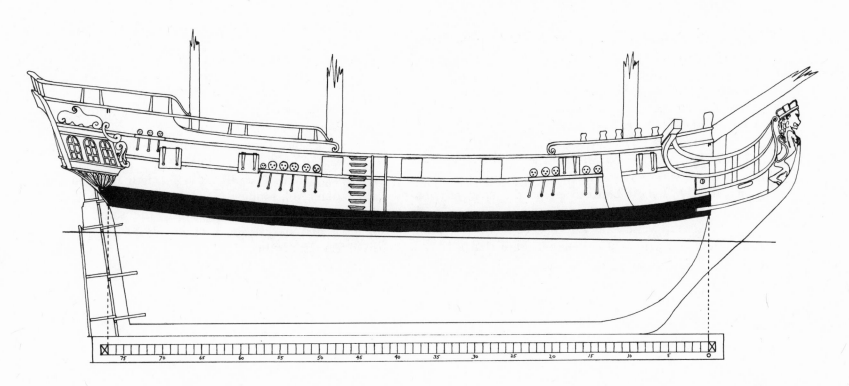

Newfoundland Fishery Ship, Bilander, and Pink

THERE is a semiprimitive oil painting of three vessels anchored in a bay on the Newfoundland coast with a fourth vessel mostly out of the picture. Experts believe the scene to represent New England vessels from the cod fisheries about 1760; hundreds of cod were shown stretched out in the foreground to dry in the sun. The largest of these three vessels was ship-rigged. She could have passed as a typical merchant ship with no windows on the quarter, but a full head, and raised forecastle and quarterdeck. We estimate her dimensions: length overall, 89'; length between perpendiculars, 72'; tonnage, 150.

The second vessel was rigged as a bilander (almost the same as a brig or a snow), and she had a full head, a raised quarterdeck, and windows on the quarter. Estimated dimensions: length overall, 75'; length between perpendiculars, 60'; tonnage, 115.

The third vessel was a pink with a sloop or cutter rig. A pink had an unusual stern that projected abaft the rudder almost to a point. For some reason, pinks were very popular among fishermen (see our drawing of *Diligence*), and the pink form persisted in fishing boats well into the nineteenth century. Estimated dimensions: length overall, 48' 6"; length between perpendiculars, 40'; tonnage, 35. This pink may have done more of the actual fishing, while the ship and the bilander may have been there merely to transport the dried fish back to Boston.

A Reconstruction of the Draft of a New England Ship used for
Fishing, built about 1750
Length between Perpendiculars 72′

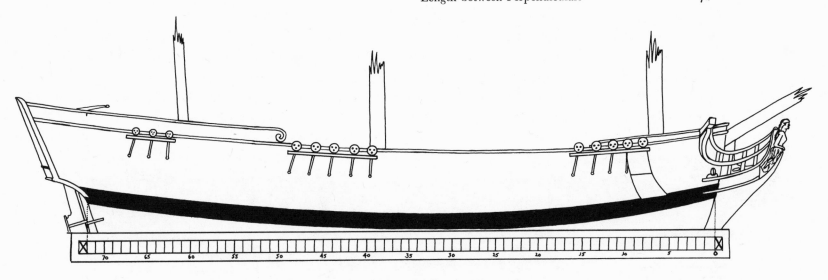

A Reconstruction of the Draft of a New England Fishing Bilander
built about 1750
        Length between Perpendiculars   60′

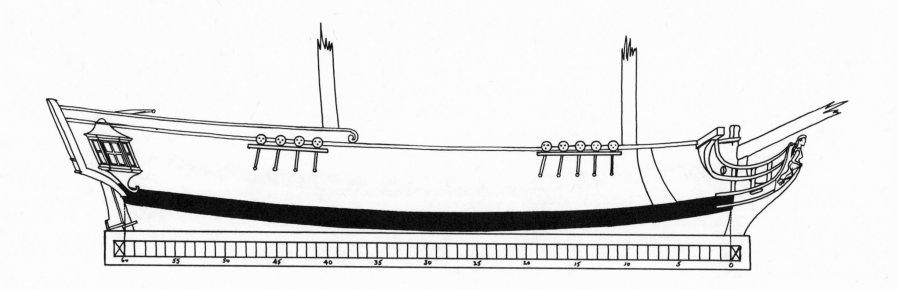

A Reconstruction of the Draft of a New England Cutter-rigged
Fishing Pink built about 1750
Length between Perpendiculars   40′

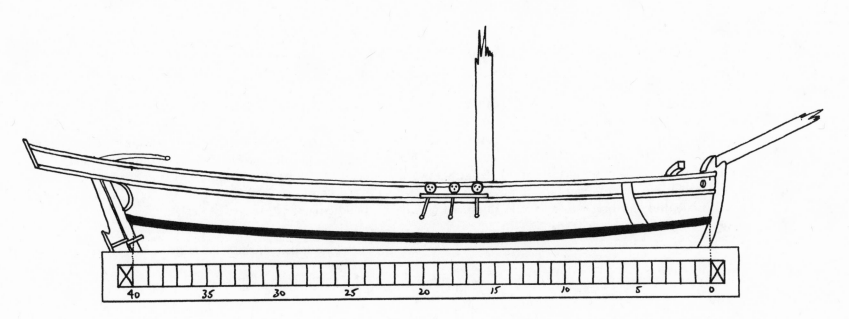

New York Brig and Sloop

IN the famous view of New York City in 1717 by Burgis a recently launched brig is shown at anchor. Allowing for the obvious distortion by the artist, which makes the vessel look higher and fatter than she was, we can see that she looked fairly typical of brigs built in England and America throughout the eighteenth century, and that the form was already well established even that early in the century. As we reconstruct her, her dimensions were: length overall, 64' 7"; length between perpendiculars, 52'; tonnage, about 75.

Just behind the brig was a simple sloop with work being done on her bottom. She is heeled over, away from the artist, which gives more of a view of her bottom than would otherwise have been available, but the method of heaving her over is not shown and therefore we can not tell exactly how much of the bottom we are seeing. She appears to be related to the famous Hudson River sloops which were both wide and fairly shallow, but she also may have been of the "Bermuda" sloop style; the engraving is not clear enough to tell which.

Dimensions: length overall, 62'; length between perpendiculars, 54'; length of keel, 47'.

A Reconstruction of the Draft of a Brig built at New York about 1717

Length between Perpendiculars   52'

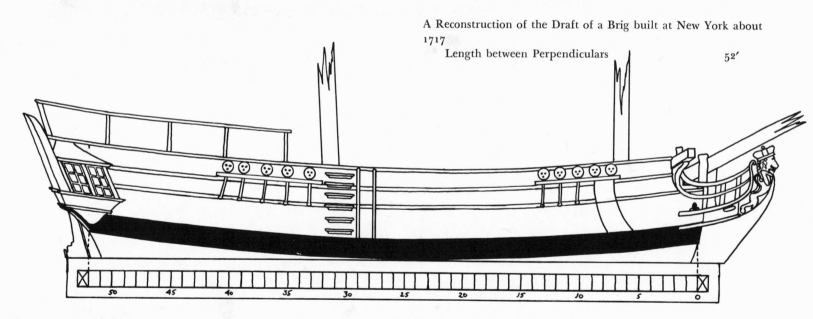

A Reconstruction of the Draft of a Sloop built at New York about
1717
Length between Perpendiculars   54'

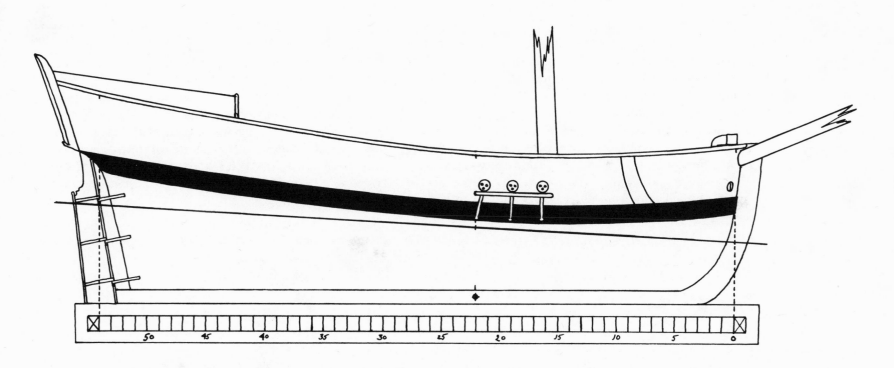

Nieuw Amsterdam and New York Yachts

NEW YORK, once known as Nieuw Amsterdam, was the largest and most important city in the Dutch possessions in seventeenth-century America. It would be fairly natural, then, for Dutch concepts of ship design to wield considerable influence in New York, even after the British had taken over the city from the Dutch. The most obviously Dutch feature that can be noticed in local vessels in pictures of seventeenth-century New York is the concept of the *Staten Jacht;* this was a sloop with a large and high cabin in the stern. We have chosen one of many from old views of the city, a yacht

from a picture dated 1661. Judging from the picture, which is unfortunately rather primitive, the yacht was quite small, although she could have been slightly bigger than we have drawn her: length overall, 41'; length between perpendiculars, 37'. It would have been possible to make comfortable overnight passages on this yacht, but the next one we have chosen, from a 1679 picture, was smaller, with no large cabin, so she would have been used strictly as a day-sailer. She was also rigged as a sloop: length overall, 37' 6"; length between perpendiculars, 33'.

A Reconstruction of the Draft of a Yacht at Nieuw Amsterdam in 1661

Length between Perpendiculars   37'

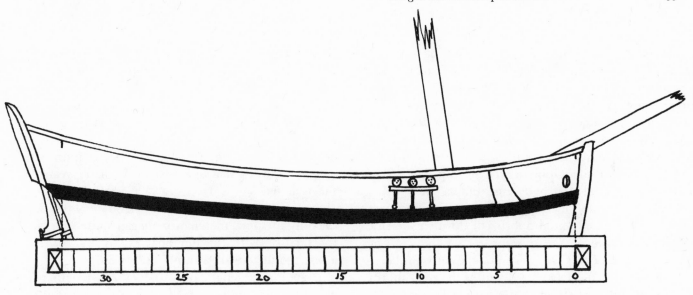

A Reconstruction of the Draft of a Yacht at New York in 1679
Length between Perpendiculars   33'

30   25   20   15   10   5   0

Yacht at Nieuw Amsterdam
From a 1661 map known as "The Duke's Plan"

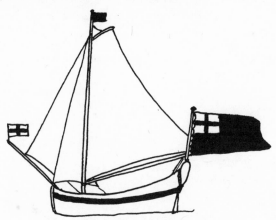

Yacht at New York
From a 1679 map

Philadelphia Ship of 24 Guns

A<small>N</small> extremely fine punchbowl of the period immediately after the Revolution is now on display at the Connecticut Historical Society. This punchbowl once belonged to Captain Robert Niles, who commanded the Connecticut privateer schooner *Spy* during the Revolution, and it has his initials elaborately drawn under the portrait of a large American ship. This ship has the exact shape of a Philadelphia merchant ship like *Alfred* (it can't actually be *Alfred* because the flag it is flying has fifteen stripes and fifteen stars, a post-Revolutionary flag), and she had eleven gunports cut through the side and another three on the quarterdeck. *Alfred, Drake, Columbus,* and *Hyder Ali* were not the only Philadelphia merchantmen to be fitted out with guns in the Revolution and used either in the navy or as privateers; it was frequently much cheaper for a shipowner to take an existing merchant ship from his fleet and fit it out with cannons than it was to build a privateer from scratch, and we believe that this is one such ship.

This ship differs from *Alfred* and the others in one important respect: this one has quarter galleries, a luxurious feature that was not found on most Philadelphia merchantmen. She has no dolphin striker, which indicates that she was built many years before the 1792 flag she is flying; in fact, we feel she was built about 1775, but that is just a guess. The closed waist of the Philadelphia merchantman can clearly be seen in the picture, with the longboat raised high on stilts to allow people to walk around underneath.

Dimensions: length overall, 111′ 6″; length between perpendiculars, 92′; length of keel, 76′; breadth, 27′; tonnage, about 300.

A Reconstruction of the Draft of a Merchant Ship fitted for 24
Guns and built at Philadelphia about 1775

Length between Perpendiculars 92'

Tonnage 300

Philadelphia Merchant Ship

THE Philadelphia Maritime Museum has very few pictures or models of early American ships, but there is one oil painting of a Philadelphia merchant ship of the period immediately after the Revolution. She flies a thirteen-stripe flag, but the canton contains a crescent moon in addition to the thirteen stars. She has quarter galleries but no guns, so she was never converted to a privateer or warship. In fact, she might have been built after the war. She has davits over the stern for the captain's gig, which was a rare sight until after the war.

Dimensions: length overall, 110' 6"; length between perpendiculars, 91' 6"; tonnage, about 300.

A Reconstruction of the Draft of a Merchant Ship built at Philadelphia about 1785
Length between Perpendiculars   91' 6"

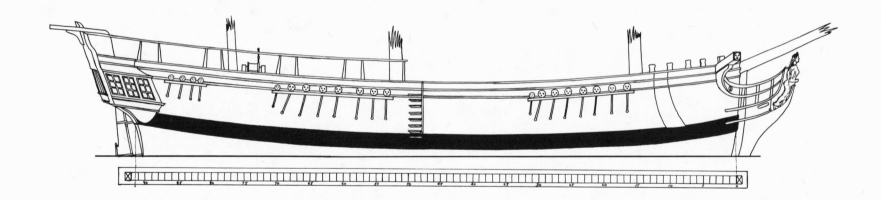

Rhode Island Ship

IT was a fairly common practice to paint an impressive ship in the background of the portrait of a prosperous eighteenth-century American merchant, and many such ship pictures survive. Because of lack of space on the canvas the majority of them are shown with stern-on-views, which tells us little about the ships, and those with broadside views are too distant and vague in most cases to enable us to reconstruct them.

However, there is one early portrait in the Newport Historical Society of Benjamin Ellery, Senior, executed about 1720, showing a fine privateer ship in the background. Most Rhode Island vessels in the Colonial period were sloops of up to 100 tons or so, but there were occasional ships as well, and this one was armed with 14 guns and also could be rowed with five oars per side. She had the characteristic stern and quarter galleries found on British ships of about the year 1700. Another painting, a view of Newport Harbor in 1740, shows an almost identical ship, and it may in fact be the same ship.

Dimensions: length overall, 91′ 2″; length between perpendiculars, 76′; breadth, 24′; tonnage, about 180.

A Reconstruction of the Draft of a 16-Gun Ship built in Rhode Island about 1720

Length between Perpendiculars	76′
Breadth	24′
Tonnage	180

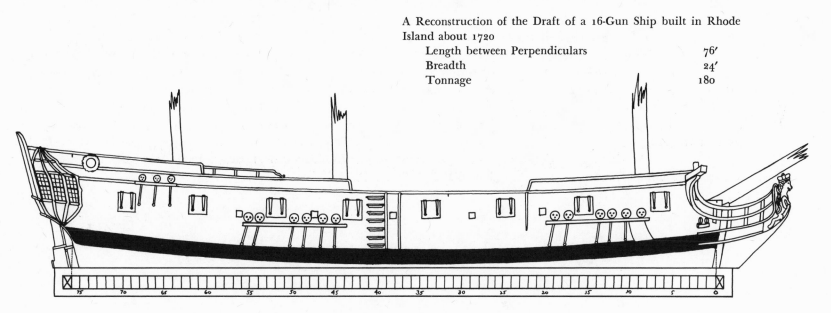

St. Lawrence River Galleys

BY 1759, due to the brilliant campaigning of James Wolfe and Jeffery Amherst, the British had captured both Louisbourg and Quebec from the French, and Montreal was the only large French settlement remaining in the northeast. Amherst carefully planned a joint attack on Montreal, with one force coming upriver from Quebec and another coming downriver from Lake Ontario. In 1760, with advice from Thomas Davies, an artist who was serving as an officer of Royal Artillery, Amherst built at least four sloop-rigged row galleys, with which he hoped he could sweep away any resistance on the St. Lawrence between Lake Ontario and Montreal. This proved to be prudent, for the French were waiting for him at Fort La Galette (now Ogdensburg, New York) with the 18-gun brig *L'Outaouaise*. Although each galley had no more than one twelve-pounder and some swivels, their superior maneuverability enabled them to capture the brig, and Montreal surrendered shortly after without firing a shot. Davies commanded one of the galleys.

Davies painted a charming picture of the engagement with *L'Outaouaise*, now at the National Gallery of Canada in Ottawa, but the picture shows little in the way of detail on the galleys. However, Davies also painted a sketch-portrait of one of the galleys with all sails set (now in the Public Archives of Canada), which, although it contains some obvious inaccuracies, is fairly useful in reconstructing the general appearance of Amherst's galleys. They had ports for as many as eleven oars a side, but the painting of the battle shows that only about six or seven of those were normally in use. The galleys had a small, raised quarterdeck aft, under which was a cabin with a large window on each side. On the raised forecastle was mounted the large cannon, which fired through a port cut slightly to the left of the stem. There were stocks for eight swivels on each side along the waist. The rig was simple: a gaff mainsail could be extended with a triangular studdingsail, and there was only one jib, set on the forestay which led to the stem; no bowsprit was indicated, although one could have been fitted. Dimensions (estimated): length overall, 60′ 8″; length between perpendiculars, 50′; length of keel for tonnage, 44′ 7″; depth in hold, 4′; draft, 4′ 2″; tonnage, about 30.

A Reconstruction of the Draft for Building His Majesty's Galleys
on the St. Lawrence River in 1760

Length between Perpendiculars	50′
Length of Keel for Tonnage	44′ 7″
Depth in Hold	4′
Tonnage	30

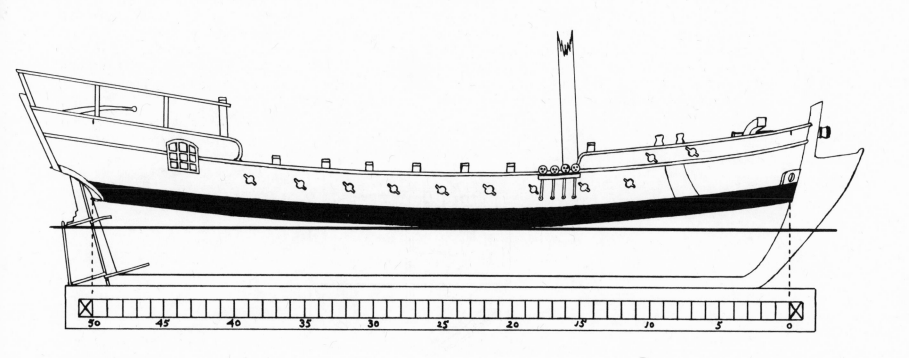

Salem Ship

At the Peabody Museum at Salem, Massachusetts, is a contemporary model of a 12-gun merchant ship of about 1750. The model may not be terribly accurate in some respects, particularly the deadrise of the midship section, which seems excessive. This ship had a raised quarterdeck and forecastle, and quarter galleries. She could well have served as a useful letter-of-marque during the Seven Years' War. The model had no scale marked on it, so we have calculated our own scale, based primarily on the size and spacing of the gunports. If our calculations are correct, this ship was small to be ship-rigged, although not as small as the Newburyport ship.

Dimensions: length overall, 86′ 3″; length between perpendiculars, 70′ 9″; length of keel, 54′ 4″; breadth, 23′ 4″; depth, 10′ 2″; draft, 11′; tonnage, about 130.

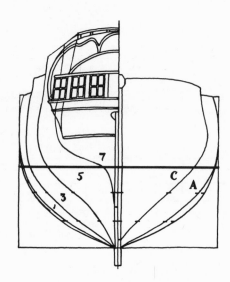

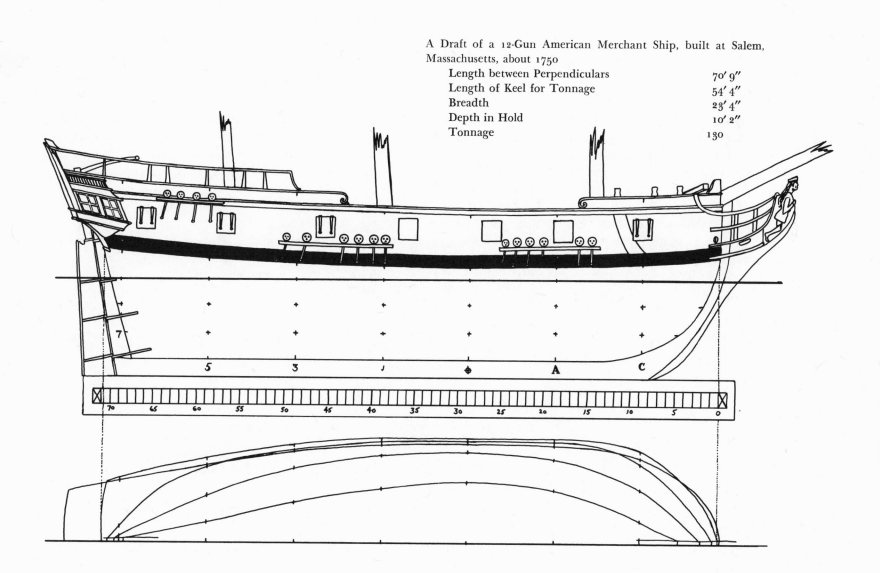

A Draft of a 12-Gun American Merchant Ship, built at Salem, Massachusetts, about 1750

Length between Perpendiculars	70′ 9″
Length of Keel for Tonnage	54′ 4″
Breadth	23′ 4″
Depth in Hold	10′ 2″
Tonnage	130

Salem Sloop

ONE of the models of early American ships at the Peabody Museum at Salem, Massachusetts, is an eighteenth-century unarmed sloop. The model was apparently used as a child's toy and could be sailed, but it is now minus its rig, its rudder, and any details of interest. Because this sloop at least reflects the general appearance of New England sloops of the mid-eighteenth century, and may even represent a specific vessel that was perhaps owned by the child's father, we have decided to include a profile of it in this book. We were not able to spend enough time with the model to take off its complete lines, and the inexact nature of the model made it seem not worth our while returning to investigate it further, especially since it was not on regular display and not readily accessible. There was no scale attached to the model, so we have reconstructed it as best we could.

Dimensions: length overall, 63′; length between perpendiculars, 55′ 4″; length of keel, 44′; breadth, 22′; draft, 11′ 9″; tonnage, about 80.

A Reconstruction of the Draft of an American Merchant Sloop,
built at Salem, Massachusetts, about 1770

Length between Perpendiculars	55' 4"
Length of Keel for Tonnage	44'
Breadth	22'
Tonnage	80

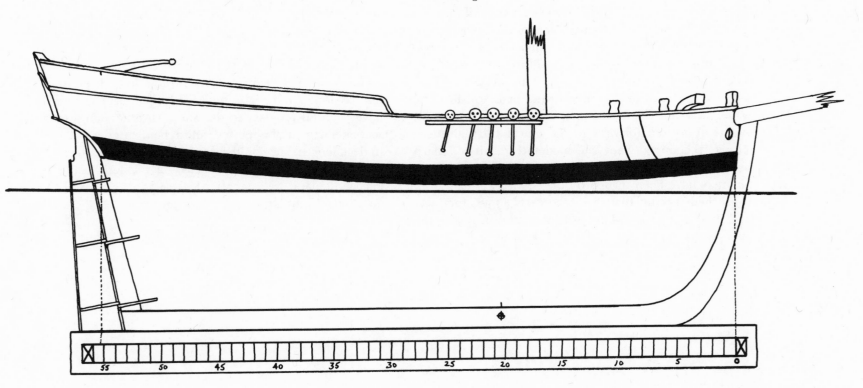

Virginia Schooner

I N David Steel's book *Elements and Practice of Naval Architecture* (published 1805) are the offsets and specifications for "a fast-sailing schooner" obviously of American build, and Chapelle thinks she was a privateer built possibly before the end of the American Revolution. Chapelle redrew her from the table of offsets, and we have made our drawing based on his. She was lightly built, with open rails instead of bulwarks, and truly looked forward to the era of the Baltimore clipper schooners. She had moderate deadrise, sharp lines, raked stem and sternpost, and a square-tuck stern. She may have been owned by the French and captured from them by the British in the early 1790s, for Steel usually obtained his plans from the Admiralty and the Admiralty was not then enlightened enough to look for such a schooner to purchase, even if they did not mind capturing one. There is no Admiralty record, however, among the incomplete lists of captures made by ships of the Royal Navy, of the capture of a schooner that matches these dimensions. She would have been very fast, as long as she was not overloaded, which would have been all too easy to do. She was rather long for a schooner rig in this period, most being under 70 feet in deck length. She could carry 12 light carriage guns.

Dimensions: length overall, 85' 2"; length between perpendiculars, 77'; length of keel, 50' 4"; breadth, 20' 2"; depth, 8'; draft, 9' 3"; tonnage, 140.

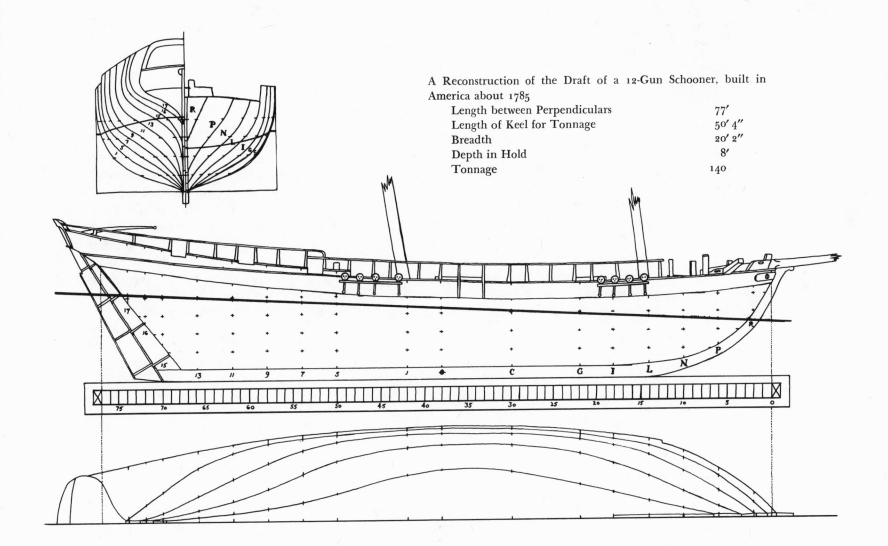

A Reconstruction of the Draft of a 12-Gun Schooner, built in America about 1785

Length between Perpendiculars	77'
Length of Keel for Tonnage	50' 4"
Breadth	20' 2"
Depth in Hold	8'
Tonnage	140

Virginia Schooner

DAVID STEEL, an Admiralty agent and publisher in the 1790s and early 1800s, wrote a number of books about design and construction of ships. In one of these, *Elements and Practice of Naval Architecture* (1805), he included the draft for an American privateer schooner of 12 light carriage guns and 10 swivels. This was a fast-looking design which Steel claimed had come from Virginia, but the word Virginia was always used rather loosely, so we may safely assume this schooner was from the Chesapeake Bay region in the period 1781–1789. The schooner was apparently owned for a while by the French and was captured by the British around 1793, although no record can be found of a captured vessel of her dimensions. She had very sharp lines and considerable deadrise, low freeboard, and quite a bit of sheer. Her stern was a square tuck, and her stem was sharply raked.

Dimensions: length overall, 86′ 8″; length between perpendiculars, 77′ 8″; length of keel, 60′ 7″; breadth, 21′ 10″; depth, 8′ 6″; draft, 12′; tonnage, 158.

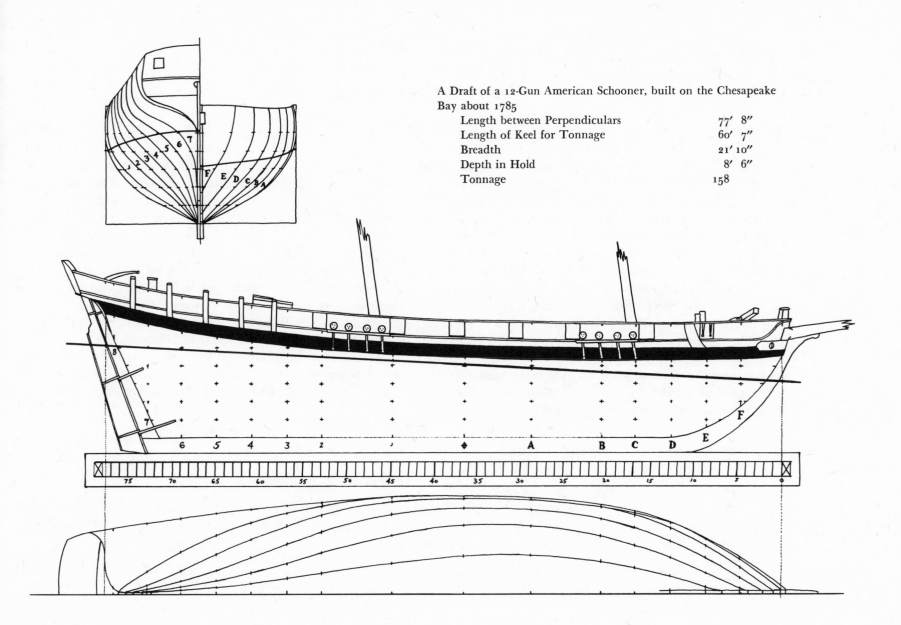

A Draft of a 12-Gun American Schooner, built on the Chesapeake
Bay about 1785

Length between Perpendiculars	77′ 8″
Length of Keel for Tonnage	60′ 7″
Breadth	21′ 10″
Depth in Hold	8′ 6″
Tonnage	158

Virginia Sloop

THE late Howard Chapelle of the Smithsonian Institution was often searching through European archives in search of records of American ships. One design that he and his researchers found that was not included in any of his books was that of a 6-gun fast sloop built in Virginia or the Chesapeake area in 1768. He apparently obtained the lines from a Dutch copy of a French drawing, and a model of her was subsequently made for the Smithsonian. Presumably she had been purchased by the French shortly after she was built.

She appears to be a transitional design, somewhere between the sloop *Mediator* and the Bermuda sloop of Chapman, on the one hand, and the two Virginia schooners found in Steel's book, on the other hand. She had the standard aft cabin with rounded roof found on the earlier designs, and she had the lower freeboard, steep deadrise, and sharp lines of the later designs. She had four gunports and four posts for swivel guns on each side. She also had oarports of a special design that enabled the blade to be retracted only at a certain angle; this caused less wear on the oars than the more normal square oarports. She was steered with a wheel, as were most small vessels with a high aft cabin. Numerous contemporary pictures show similar sloops in the Chesapeake, Bermuda, Jamaica, and all over the West Indies, so this sloop was far from unusual.

Dimensions: length overall, 53′ 7″; length between perpendiculars, 48′ 7″; length of keel, 40′ 9″; breadth, 16′; depth in hold, 6′ 2″; draft, 7′ 10″; tonnage, about 42.

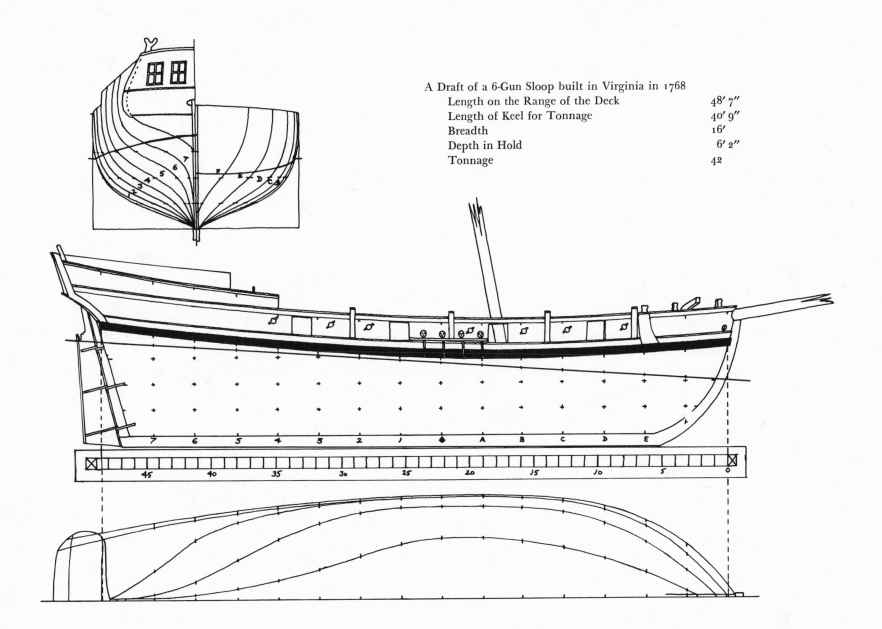

A Draft of a 6-Gun Sloop built in Virginia in 1768
Length on the Range of the Deck   48′ 7″
Length of Keel for Tonnage   40′ 9″
Breadth   16′
Depth in Hold   6′ 2″
Tonnage   42

Selected Bibliography

Books

Albion, Robert Greenhalgh. *Forests and Sea Power: The Timber Problem of the Royal Navy, 1652–1862*. Cambridge, Mass.: Harvard University Press, 1926.

Allen, Gardner W. *A Naval History of the American Revolution*. 2 vols. Williamstown, Mass.: Corner House, 1970.

————. *Massachusetts Privateers of the Revolution. Massachusetts Historical Society Collections*, vol. 77. Boston: Massachusetts Historical Society, 1927.

Archibald, E. H. H. *The Wooden Fighting Ship in the Royal Navy, 897–1860*. London: Blandford, 1968.

Baker, William A. *Colonial Vessels*. Barre, Mass.: Barre, 1962.

————. *Sloops & Shallops*. Barre, Mass.: Barre, 1966.

Bird, Harrison. *Navies in the Mountains*. New York: Oxford University Press, 1962.

Bondriot, Jean. *Le vaisseau de 74 canons*. 4 vols. Grenoble: Éditions des Quatre Seigneurs, 1973–1977.

Brewington, M. V. *Shipcarvers of North America*. Barre, Mass.: Barre, 1962; reprint ed., New York: Dover Paperbacks, 1976.

————, and Brewington, Dorothy. *Marine Painting & Drawings in the Peabody Museum*. Salem, Mass.: Peabody Museum, 1968.

Brown, Vaughan W. *Shipping in the Port of Annapolis, 1748–1775*. Annapolis, Md.: Naval Institute Press, 1965.

Bryant, Samuel W. *The Sea and the States*. New York: Thomas Y. Crowell, 1947; paperback ed., 1967.

Chapelle, Howard I. *American Small Sailing Craft*. New York: W. W. Norton & Co., 1951.

————. *The Baltimore Clipper*. 1930. Reprint. New York: Bonanza, 1976.

————. *History of American Sailing Ships*. New York: W. W. Norton & Co., 1935.

————. *History of the American Sailing Navy*. New York: W. W. Norton & Co., 1949.

————. *The Search for Speed Under Sail, 1700–1855*. New York: W. W. Norton & Co., 1967.

Chapman, Henrik Af. *Architectura navalis mercatoria*. 1968. Reprint. New York: Praeger, 1972.

Clark, William Bell. *Ben Franklin's Privateers*. New York: Greenwood, 1969.

————. *Captain Dauntless*. Shreveport, La.: Louisiana State University Press, 1949.

————, and Morgan, William James, eds. *Naval Documents of the American Revolution*. 7 vols. to date. Washington, D.C.: U.S. Government Printing Office, 1964–1976.

Coggins, Jack. *Ships and Seamen of the American Revolution*. Harrisburg, Pa.: Stackpole, 1969.

Colledge, J. J. *Ships of the Royal Navy: An Historical Index*. Vol. 1. Newton Abbott, Devon, England: David & Charles, 1969.

Dickerson, Oliver. *The Navigation Acts and the American Revolution*. 1951. Reprint. Philadelphia: University of Pennsylvania Press, 1974.

Dodge, Ernest S. *Beyond the Capes*. Boston: Little, Brown, 1971.

Dupuy, Trevor N. *The Military History of Revolutionary War Naval Battles*. New York: Franklin Watts, 1970.

Eastman, Ralph M. *Some Famous Privateers of New England.* Boston: State Street Trust Co., 1928.

Evans, Cerinda W. *Some Notes on Shipbuilding and Shipping in Colonial Virginia.* Newport News, Va.: Mariners Museum, 1957.

Falconer, William. *An Universal Dictionary of the Marine.* London, 1769; reprint ed., Newton Abbott, Devon, England: David & Charles, 1970.

Fowler, William M., Jr. *Rebels Under Sail.* New York: Scribners, 1976.

Gardner, John. *Sail.* Warships of the Royal Navy, vol. 1. London: Evelyn, 1968.

Goldenberg, Joseph A. *Shipbuilding in Colonial America.* Charlottesville, Va.: University of Virginia Press, 1975.

Graham, Gerald S. *The Royal Navy in the War of American Independence.* London: Her Majesty's Stationery Office, 1976.

Grimwood, V. R. *American Ship Models and How to Build Them.* New York: W. W. Norton & Co., 1942.

Hutchinson, William. *A Treatise on Naval Architecture.* London: 1794; reprint ed., London: Conway Maritime Press, 1969.

Jackson, John W. *The Pennsylvania Navy, 1775–1781.* New Brunswick, N.J.: Rutgers–The State University Press, 1974.

Jackson, Melvin H., and Miller, Helen Hill. *Tobacco and the "Brilliant."* Washington, D.C.: Smithsonian Institution, 1976.

Kaminkow, Marion, and Kaminkow, Jack, eds. *Mariners of the American Revolution.* Baltimore: Magna Carta, 1967.

Laing, Alexander. *American Sail.* New York: E. P. Dutton, 1961.

————. *Seafaring America.* New York: American Heritage, 1974.

Longridge, C. Nepean. *The Anatomy of Nelson's Ships.* London: Percival Marshall, 1955.

MacGregor, David R. *Fast Sailing Ships, 1775–1875.* Lymington, Hampshire, England: Nautical Publishing Co., Ltd., 1973.

Mahan, Alford Thayer. *The Influence of Seapower upon History, 1660–1783.* 1890. Reprint. New York: Hill & Wang, 1957.

————. *The Major Operations of the Navies in the War of American Independence.* Boston: Little, Brown, 1969.

Manning, T. D., and Walker, D. F. *British Warship Names.* London: Putnam, 1959.

Marcus, G. J. *Heart of Oak: A Survey of British Sea Power in the Georgian Era.* London: Oxford University Press, 1975.

McCusker, John J. *Alfred, the First Continental Flagship.* Washington, D.C.: Smithsonian Institution, 1973.

McKee, Christopher. *Edward Preble.* Annapolis, Md.: Naval Institute Press, 1972.

Middlebrook, Louis F. *History of Maritime Connecticut During the American Revolution.* 2 vols. Salem, Mass.: 1925.

Miller, Nathan. *Sea of Glory: The Continental Navy Fights for Independence, 1775–1783.* New York: David McKay, 1974.

Morgan, William James. *Captains to the Northward.* Barre, Mass.: Barre, 1959.

Morison, Samuel Eliot. *John Paul Jones, A Sailor's Biography.* Boston: Little, Brown, 1959.

Nance, R. Morton. *Sailing Ship Models.* London: Holton & Truscott Smith, 1924.

Preston, Antony; Lyon, David; and Batchelor, John H. *Navies of the American Revolution.* Englewood Cliffs, N.J.: Prentice-Hall, 1975.

Rider, Hope S. *Valour Fore and Aft.* Annapolis, Md.: Naval Institute Press, 1976.

Henry Huddleston Rogers Collection of Ship Models. Annapolis, Md.: Naval Institute Press, 1972.

Rosa, Narcisse. *La construction des navires à Quebec et les environs.* Quebec.

Roscoe, Theodore, and Freeman, Fred. *Pictorial History of the U.S. Navy.* New York: Scribners, 1956.

Sheffield, William P. *Rhode Island Privateers and Privateersmen.* Newport, R.I.: 1883.

Smith, Myron J. *Navies in the American Revolution: A Bibliography.* Metuchen, N.J.: Scarecrow Press, 1973.

Smith, P. C. F. *Captain Samuel Tucker (1747–1833) Continental Navy.* Salem, Mass.: Essex Institute, 1976.

————. *Fired by Manly Zeal*. Salem, Mass.: Peabody Museum, 1977.

————, ed. *The Frigate Essex Papers*. Salem, Mass.: Peabody Museum, 1974.

————, ed. *The Journals of Ashley Bowen (1728–1813) of Marblehead*. 2 vols. Salem, Mass.: Peabody Museum, 1973.

Stout, Neil R. *The Royal Navy in America, 1760–1775*. Annapolis, Md.: Naval Institute Press, 1973.

Syrett, David. *Shipping and the American War 1775–83*. London: Athlone Press, 1970.

Van Powell, W. Nowland. *The American Navies of the Revolutionary War*. New York: G. P. Putnam's Sons, 1974.

————. *War at Sea for Liberty*. Memphis, Tenn.: Memphis Council, Navy League of the U.S., 1975.

Wilbur, C. Keith. *Picture Book of the Revolution's Privateers*. Harrisburg, Pa.: Stackpole, 1973.

Wilcox, Leslie. *The War of Independence: A Bicentennial Exhibition of Marine Paintings*. Bethesda, Md.: Wm. Blair, Ltd., 1976.

Periodicals

The American Neptune (Quarterly). Peabody Museum, Salem, Mass.

Model Ships & Boats (Bimonthly), edited by Frank W. Miller. Model Ships & Boats, Inc., New York, New York.

The Model Shipwright (Quarterly). Conway Maritime Press, Greenwich, London, England.

Nautical Research Journal (Quarterly), edited by Merritt A. Edson, Jr. Nautical Research Guild, Washington, D.C.

GENERAL INDEX

d'Abbans, Count Jouffrey, 214
Aboukir Bay, Battle of, 126
Académie des Sciences (Paris), 214
Adams, John, 77
Admiralty models, 11
Alexander, Charles, 110
Alfred, English King, 9, 40
Algeciras Bay, Battle of, 238
Allen, Ethan, 179
Allen, Thomas, 141
America's Cup races, 66
Amherst, General Jeffery, 212, 332
Andrews, John, 236
Archibald, E. H. H., 10
Armada, Spanish, 10
Arnold, General Benedict, 84, 146, 162, 172, 188, 240, 248, 276, 284, 286, 290, 292, 294, 296, 297
Athenaeum (Portsmouth, N.H.), 46
Attoo, Hawaiian chief, 92
Austrian Succession, War of, 8
d'Auxiron, Count, 214

Bailey Collection, iii
Baker, William A., 135, 282
Barney, Joshua, 144, 145, 258, 286
Barnsby, Henry, 46
Barry, John, 34, 40, 45, 174, 228, 257, 284
Basque Roads, Battle of, 126
Bath Marine Museum (Maine), 282
Baugean (French artist), 228, 229

Bayard, John, 206
Bazely, John, 176
Biddle, Nicholas, 230
Bilander, ill. 5
Black Prince, see Edward, Prince of Wales
Blunt, John S., 50
Boston Museum of Fine Arts, 222
Bostonian Society, The, 166
Boudriot, Jean, 211, 226, 256
Bouteille, Jean, 110
Bowen, Ashley, 58, 62, 113, 155, 219, 227, 246, 274, 299
Breton (artist), 238
Brewington, Marion, 206
Brig, ill. 4
Brisbane, John, 128
Bristol Historical Society (Rhode Island), 222
Broughton, Nicholas, 155
Brown, John, 128, 143, 145, 287
Brown, Nicholas, 206
Bruckshaw, Robert V., 123
Bunbury, Captain, 62
Burgis, William, 125, 304, 324
Burgoyne, General John, 284
Burling, Lancaster, 110, 284
Bushnell, David, 280
Bushnell, Ezra, 280

Cabot, John (or Giovanni), 82
Caldwell, James, 206
Calhoun's Shipyard, 132
Canada, National Gallery of (Ottawa), 212, 332
Canada, Public Archives of

(Ottawa), 51, 84, 146, 240, 292, 294, 332
Carleton, Lady Maria, 188
Carleton, Sir Guy, 84, 162, 188
Carnes, John, 200
Carron Foundry, 16
Castries, Marquis de, 48
Champlin, Samuel, 122
Chapelle, Howard I., iv, 34, 68, 98, 108, 145, 157, 186, 222, 231, 235, 290, 338, 342
Chapman, Fredrik Henrik af, 34, 82, 252, 300, 342
Charles I, British King, 10, 206, 232
Charles II, British King, 10
Clark, Mark, 236
Cleveley, Robert and John, Jr., 176
Coates, Warwick, 110
Coit, William, 141, 142
Colledge, J. J., 244, 266
Collier, Sir George, 97, 286
Color schemes, 25, 27, 31
Congress, Library of (Washington, D.C.), 134
Connecticut Historical Society, 72, 122, 141
Construction techniques and materials, 23, 24, 25
Conyngham, Gustavus, 242, 268
Cook, Captain James, 8, 29
Cornè, Michel Felice, 53
Cotton, John, 284
Courter, Harmon, 206
Crary, Humphrey, 72
Crépin, Louis-Philippe, 143, 145

Cromwell, Oliver, 206
Crymes, Lieutenant, 54
Cuddalore, Battle of, 126
Cunningham, Gustavus, see Conyngham, Gustavus
Cutter, ill. 4

Dacres, J. R., 84
Dacres, Richard, 84
Davidson, Samuel, 257
Davies, Thomas, 212, 332
Davis, C. G., 118
Dean, Stewart, 118
Deane, Silas, i, 82, 104
Degge, James, 45
Digby (shipwright), 282
Dimon, George, 62
Disneyland, 93
Dodd, Robert, 38, 54, 164
Dogger Bank, Battle of, 82
Dougherty, Henry, 257
Douglas, Captain, 204
Drake, Admiral F. S., 126
Drake, Sir Francis, 10, 42
Drew, John, 13
Dudingston, William, 135

Edes, Jonathan, 43
Edson, Merritt A., Jr., iv
Edward III, English king, 40
Edward, Prince of Wales, 40, 42
Effingham, Lord Howard of, 284
1812, War of, 7, 15, 25
Eldred, Peleg, 122
Elizabeth, English queen, 9

Ellery, Benjamin, Sr., 331
Elliott, William, 73
"Establishments," 10, 11
d'Estaing, Admiral Hector, Count, 128
Evans, Oliver, 216
Exmouth, Lord Edward, *see* Pellew, Edward
Exshaw, Captain, 274
Eyre shipyard, 230

Finisterre, Battle of, 123
Fitch, John, 214–216
de Follenay, Count, 214
Fort Ticonderoga Museum, 148, 179, 292
Fotheringham, Captain, 132
Fox, Charles James, 132
Franklin, Benjamin, 73, 114, 186, 242, 263
Fulton, Robert, 216

Gates, General Horatio, 137, 292
Gayton, Admiral Clark, 108
Geddes, George, 98
George III, British king, 206
Gérard, Conrad Alexandre, Ambassador, 96
Gillon, Alexander, 263, 265
Glorious First of June, Battle of the, 126
Glover, General John, 155
Gondola, *ill. 7*
de Grasse, Admiral François, Count, 126, 154
Gray, Robert, 92, 170
Green, John, 116
Greene, Jacob and Griffin, 128
Greenleaf & Cross, 77, 90, 152, 318
Greensleaf, Jonathan, 318
Grenville, Sir Richard, 242
Grice & Company, 284
Grimwood, V. R., 206
Grinnell, Thomas, 284

Grush, John, 137
Gunboat, *ill. 8*

Hacker, Hoysted, 94, 222
Hackett family, 43, 48, 190, 228. 232
Hahn, Harold, 206
Hall, Lieutenant, 42
Hallock, William, 174
Hallowell, Benjamin, 70, 75, 266
Hampden, John, 232
Hancock, John, 152, 177
Haraden, Jonathan, 139
Harding, Seth, 96, 142
Harmon, John, 141
Harvard College, 46
Haswell, Robert, 170
Hayden, Uriah, 141
Hayley, Mary, 110
Hazard, John, 220, 222
Hazelwood, John, 110, 257
Heeltapper, 5, 261
Henry, William, 214
Henry VIII, English king, 9
Hewitt, Charles, 223, 287
Hill, Thomas, 137
Hinman, Elisha, 40, 286
Hodge, John, 110
Hodge, William, 242, 268
Holland (shipbuilder), 64, 123
Holman, Francis, 77, 131, 132, 152, 154, 174, 176, 220, 222, 302
Hood, Admiral Samuel, Viscount, 126
Hopkins, Esek, 40, 82, 223, 287
Hopkins, John Burroughs, 82, 287, 289
Hopkins, Governor Stephen, 137
Howe, General Sir William, 274
Hughes, Admiral Sir Edward, 126
Hull, John, 214
Hull design, 5, 8, 9, 13, 14, 15, 21, 23, 31, 32, 33, 34
Humphreys, Joshua, 48, 66, 174, 186

Hunt, John, 282
Hunter, John, 134
Hyder Ali, Prince, 143

Independence National Historical Park (Philadelphia), 48

Jay, John, 96
Jenkins' Ear, War of, 8, 113
Johnson, Henry, 174, 176
Johnston, George, 158
Johnston, Henry, 128
Jones, John Paul, 34, 40, 42, 44, 45, 48, 60, 73–75, 145, 208, 222, 259, 263
Joyner, John, 265

Kaiana, Hawaiian chief, 204
Keats, Captain, 238
Kendrick, John, 92, 170
Ketch, *ill. 6*
Knatchbull, Captain C., 126
Knowles, James A., 46

Lafayette, Marquis de, 44
Landais, Pierre, 43, 44, 45, 60, 73
de Langara, Admiral Don Juan, 126
Langbehn, Carl, 282
Lawrence & Tudor, 284
Lee, Arthur, 45
Lee, General Charles, 172
Lee, Ezra, 280
Linois, Admiral, 238
Loring, Captain Joshua, 148
Loring, Joshua, Jr., 148n
Louis XVI, French king, 263
Lugger, *ill. 9*
Luny, Thomas, 82
Luxembourg, Duke de, 263, 265

McClenahan, Blair, 120
McCusker, John J., Jr., 42
McNeill, Hector, 77
MacPhaedris House (Portsmouth, N. H.), 13
Manley, John, 104, 152
Mariners Museum (Newport News), *iii*, 34, 222, 252
Maryland Historical Society (Baltimore), 160
Massachusetts Historical Society, 177
Mayes, William, Jr., 202
Meares, John, 92, 204
Melgareso, Don Francisco, 126
Merchants' Coffee House (Philadelphia), 45
Metcalf, Simon, 308, 313
Middlebrook, Louis F., 106
Model shipwright, 206
Montgolfier, Joseph Michael, 214
Montgomery, General Richard, 162, 258
Moreno, Admiral Don Juan de, 238
Morris, Colonel, 125
Morris, Robert, 40, 45, 116, 144
Mugford, James, 155
Munro, James, 66, 143
Musée de la Marine (Paris), 11, 43, 100, 110, 112, 131, 228
Museo Naval (Madrid), 11, 238, 239
Mutiny on the Bounty, 27
Mystic Seaport, 50, 118, 194

National Archives (Washington, D.C.), 48
National Maritime Museum (Greenwich), *ii*, 11, 34, 51, 56, 68, 75, 76, 79, 80, 81, 84, 85, 86, 87, 90, 91, 97, 100, 101, 102, 103, 108, 109, 123, 124, 126, 145, 150, 152, 153, 172, 173, 176, 180, 181, 182, 183, 184, 185, 188, 189,

192, 193, 196, 197, 200, 201, 207, 208, 209, 210, 211, 228, 229, 236, 237, 244, 245, 248, 249, 261, 262, 266, 267, 270, 271, 272, 273, 276, 277, 284, 285, 286, 287, 289, 290, 291, 292, 302, 306, 307
Nautical Research Journal, 206
Nederlands Scheepvart Museum (Amsterdam), 11
Nelson, Almiral Horatio, Lord, 108, 230
New Jersey State Museum, 116
Newport Historical Society, 331
Newport *Mercury,* 287
New-York Historical Society, 38
New York Public Library, 190, 250
Nicholson, James, 160, 284, 286
Nicholson, John, 160
Nicholson, Samuel, 104, 114
Niles, Robert, 328
Nixon, John, 40

Oakes, Captain, 272
O'Brien, Jeremiah, 217
Old Granary Burying Ground (Boston), 278
Olney, Joseph, 82
Ormsbee, Elijah, 216
Ozanne, Nicolas, 229
Ozanne, Pierre, 100, 234

Paine, Thomas, 45
Papin, Denis, 214
Paris, Admiral, 34, 265, 313
Parke, Captain Matthew, U.S.-M.C. 43, 45
Parker, Timothy, 142
Peabody Museum (Salem), 43, 58, 70, 77, 79, 131, 139, 140, 152, 154, 155, 157, 200, 219, 263, 265, 316, 318, 334, 336
Peale, Charles Willson, 160
Pearson, Richard, 259

Pease, Martin, 166
Peck, John, 66, 116, 194, 236
Pellew, Edward, 84
Penobscot Bay Expedition, 79, 141, 222, 234, 286, 289
Perkins Jabez, 122
de la Pérouse, Jean François, Count, 60
Perry's Shipyard, 60
Philadelphia, Historical Society of, 116
Philadelphia Maritime Museum, 330
Phillips Andover Academy Museum, 222
Phippen, J., 263
Pickering, Thomas, 232
Pickering, Timothy, 139
Pigot, Admiral Hugh, 200
Pirates, 202
Poor Richard's Almanac, 73
Popham, Sir George, 282
Pownalborough Court House (Dresden, Maine), 217–218
Preble, Edward, 79
Prince, Job, 190
Pringle, Thomas, 188
Privateers, 8
Providence *Gazette & Country Journal,* 192

Quiberon Bay, Battle of, 123, 128
Quincy family, 70

Raleigh, Sir Walter, 228
Randall's Shipyard, 259
Randle, C. (artist), 146, 240, 250, 292, 294
Rathbun, John Peck, 34, 222
Read, Thomas, 45, 230, 257
Reid, Lieutenant, 177
Remick, Christian, 177
Rhode Island Historical Society (Providence), 222

Rider, Hope, 222
Rigging, 1, 6, 17, 19, 20
Rigs, 5, 20, 21
de Rochefort, Sieur Fauré, 131
Rodney, Admiral Sir George Brydges, 68, 126
Rogers, Captain, 143
Roosevelt Collection (Hyde Park, N.Y.), 42, 222
Ropes, David or John, 164
Roux, Antoine, 166
Row galley, *ill. 5*
Royal Collection (Windsor Castle,) 51, 84, 292
Rumford, Count, *see* Thompson, Benjamin
Rumsey, James, 216
Russell, William, 206

Salter, Captain, 234
Saltonstall, Dudley, 40, 286, 289
Saltonstall, Nathaniel, 141
Saumarez, Admiral Sir James, 238
Savage, Edward, 225
Sayer & Bennett, 172, 290, 292
Schank, John, 162, 188, 276, 308
Schooner, *ill. 13*
Schuyler Collection (N.Y.), 250
Science Museum, London, 11, 168, 169, 254
Selkirk, Earl of, 234
Selman, Archibald, 155
Serres, Dominic, 38, 284, 286
Seven Years' War, 8, 9, 231, 274, 276, 334
Seymour, Commodore, 257
Shaw, Major, 190
Shaw, Nathaniel, 141
Shelley, Giles, 202
Sherlock, Simon, 257
Ship (rig), 10, 11
Shirley, Governor Henry, 142
Simpson, Thomas, 38, 42, 234
Skene, Philip, 179, 180
Skillin, Simeon, 190

Skimmer, John, 137
Sloop, *ill. 12*
Smedley, Samuel, 106
Smith, Jabez, Jr., 278
Smith & Rhuland, Ltd., *ii*
Smithsonian Institution, *i*, 11, 80, 123, 294, 342
Snow, *ill. 6*
Spain, National Archives of (Madrid), 282
Stalkaart, Marmaduke, 186
Statens Sjohistorika Museum (Sweden), 252
Steel, David, 338, 340, 342
Stevens, John, 216
Stone, William, 160
Sussel Collection, 303

Talbot, Silas, 34, 143
Talman & Bowers, 223, 287
Taylor, John, 123
Tew, Thomas, 202
Thompson, Benjamin, 120, 186
Thompson, Thomas, 228
Timber, 6, 7
Todd, Joseph, 88
Trevett, Samuel Russell, 58
Trumbull, Governor John, Sr., 106, 278, 286
Truxton, Thomas, 98
Tucker, Samuel, 77, 155

U.S. Marine Corps Museum (Quantico), 42
U.S. Naval Academy Museum (Annapolis), 11, 43, 73, 120, 143, 145

Valcour Island, Battle of, 84, 146, 162, 179, 188, 240, 250, 251, 276, 290, 292, 294, 296, 297, 306
Vancouver, George, 92
Van Powell, W. Nowland, *iii*

INDEX OF SHIPS

l'Abenakise, French Navy Frigate (1756), 36, *ill. 37*, 211, 226, 256

A Bien Acquis, frigate, *see l'Abenakise*

Achilles, British warship, 139

Actaeon, British frigate (1775), *ill. 8*

Admiral Duff, British warship, 79

Admiral Keppel, British corvette, 142

Adventure, American sloop (1792), 92, 204

Alert, British cutter (1778), 175

Alexander, American frigate (1780), 38, 39, *ill. 39*, 48

Alfred, Continental ship (ca. 1774), 40–42, *ill. 41, 42*, 80, 180, 182, 184, 222, 228, 234, 257, 328

l'Algonquin, French corvette (1753), 36

Alliance, Continental frigate (1777), 39, 43–45, *ill. 43, 44, 45*, 48, 60, 73, 96, 145, 190, 259

l'Amazone, French frigate, 60

America, British warship (1777), 50

America, Continental battleship (1778), 48–50, *ill. 49*, 96, 190

America, Continental frigate (1776), *see Warren*, Continental frigate

America, Royal Navy ship (1748), 46, *ill. 47*, 75

America of Charleston, merchant ship, 53, *ill. 53*

American, Continental gondola (1775), 51–52, *ill. 51, 52*

American Convert, gondola, *see American*

Amérique, French battleship (1787), 50

Amiable, American brig, 38

Amsterdam, American brig (ca. 1777), 54–55, *ill. 55*, 164

Andrew Doria, Continental brig (ca. 1775), 82, 160

Ant, Royal Navy schooner (ca. 1788), 56–57, *ill. 57*, 68

Argo, American warship (ca. 1780), 58–59, *ill, 58–59*

Ariadne, British frigate (1776), 42

Ariel, frigate (1777), 60–61, *ill. 61*

Artois, British frigate (1794), 100

Assurance, British warship (1780), 236

Astrea, British frigate (1781), 265

Atalanta, British corvette (1775), 45

Atlantic, American merchant ship, 62–63, *ill. 63*

Aurora, frigate, *see l'Abenakise*

Badger, Royal Navy brig, *see Defence*, American brig

Baille, British ship, 104

Baltick, American schooner, 155–157, *ill. 156, 167*

Barbadoes, corvette, *see Rhodes*

Basilisk, fireship, *see London*

Bateau, 293, *ill. 293*

Beaver, American brig (1772), 92, 93

Beaver, British corvette (1761), 206

Beaver's Prize, corvette (ca 1774), *see Oliver Cromwell*, American privateer

Bedford Galley, Royal Navy ship (1697), 6, 64–65, *ill. 65*, 123

Belisarius, American frigate (ca. 1780), 66–67, *ill. 67*, 143

Bellerophon, British battleship (1786), 36

Berbice, American schooner (ca. 1780), 68–69, *ill. 69*

Bermuda schooner, 299, *ill. 299*

Bermuda sloop, 300–301, *ill. 301*

Bethel, American warship (ca. 1746), 70–71, *ill. 70, 71*

Bird, American sloop, 266

Black Prince, American ship, *see Alfred*

Black Princess, American warship (ca. 1776), 72, *ill. 72*

Blast, fireship, *see Brilliant*

Bon Acquis, frigate, *see l'Abenakise*

Bonhomme Richard, Continental warship, 36, 43, 44, 73–75, *ill. 73, 74*, 225, 259

Boston, Continental frigate (1776), ii, 77–79, *ill. 77, 78*, 96, 104, 105, 132, 137, 152, 154, 223, 234, 235, 318

Boston, Continental gondola (1776), 294–296, *ill. 296*

Boston, Royal Navy ship (44 guns, 1748), *see America*, Royal Navy ship

Boston, Royal Navy ship, (32 guns, 1692), 64

Boston, Royal Navy ship (24 guns, 1748), 46, 75–76, *ill. 76*, 266

Boston brig, 302, *ill. 302*

Boston Light, sloop off, 304–305, *ill. 304, 305*

Boston merchant ship, 303, *ill. 303*

Bounty, British transport, 27

Bourbon, Continental frigate (1780), 96–97, *ill. 97*

Bricole, La, French warship, 75, 225

Brilliant, American merchant ship (ca. 1775), 80–81, *ill. 81*, 228

Cabot, Continental brig (ca. 1775), 82–83, *ill. 83*

Canada, Le, French corvette (1742), 36

Canso, British warship, 42

Caribou, Le, French corvette (1744), 36

Carleton, Royal Navy schooner (1776), 84–85, *ill. 85*, 162

Castor, Le, French corvette (1745), 36

Cato, American brig, *ill. 82*

Cerberus, British frigate (1758), 94

Cerberus, British frigate (1779), 158

Chaleur, Royal Navy schooner (ca. 1762), 86–87, *ill. 87*

Charleston, frigate, *see Boston, Continental* frigate (1776)

Charming Jenny, American ship (1761), 88–89, *ill. 89*

Charming Molly, British ship, 258

Chatham, British warship (1758), 143

Cherokee, transport, *see Codrington*

Chesapeake, U.S. frigate (1799), 7

Chichester, British battleship (1753), 36

Clearwater, American sloop, 118

Codrington, American merchant ship (1773), 90–91, *ill. 91*

Columbia, American merchant ship (1773), 92–93, *ill. 92, 93,* 170, 214

Columbia Rediviva, American ship, *see Columbia*

Columbus, Continental warship (ca. 1775), 94–95, *ill. 94, 95,* 328

Confederacy, Continental frigate (1778), 96–97, *ill. 97,* 104, 142, 258

Confederate, frigate, *see Confederacy*

Congress, American privateer (ca. 1781), 98–99, *ill. 99,* 145

Congress, Continental frigate (1776), 110, 284–286, *ill. 285*

Congress, Continental galley (1776), 162, 290–292, *ill. 291,* 292

Connecticut, Continental gondola (1776), 294–296, *ill. 296*

Constellation, U.S. frigate (1797), *i*

Constitution, U.S. frigate (1797), *i, iii,* 25, 97, 186, 190, 200, 265

Convert, gondola, *see American*

Cormorant, corvette, *see Rattlesnake*

Countess of Scarborough, British warship, 208

Coureuse, La, American schooner (ca. 1785), 100–101, *ill. 101*

Culloden, British battleship (1776), 143

Cupid, Royal Navy transport (ca. 1774), 102–103, *ill. 103,* 206, 208

Cyrus, British corvette, 106, 142

Daphne, British frigate (1776), 142

Dauphin, Le, frigate, *see Delaware*

Deane, Continental frigate (1777), 79, 95, 104–105, *ill. 105,* 258

Defence, American brig (1776), 108–109, *ill. 109*

Defence, American ship (1775), 106–107, *ill. 107,* 142

Delaware, Continental frigate (1776), *ii,* 105, 110–112, *ill. 111, 112,* 142, 154, 257

Despatch, transport, *see Codrington*

Diana, sloop, 220

Diligence, American snow (1739), 113, *ill. 113,* 320

Diligent, British brig, 222

Diligent, British survey ship, 217

Diomede, British warship (1781), 265

Dolphin, Continental cutter (ca. 1770), 114–115, *ill. 114, 115*

Drake, Royal Navy corvette (ca. 1774), 40–42, *ill. 41,* 182, 184, 234, 328

Druid, transport, *see Brilliant*

Duc de Duras, Le, French ship, *see Bonhomme Richard*

Duc de Lauzun, Le, French ship, 45

Eagle, American sloop (ca. 1776), *ill. 246*

Eagle, British warship (1774), 280

Earl of Egmont, Royal Navy schooner (1768), 261–262, *ill. 262*

Edward, British sloop, 174

Effingham, Continental frigate (1776), 160, 230, 284–286, *ill. 285*

Eliza, American schooner, *see Franklin*

Empress of China, American ship (1783), 66, 116–117, *ill. 117*

Endeavour, British transport, 8

Enterprise, Continental sloop (1775), 146–147, *ill. 146, 147,* 172, 250

Experiment, American sloop (ca. 1784), 118–119, *ill. 118, 119*

Experiment, American steamboat (1788), 214

Fair American, American brig (ca. 1776), 120–121, *ill. 121*

Fair American, Connecticut brig (ca. 1780), 122, *ill. 122*

Fairy, British corvette (1778), 194

Falcon, American sloop, *see Hornet*

Falkland, Royal Navy ship (1690), 6, 64, 123–124, *ill. 124,* 252

Fancy, American yacht (ca. 1717), 125, *ill. 125*

Favourite, British corvette (1757), 86

Felice, British exploration ship, 204

Felucca (1786), 313–314, *ill. 314*

Feniks, Russian boat (1794), 93, 204

Fenix, Spanish battleship (1749), 50, 126–127, *ill. 127*

Flora, American/British/French frigate (ca. 1770), 77, 128–131, *ill. 129, 130, 131, 132,* 152

Flore, La, frigate, *see Flora*

Fly, Continental sloop (ca. 1774), 160, 227, 230, 246

Foudroyant, British battleship (1774), 174

Fox, frigate (1773), 77, 131, 132–133, *ill. 133,* 152

Franklin, American schooner, 155–157, *ill. 156, 157*

Fury, Royal Navy sloop (ca. 1775), 134, *ill. 134*

Galatea, British frigate (1776), 242

Galatea, British frigate (1794), 100

Gaspée, Royal Navy schooner (ca. 1763), 135–137, *ill. 136*

Gates, Continental galley (1776), 290–292, *ill. 291*

General Gates, Continental corvette (1777), *ii,* 137–138, *ill. 138,* 141, 143, 232

General Monk, corvette, *see General Washington*

General Pickering, American corvette (ca. 1780), 139–140, *ill. 139, 140*

General Putnam, American corvette (1778), 141–142, *ill. 142,* 286, 289

General Washington, Continental corvette (1779), *ii, iv,* 66, 98, 120, 143–145, *ill. 143, 144, 145,* 154, 208, 286, 287

George, Royal Navy sloop (1775), *see Enterprise*

Gibraltar, battleship, *see Fenix*

Glasgow, British frigate (1756), 40, 42, 82, 94

Golden Eagle, British schooner, 139

Golden Hinde, English galleon (1577), 10

Grana, Spanish frigate, *ill. 26*

Grand Duchess of Russia, British ship, 134

Grand Turk, American ship, 116
Grasshopper, transport, *see London*
Guerrière, British frigate (ca. 1800), 84

Hague, American frigate (1777), *see Deane*
Halifax, Royal Navy sloop (ca. 1759), 148–149, *ill. 149*
Hall, British ship, 116
Hallifax, Royal Navy schooner (ca. 1765), 150, 151, *ill. 151*
Hampden, American brig (ca. 1777), 48, 190, 232–235, *ill. 233, 234*, 286, 289
Hampden, Continental brig (ca. 1775), 232
Hancock, Continental frigate (1776), 77, 79, 132, 137, 143, 152–154, *ill. 152, 153*, 190, 258, 286, 318
Hannah, American schooner, 155–157, *ill. 155, 156, 157*
Harlequin, American corvette (ca. 1778), 158–159, *ill. 159*
Harriet, American sloop (ca. 1783), 118
Harrison, American schooner, 155
Hawke, British warship, 261
Hermenegildo, Spanish battleship, 238
Hermione, La, French frigate, 152
Hero, American frigate (ca. 1760), 112, 231
Holker, American brig, 120
Hope, American sloop (ca. 1780), *ill. 192*
Hornet, Continental sloop (ca. 1774), 160–161, *ill. 160, 161*, 230
Hussar, frigate, *see Protector*

Hyder Ali, American warship, 120, 143, *ill. 143*, 144, 145, 328

l'Indien, frigate (1777), *see South Carolina*
Industrious Bee, American brig, 137
Industry, British ship, 128
Inflexible, Royal Navy corvette (1776), 162–163, *ill. 163*, 248
Intrepid, British warship (1770), 258
Invincible, Royal Navy radeau, 148
Iphigenia, British exploration ship, 204
Iris, frigate, *see Hancock*

Jack, American warship (ca. 1781), 54, 122, 164–165, *ill. 164, 165*
Jaramas, Swedish frigate, *ill. 30*
Jersey, Continental gondola (1776), 294–296, *ill. 296*
John Barrington, British ship, 143
Juno, American merchant ship, 206
Junon, La, French frigate, 132

Katharine, American ketch (ca. 1767), *see Liberty*, Continental ketch
Katy, American brig. (ca. 1788), 166, *ill. 166, 167*
Katy, American sloop, *see Providence*, Continental sloop

Lady Hamond, Royal Navy schooner (1788), 168–169, *ill. 169*
Lady Washington, American schooner (ca. 1776), *ill. 155*

Lady Washington, American sloop (ca. 1780), 92, 170–171, *ill. 171*, 315
Lake Champlain gunboats (1775–1776), 297–298, *ill. 298*
Lake Champlain sloops (1776), 306–307, *ill. 307*
Lark, British frigate (1762), 223
Lee, American schooner (ca. 1774), 155
Lee, Continental cutter (1775), 146, 172–173, *ill. 172, 173*, 250, 252, 290
Lexington, Continental brig (ca. 1773), 174–176, *ill. 174, 175, 176*
Liberty, American sloop (ca. 1765), 177–178, *ill. 177, 178*
Liberty, Continental ketch (ca. 1767), 146, 179–180, *ill. 179, 180*
Lightning, fireship (1774), *see Lovely Lass*
Lily Ann, American brig (1775), *see Defence*, American ship
Liverpool, British frigate (1758), 174, 257
London, American merchant ship, 180–181, *ill. 181*, 228
Lord Camden, American ship (1775), 42, 182–183, *ill. 183*, 184
Louisbourg sloop, 315, *ill. 315*
Lovely Lass, American merchant ship (1774), 184–185, *ill. 185*
Loyal American, Royal Navy frigate (1782), 120, 186–187, *ill. 187*
Loyal Convert, gondola, *see American*
Lynch, American schooner (ca. 1774), 155

Machias Liberty, American sloop (ca. 1770), *see Polly*
Magnifique, Le, French battleship, 48

Margaretta, British schooner, 217
Maria, Royal Navy schooner (1776), 188–189, *ill. 189*
Maria Wilhelmina, American merchant ship (1774), 190
Mariner, American yacht, 66
Mars, Dutch frigate, *ill. 28*
Martha, British brig, 77
Martre, Le, French warship (1747), 36
Massachusetts, American merchant ship (1789), 190–191, *ill. 191*
Mayflower, English merchant ship, 10
Medea, British frigate (1778), 66, 79
Mediator, British warship (1782), 38
Mediator, Royal Navy sloop (ca. 1741), 192–193, *ill. 193*, 342
Mellish, British transport, 42, 222
Ménagère, La, French ship, 38
Mercury, American schooner (ca. 1781), 194
Mercury, Continental brig (ca. 1776), 194–195, *ill. 195*
Metcalf's Corvette (1777), 308, 312, *ill. 312*
Metcalf's Radeau (1777), 308–309, *ill. 309*
Metcalf's Schooner (1777), 308, 311, *ill. 311*
Metcalf's Sloop (1777), 308, 310, *ill. 310*
Mexico, Spanish ship (ca. 1730), 196–197, *ill. 197*
Milford, British frigate (1759), 40, 82
Minerva, American brig, 82, 220
Mohawk, American corvette (1779), 122, 164, 200–201, *ill. 200, 201*
Mohawk, Royal Navy snow (1759), 198–199, *ill. 199*
Montague, British brig, 137

[354]

Montgomery, American corvette (1775), 110, 257–258, *ill. 258*

Montgomery, Continental frigate (1776), ii, 110–112, *ill. 111,* 284

Nancy, American brig, 174

Nassau, American pirate ship (ca. 1695), 202–203, *ill. 203*

Newburyport ship (1752), 318–319, *ill. 319*

Newburyport ship (ca. 1760), 316–317, *ill. 316, 317,* 334

Newfoundland Fishery bilander (ca. 1750), 320, 323, *ill. 323*

Newfoundland Fishery pink (ca. 1750), 320, 322, *ill. 322*

Newfoundland Fishery ship (ca. 1750), 320–321, *ill. 321*

New Haven, Continental gondola (1776), 294–296, *ill. 296*

New York, Continental gondola (1776), 294–296, *ill. 296*

New York, U.S. frigate (1799), 186

New York brig (ca. 1717), 324, *ill. 324*

New York sloop (ca. 1717), 324–325, *ill. 325*

New York yacht (ca. 1675), 326–327, *ill. 327*

Nieuw Amsterdam yacht (ca. 1660), 326–327, *ill. 326, 327*

Northwest America, lugger (1788), 204–205, *ill. 204, 205,* 214

Observer, brig, *see Amsterdam*

Oliver Cromwell, American corvette (1776), 106, 110, 141–142, *ill. 142,* 206, 278

Oliver Cromwell, American privateer (ca. 1774), 102, 145, 206–208, *ill. 207,* 225, 287

Onondaga, Royal Navy snow (1759), 198

Ontario, Royal Navy brig (1780), 209–210, *ill. 210*

l'Original, French battleship (1750), 36, 211, *ill. 211*

Orpheus, British frigate (1780), 96

l'Outaouaise, French Navy brig (ca. 1757), 212–213, *ill. 212, 213,* 332

Patty, American merchant ship, 62–63, *ill. 63*

Pearl, British frigate (1762), 174

Perseverance, American steamboat (1786), 214–216, *ill. 215*

Phaeton, British frigate (1782), 131

Philadelphia, Continental gondola (1776), i, 294–296, *ill. 294, 296*

Philadelphia merchant ship (ca. 1785), 330, *ill. 330*

Philadelphia ship of 24 guns (ca. 1775), 328–329, *ill. 329*

Pitt, brig, *see Defence,* American brig

Polly, American sloop (ca. 1770), 217–218, *ill. 217, 218*

Pomone, British frigate (ca. 1793), 100

Pompey, merchant ship, *see America of Charleston*

Porto, corvette, *see Harlequin*

Postillion, American merchant ship (ca. 1780), 219, *ill. 219*

Prince of Orange, British ship, 268

Protector, American frigate (1779), 77–79, *ill. 78*

Prothée, British warship, 244

Providence, Continental frigate (1776), 79, 206, 220, 223–225, *ill. 223, 224, 234,* 284, 287

Providence, Continental gondola (1776), 220, 294–296, *ill. 296*

Providence, Continental sloop (ca. 1769), i, ii, 40, 82, 137, 220–222, *ill. 220, 221,* 265, 286, 289

Pyroscaphe, French steamboat (1783), 214

Quebec, British frigate (1781), 143, 265

Quebec, Le, French frigate (1757), 36, 211, 226, *ill. 226*

Queen of France, Continental frigate, 223, 225, 234, 235, 287

Race Horse, American sloop (ca. 1750), 227, *ill. 227*

Rainbow, British warship (1747), 77, 97, 132, 152, 154

Raleigh, Continental frigate (1776), 39, 40, 43, 48, 80, 154, 180, 190, 228–229, *ill. 228, 229,* 232, 235, 278, 286

Randolph, Continental frigate (1776), 39, 48, 96, 120, 160, 194, 230–231, *ill. 231,* 257

Ranger, Continental corvette (1777), ii, 38, 42, 48, 79, 137, 143, 190, 223, 232–235, *ill. 232, 233, 234,* 263

Rattlesnake, American corvette (1780), 66, 236–237, *ill. 237*

Real Carlos, Spanish battleship (1787), 238–239, *ill. 239*

Reconnaissance, La, frigate, *see Flora*

Reprisal, Continental cutter, 174

Resistance, American brig, 278

Resolution, British transport, 29

Resolution, British transport, *see Drake*

Restoration, corvette, *see Oliver Cromwell,* American corvette

Revenge, Continental cutter (ca. 1776), 242–243, *ill. 243*

Revenge, Continental schooner (1776), 240–241, *ill. 240, 241*

Rhode Island ship (ca. 1720), 331, *ill. 331*

Rhodes, American corvette (ca. 1779), 244–245, *ill. 245*

Robin, American sloop (ca. 1750), 246–247, *ill. 247*

Roebuck, British warship (1774), 79, 96, 257

Romney, British warship (1762), 177

Rose, British frigate (1756), ii, iii, iv, 220, 274

Royal George, British battleship (1756), 248

Royal George, Royal Navy corvette (1777), 248–249, *ill. 249,* 306

Royal Savage, Continental schooner (1775), 146, 172, 250–252, *ill. 250, 251,* 290

St. Ann, schooner (1736), 252–253, *ill. 253*

St. Helena, American merchant ship (ca. 1775), 254–255, *ill. 254, 255*

St. John, Royal Navy schooner (ca. 1763), i, 135–137, *ill. 135, 136*

Saint-Laurent, Le, French warship (1748), 36, 211, 256, *ill. 256*

St. Lawrence River galleys, 332–333, *ill. 333*

Salem ship (ca. 1750), 334–335, *ill. 334, 335*

Salem sloop (ca. 1770), 336–337, *ill. 337*

Sally, American ship, *see Columbus*

Santa Gertrudis la Magna, lugger (1788), *see Northwest America*

Saratoga, Continental corvette (1777), *ii,* 95, 104, 137, 143, 232, 257–258, *ill. 258*

Savage, British corvette (1778), 98

Seneca, Royal Navy snow (ca. 1763), 198

Serapis, British warship (1779), 43, 44, 73, 75, 208, 259–260, *ill. 260*

Shannon, British frigate (1806), 7

Sir Edward Hawke, Royal Navy schooner (1768), 261–262, *ill. 262*

Sirenne, La, French frigate, *ill.* 22, 225

Solebay, British frigate (1763), 98

South Carolina, American frigate (1777), 15, 263–265, *ill. 263, 264*

Speedwell, British ketch (1752), 194

Spitfire, Continental gondola (1776), 294–296, *ill. 296*

Spy, American schooner, 328

Success, Continental gondola (1776), 294–296, *ill. 296*

Sultana, Royal Navy schooner (1776), 150, 266–267, *ill. 267*

Superb, British battleship (1798), 238

Surprise, Continental lugger (ca. 1770), 174, 268–269, *ill. 268, 269*

Susan Constant, English merchant ship, 10

Swift, American brig (ca. 1778), 270–271, *ill. 271*

Swift, American pilot-schooner (ca. 1786), 272–273, *ill. 273*

Swift, British vessel (8-gun), 270

Swift, British vessel (16-gun), 270

Sybil, British frigate (1779), 45

Sylph, transport (1774), *see Lovely Lass*

Tattamagouche, British survey ship, 217

Thames, British frigate (1758), 79

Thornton, transport (ca. 1756), 274–275, *ill. 275*

Thunderer, Royal Navy radeau (1776), 276–277, *ill. 277*

Tobago, see Trumbull, American privateer

Tonnant, Le, corvette, *see Rattlesnake*

Tracy, American warship, 60

Trepassey, British corvette (1779), 45

Triumph, Loyalist warship, 60

Truite, La, American/French frigate, 225

Trumbull, American merchant ship, 278–279, *ill. 278, 279*

Trumbull, American privateer (ca. 1777), 286

Trumbull, Continental frigate (1776), 143, 154, 278, 284–286, *ill. 285,* 289

Trumbull, Continental galley (1776), 290–292, *ill. 291, 292*

Turtle, Continental submarine (1775), 214, 280–281, *ill. 281*

Tyrannicide, American warship, 139

Unicorn, British frigate (1748), 36

Unicorn, British frigate (1776), 29, 228

Union, British warship, 142

United States, American ship (1776), *see Delaware*

United States, U.S. frigate (1797), 265

Unity, American sloop, 217

Unity, British transport, 155

Vestal, British frigate (1757), 128

Vestal, British frigate (1779), 120, 194

Vestale, La, frigate, *see Flora*

Vigilant, British ship, 134

Viper, British corvette, 104

Virginia, American pinnace (1607), 282–283, *ill. 282, 283*

Virginia, Continental frigate (1776), 39, 284–286, *ill. 284, 285*

Virginia schooner I (ca. 1785), 338–339, *ill. 339,* 342

Virginia schooner II (ca. 1785), 340–341, *ill. 341,* 342

Virginia sloop (1768), 342–343, *ill. 343*

Wallace, American corvette (1775), *see Montgomery,* American corvette

Warren, American schooner, 155

Warren, Continental frigate (1776), 206, 223, 286, 287–289, *ill. 287, 288,* 289

Washington, American schooner, 155

Washington, Continental frigate (1776), 160, 230–231, *ill. 231,* 284

Washington, Continental galley (1776), 162, 188, 290–292, *ill. 290, 291*

Wasp, Continental schooner, 160

Watt, British warship, 286

Welcome, American sloop, 306

Wild Duck, American brig (ca. 1773), *see Lexington*

Yarmouth, British warship (1748), 230

Ye Terrible Creture, American ship, 206